WITHDRAWN

APR 1 5 2010

D1606027

The War in Words

The War in Words

Reading the Dakota Conflict through the Captivity Literature

Kathryn Zabelle Derounian-Stodola

UNIVERSITY OF NEBRASKA PRESS | LINCOLN & LONDON

Revised portions of the preface originally appeared in the author's "The Accidental Colonialist: Notes on Academic Choice and Identity," *Society of Early Americanists Newsletter* 17, no. 2 (Autumn 2005): 3–7. Used by permission.

Revised portions of chapter 1 originally appeared in the author's "'Many persons say I am a "Mono Maniac"': Three Letters from Dakota Conflict Captive Sarah F. Wakefield to Missionary Stephen R. Riggs," *Prospects: An Annual of American Cultural Studies* 29 (2004): 1–24. Copyright © 2005 Cambridge University Press. Used by permission.

Revised portions of chapter 3 originally appeared in Colin T. Ramsey and Kathryn Zabelle Derounian-Stodola, "Dime Novels," in *A Companion to American Fiction, 1780–1865*, ed. Shirley Samuels, 262–73 (London: Blackwell Publishing, 2004). Used by permission.

© 2009 by the Board of Regents
of the University of Nebraska
All rights reserved
Manufactured in the
United States of America
∞
Library of Congress
Cataloging-in-Publication Data
Derounian-Stodola, Kathryn Zabelle, 1949–
The war in words: reading the Dakota
conflict through the captivity literature /
Kathryn Zabelle Derounian-Stodola.
    p.   cm.
Includes bibliographical references and index.
ISBN 978-0-8032-1370-8 (cloth : alk. paper)
1. Dakota Indians—Wars, 1862–1865—
Personal narratives. 2. Indian captivities—
Minnesota. 3. Captivity narratives.
4. Prisoners in literature. I. Title.
E83.86.D47 2009
973.7—dc22
2008036586

Set in Iowan Old Style by Bob Reitz.
Designed by R. W. Boeche.

For Bob, with love

Contents

Part 1. European Americans Narrating Captivity

Part 2. Native Americans Narrating Captivity

Illustrations

Map

Figures

Preface

This book on the Dakota War captivity and confinement narratives refused to be rushed despite my desire to complete it.[1] I began my research at the Newberry Library in fall 1999, during a sabbatical from the University of Arkansas at Little Rock, and for the next two years I just kept reading. Then, in 2001, I made the first of half a dozen research trips to the Minnesota Historical Society and elsewhere to consult primary sources. As I came to appreciate the complexity and sensitivity of the Dakota Conflict, I was glad that the book came together as slowly as it did. Over the years *The War in Words* has benefited from the input of many readers, and together we have tried to do justice to the narratives and their narrators.

The following people helped me establish not necessarily the truth but the truths of the Conflict, and I am indebted to them. Alan R. Woolworth, Research Fellow Emeritus at the Minnesota Historical Society, was extremely generous in sharing his time, knowledge, and materials from 1999 onward, especially at the project's beginning stages. Through Alan I met other researchers working specifically on Dakota War history. Carrie R. Zeman, an independent scholar in Minnesota researching many aspects of the Dakota War, read the entire manuscript several times, clarifying dozens of points and sending me all kinds of additional data, including her own work. Walt Bachman, who has written a biography of Joseph Godfrey and is currently completing a study of the postwar trials, kindly shared his considerable knowledge of arcane aspects of the Conflict, especially concerning legal issues.

Elden Lawrence provided detailed commentary on several sections of *The War in Words* as a descendent of Lorenzo Lawrence, author of one of the book's core texts. Elroy Ubl provided a fine photograph of

Joseph Godfrey's gravestone that I have reproduced in my book, and photographic historian Curtis Dahlin facilitated access to contemporaneous images of people and places in this study. Darla Gebhard, research librarian at the Brown County (Minnesota) Historical Society, promptly responded to requests for photocopies, photographs, and information. Feedback—some cursory, some comprehensive—from the following scholars helped me think through aspects of this book: Patricia Albers, Eric Gary Anderson, P. Jane Hafen, Annette Kolodny, Bonnie Sue Lewis, Neil McKay, and Waziyatawin Angela Wilson. I was particularly pleased to receive encouragement from Virginia Driving Hawk Sneve, the only living author of one of my core texts, concerning my analysis of her novel *Betrayed*. I would also like to acknowledge other relatives and descendents of several core figures in this book whom I contacted: Kathleen Backer, Ernest W. Coursolle, Joyzelle Godfrey, Jane Hayden-Hart, Anne Leck, Louise Otten, Kim Rossina, Raymond W. Schwan, and Roberta Schilling Shipps. Particular thanks to Ernest W. Coursolle and Jane Hayden-Hart for their many e-mails clarifying the complicated genealogy of their great-great-grandfather Joseph Coursolle and directing me to other material.

My colleague Daniel F. Littlefield at the University of Arkansas at Little Rock, director of the American Native Press Archives, offered assistance, expertise, and support at important points during this project. LaVonne Brown Ruoff gave me guidance and provided contacts on several occasions. And A. Robert Lee, who taught me as an undergraduate at the University of Kent at Canterbury more years ago than either of us cares to admit, furnished valuable feedback on the project and on theoretical dimensions of American Indian literatures. I would also like to thank the two scholars who reviewed the manuscript for the University of Nebraska Press. They supplied unusually detailed and constructive criticism that has strengthened the final product considerably. Despite the help of so many people, I take full responsibility for the book's remaining errors.

Organizations as well as people supported the research and writing of *The War in Words*. In 1999 I received a Newberry Library/South Central Modern Language Association Short-Term Fellowship to travel to Chicago and begin research at the Newberry during my sabbatical. The Office of Research and Graduate Studies at the University of Arkansas at Little Rock gave me funds that covered several research visits to the Minnesota Historical Society, and other sites, from 2001 to 2003. While I was there, the society kindly accorded me office and photocopying privileges. In summer 2003 a very welcome Summer Stipend from the National Endowment for the Humanities provided time to synthesize material, draft the introductory sections, and regain momentum.[2]

When the time came to request images to be included in this book, the following organizations generously waived or reduced their use fees and expedited the reproduction process: the Minnesota Historical Society, the Brown County (Minnesota) Historical Society, the Chippewa County (Minnesota) Historical Society, the Nebraska State Historical Society, the South Dakota State Historical Society, the Denver Public Library, and the Newberry Library. I am particularly grateful to geographer Jerry Hanson, one of my colleagues at the University of Arkansas at Little Rock, who at short notice kindly produced the map of Dakota War sites used in this book.

I would also like to add a personal note on how I became interested in captivity narratives in the first place. For twenty-five years I have worked on various projects in the field of captivity narrative studies, *The War in Words* being the latest contribution. In 2004, while preparing a talk on how scholars become interested in specific research areas, I encountered the work of Albert Bandura, one of the twentieth century's most influential psychologists and the father of Social Cognitive Theory.[3] Bandura believes that "under certain conditions . . . fortuitous events set in motion constellations of influences that alter the course of lives."[4] He defines a chance event as an unintentional meeting of strangers and elaborates, "Although the separate chains of events in a

chance encounter have their own causal determinants, their intersec-
tion occurs fortuitously rather than by design."[5]

As with many other researchers, my first unexpected exposure to
the field was tied to an individual mentor. I was originally interested
in twentieth-century American literature when I left England to study
at Penn State in the 1970s. Once there, however, I met the formidable
bibliographer and early Americanist Harrison T. Meserole and joined his
cadre of graduate students. He introduced me to Mary Rowlandson's
captivity narrative, first published in 1682, and the rest is history. I very
much regret that he did not live to see this book appear in print.

Commitments to knowledge, ideology, and aesthetics are ways in which
individuals define themselves personally and professionally. Ideology
reinforces sense of self, and sense of self reinforces ideology. Theorist
Anthony Giddens explains: "Self-identity is not a distinctive trait, or even
a collection of traits, possessed by the individual. It is *the self as reflexively
understood by the person in terms of his or her biography*."[6] A coherent sense
of identity is achieved by ordering one's own life narratives. Further,
reaching back to the past and forward to the future positions people
for the greatest fulfillment individually and collectively, for negotiating
and engaging with what Giddens terms "life politics."[7]

So how did I combine my own self-narratives with what the world
tells about me? Apart from Harry Meserole, one of my other teachers
at Penn State was Philip Young, a Hemingway scholar who used to
mock his institutional designation there as "Our Hemingway Man."[8]
Sometimes I wonder if I haven't become "Our Captivity Narrative
Woman" at my own university and beyond. I continue to be drawn to
captivity narratives, I believe, because my own ethnic background is
so very mixed (English, Armenian, German Jewish, Irish) and because
the texts enact culture clashes, culture-crossing, cultural confusion,
and cultural exchange, which I find fascinating. These narrative pat-
terns are both familiar and familial to me.

My father used to tell the haunting story of a distant Armenian relative whom he remembered from the 1920s only as "Mariam." During the deportations of Armenians from Turkey before the First World War, twelve-year-old Mariam was driven into a column of women and children on a forced march. En route, Kurdish villagers sometimes carried women into concubinage or took children to act as servants or to replace lost family members. Initially a Kurdish family abducted Mariam to be a servant, but later she became the common-law wife of one of the family's sons. Although she was tattooed on her face according to Kurdish custom and bore a child, she clung to her Armenian identity—encompassing a different language, religion, and culture—and escaped her captivity about four years later, willingly abandoning her Muslim spouse and child. Mariam not only readapted to her culture of origin, Christian Armenian society, she had never really lost it. In retelling this family story I memorialize and re-create Mariam and also its original teller, my father, who died in 2005.

I first wrote on Dakota War captivity narratives in *The Indian Captivity Narrative, 1550–1900*, the book I coauthored in 1993 with my colleague and friend James A. Levernier. There I used the stories by Jannette DeCamp Sweet, Nancy McClure Faribault Huggan, and Mary Schwandt Schmidt to signify the complexity of many other women's experiences as captives and writers. The sheer variety of these three women's responses to the Dakota War was the spark for *The War in Words*. But another connection fueled my interest in Minnesota history and storytelling. My husband's family is from St. Paul, and we retain a close link with Minnesota (even though we live in Arkansas) because we own a cabin in the Superior National Forest that my in-laws bought in the 1960s. It is in Ojibwe, not Dakota, country, but I have been able to write parts of this book in the quiet of our cabin on Gust Lake. For the ties to land and family that the cabin represents—the home-away-from-home that we both love so dearly—I dedicate this book to my husband, Bob.

September 2007

List of Narratives and
Their Chronological Contexts

To introduce readers to the twenty-four figures in this book who wrote about the Dakota War, and to allow for easy reference to them, I list entries below alphabetically under the primary subject.[1] Then I record multiple versions of narratives (sometimes with different authors) under the primary subject's name, in chronological order of publication. Since most of these narratives are little-known, I also furnish basic descriptive information so readers are more prepared when they read my later, more detailed analyses.[2] Finally, in a separate section I survey the general chronological contexts of these accounts.

List of Narratives
Jerome Big Eagle (Wamditanka) (1827–1906)

"Evidence Taken by the Indian Peace Commission . . . June 15, 1868." Big Eagle's Testimony. In *Papers Relating to Talks and Councils Held with the Indians in Dakota and Montana Territories in the Years 1866–1869*. Washington DC: Government Printing Office, 1910. 93–94.
"A Sioux Story of the War." Published in the *St. Paul Pioneer Press*, 1 July 1894. Republished in *Collections of the Minnesota Historical Society* 6 (1894): 382–400.

Big Eagle (Wamditanka) held many leadership positions among the Mdewakanton Dakotas and led his band at several major battles during the Dakota War. He surrendered to the U.S. military and was originally sentenced to death. After his reprieve he went to prison in Davenport, Iowa. Pardoned in 1864, he moved to the Crow Creek and Santee Reservations and finally settled near Granite Falls, Minnesota. "A Sioux Story of the War," published in 1894, is considered the most important of the accounts by Dakota combatants and leaders. It uses various forms of captivity rhetoric and discusses his incarcerations.

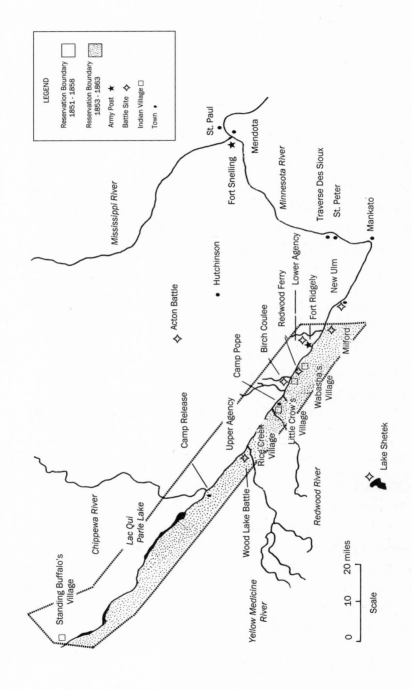

LEGEND

Reservation Boundary 1851 - 1858 ☐
Reservation Boundary 1853 - 1863 ▨
Army Post ★
Battle Site ◇
Indian Village ☐
Town •

Mississippi River

St. Paul
Mendota
Fort Snelling
Minnesota River
Traverse Des Sioux
St. Peter
Mankato

Hutchinson
Acton Battle
Camp Pope
Birch Coulee
Redwood Ferry
Lower Agency
Fort Ridgely
New Ulm
Milford

Camp Release
Upper Agency
Rice Creek Village
Little Crow's Village
Wabasha's Village

Chippewa River
Lac Qui Parle Lake
Wood Lake Battle
Redwood River
Lake Shetek

Standing Buffalo's Village
Yellow Medicine River

Scale
0   10   20 miles

Map of Dakota War sites. Drawn by Jerry Hanson, University of Arkansas at Little Rock. Used with permission.

Samuel J. Brown (1845–1925)

"Captivity of the Family of Joseph R. Brown." In Isaac V. D. Heard, *History of the Sioux War and Massacres of 1862 and 1863*. 1863. 2nd ed., New York: Harper, 1864. Rpt., Millwood NY: Kraus, 1975. 202–8.

"In Captivity: The Experience, Privations and Dangers of Sam'l J. Brown, and Others, while Prisoners of the Hostile Sioux, during the Massacre and War of 1862." Published in the *Mankato Weekly Review*, 30 March to 11 May 1897. Reprinted in pamphlet form by the *Mankato Review*; by the U.S. Senate, titled *In Captivity* . . . , 56th Congress, 2nd session, 1900; and within "Deposition of Samuel J. Brown," *Sisseton and Wahpeton Bands of Dakota Sioux Indians v. the United States*, 1901–7, U.S. Court of Claims No. 22524. Part 1, 1901, 25–74.

George G. Allanson. *Stirring Adventures of the Joseph R. Brown Family*. 1933. Rpt., Wheaton MN: Wheaton Gazette, 1947.

Samuel J. Brown was the son of Joseph R. Brown, Indian agent to the Dakotas until 1861, and Susan Frenier Brown, who was Franco Dakota. Seventeen-year-old Samuel was captured along with other family members while escaping from their home near the Upper Sioux Agency. They stayed with Little Crow for several days and were then rescued by their Dakota relatives and taken to Fort Ridgely. Brown became a scout with General Sibley's forces for several years. He told the story of his family's captivity many times, most famously in the 1897 publication *In Captivity*.

Joseph Coursolle
(Joe Gaboo, Joe Caboo, Joe Gabbro) (ca. 1830–before 1893)

Clem Felix. "The Ordeal of Hinhankaga." As told to F. J. Patten. Ca. 1962. Typescript. Minnesota Historical Society Library.

This is a transcription of an oral narrative told to an amateur historian by Joseph Coursolle's grandson, Clem Felix, which remained unpublished until 1988. The romanticized story tells how Joseph Coursolle, son of a French Canadian man and a Dakota woman, escaped from the Lower Sioux Agency with his wife and baby but how their two young daughters were captured for six weeks and rescued at Camp Release. Recast as a kind of frontier story of bravery and endurance, the narrative also includes historical information about phases of the Dakota War in which Coursolle acted as a scout.

Edward Sylvester Ellis (1840–1916)

Indian Jim: A Tale of the Minnesota Massacre. Beadle's Dime Novels, no. 67, 1 April 1864. London: Beadle and Co., 1864. Reprinted in Beadle's American Library (London edition of Dime Novels), no. 40; Pocket Novels, no. 28; Boy's Library, no. 94; New Dime Novels, no. 576; Boy's Library, no. 109.

Indian Jim is a dime novel published in 1864 fictionalizing aspects of the Dakota War and using it as background for a captivity narrative. Details indicate that Ellis included historical persons and events to authenticate his novel. One of the most prolific and well-known of all the nineteenth-century dime novelists, Ellis adapted captivity as a subject in many other works, including two later novels that traded on the Dakota War in the popular imagination, though their connection to it was actually very slight: *Red Plume* (1900) and *The Story of Red Feather: A Tale of the Frontier* (1908). Like some other dime novelists, Ellis was interested in melding the two genres of the Indian captivity narrative and the dime novel.

Joseph Godfrey (Otakle) (1835–1909)

Testimony. U.S. Army, Military Commission, Sioux War Trials: 1862. Case #1. Original documents at National Archives, Washington DC. Senate Records 37A–F2. Original Transcripts of the Records of Trials of Certain Sioux Indians Charged with Barbarities in the State of Minnesota.
"Godfrey's Statement." In Isaac V. D. Heard, *History of the Sioux War and Massacres of 1862 and 1863.* 1863. 2nd ed., New York: Harper, 1864. 191–201.

Joseph Godfrey (Otakle), the son of a French Canadian man and a slave woman, was a slave himself until he ran away from an abusive master to live among the Dakotas. In his twenties he married Takanheca, a Native woman, and became culturally Dakota. During the Dakota War he fought in major battles but claimed that he was coerced into doing so. Godfrey played an important role in the postwar trials by implicating other Dakotas and sending them to the gallows. Although originally sentenced to death, he was granted a stay of execution and imprisoned instead. Released in 1866, he lived out his days on the Santee Reservation. The story of his own and others' captivity is included in court testimony and in Isaac Heard's *History of the Sioux War*.

Good Star Woman
(Wicahpewastewin, Dorine Blacksmith) (1854–after 1930)

Frances Densmore. "A Sioux Woman's Account of the Uprising in Minnesota." [1938]. Typescript. Frances Densmore Papers. Minnesota Historical Society Library.

Good Star Woman (Dorine Blacksmith) was born near the Upper Sioux Agency and was about eight when the Dakota War broke out. Although her family tried to avoid involvement in the hostilities, she and other relatives were confined at the Fort Snelling camp for noncombatants and then at the Crow Creek Reservation. Eventually she returned to Minnesota and lived with the Prairie Island band near Red Wing. Good Star Woman's account, translated by her daughters and recorded in the 1930s by the noted ethnologist Frances Densmore, provides an unusual perspective, since very few Native women had spoken publicly of their wartime experiences up to then.

Isaac V. D. Heard (1834–1913)

History of the Sioux War. 1863. 2nd ed., New York: Harper, 1864. Rpt., Millwood NY: Kraus, 1975.

Heard's book provides an extensive early history of the Dakota War by a lawyer, soldier, scholar, and recorder at the postwar military hearings. It includes many first-person and third-person accounts of captivity within its pages and strives to be comprehensive. Traditionally it has been considered the most trustworthy of the histories published shortly after the Dakota War, but this reputation is misleading, as the book reveals its author's many biases.

Nancy McClure Faribault Huggan (1836–1927)

"Story of Nancy McClure. Captivity among the Sioux." *Collections of the Minnesota Historical Society* 6 (1894): 438–60. Taken from a series of eight letters McClure wrote to Return I. Holcombe, 13 April–14 June 1894. Return I. Holcombe Papers. Minnesota Historical Society Library.

Letter to William R. Marshall. May 1894. Dakota Conflict of 1862 Manuscripts Collections. Minnesota Historical Society.

"Statement of Nancy Huggins, Wa-Pa-Let (Hat)." Interview with Frank Hopkins. 29 October 1926. Manuscript Notebooks. Fort Ridgely State Park and Historical Association Papers. Minnesota Historical Society.

Thomas Hughes. *Old Traverse des Sioux.* St. Peter MN: Herald, 1929.

Nancy McClure was the child of James McClure, an Anglo officer at Fort Snelling, and Winona, a Dakota woman. She lived with her mother and stepfather until she was fourteen and attended a mission school. After her mother's death in 1851 she moved to be with her grandmother at Traverse des Sioux but soon married a Franco Dakota trader, David Faribault Sr. Nancy, her husband, and her daughter were captured as they escaped from their farm near the Lower Sioux Agency. She wrote down her story in 1894 and went on to retell it a number of times in her later years.

Benedict Juni (1852–1922)

Held in Captivity. New Ulm MN: Liesch-Walter, 1926. Rpt., New Ulm MN: L. F. & R. W. Juni, 1961.

This text is a first-person captivity narrative written in old age by a German American boy captured near New Ulm. Told as a boy's adventure story reminiscent of *The Adventures of Huckleberry Finn,* the story presents the Dakotas sympathetically and shows eleven-year-old Juni's rapid acculturation to Dakota life. Juni characterizes his captivity among the Dakotas as benevolent but his experience at Camp Release, with all its privations, as the real captivity he had to endure.

Lillian Everett Curtiss Keeney (ca. 1856–1923)

Typescript of a letter sent to Harper M. Workman, 2 August 1894. In Neil Currie, comp., "Information on Victims of the Lake Shetek Massacre Obtained by Correspondence and Personal Testimony." Dakota Conflict of 1862 Manuscripts Collections. Minnesota Historical Society.

This text is a captivity narrative in the form of a personal letter sent in middle age by a traumatized survivor of the Lake Shetek attack. Only six when she was captured, Lillian Everett was rescued and reunited with her father after five months of captivity with White Lodge's band of Dakotas. This unpublished account is interesting for its narrative gaps and its detached tone. Lillian Everett Keeney remembered surprisingly little of her captivity, but what she did remember was nightmarish.

Lorenzo Lawrence (Towanetaton) (ca. 1822–1897)

"Story of Lorenzo Lawrence." 1895. Lorenzo Lawrence Papers. Minnesota Historical Society Library
"The Statement of Lorenzo Lawrence." In Henry B. Whipple, *Lights and Shadows of a Long Episcopate*. New York: Macmillan, 1912. 114–18.
Elden Lawrence. *The Peace Seekers: Indian Christians and the Dakota Conflict*. Sioux Falls SD: Pine Hill Press, 2005.

Lorenzo Lawrence was born near Big Stone Lake, Minnesota, about 1822 and was an early Dakota convert to Christianity. He attended several schools in Minnesota and Ohio and cofounded the Hazelwood Republic near the Upper Sioux Agency, a group of Dakotas who adopted certain European American practices. In 1861 he successfully obtained American citizenship. Lawrence's 1862 postwar statement and the longer written account he titled "Story of Lorenzo Lawrence" in 1895 describe his rescue of ten captive women and children and his own economic captivity and hardship after the war despite his courageous actions.

Harriet E. Bishop McConkey (1817–1883)

Dakota War Whoop; or, Indian Massacres and War in Minnesota. St. Paul: D. D. Merrill, 1863. Rev. ed., St. Paul: For the Author, 1864. Rpt., Chicago: Lakeside Press, 1965.

An early belletristic history of the Dakota War claiming to be definitive but actually filled with factual errors and racist rhetoric, this book
includes many captivity narratives as well as military documents and
other forms of first-person testimony. It was written by a New England
schoolteacher who opened the first schoolhouse in St. Paul. McConkey was never a captive but incorrectly fancied herself the premier
historian of the war.

Paul Mazakutemani (Little Paul) (ca. 1806–1885)

Holograph manuscript in Dakota. 32 pages. 1869. Minnesota Historical Society Library.
Translated by Stephen R. Riggs and published as "Narrative of Paul Mazakootemane,"
Collections of the Minnesota Historical Society 3 (1870–80): 82–90.

Born about 1806 at Lac Qui Parle, Minnesota, Paul Mazakutemani (Little
Paul) learned to read and write in Dakota, converted to Christianity,
took up farming, and helped to organize the Hazelwood Republic of
assimilationist Dakotas. In 1869 he wrote an autobiographical narrative
in Dakota that he sent to missionary Stephen Riggs, who translated
and published it. It falls into Native traditions of telling but also can
be seen as a captivity narrative that includes the stories of his own
and others' captivity or confinement. According to Riggs, the narrative
"gives an inside view of the late Sioux outbreak" (original emphasis).

Martha T. Riggs (Martha Morris) (1842–1910)

"Letter: The Flight of the Missionaries." Published in the *Cincinnati Christian Herald*, ca.
1 October 1862. Reprinted in Stephen R. Riggs, *Mary and I: Forty Years with the Sioux*.
Chicago: Holmes, 1880. Rpt., Williamstown MA: Corner House, 1971. 171–78.

Martha Riggs, the daughter of Presbyterian missionary Stephen Riggs,
provides a pro-Dakota, first-person impression in this protest letter.
The narrative shows the escape party from the Upper Sioux Agency,
of which she was a member, as captive to the elements rather than to
Indians, though always fearful of further attacks. It contains a vehement defense of those Christian Dakotas who were not among the

militants and an equally vehement censure of the government's continued mistreatment of the Dakotas.

Jacob Nix (1822–1897)

Der Ausbruch der Sioux-Indianer in Minnesota, im August 1862. Milwaukee: Zahn, 1887.
The Sioux Uprising in Minnesota, 1862: Jacob Nix's Eyewitness History. Trans. and ed. Don
    Heinrich Tolzmann. Indianapolis: Max Kade German-American Center, 1994.

Jacob Nix, who commanded the volunteers at New Ulm who fended
off the first Indian attack in 1862, was born in Germany. He came to the
United States after fighting in the German Revolution of 1848, and he
and his family moved to New Ulm in 1855. Nix's account, published in
German in 1887, recognizes the contributions of New Ulm's German
inhabitants to state and national affairs and uses the captivity narrative
not just for anti-Indian propaganda but for anti-Anglo propaganda too.
Nix responds to the nativist interpretation of the Conflict by presenting himself and the New Ulm settlers as new patriots.

Mary E. Schwandt Schmidt
(Mary Schwandt, Mary Schwandt-Schmidt) (1848–1939)

"Narrative of Mary Schwandt." In Charles Bryant and Abel Murch, *A History of the Great Mas-
    sacre by the Sioux Indians in Minnesota.* Cincinnati: Rickey and Carroll, 1864. 335–42.
"The Story of Mary Schwandt. Her Captivity during the Sioux 'Outbreak'—1862." *Col-
    lections of the Minnesota Historical Society* 6 (1894): 461–74. Reprinted in Don Heinrich
    Tolzmann, ed., *German Pioneer Accounts of the Great Sioux Uprising of 1862.* Milford OH:
    Little Miami Publishing Company, 2002. 8–25.
"Recollections of the Indian Massacre of 1862 in Minnesota." Address before the Colonial
    Dames of America in Minnesota. St. Paul, 25 October 1915. Mary Schwandt Schmidt
    Papers. Minnesota Historical Society.
"Recollections of My Captivity among the Sioux the Year of 1862." Ca. 1929 (n.d.). Mary
    Schwandt Schmidt Papers. Minnesota Historical Society.

Mary Schwandt was captured near New Ulm at the beginning of the
war, along with two other young women. After several days she was
adopted by a Dakota woman, Snana, also called Maggie Good Thunder (later Maggie Brass). Maggie Good Thunder protected Schwandt

and at war's end handed her over to the authorities at Camp Release. Schwandt's story first appeared in Bryant and Murch's *History* in 1864. After many years of silence Schwandt told a different version of her story in 1894, focusing on her adoptive mother's kindness. The two women were reunited and met regularly in the 1890s. Thereafter Schwandt Schmidt wrote down multiple versions of her captivity narrative and delivered many talks on the subject.

Snana (Maggie Brass) (1839–1908)

"Narration of a Friendly Sioux." [1900?]. Minnesota Historical Society Archives. Minnesota Historical Society Library. Published in *Collections of the Minnesota Historical Society* 9 (1901): 426–30.

"Deposition of Mrs. Maggie Brass." Evidence for Defendant, Court of Claims No. 22524. *Sisseton and Wahpeton Bands of Sioux Indians v. the United States*, 1901–7, part 2, 379–85.

Snana (Maggie Good Thunder, later Maggie Brass) and her husband, Wakinyanwaste (Andrew Good Thunder), were early Dakota converts to the Episcopal mission effort. During the Dakota War they were among the peace faction. In 1894 Maggie Brass was reunited with Mary Schwandt Schmidt, whom she had rescued and adopted during the Dakota War. Return Holcombe, the journalist to whom Schwandt Schmidt told her story, interviewed and corresponded with Brass and published her narrative in 1901. In popular culture Snana/Maggie Brass is Minnesota's Pocahontas.

Virginia Driving Hawk Sneve (1933–)

Betrayed. New York: Holiday House, 1974.

This young-adult novel by contemporary Sioux author Virginia Driving Hawk Sneve takes as its subject the Fool Soldiers' historical rescue of nine captives from the Lake Shetek attack. The Fool Soldiers were a group of Lakota youths led by Waanatan (Martin Charger), and the novel contrasts the points of view of Waanatan and of captive Sarah Duley. Unlike the negative stereotypes of Native Americans so prevalent in the traditional white-authored captivity literature, this narrative presents captors, captives, and rescuers sympathetically and interchangeably.

Cecelia Campbell Stay (1848–1935)

"The Massacre at the Lower Sioux Agency, August 18th, 1862." Typescript. 1882. Provincial Archives of Manitoba, Winnipeg MB.

Interview with Alexander Seifert et al. 5 August 1924. In Alexander Seifert, comp., "Notes of Committee Selecting Historical Data from New Ulm, Minn." 5–6 August 1924. Typescript. Dakota Conflict of 1862 Manuscripts Collections. Minnesota Historical Society.

"Camp Relief [Release] in 1862." [1924?]. Undated typescript. In Celia M. Campbell Stay, "Reminiscence and Biographical Data." Dakota Conflict of 1862 Manuscripts Collections. Minnesota Historical Society.

Cecelia (often called Celia) Campbell Stay was born into a Franco-Irish-Dakota family in 1848. They lived in 1862 at the Lower Sioux Agency, where her father, Antoine J. Campbell, was a government interpreter. During the war the family was captured but then defended by other Dakotas and protected by Little Crow. Cecelia Campbell was an observant thirteen-year-old in 1862 and recalled events later on from that vantage point. Between 1882 and 1925 she provided at least three English versions of her family's wartime role.

Jannette DeCamp Sweet (1833–after 1912)

"In the Hands of the Sioux: A California Woman's Captivity among Savages." 7 pages. Typescript of article possibly appearing in *San Francisco Call*, April 1892. Brown County Historical Society, New Ulm MN.

"Mrs. J. E. DeCamp Sweet's Narrative of Her Captivity in the Sioux Outbreak of 1862." *Collections of the Minnesota Historical Society* 6 (1894): 354–80.

Jannette and Joseph DeCamp married in Ohio, then settled in Shakopee, Minnesota, in 1855. They moved to the Lower Sioux Agency in 1861 so Joseph could run the sawmill, and Jannette says that soon she was accustomed to living among the Dakotas. On 18 August, when the Lower Agency was attacked, Jannette was there with her three young sons, though Joseph had gone to St. Paul on business. Lorenzo Lawrence rescued her and her children and escorted them to Fort Ridgely. DeCamp Sweet's narratives, especially the one published in 1894, stress the traumas of captivity.

Helen Mar Carrothers Tarble (1843–after 1912)

The Story of My Capture and Escape during the Minnesota Indian Massacre of 1862. St. Paul: Abbott, 1904.

Thirteen-year-old Helen Mar married James Carrothers in 1856 and moved to an isolated cabin in Renville County, Minnesota. Often alone while James worked at the Lower Sioux Agency, Helen became friends with the nearby Dakotas. Native women attended her when she gave birth to her first child at fifteen, and a Dakota shaman instructed her in traditional remedies. Although she was captured during the war, her knowledge of Dakota culture and language helped her to cope better than many others. A Native woman facilitated her escape to Fort Ridgely.

Sarah F. Wakefield (1829–99)

Six Weeks in the Sioux Tepees: A Narrative of Indian Captivity. Minneapolis: Atlas, 1863. 2nd ed., Shakopee MN: Argus, 1864.
Modern reprints of the 1864 edition: June Namias, ed., Six Weeks in the Sioux Tepees, Norman: University of Oklahoma Press, 1997, and Kathryn Zabelle Derounian-Stodola, ed., Women's Indian Captivity Narratives. New York: Penguin, 1998. 241–313.

Doctor's wife Sarah Wakefield wrote this first-person captivity narrative after being captured while leaving the Upper Sioux Agency and protected for six weeks by a Dakota man she called Chaska (We-chank-wash-ta-don-pee). The most famous of all the captivity narratives arising from the Dakota War, Wakefield's account is a cultural critique and condemnation of the Dakotas' (and her own) treatment by the U.S. military and the government. Wakefield fervently defends Chaska, who was nevertheless one of the thirty-eight Dakotas hanged at Mankato.

Esther Wakeman (Mahpiyatowin) (1845–after 1885)

"Narrative." In Mr. and Mrs. Harry Lawrence, "The Indian Nations of Minnesota: The Sioux Uprising." In *Minnesota Heritage: A Panoramic Narrative of the Historical Development of the North Star State*, ed. Lawrence Brings. Minneapolis: Denison, 1960. 80–82.

Born in 1845, Esther Wakeman married White Spider (John C. Wakeman), Little Crow's half brother, about 1861. They lived at the Lower Sioux Reservation and supported Little Crow during the war. In September 1862 they fled the state but surrendered in January 1864. Afterward Esther Wakeman was confined at Fort Snelling and then the Crow Creek Reservation. The Wakemans returned to Minnesota in the 1880s. Esther told her story to her daughter, who passed it down as part of the family's oral history. This account reflects the viewpoint of a close relative and ally of Little Crow.

Urania S. Fraser White (1825–after 1901)

"Captivity among the Sioux, August 18 to September 26, 1862." *Collections of the Minnesota Historical Society* 9 (1898–1900): 394–426.

Urania and Nathan White were married in 1845. Two years later they moved to Wisconsin and stayed there for fifteen years. But in the spring of 1862 they moved again, to Minnesota. The family was attacked at the beginning of the Dakota War, and White's eldest son was killed and scalped. Another son escaped, but Urania White, her daughter Julia, and her baby boy were captured. An Indian couple adopted and protected White. Her account shares with only a handful of other captivity narratives a detailed articulation of extreme psychological trauma.

Chronological Contexts of the Dakota War Captivity Narratives

Not all the early accounts generated by the Dakota War fall into the genre of the captivity or confinement narrative, but many of them do. The first captivity narrative I discuss in my book is Martha Riggs's protest letter published in a newspaper and a church circular in 1862. It uses captivity as a vehicle to defend Christianized Dakotas and was so powerful that Riggs's father reprinted it twelve years later in his autobiography, *Mary and I: Forty Years with the Sioux* (1880). Martha Riggs's letter was one of many on-the-scene reports covering captivity and appearing in local and national newspapers and magazines.

Mary Renville and John Renville's *Thrilling Narrative of Indian Captivity* and Sarah Wakefield's *Six Weeks in the Sioux Tepees* were the earliest individual captivity narratives to be separately published. Both came out from the Atlas Publishing Company in 1863, and both, in their own ways, were controversial. These individual narratives by survivors joined cumulative assessments by historians and antiquarians that began to flood the market as soon as the Dakota Conflict was over. Dakota War and Civil War accounts echoed each other for a while and vied for readers. But the Civil War was only partway through its five-year campaign in 1862, so accounts were ongoing and undigested. On the other hand, the Dakota Conflict was over within weeks, so the work of interpreting it could begin more quickly.

By 1863 Harriet Bishop McConkey, Isaac Heard, and Sarah Wakefield had all published first editions of their texts that were popular enough to warrant expanded second editions the following year. McConkey and Heard used captivity narratives within overall histories of the Dakota War mostly to record and legitimate the government's response. McConkey's *Dakota War Whoop* and Heard's *History of the Sioux War* included first-person accounts over which the subjects had little or no control, such as those by Joseph Godfrey and Samuel Brown. In later life Brown was able to return to the topic of his family's captivity and provide his own version of events. Joseph Godfrey, however, did not furnish any other written accounts of his role in the war but presumably passed down his oral history to his family. Wakefield published *Six Weeks in the Sioux Tepees* in 1863 to proclaim her own and her protector's innocence of any sexual wrongdoing and to protest government policies against the Dakotas.

Mary Schwandt's sensationalized captivity narrative first appeared in Bryant and Murch's 1864 *History* with some—probably much—editorialization. Like Samuel Brown, Schwandt retold her captivity tale in later life and reclaimed her own life story in numerous written and spoken texts after 1894. Helen Carrothers Tarble's story also first appeared in Bryant and Murch's *History*, then came out again in the *St. Paul Pioneer Press* in 1894 and finally, in a separately published version, in 1904. The Dakota War quickly became the stuff of fiction, as seen in Edward Ellis's dime novel *Indian Jim*, published in 1864, just two years after the hostilities ended. Although dimes were still in their infancy, Ellis's book incorporated what were already popular generic themes of captivity and frontier romance. From then on the Dakota War formed the basis for other dime novels and fictionalized captivity narratives.

Few Native accounts were published in the decades immediately following the Dakota War, and those that were appeared in books produced by non-Natives. The words of individual Indians can be recouped contemporaneously through oral statements (for example, Joseph Godfrey's testimony in the Military Commission hearings), and some of these constitute captivity narratives of the subjects themselves or of others. Yet even here the evidence is often mediated through translation and editorialization. The 1880s, however, saw the composition if not actual publication of texts by Paul Mazakutemani and Cecelia Campbell Stay and by other hitherto underrepresented constituencies, such as German Americans. Jacob Nix's history, *The Sioux Uprising in Minnesota*, was published in 1887 to mark the twenty-fifth commemoration of the war, but it reached a limited readership because Nix wrote it in German.

In the 1890s a large number of captivity narratives appeared in various media, including local newspapers and *Collections of the Minnesota Historical Society*. Historians and journalists like Return Holcombe and Thomas Hughes collected and edited these narratives by European

Americans and Native Americans alike. Perhaps the interest in Dakota Conflict accounts marked a wish to document the state's turbulent early years for a new generation, or perhaps antiquarians and ethnographers wanted to record first-person accounts before the subjects died. The narratives of Jannette DeCamp Sweet, Nancy Huggan, Mary Schwandt Schmidt, and Big Eagle all appeared in the 1894 volume of *Collections of the Minnesota Historical Society,* and Lorenzo Lawrence's manuscript account—while not published until 1988—was submitted to the Minnesota Historical Society that same year. Further, the 1894 Columbian Exposition in Chicago emphasized and even exhibited Native Americans and, through the efforts of the anthropologist Franz Boas, introduced attendees to the new discipline of anthropology.[3] Like other states, Minnesota had its own pavilion there, and the organizers back home may have looked to Minnesota's most famous war for publishable material just after the Exposition ended.

In the early twentieth century the Minnesota Historical Society still wished to collect and publish captivity narratives and other material about the Dakota War. Hence the stories of Maggie Brass (Snana) and Urania White appeared in the pages of its *Collections,* the former in 1901 and the latter in 1904. Benedict Juni published his longer account as a separate book in 1926. Narratives by Dakotas and those from a mixed background were collected and printed more routinely later in the twentieth century. Some of these stories represented originally oral accounts that were finally transcribed and published. For example, as an old lady in 1934, Dakota War survivor Good Star Woman agreed to recount her experiences to ethnologist Frances Densmore. And the captivity accounts of Esther Wakeman and Joseph Coursolle were passed down within their families and then transcribed in the 1960s. In fact, the publication of Wakeman's story and the recording of Coursolle's in 1962 may signal a resurgence of interest marking the centenary of the Dakota War. In 1978, when the publishing industry recognized the need for young-adult novels by and about Indians, Virginia Driving

Hawk Sneve took the captivity of women and children from Lake Shetek as the basis for *Betrayed*.

Legal proceedings after the Dakota War may also have prompted participants and others to remember events and to tell their stories.[4] For instance, the histories by Isaac Heard and Charles Bryant and Abel Murch adapt testimony taken during the U.S. Army's Military Commission hearings in fall 1862 to try Indians and establish their wartime actions. First versions of the captivities of Mary Schwandt, Joseph Godfrey, and Samuel Brown came from this testimony, plus additional information the subjects might have furnished privately. The next year various parties gave evidence before the Sioux Claims Commission for property losses incurred in the war. Being forced to recall this information may have provided the impetus for claimants to write down their experiences in more detail and eventually publish or authorize a narrative. This could have been the case with Sarah Wakefield, for example. She and her husband made large claims for losses, and although much of the Claims Commission testimony is no longer extant, the Wakefields prudently kept a copy of their claim, which has survived.

The Office of Indian Affairs Report for 1866 mentions awards of between fifty and twenty-five hundred dollars for Dakotas who were progovernment during the Conflict. The thirty-five Dakotas to whom rewards were given probably furnished testimony, and this information may have formed the basis for accounts published later, for example, Lorenzo Lawrence's testimony, which Bishop Henry Whipple included decades later in his book *Lights and Shadows of a Long Episcopate*. Also, in 1868 Congress charged the Indian Peace Commission to find ways to placate Native Americans and deter war. Information taken by the commission may have been the basis for information on Dakotas rescuing captives. In 1885 traders and their survivors instigated a lawsuit for business losses during the Dakota War. The Special Commission of the Indian Division of the Secretary of the Interior heard the claims, which included Joseph Coursolle's account of his escape in 1862.

Other accounts of captivity and confinement may have been prompted by testimony during the Sisseton and Wahpeton bands' claims against the U.S. government in 1901. Settlements to the Sissetons and Wahpetons—including restoration of annuities—were not made until 1907, the same year that the Mdewakanton and Wahpekute bands began their suit for restoration of treaty rights. At stake in 1901 was the extent to which the Sissetons and Wahpetons (from the Upper Sioux Agency) had joined militant Mdewakantons and Wahpekutes (from the Lower Agency) during the Dakota War. Captivity narratives by Natives and non-Natives may have affected public sentiment concerning these claims, especially within the state of Minnesota. The publication of Maggie Brass's captivity narrative about Mary Schwandt in the 1901 volume of *Collections of the Minnesota Historical Society*, for example, was well-timed in terms of possibly softening non-Native Minnesotans' sentiments toward the Dakotas forty years after the war.

Methodology

To know what took place summary is enough. To learn what happened requires multiple points of address and analysis. | Toni Morrison, "Introduction: Friday on the Potomac" (1992)

The words used to describe war have a great deal of work to do: they must communicate war's intensity, its traumas, fears, and glories; they must make clear who is right and who is wrong, rally support, and recruit allies; and they must document the pain of war, and in so doing, help to alleviate it. | Jill Lepore, *The Name of War: King Philip's War and the Origins of American Identity* (1999)

The reason to assess the works that claim to be telling the life histories of Indians cannot be said to be just a war of words. It is, in fact, a war for the future of Indian intentions. Art and literature and storytelling are at the epicenter of all that an individual or a nation intends to be. | Elizabeth Cook-Lynn, *Anti-Indianism in Modern America: A Voice from Tatekeya's Earth* (2001)

The six-week Dakota War of 1862 has always attracted attention from European American historians, ranging from early books like Isaac Heard's *History of the Sioux War* (1863) to contemporary ones like Gary Clayton Anderson's *Kinsmen of Another Kind: Dakota-White Relations in the Upper Mississippi Valley, 1650–1862* (1984).[1] Recent years have also seen a growing public response from Dakota scholars, tribal leaders, activists, and elders such as Elizabeth Cook-Lynn, Elden Lawrence, Floyd Red Crow Westerman, and Waziyatawin Angela Wilson concerning historical memory and oral history.[2] Yet literary critics have paid little attention to the war and the many narratives it engendered. My contribution to Dakota War scholarship is part literary history, part textual analysis, part historiography, and part cultural contextualization of twenty-four captivity or confinement narratives by and about people involved in the hostilities.

Some of these accounts were originally oral, but most of them fall within the written captivity narrative tradition. Privileging texts, authors, textual production, and contemporary readership helps to situate individual interpretations of captivity and expose the complicated nexus of politics, cultures, identities, and ethnicities at the heart of the Conflict. Thus my title, *The War in Words*, has a double meaning: "the *war* in words," meaning the different ways that information about the war appears in oral and print culture; and "the war in *words*," meaning the range of perspectives about the war created and fought in the texts under discussion.

Using different forms of testimony, I aim to see anew "how issues of biography and history are neither simply represented nor simply reflected, but are reinscribed, translated, radically rethought and fundamentally worked over by the text."[3] Because I do not want to perpetuate misinformation about the war — and there is a lot — I draw attention to blatant inaccuracies within the accounts. But I recognize the difficulty and in the end the inadvisability of establishing a master narrative. Instead, like Tzvetan Todorov, I seek "the path of dialogue. I question, I transpose, I interpret these texts; but also I let them speak (whence so many quotations) and defend themselves."[4] Through the surviving traces of multiple captivity narratives, this book reveals the Dakota War's persistence in historical memory and joins a larger conversation within the United States about ethnicity, identity, war, memory, and narrative.

Although many of the Indian wars generated stories, the Dakota Conflict is unusual in the sheer number of accounts that found their way into print, probably because the war was, and continues to be, bitterly contested. Depending on the definition of "narrative accounts," dozens if not hundreds of versions of the war and its aftermath exist.[5] And the number increases dramatically when stories within longer works are counted, not just separately written ones, plus unpublished and oral material. From this corpus I selected twelve texts by European

Americans and twelve by Native Americans.[6] The authors are men
and women from varied ethnic backgrounds and social strata whose
works were composed and published from 1862 to 1978. Yet of course
even this number of accounts cannot constitute the definitive word
on the war. No number could. In the end the narratives are representative only insofar as they signify a series of complex, contesting,
kaleidoscopic responses.

In keeping with my primary interest in the textual and cultural aspects
of the Dakota Conflict stories, I focus on the rich literary genre called
the captivity narrative. I hold that captivity functioned as metonymy
for the wars between European Americans and Native Americans
and that it also held typological power in its associations with the
Bible. Politically and personally, writing of these wars especially in the
nineteenth century invariably involved a rhetorical engagement with
captivity. In other words, captivity provided a symbolic shorthand that
came to actually define these wars. Thus my selected stories not only
provide different perspectives on the Dakota War but also illustrate
variations of the basic captivity, or confinement, narrative.

I also chose captivity narratives as a vehicle because they are the
most familiar kinds of war narratives, encompassing, in the larger
sense, any story with captors (the empowered, the winners) and captives (the disempowered, the losers). This general definition is useful
since it accommodates such distinct, but cognate, literary forms as
the prison account, the slave narrative, the prisoner-of-war story, the
spiritual autobiography, the providence tale, the Indian boarding school
biography or autobiography, the UFO abduction story, the convent
captivity narrative, the sentimental novel of seduction, and of course
the Indian captivity narrative. The captivity narrative's wide generic
web encompassing auto/biographical, historical, and fictional texts
enacts contact between people of different cultures and provides what
might be termed "cross-cultural conversations."[7] This book shows
the power and pervasiveness of captivity in American culture both

literally and metaphorically, and it contributes to the evolving field of captivity narrative studies by being the only monograph to date about the captivity narratives generated by a single white/Indian war.

Both Native and non-Native theorists see connections among these cognates of the captivity narrative, including Gerald Vizenor (Ojibwe), who observes, "The narratives of slavery, captivity, abduction, and servitude by slavers, colonists, natives, *indians* [*sic*] and others have in common a moral resistance to dominance, the case of survivance over victimry."[8] The specific ways that scholars have engaged with the captivity narrative tradition receive fuller treatment later in the book. But although the image of American Indians capturing European Americans is part of the national colonial ideology, large numbers of Natives were captured in the Americas. Anthropologist Pauline Turner Strong indicates that "in numerical terms the captivity of English colonists pales in comparison to the abduction, imprisonment, and enslavement of Indians by the English."[9] Thus both groups experienced captivity in the historical record, and both told stories about their confinements.

After this methodology comes a chapter titled "Historical Perspectives on the Dakota War," followed by a series of chapters within the book's two main parts, "European Americans Narrating Captivity" and "Native Americans Narrating Captivity," arranged chronologically by date of composition and/or publication, by subject author(s), and by variations on the captivity or confinement narrative prototype. For example, in part 1 the first chapter is titled "Martha Riggs Morris and Sarah Wakefield: Captivity and Protest." It considers texts by Riggs Morris and Wakefield published in 1862 and 1863 respectively, it contextualizes biographical information about the two women, and it shows how their texts employ captivity narratives as protest literature. But predictably the chapter designations and the narratives within chapters are not as discrete as they seem: they deliberately overlap to create a syncretic study of the Dakota War.

Why did I organize the majority of the book within two main sections called "European Americans Narrating Captivity" and "Native Americans Narrating Captivity"? This structure arose as I recognized the individual ideologies and identities within the two groupings and decided to privilege a comparative ethnicities approach rather than a thematic one blending the figures and stories. Dakota voices, I felt, needed to be heard separately from non-Dakota ones, especially since the latter have dominated historical discourse and popular culture.

Such an organization also underscores the discrepancies between Indigenous and non-Indigenous versions of history, especially war history. "For the Eastern Dakota," asserts Dakota historian Waziyatawin Angela Wilson, "this is nowhere more evident than in accounts surrounding the U.S.-Dakota War of 1862."[10] The impact of this war on the Dakotas reinforces the gulf between Natives and non-Natives at the time because the Conflict "remains the major point of demarcation in Dakota history. . . . It was not just the fact that Dakota people were severed from the land that defined who we were, it was not just being confined to reservations in new lands, nor was it just the sense of disconnection suffered by the people. It was all these factors combining to change our relationship with the rest of the world, altering our existence with a seeming finality and irrevocability."[11]

The book's two-part division therefore clarifies that the experience and recollection of captivity during the Dakota War differed according to a person's real or perceived ethnicity in the 1860s and even later. Up to about 1837, which marked the beginning of major treaties in which Dakotas lost land and settlers trickled and then flooded into what became the state of Minnesota, the boundaries between Natives and non-Natives were porous when people originally from one culture lived in or adopted some of the other culture's lifeways. Indeed, as in many frontier communities, various forms of exchange between the groups existed as they attempted to cohabit and adjust. From the late 1830s to the late 1850s underlying problems threatened but did not necessarily sunder existing kinship ties.

But in 1862 any shared terrain dramatically disappeared, at least for a while.[12] By way of example, Annette Atkins compares two figures who moved between cultures before the Conflict: Dakota chief Little Crow (Taoyateduta) and Philander Prescott, a white man married to a Dakota woman. However, when the Dakota War erupted both men "were caught up in the rage. Whatever territory they had shared was ripped into two separate and explicitly racial camps. There was no middle ground to meet or stand on."[13] Wartime conditions thus forced Natives and non-Natives to view events through the lens of race and ethnicity, and their stories of captivity and confinement reflect this.

Although I treat the narratives and their narrators individually, at times I acknowledge the presence of group characteristics that also support my section divisions: for example, a predictable emphasis on victimization during captivity in some (but by no means all) European American women's texts; a different timeframe for publication of the European American and Native American texts, with the former tending to appear before the latter; and evidence that the Dakota women's narratives reflect cultural transformations in their lives since so many of their menfolk were absent or dead.[14] By "group characteristics" I do not, of course, mean essentialist racial qualities but rather rhetorical, political, and cultural strategies the subjects/authors used as consciousness, not category, for identity and survival.[15] Maybe the ideal organization for the book would have been to write twenty-four discrete chapters regardless of "cultural communities" — a phrase Albert Memmi prefers to the erroneous concept of biologically distinct races — and this was an early possibility.[16] But ultimately, having so many short chapters was neither reader-friendly nor practical.

I also opted for this structure recognizing the increased academic attention to ethnicity, race, and nation, specifically to "comparative ethnicities studies."[17] Much of the discussion here obviously concerns European American and Native American ethnicities, yet the case of

Joseph Godfrey, while unusual, is a reminder of just how ethnically blended 1860s Minnesota could be. Godfrey came from a black/white (French) background; was brought up by people from a Franco Dakota background; serially married several Dakota women; lived first as a slave among whites and then as a Dakota; and spoke French and Dakota well but English somewhat hesitantly, at least at the time of the Conflict. Godfrey thus exemplifies the pre-twentieth-century reality that mixed-race Americans were probably not black/white, as often assumed, but far more likely black/Indian/white.[18] A survey of some nineteenth-century racial attitudes and then some twentieth-century approaches, especially the growing amount of literature on "whiteness," provides a useful perspective on this study of Dakota War texts.

Looking at nineteenth-century views of individuals who were part Indian and part white is one way to measure prevailing beliefs about the background and evolution of different races.[19] These bicultural people formed the focus of groups such as philanthropists, who believed that Indians could be "civilized," and also of other constituencies, who debated whether they formed a new race or whether they were "the hybrid offspring of two separate species."[20] Such issues involved the originary theories of two camps: the monogenists (who thought that all human beings, despite their racial markers, were a single species descended from the same evolutionary parents and who pointed to human procreation as proof) and the polygenists (who thought that human beings belonged to different races, which were created separately, and that joint racial offspring were anomalies). Needless to say, both groups exhibited colonialist ideologies.

Initially many monogenists saw Indian/white unions, rather than wars, as the preferred method of "whitening" or "civilizing" Indians, but prejudice against miscegenation meant it was impossible to put this into widespread practice. Regarding skin color, for example, the eighteenth-century New England scientist Samuel Williams stated that the children of Indian/white parents would be white within three generations rather than the five required for children of black/white parents.[21] The monogenists therefore saw bicultural persons as catalysts in the process of total Indian assimilation. Among the white authors in this study Martha Riggs Morris and Sarah Wakefield reflect the applied (but only superficially benevolent) aspects of monogenism.

By the 1830s, with Native Americans understandably fighting land theft in clashes with European Americans and resisting comprehensive adoption of formal (Western) education, farming, Christianization, and intermarriage, the polygenists' views got the upper hand; they were further supported by pseudoscientific approaches to craniology and hybridity. Because Native Americans did not change as rapidly as had been anticipated, many European Americans called for Indian removal west of the Mississippi (there were also, of course, even more compelling arguments for removal). In fact, "Indian Removal as it developed between 1815 and 1830 was a rejection of all Indians as Indians, not simply a rejection of unassimilated Indians who would not accept the American lifestyle."[22]

As this initiative went into effect and the problem seemed literally to move further away for Northeasterners and Midwesterners, the need to modify Native culture lost urgency. Besides, America was becoming more preoccupied with other racialized ethnic issues to do with slavery, the status of free blacks, the Mexican War, and the influx of Asian and European immigrants. Furthermore, bicultural people overall had not proved to be agents for change, as seen in their role in frontier wars including the Dakota Conflict, where they could not be counted on to support colonial expansionist ambitions. Their position therefore pushed them, in the prevailing nineteenth-century mindset, closer to Native than to white identity, culture, and political ideology.

A more recent examination, however, concludes that generalizing about nineteenth-century beliefs on "Indian-white race-mixing is quite perilous. The more one scrutinizes the historical record, the more evident it becomes that, overall, these attitudes were remarkably diverse, ambivalent, contradictory, subjective, and changeable over time."[23] Not only the historical record but also the literary record illustrates a tension between received theoretical assumptions on one hand and practical applications and lived experience on the other. This point may help to explain, for instance, the divergent presentations of Dakotas in many of this book's European American core texts. Jannette DeCamp Sweet, Helen Carrothers Tarble, and Edward Ellis, to take only a few examples, could talk about individual Dakotas who helped whites but elsewhere — sometimes in the same text — excoriate the entire Dakota nation for its savagery.

Just about all the non-Native works under consideration reveal the need to deal with "the character of the Indian" in more or less detail, indicating the authors' awareness that readers expected them to tackle this question. In the first-person accounts especially European Americans often measured Native American nature by the capacity for warfare. This could happen regardless of colonists' favorable prewar interactions with the Dakotas and regardless of their generous, even kind, treatment during captivity. Personal experience frequently gave way to widespread prejudice as the Dakota Conflict seemed to prove that derogatory typecasting of Indians was warranted.

Apart from European American views of Indians, the Native texts themselves not only showed what their usually white mediators wanted them to show but could and did reveal the Native subjects manipulating or controlling material. Some of these accounts present Dakotas in very positive roles for a predominantly white readership in order to reverse negative stereotypes and suggest the need for common ethical behavior. Nancy Huggan, for instance, whose father was English and whose mother was Dakota, proclaims that she was always "white" in her leanings despite her Dakota upbringing. Maggie Brass (Snana) indicates her strong maternal attachment to Mary Schwandt, the captive whom she adopted and protected during the war. And Paul Mazakutemani (Little Paul), an early Christian convert, spends a good deal of time in his account establishing how he helped many captives and thus put Christianity into practice.

The texts by bicultural subjects in particular reflect the complex cultural identities that affected race relations in the mid-nineteenth century. Some Native scholars believe that the roles such people adopted were "numerous and varied."[24] But others, like Diane Wilson, author of the 2006 memoir *Spirit Car: Journey to a Dakota Past*, think their roles were more polarized within Minnesota: "Torn between two cultures, mixed-blood children grew up with varying degrees of loyalty to both sides, depending on which community they were raised in. Some identified closely with their tribe, spoke only Dakota, and became influential in tribal councils. Others adopted the lifestyle of whites, learning to farm, speak French or English, and read and write. The uncertainty over a mixed-blood person's cultural loyalty created a cultural limbo that persists to this day."[25]

Despite how nineteenth-century European Americans considered other groups and how those people tried to present themselves, a growing amount of theory now exists to complicate notions of race and ethnicity and to contribute to the field of whiteness studies. A modern historical truism holds that notions of *race* were rooted in slavery and other forms of imperialism, while notions of *ethnicity* were rooted in the large numbers of European immigrants coming to the United States in the early twentieth century.[26] In fact, new waves of migration into the twenty-first century affect ongoing modifications of both terms as debates continue to rage on definitions and theoretical approaches.

As in earlier times, a major distinction even in modern methodologies is cultural assimilation versus racial essentialism, though recent commentators tend to recognize both the differences and the similarities in the social construction of ethnicity. For example, according to one scholar: "Different ethnic groups retain their own unique stories, insights and reflections, triumphs and tragedies from their sojourns through American life. None of that can take away from the deep structural parallels, especially in the processes of racial oppression, in struggles for survival and resistance, and in efforts to maintain cultural and social integrity and identity. These create the dynamic social framework that brings us together."[27]

Further, class, gender, nation, and region contribute to the fluidity of racialization and modify it radically. This book's division into chapters on texts by and about European Americans and by and about Native Americans attempts not only to recognize and explore racialized ethnicities but also to show the comparative flexibility of some individuals as they moved within and between groups (Helen Tarble, Sarah Wakefield, Samuel Brown, Nancy Huggan, and Cecelia Stay, for example). I believe that all the focus figures in the book contribute to "a complex, contradictory world where ethnicity is both given and contested."[28] Yet, as with my Armenian relative Mariam, discussed in the preface, I also believe these figures assert their identities within their narratives, no matter how problematic or nuanced.[29]

Historians and other theorists in the area of whiteness studies, who explore "the *construction* of whiteness — how diverse groups in the United States came to identify, and be identified by others, as white — and what that has meant for the social order," recognize that whiteness is not physically self-evident.[30] It is now well-known that many ethnicities, including the Irish and German immigrant populations, were not automatically considered white on arrival in terms of class, religion, and social status. They had to grow into whiteness. So to outline the process by which these groups "became Caucasians is to recognize race as an ideological, political deployment rather than as a neutral, biologically determined element of nature."[31] As experienced, then, whiteness is just another type of "social, political, economic, and cultural capital."[32]

Current research suggests that European immigrants to Minnesota spoke at least eleven languages on arrival and that for a surprising number English was their second or even third language.[33] Certainly, both the Anglo white and the Dakota populations in Minnesota tended to see the German immigrants, for example, as less empowered — and thus less white, in a way — than the settlers of English descent. So my study includes German American figures, whose texts reveal the attitudes of other ethnic groups toward them. It also expands the relative dearth of information on German Americans in Minnesota.

Some racialized ethnicities not only aspired to the more powerful position of being white but actually lived it through the phenomenon of passing. In Minnesota those from an Indian/white background had more opportunity for incorporation into white culture either overtly (by taking a white spouse, for example) or covertly (by passing). Class and gender inflected that ability. For example, some second-generation male missionaries married assimilated Dakota women, though apparently none of the daughters of pioneer missionaries married Dakota men.[34] The situation of spouses John and Mary Renville, Dakota and white authors respectively of a text that I examine in my conclusion, is thus very unusual, since in 1862 only a few other Native men, such as John Other Day and Angus Brown, were known to have non-Native wives.

Future scholarship on whiteness studies should show, among other things, "greater attention to historical and geographical context, more precision in delineating the multiple meanings of 'whiteness,' [and] . . . more sustained treatment of actual lived relations."[35] Moreover, educators like me and studies like mine should encourage others to investigate how the many constructions of race have helped to shape relationships and identities in the United States.[36] This book also tries to make better known the people and texts from what is considered a localized war and to contribute to the new field of public memory studies.

Nevertheless I acknowledge that some readers will find my book controversial. First, the Dakota War itself remains contested between and within the Native and non-Native communities, especially in Minnesota, so separating the narrative analysis into two parts may seem like embracing a simplistic division rather than encouraging a complicated dialogue filled with interruptions and overlapping voices. Second, the emphasis on race and ethnicity in the book's two main sections might be seen as a reactionary reinforcement of essentialist binaries. Instead I intend this split to signify that individuals in the mid-nineteenth century and later were often assigned an inflexible identity within the prevailing political ideology and spoke from that position at the same time that they reinforced or subverted it. The two sections give European Americans and Native Americans equal say and equal space concerning the same war, which affected both groups.

Third, some critics may object to this comparison of literary traditions and texts on the grounds that a multicultural approach is inappropriate for American Indian materials. Specifically they may take issue with my decision to apply the term *captivity narrative* to Native texts. One reason is that "captivity narrative" has been synonymous with "Indian captivity narrative" within the mainstream literary tradition in which European Americans told stories of being captured by Native Americans. Those stories often presented Indians stereotypically and negatively in what amounted to blatant anti-Indian propaganda. Nevertheless some Native commentators are now reclaiming the term *captivity narrative* to apply to stories of Indians held hostage in various ways or to retell from an Indigenous viewpoint the stories of non-Native hostages.

My exploration of the Dakota Conflict narratives reveals Minnesota frontiers, borderlands, and inhabitants that have hitherto received little critical attention. To uncover them I use whatever interpretive strategies the complex material itself seems to warrant on a case-by-case basis. In the words of Toni Morrison, employed in one of the earlier epigraphs, *The War in Words* does not just want to "know what took place"; it wants to "learn what happened" through "multiple points of address and analysis."[37] But before I can contextualize and analyze each particular story, I must present the Conflict's general historical dimensions.

Historical Perspectives on the Dakota War

The best that the most honest and conscientious can do often, is to approximate to the truth. Take for example almost any separate fact in the Sioux outbreak, and there is room for a good many different versions. Different witnesses saw different parts, and observed from different stand-points, and hence the narratives will be somewhat different. The business of the historian is to pick out the truth from different and even conflicting statements. Frequently this is by no means an easy undertaking. Frequently there is room for a doubt. | Stephen R. Riggs, "History of the Sioux War by Isaac V. D. Heard" (1863)

The narratives that have been told by whites differ considerably from the narratives told by Indians. | Elizabeth Cook-Lynn, *Anti-Indianism in Modern America: A Voice from Tatekeya's Earth* (2001)

There have been many versions and interpretations of Dakota history and readers, like a hung jury, are persuaded first by one version and then another. Dr. Lawrence believes that somewhere in all the collaboration and controversy, there is an element of truth. After sorting through the many documents, testimonials and historical accounts, in the final analysis . . . history must tell its own story. | Elden Lawrence, *The Peace Seekers: Indian Christians and the Dakota Conflict* (2005)

In 1862, it [the Minnesota River] was at the center of a cataclysmic event that still colors relationships in the valley: "The anger and hatred is so bad I don't think we'll ever find the truth about what happened," says David Larsen, former chairman of the Lower Sioux Dakota tribal council. | Beth Gauper, "River with a Past" (2006)

For something characterized as a "cataclysmic event," the U.S.-Dakota War of 1862 is not widely known today even in Minnesota, let alone outside it.[1] So it seems prudent to establish a basic chronology, beginning with the act that actually triggered the hostilities. Yet starting at this point is already problematical since that catalyst was, of course, the shortest of short-term causes. It alone didn't cause or create the war, any more than the murder of Archduke Ferdinand did the First World War, which is probably the most famous example of a war's immediate cause being among the least important of contributing factors overall. The chronology below ends with the removal from Minnesota of 1,316 innocent Dakotas to the Crow Creek Reservation in modern-day South Dakota. Concluding at this point is also questionable, because although many Dakotas perished at Crow Creek, survivors were moved after three years to Santee, Nebraska, and yet more dispersed or eventually returned to their traditional homelands. Crow Creek was not the end of anything, just the point at which I choose to stop and provide a (false) sense of closure.[2]

Any chronology too raises issues of inclusion and exclusion. It could be factual yet still biased depending on what is left in and out. So although the sequence of events in the Dakota Conflict is well-established, it is much too reductive for such a complex war. Throughout, this book will continue to adjust, augment, and align the chronology as well as several central questions from European American and Native American perspectives: What took place? Why? Who was involved? What were the aftershocks? Who told or wrote about it? How did it come to be written, published, narrated, or disseminated? Who read about it? The answers to these questions will differ from person to person and text to text.

17 August 1862: Four young Dakota hunters kill five white settlers at Acton, precipitating a war between Dakota resistance fighters on one side and European Americans and Dakota sympathizers on the other.

18 August 1862: Groups of Mdewakanton Dakotas led by Little Crow attack the Lower Sioux (Redwood) Agency and ambush troops at Redwood Ferry. Fighting spreads to the Upper Sioux (Yellow Medicine) Agency and other off-reservation sites.

19 August 1862: The Dakota assault on Fort Ridgely is unsuccessful. Henry H. Sibley is appointed commander of the volunteer troops.

19–20 August 1862: Dakota forces try to overrun the mostly German settlement of New Ulm, but its citizens maintain control of the town.

20–21 August 1862: A few days after war commences some outlying settler communities are attacked and captured in the southern and western parts of the state. A group at Lake Shetek is particularly hard hit.

22 August 1862: The Dakotas' second, main, attack on Fort Ridgely fails.

23 August 1862: Another Dakota attempt to capture New Ulm is unsuccessful.

1–2 September 1862: A surprise ambush by Dakotas at the Battle of Birch Coulee inflicts severe casualties on an army burial detail of about 170 men.

3 September 1862: Opponents skirmish at Acton, and Dakotas attempt to take over Fort Abercrombie but do not manage to do so.

3–4 September 1862: A raiding party led by Little Crow loots and burns around the towns of Forest City and Hutchinson.

6 September 1862: A second Dakota attempt to capture Fort Abercrombie is also unsuccessful.

23 September 1862: Dakotas mass for a last all-out assault on U.S. troops at the Battle of Wood Lake. After some initial success they are defeated. Hundreds of Dakotas leave Minnesota and begin to disperse north, into Canada, and west, onto the prairies.

26 September 1862: The army led by Sibley reaches Camp Release, a site where progovernment Dakota factions and others gather with several hundred captives, for the formal surrender and handover of hostages.

28 September 1862: Sibley appoints a military commission to try Indian participants; it condemns 303 of them to death. Later President Lincoln reduces the execution list to thirty-nine but takes no action on the rest, who go to prison.

Figure 1. Prison camp below Fort Snelling for uncondemned Indians, 1862–63. Photo by Benjamin Franklin Upton. From the Collections of the Minnesota Historical Society. Used with permission.

9 November 1862: Almost 1,700 untried Dakota men as well as dependents of the prisoners are marched to St. Paul and placed in a camp near Fort Snelling at the same time as the prisoners themselves are marched to a prison in Mankato.

26 December 1862: Thirty-eight Dakotas are hanged at Mankato (one on the original list is reprieved), and hundreds remain imprisoned there.

Spring 1863: The Dakota convicts are sent to a prison camp in Davenport, Iowa, where they are jailed until pardoned in one to three years. Thirteen hundred and sixteen innocent Dakotas and prisoners' dependents are removed to the Crow Creek Reservation in Dakota Territory.[3]

But some contemporary Dakotas describe a different version of events and use different terminology, including Southwest State University professor Chris Mato Nunpa, speaking about the Dakota Commemorative March of 2002:

The purpose of the march was to remember and honor the 1,700 Dakota People, primarily women and children (non-combatants), who were forced-marched 150 miles from the Lower Sioux Community to the concentration camp at Fort Snelling. The event was conducted by relatives and descendents of those 1,700 Dakotas and was the beginning of healing and recovery from the traumatic events of 1862.

One issue the debate has highlighted is the matter of perspective and terminology. The reader can see at least two distinct perspectives, a status quo perspective representing the colonizer/white academic structure, which perspective we all—red, white, black, yellow, etc.—have been taught in the educational systems of the U.S. The other is an emerging Indigenous perspective, or more specifically, a Dakota perspective, which generally has been suppressed, attacked, disregarded, or dismissed. These two perspectives, generally, are inherently opposed to each other.[4]

Mato Nunpa then shows how a European American perspective tends to sanitize language so that Dakotas "died" on the forced march or entered "internment camps" at Mankato and Fort Snelling, while a Dakota perspective would be more likely to use the words "murdered" and "concentration camps" instead. He agrees with those genocide scholars who look at what happened to Native peoples in the United States and Canada in terms of "'genocide,' 'crimes against humanity,' [and] 'ethnic cleansings,'" rather than as regrettable outcomes of war.[5] Making explicit comparisons between Jews and Native Americans, Mato Nunpa claims that, like the Germans during the Holocaust, the U.S. government often used Christianity to rationalize its actions against ethnic others.

Dakota scholar, writer, and activist Elizabeth Cook-Lynn reinforces Mato Nunpa's points in her own work but further problematizes events and their significances. So, for example, she coins the term "anti-Indianism" as a parallel to "anti-Semitism" and shows how both phenomena originated in religious discrimination.[6] It was not enough for Natives and Jews to relinquish faith and identity, because they could not change what the dominant culture perceived as their race. Cook-Lynn agrees that a Dakota incarceration site such as the Crow Creek Reservation functioned like a concentration camp, but she adds to the ongoing discussion of Dakota removal a sense of continuity predating European expansionism.

Thus she points out that Dakotas as well as other Indians had lived from time immemorial in the Crow Creek area. And Dakotas "had complex relationships with their relatives, the Lakotas and the Nakotas, in addition to intertribal and political and cultural ties to their neighbors, the Winnebagoes and the Arapahoes and the Cheyennes, who also possessed the territory in their hearts and in their religions."[7] Crow Creek was and is a sacred place, for it links the land with the people's origin stories.[8] Therefore the removal to Crow Creek involved connection as much as disruption, and its significance is even more complex than it appears.

The distinction here between history and memory might be described in these terms: "The concepts of history and memory represent two attitudes toward the past, two streams of historical consciousness that must at some point flow together. . . . Memory is often owned; history, interpreted."[9] At the "confluence of history and memory" lessons can be learned about the multiple ways that individuals, communities, and nations make use of the past.[10] So tribal literature and memory almost invariably differ from Western literature and memory, as indicated in the epigraph above by Elizabeth Cook-Lynn. Even so, the role of memory and narrative in wars like the Dakota War, the Civil War, and the Vietnam War can also reveal commonalities because "if war is a culturally specific invention, then the rumor of war, as a narrative reconstruction of constructed events, is doubly imbued with the assumptions, values, and purposes of human culture. In some cases the war story endorses the values of the dominant ideology; in other cases it calls them into question. Thus the war story, like war itself, is politics by other means."[11]

A recent study of memory reinforces the notion that memory is created through a host of personal, cultural, and historical contexts.[12] Specifically memory shapes itself into narrative, with personal recollections differing from public ones, and with traumatic and nontraumatic events encoded into "semantic" memory, meaning remembrances that people don't know how they learned, and "episodic" memory, meaning remembrances that people can clearly situate in a particular time and place.[13] Although memory can assume the form of a story, our recollections can be formed or elicited by other people; in this case "the past is created through narrative rather than being translated into narrative."[14] Examining a series of Dakota Conflict captivity narratives reveals the complex interplay of narrative and memory.

In Minnesota the Dakota Conflict is sometimes called "the other Civil War" because it ravaged the state at the same time as the wider Civil War.[15] This dual wartime involvement suggests the inherent difficulties of remembering, discussing, differentiating, and historicizing trauma and also indicates why the regional Dakota War has been overshadowed by the concurrent national campaign. The Dakota Conflict's main participants were European Americans and their Dakota allies, who fought against Dakotas defending their homelands from further encroachment. Under different circumstances the incident near Acton on 17 August 1862 could have been contained; instead it fueled the ongoing struggle for Dakota identity and cohesion.

Certainly the Dakotas' sense of siege had been aggravated by "rapacious traders, ethnocentric missionaries, white men's decimating diseases, inept Indian Bureau officials, equivocating United States government representatives, and deplorably conflicting military policies," as well the growing number of "land-hungry settlers."[16] But by the late 1850s a less stereotypical rationale for the hostilities emerged as European Americans challenged traditional Dakota culture on a variety of fronts. The wider issue of imposed cultural change, not just a series of separate grievances, was the major reason Dakotas went to

Figure 2. The execution of thirty-eight Dakota Indians at Mankato, Minnesota, 26 December 1862, by W. H. Childs. From *Frank Leslie's Illustrated Newspaper*, 24 January 1863, p. 285. From the Collections of the Minnesota Historical Society. Used with permission.

war in 1862.[17] European Americans too were trying to consolidate an identity in Minnesota, which had obtained statehood only in 1858.

When the war ended in late September 1862, with substantial loss of life on both sides, the U.S. government removed or imprisoned hundreds of Dakotas, conducted hasty and illegal trials, and sent thirty-eight to the gallows on 26 December 1862 in the largest mass execution in American history.[18] Then in February 1863 the government unilaterally abrogated treaties with the Dakotas regardless of individuals' involvement in the Conflict and authorized further reprisals and executions in the next few years, following continued skirmishes to the West. Some see the U.S.-Dakota Conflict as the first step toward the infamous Battle at Wounded Knee, which seemed to symbolize the annihilation of Sioux culture so many whites had wanted for so long.[19]

As a young man Sitting Bull (Tatanka Yotanka) visited the exiled Dakotas at the Crow Creek Reservation. In Dee Brown's reconstruction of this event, "He looked with pity upon his Santee cousins and listened to their stories of the Americans who had taken their land and driven them away. . . . Soon they [the European Americans] would take the buffalo country unless the hearts of the Indians were strong enough to hold it. He resolved that he would fight to hold it."[20] His defiance led him to an initial victory over Custer at the Battle of the Little Bighorn. Though embattled, his cousins the Dakotas did survive, and like other Native nations, their stories contributed to their survival.

The Dakotas are the easternmost members of the larger Sioux Nation, which also includes the western, Plains, or prairie Lakotas (Tetons) and the Middle Dakotas—sometimes incorrectly called Nakotas (Yanktons and Yanktonais). The names "Dakota," "Lakota," and "Nakota" are primarily modern linguistic labels denoting three different dialects of the same original language and people who were all at one time called Dakotas. At the point of early contact with Europeans in the mid-seventeenth century, there were seven bands or council fires in the territory that became Minnesota. By 1862 the Yanktons, Yanktonais, and Tetons had been displaced west of Minnesota. But the eastern-most tribes within the state still referred to themselves as Dakotas (or Santees) and consisted of four bands: the Mdewakantonwan or Mdewakantons (Spirit Lake People), the Wahpekute (Shooters among the Leaves People), the Wahpetonwan or Wahpetons (People Dwelling among the Leaves), and the Sissetonwan or Sissetons (People of the Fish Villages), which were further subdivided. European Americans, Dakotas, and an ever-growing number of mixed bloods coexisted for almost two hundred years, primarily through their mutual involvement in the fur trade. But in 1805 the Sioux Nation and the U.S. government signed the first of a series of treaties exchanging land for money.[21]

Continued contact and conflict between European Americans and Dakotas resulted in more treaties. According to the Treaty of 1837 and the two treaties signed in 1851, called the Treaty of Traverse des Sioux and the Treaty of Mendota, the Dakotas ceded huge land claims in what became Minnesota for annuities and, eventually, large-scale settlement on two reservations: the Lower Sioux Reservation for the Mdewakantons and Wahpekutes and the Upper Sioux Reservation for the Sissetons and Wahpetons. The town that formed the Lower Sioux Reservation's administrative center was known as both Redwood and the Lower Sioux Agency. Pajutazee, Yellow Medicine, and the Upper Sioux Agency were the names used for the Upper Sioux Reservation's administrative center, which also dealt with matters involving the combined Upper and Lower Sioux reservations system.

Though the government and the missionaries shared the same imperial agenda of "civilizing" the Dakotas, they approached this aim differently. The government's priority was to make the Dakotas farmers first, whereas the missionaries' priority was to make them Christians first.[22] Government policies compelled the Dakotas to stop going on war parties; to relinquish communal living and adopt the basic nuclear family, plus dependents, model; to provide their own food by subsistence agriculture, supplemented if necessary by hunting and warehouse allotments; to cut their hair and adopt European dress; and to send their children to government-run schools on the reservations. Dakotas who farmed could continue to practice their own religion if they wished, though the government expected that Christian conversion would likely follow acculturation to other non-Native practices. But in fact, many of these Dakotas continued to adhere to their traditional belief systems without government intervention. The missionaries, however, realized that Christians often became farmers, rather than the other way around, partly because traditional beliefs and lifeways were intertwined. Indeed, the evangelists tried to model this behavior themselves by being Christians, first and foremost, who farmed to support their families.

At some level, overtly or covertly, government bureaucrats and missionaries both understood that these "civilizing" requirements, especially placing nuclear families on subsistence farms, undermined traditional Dakota kinship and spirituality, causing instability and conflict.[23] Further, successive agents to the Dakotas hastened the pace of agricultural assimilation by providing even greater incentives than before. After 1858 the Dakotas who farmed were entitled to much larger annuity benefits, augmented from a treaty-stipulated "civilization" fund, than those who did not farm. As the Dakota chief Big Eagle (Wamditanka) put it: "Then the whites were always trying to make the Indians give up their life and live like white men—go to farming, work hard and do as they did—and the Indians did not know how to do that, and did not want to anyway. It seemed too sudden to make such a change."[24]

Here is a description of the basic setting at the two agencies on the eve of war. At or near the Lower Sioux Agency there were one Wahpekute and nine Mdewakanton bands on the southwest bank of the Minnesota River. The Mdewakanton bands of Big Eagle, Little Crow (Taoyateduta), Blue Earth (Mankato), and Traveling Hail (Wasuheyadan) lived quite close to the agency, while those of The Shooter (Wacouta) and Red Standard (Wabasha), as well as the Wahpekute band of Red Legs (Hushasha), had established villages toward the southern end of the reservation. A small number of Mdewakantons from Shakopee's band, as well as some Wahpetons, lived about fifteen miles north of the agency, near the mouth of Rice Creek. Several of these Rice Creek Indians were the ones involved in the Acton incident.[25]

In the same year the situation at the Upper Sioux Agency was somewhat different for the approximately four thousand Sissetons and Wahpetons, who were more conciliatory toward the European Americans during the war. Interestingly, they had been less so before 1862 and also technically had not adopted as many of the government and missionary requirements. In addition to those Indians living near the agency, others settled about three miles away, near the Pajutazee (Yellow Medicine) mission operated by the Presbyterian missionary and doctor Thomas Williamson and his family. Three miles above the Pajutazee mission Presbyterian Stephen Riggs established his own

Hazelwood (sometimes spelled Hazlewood) mission in 1854 and the "Hazelwood Republic" of Christian and assimilationist Dakotas. Both the Williamson and the Riggs missions were focal points for many Native sympathizers or converts, with whom the ministers had worked for decades.[26]

Minnesota in the early 1860s was also seeing an influx of immigrants from Europe and newcomers from the settled East, who viewed the state as the unsettled West. On first arrival many of them voiced their physical and psychological displacement in letters and in the captivity narratives I discuss later. Minnesota was thus a locus of cultural interpenetration and interaction, and Minnesotans' many texts at this time fit this assessment by Annette Kolodny: "By acknowledging the many different configurations of indigenous peoples, immigrants, and emigrants who came in contact over time on a variety of landscapes, we allow the literatures of the frontiers to stand—accurately, at last—as multilingual, polyvocal, and newly intertextual and multicultural. . . . Indeed, the study of frontier literary history—like American literary history in general—should properly be marked by endlessly proliferating, multiple, competing narrative designs."[27] Native authors and critics such as Kimberly Blaeser (Ojibwe) also appropriate the term "frontier" or "frontiers," especially as opposed to the loaded term "territory." Blaeser's phrase "post-Indian frontier" refers to "a trans-cultural zone" for contact, whereas "territory" means a place emptied of Indians and filled by whites.[28] My exploration of the Dakota Conflict captivity and confinement narratives reveals the heterogeneity and volatility of Minnesota's many frontiers.

In fact, these texts serve as verbal equivalents of the Native and non-Native sites of contact in Drex Brooks's photograph collection *Sweet Medicine: Sites of Indian Massacres, Battlefields, and Treaties*. The conclusion to Brooks's book, an essay by Western historian Patricia Nelson Limerick titled "Haunted America," discusses the complexity of war stories and provides an antidote to mainstream America's belief that all whites and all Indians were polarized into two homogeneous camps.[29] Reality was much more complicated, with individuals making their own moral judgments and aligning themselves with groups to which they did not, at first glance, seem to belong. For even though war encouraged nationalistic or sovereign identity, no group was a monolithic entity. Deep divisions and differences existed, though they might not be readily apparent. Such was certainly true in the Dakota War, where among whites, for example, we see the pro-Indian, antigovernment stance of Sarah Wakefield's *Six Weeks in the Sioux Tepees* alongside the vehemently anti-Indian, propagandist intent of Harriet Bishop McConkey's *Dakota War Whoop*, both published in 1863.

Dakota narratives and perspectives are also diverse. Native people's stories, says a Dakota historian, "are testimony to the richness, variety, detail, and complexity of the interpretations of history. Our role as historians should be to examine as many perspectives of the past as possible—not to become the validators or verifiers of stories, but instead to put forth as many perspectives as possible."[30] The role of literary critics, too, is to examine many pasts, many perspectives, many texts, in an attempt to hold the resulting "multilayered vision" together.[31] But confronting the details of this war remains profoundly unsettling in Minnesota and the Dakota diaspora because it was "an epochal event . . . whose consequences continue to ripple through" Dakotas' lives.[32] Sisseton Wahpeton Dakota Florestine Kiyukanpi Renville observed, "I think something terribly traumatic happened to our people during and after the 1862 war in Minnesota."[33] A year later, in 2002, she offered one coping mechanism for this ongoing trauma: "We are trying to heal ourselves physically, emotionally, and spiritually, and dealing with our historical past is one of the biggest steps toward that goal."[34] That same year marked the first of what have become biennial Dakota Commemorative Marches, from the Lower Sioux Agency to Fort Snelling.[35]

On the Web site of the Sisseton-Wahpeton Oyate of the Lake Traverse Reservation, spokesman Ed Red Owl shows how the Conflict is viewed in tribal historical memory: "Often it has been said by the Old People that the civilized way of life of the eastern Dakota bands came to an end at the time of the execution of the 38 eastern Dakota leaders at Mankato."[36] While European Americans believed that the "uncivilized" Dakotas were finally beaten at war's end, Natives viewed this as a time when their civilized life actually ended. Changes in and challenges to traditional Dakota culture had been ongoing ever since initial contact with whites, but like many ravaging wars, the Dakota Conflict marked a turning point in communal memory.

Palliative efforts to heal the rifts within and between communities include serial renaming of the war—from early, often pejorative, names like the "Minnesota Massacre," "Little Crow's War," and the "Great Sioux Uprising of 1862"; to the "Dakota War" a while later; and then to the more neutral "U.S.-Dakota Conflict of 1862" or just "the Conflict." (Similarly, participants in the civil war between Protestants and Catholics in Northern Ireland in the late twentieth century refer to it simply as "the troubles.") Currently a number of phrases are in use.[37] One hundred and twenty-five years after the war the state of Minnesota agreed to designate 1987 "the year of reconciliation." Clearly Minnesotans felt that reconciliation had not yet been achieved.[38]

The essay by Patricia Nelson Limerick mentioned earlier, "Haunted America," looks at a dozen generalizations that can be made about prewar, wartime, and postwar interactions between European Americans and Native Americans. She applies her points to the Modoc War of 1872–73 but claims that they hold true for many white/Indian wars. Indeed, applying these general characteristics to the Dakota War lays the groundwork for the much more particularized accounts discussed later in this book and anticipates my conclusion that the causes, progression, and consequences of such hostilities are not easily recovered or recounted. The war's significances can only be approached through a range of texts whose words endlessly spar with each other but do not ultimately reach any overarching truth.

Prewar Contact

Two observations by Limerick about prewar contact between Natives and non-Natives hold, first, that wars did not occur in a vacuum but were the culmination of a history of contact and interaction, and second, that when government representatives intervened early on to halt potential hostilities, they often made things worse.[39]

Typically, before a war began extensive contact between colonizers and colonized had already taken place. One obvious marker of this contact was the growing presence of people from a bicultural background. Usually the children of white men and Indian women, they adopted multiple roles in both communities. Various ethnohistorical studies show their importance in the long history of Dakota/white contact. By the nineteenth century economic relations between Dakotas and non-Dakotas were increasingly characterized by kinship connections, for "traditionally, Dakota families have included a web of extended family (cousins, aunts, uncles, grandparents) that include relatives by blood, and relatives by deed and choice."[40] In this way explorers and traders, for example, married into Dakota bands and essentially became Dakotas. While these kinship ties were already unraveling by 1862, the Dakota War severely tested and in some cases completely sundered them.

Before a war broke out government representatives often tried to settle existing problems, but instead of clarifying the issues these men obscured them and actually precipitated the fighting.[41] In the Dakotas' case treaties required the government to provide regular annuity payments and food allocations, but as the Civil War got under way Congress delayed the annual appropriations, with disastrous consequences.[42] Also, as already noted, the traders and the government treated those Indians who were willing to adopt European ways differently from those Indians who did not. Further identity confusion ensued when Dakotas adopted some but not all of these practices—Christianity, for example.

Another hindrance to continuity in white/Indian matters was the fact that Indian agents were political appointees who changed with new administrations. In 1861 Abraham Lincoln replaced the experienced but corrupt agent Joseph Brown with the inexperienced but idealistic newcomer Thomas Galbraith. This change in agents further destabilized an already delicate situation within the state, and Galbraith became the natural scapegoat for the hostilities. Certainly, some Dakotas blamed Galbraith for the growing tension that culminated in the Conflict. For example, in a letter to Henry Sibley trying to explain what had caused the fighting, Little Crow said, "For what reason we have commenced this war I will tell you, it is on account of Maj. Galbrait [sic]."[43] So the government's involvement at both local and national levels hindered, not helped, the groups that were trying to coexist. By fostering discord and distrust government intervention paved the way for hostility.

Early Wartime Contact

When war actually broke out three other aspects might be noted during its early stages, according to Limerick: initial violent acts on both sides were often impulsive, not premeditated; European Americans saw themselves as victims, not oppressors, when Natives tried to reclaim their rightful lands; and Indians often won early victories, partly because whites underestimated them.[44]

First, brutal acts precipitating a war were often hasty; only in hindsight might they be seen as preliminaries in a prolonged conflict.[45] Further, those wanting to fight might take action early on without seeking advice from leaders or elders. After combat, when they could speak more freely, leaders on both sides often said that they had not wanted to wage war in the first place and condemned the insurgents. Among Native Americans the fighters were frequently young men wishing to prove their prowess, while among European Americans they were settlers wanting to consolidate their land claims or soldiers hoping to rout the Indians quickly. There were many claims of hotheadedness at the start of the Dakota War. The account of Lightning Blanket (Hachinwakanda), for instance, says that after discussions on 19 August 1862 about whether to extend the hostilities, "The young men were all anxious to go."[46]

Hunger also played a role in causing Native Americans to fight, since European American settlement changed traditional hunting and subsistence practices. By 1862 the nation's preoccupation with the Civil War had led the government to delay its treaty obligations to provide food and money to the Dakotas. The autumn harvest on the reservations had been very poor, and the severe winter of 1861 caused much hardship. By July 1862, when the Dakotas began to assemble for their annuities, inadequate distribution of available food, plus the unexpectedly long wait for the late payments, caused great suffering.[47]

Most of the Dakota Conflict narratives agree on the basic scenario that actually triggered the war. But I will take the details from Big Eagle's account, because he says he got them firsthand from Dakotas involved in the Acton incident: Four hungry young Dakota men went hunting near Acton on 17 August 1862; they found a hen's nest with some eggs, and one wanted to take the eggs, but another said it was a bad idea because the hen belonged to a settler and they might get into trouble. The first man accused the second of cowardice concerning whites; the second man said that he was no coward and would prove it by going to the settler's home and killing him. The second man dared the first man to accompany him. Finally all four Dakotas went to the house of the settler, Robinson Jones, but he became alarmed and set off for his son-in-law's place nearby. The Indians followed and killed three men and two women there.[48] The four Dakotas—whose names were Sungigidan (Brown Wing), Ka-om-de-i-ye-dan (Breaking Up), Nagi-wi-cak-te (Killing Ghost), and Pa-zo-i-yo-pa (Runs against Something When Crawling)—fled to their home camp on the Lower Reservation; talked to other Mdewakantons, who argued for combat not surrender; and then sought the support of Little Crow (Taoyateduta),

the most influential Mdewakanton leader.[49] Thus the war that killed
hundreds of people from all backgrounds and led to Dakota death and
displacement began as a fight over food.

While the opening salvo of a white/Indian war was often impulsive
and individualistic, opponents were apt to judge all members of the
other side as equally guilty.[50] This was especially true in warfare that
European Americans considered to be Indian-initiated. As stereotyping
and hysteria set in, leaders on both sides found themselves pressured
into war, or into continuing combat, because they blamed the opposition
indiscriminately. Such was definitely the case in the Dakota Conflict.
Evidence strongly suggests, for example, that the Dakota leaders Little
Crow, Big Eagle, and Joseph Wabasha joined the war effort somewhat
reluctantly, though once committed, they participated in major battles.
And Ernest Wabasha, a descendent of Joseph Wabasha, said of his
ancestor: "When the outbreak came, Wabasha III told his family that
he wasn't going to kill anybody. He rode with them in battles, but he
kept a lot of white prisoners from being killed by people who wanted
to kill everybody white."[51]

The next pattern Limerick establishes, which might be apparent
from the early days of war until its end, is that when Indians tried
to reclaim land and expel intruders from contested territory, European Americans saw themselves as innocent and victimized but their
opponents as guilty and aggressive.[52] Because the settlers and the
military were unwilling to grant their own complicity in causing the
fighting, they resorted to ethnic stereotyping to defend their actions.
This resulted in European Americans labeling themselves civilized,
progressive, and good, and the Indians savage, primitive, and evil.
Once European Americans had established these rationalizations for
war, they felt that the Indians had asked for trouble and must expect
severe punishment. Of course this is the standard, simplified response
in countless white-authored captivity narratives, but interestingly, it
sometimes exists alongside a more balanced, individual assessment.

In other words, the Dakota Conflict narratives by European Americans sometimes show the authors giving in to their own as well as readers' expectations of savage Indian stereotypes, but they sometimes give details about "good" Indians or "bad" whites. However, a white person's experience of kindness among Indians is usually tempered by racist rhetoric somewhere in the text to show that the "good" Indians are exceptions who only prove the rule.

For instance, soldier Jacob Nix, who helped defend the German town of New Ulm against the first Dakota attack, says that corrupt traders were the primary reason why the normally peaceful Indians changed "to veritable beasts, compared to which the tiger of the East Indian jungles might be considered a sympathetic creature."[53] Yet even after acknowledging the role of sympathetic Dakotas such as John Other Day, Nix continues to brand all Dakotas with the racist tags "bloodthirsty Redskins" and "murderous Indian firebugs."[54] As might be expected, narratives by and about white women and children were particularly prone to present the victim/victimizer model. So, for example, Jannette DeCamp Sweet, wife of the Redwood Agency sawmill's manager in 1862, spends time in her captivity narrative describing the Indians' harassment of three teenage German girls, Mary Schwandt, Mattie Williams, and Mary Anderson. But she also credits Dakotas like Lorenzo Lawrence, who helped her and other captives.

A third early wartime characteristic suggests that wars frequently began with a victory for the Indians, partly because European Americans misjudged their opponents' capabilities.[55] One example of the Dakotas' tactical shrewdness concerns their understanding that Minnesota was poorly defended as a result of the Civil War. The most significant troop reduction on the Minnesota frontier occurred in 1861, when the War Department closed the artillery school at Fort Ridgely and withdrew regular army troops and cavalry for the Civil War effort, substituting untrained volunteers.[56] Then on 17 July 1862 Congress authorized a draft of three hundred thousand men, with specific state quotas, to shore up the Union position. To meet Minnesota's share quickly local authorities offered financial incentives to enlist. As a result, Indian agent Galbraith assembled a company called the Renville Rangers, at least a quarter of whom were of mixed race.[57]

But conscription left the Minnesota frontier so vulnerable that one contemporary estimated that fewer than two hundred troops remained to deal with state emergencies, though about one thousand civilian men in local militia units could also be mustered.[58] For months before the Conflict finally broke out, Dakotas may have planned to exploit weaknesses like these. They also interpreted the growing Union war effort as evidence that the South might actually win, which could lead to a favorable change in Indian affairs. A few whites later realized the significance of the Dakotas' ability to take advantage of the Civil War by waging a statewide war. Stephen Riggs, for example, exclaimed, "If there had been no Southern war, there would have been no Dakota uprising and no Minnesota massacres!"[59]

At all events, after the four Dakotas killed the people at Acton and sought Little Crow's support for continued hostilities, initial Dakota victories followed in the attack on the Lower Sioux Agency and the ambush of Minnesota infantry at Redwood Ferry, both on 18 August. But despite their superior numbers, the Indians were unable to capture Fort Ridgely or overrun New Ulm after several attempts a few days later. In Big Eagle's famous words, "We thought the fort was the door to the valley as far as to St. Paul, and that if we got through the door nothing could stop us this side of the Mississippi. But the defenders of the Fort were very brave and kept the door shut."[60] There was a brief Dakota resurgence at the two-day Battle of Birch Coulee, which began on 1 September. Yet when the Dakota war faction decided on one last decisive engagement after this success, it could not withstand the fourteen-hundred-strong U.S. army that had by then assembled. Commanded by Minnesota entrepreneur and politician Henry H. Sibley (who was promoted from colonel to general during the hostilities), the troops defeated the Dakotas at the Battle of Wood Lake on 23 September. After that, despite some other skirmishes, the prowar Dakotas could not claim any further victories.

Contact in the Midst of War

Once widespread fighting had taken place, according to Limerick, four other generalizations about white/Indian wars can be made. First, Indians often fought on both sides of hostilities, and second, whites could be disunited too, as when missionaries defended Indians and opposed military intervention or reprisals. A third aspect of warfare that manifested itself at the height of hostilities concerns Natives' knowledge of the land and its resources, which put whites at a real disadvantage, despite their usually superior numbers. Fourth, while Native and non-Native fighters tried to distinguish between combatants and noncombatants on the other side, confusion and prejudice made this very difficult to do.[61]

Applying the first of these observations to the Dakota Conflict, we see that the traditional concept of a polarized war, with Native Americans on one side and European Americans on the other, is absurd, because some Indians fought with and some against whites.[62] To think, for example, that all Dakotas, let alone all Native Americans, would or could rise against European Americans in some pan-Indian revolt is overly simplistic. This notion refuses to accept that Indians were shrewd diplomats ready to form useful alliances against their enemies—both Native and white—just as other nations did. From the very beginning Dakotas responded very differently to the unfolding war in Minnesota, acting as both hawks and doves and showing "the entire range of cultural responses and political and religious views."[63]

An interesting example suggesting the large number of Dakota accommodationists occurs in missionary Gideon Pond's impassioned 1863 report titled, "True History of the Indian Outbreak in Minnesota." Pond wished to exonerate the numerous reservation Dakotas who had no advance warning of the initial attacks, took no part in them, and later stole supplies only because they saw their rightful provisions disappearing: "They did not know of it [the attack] until considerable advance had been made in the work of destruction, but were, at the time, about their ordinary affairs, and as much surprised to find what was transpiring as were their white neighbors."[64] Pond then shows that there were, to use his term, as many "un-hostile" as hostile Dakotas and that a significant number of the almost four hundred men originally condemned to death did not fight against whites and were innocent of actual or intended murder.

At every stage of the Dakota Conflict diverse Dakota factions argued about strategies and alliances. Gradually the progovernment Dakotas took over, particularly after the unsuccessful Dakota attacks on Fort Ridgely and New Ulm. Following these defeats, when the warring Mdewakantons moved north from Little Crow's village at the Lower Sioux Agency into Sisseton and Wahpeton territory at the Upper Sioux Agency, debates erupted among the Dakota bands about the hundreds of white and mixed-race captives. Two basic blocs emerged: Mdewakantons who wanted to prolong the war; and Sissetons and Wahpetons, plus conciliatory Mdewakantons, who wanted to end it by returning the hostages to Sibley.[65] Once he was involved in the fighting, Little Crow remained the foremost leader of the "war party," which also included Big Eagle, White Spider, and Lightning Blanket. Prominent in the "peace party" were such figures as Paul Mazakutemani (Little Paul), Lorenzo Lawrence (Towanetaton), Wabasha, Taopi (Wounded Man), and Gabriel Renville (Tiwakan).[66]

Limerick's next prototype indicates that whites were often disunited too and resisted, or even fought, each other in person or in print.[67] Neither Native Americans nor European Americans necessarily supported their group if individual survival, conscience, or reputation was at stake. For instance, some missionaries criticized their own culture for the conditions that precipitated the Conflict and justified a Dakota response, such as immoral treatment of Dakota women by soldiers and agency employees (including rape and concubinage), broken treaties, stolen land, and unprovoked aggression. They argued that this behavior certainly did not represent the "civilizing" Christian influence that whites were supposed to exemplify.

Understandably, missionaries like the Congregationalists Samuel Pond and Gideon Pond and the Presbyterians Thomas Williamson and Stephen Riggs—all of whom had been approved for mission work by the umbrella evangelical organization the American Board of Commissioners for Foreign Missions—were torn during the war by concern for their own safety and by responsibility toward the many Dakota converts with whom they had longstanding ties.[68] Nevertheless, especially when they saw the government's callous treatment of the Dakotas after the Conflict, they sometimes spoke out and took unpopular moral positions. To use a specific example, Martha Riggs, one of Stephen Riggs's daughters who continued his missionary work with the Dakotas, published a forceful defense of the Dakotas and a moral challenge to her readers in 1862.[69]

Conflicting arguments about military strategy and appropriate credit for victories also found their way into print. A case in point is Jacob Nix's eyewitness history. As the commander of the German townspeople during the first Dakota assault on New Ulm, Nix successfully defended it until reinforcements under Colonel Charles Flandrau were able to repulse a second attack. Nix published his account partly because he felt that Flandrau had taken the credit for both campaigns and partly because he believed that the Anglo histories had not properly recognized the Germans' role. It is significant that these two models of transgressive commentary, by Martha Riggs and by Jacob Nix, came from members of gender, religious, or ethnic minorities who themselves felt misunderstood or oppressed.

A third characteristic evident in the midst of U.S.-Indian wars is that guerilla warfare helped to undermine the government's superior firepower and wealth, at least temporarily.[70] The fact that the warring Dakotas knew the land obviously meant that they were able to move across it more easily than the military, though the help of progovernment Dakotas and Indian scouts familiar with the territory mitigated this problem for the troops. Even so, some of the captives criticized Sibley for his slowness in reaching Camp Release, where the pacifist faction waited with the captives, and for his initial reluctance in pursuing and capturing Little Crow and his men.

With inevitable defeat looming locally, knowledge of the land enabled around 250 Mdewakantons to flee westward with Little Crow. There he tried to forge an alliance with the Plains bands of Sissetons, Wahpetons, Yanktons, Yanktonais, and Tetons to defeat the U.S. government. When this attempt failed Little Crow slipped back to Minnesota with his son Wowinape (Thomas Wakeman) and a few others. He had been able to elude the government troops for almost a year and was killed by a farmer while foraging for food, not by the U.S. military while fighting.

The fourth generalization is that both groups found it hard to separate soldiers from civilians. This was partly owing to confusion and mistaken identity of individuals and partly owing to prejudice and hatred of an entire group. European Americans, for example, saw Native men living with their families in order to protect them but also saw that they could rapidly change from family members to fighters. Ironically, while European Americans found the status of bicultural people hard to read and were quick to brand them as rebels, Native Americans too found the loyalty of bicultural people suspect.

The account of Joseph Godfrey (Otakle) illustrates these points. The son of a French/Canadian voyageur and a slave woman, Godfrey was brought up as a slave in the household of a fur trader, then escaped bondage to live among the Dakotas.[71] Godfrey's testimony was first recorded in the U.S. Army Military Commission transcripts of wartime involvement, though the better-known source is within court recorder Isaac

Heard's *History of the Sioux War*. Godfrey's testimony repeatedly states that the Dakotas forced him to fight and that he did so to save his skin. Contradicting him, several white captives and commentators argued that he fought voluntarily and brutally. Godfrey was the first man to be tried, but his testimony against others helped sway the court to recommend that his death penalty be commuted to a ten-year sentence.

Postwar Contact

As war ended, states Limerick, three other characteristics of white/ Indian wars manifested themselves. First, while European Americans and Native Americans might be quick to get into a war, they often had trouble getting out of it. Second, while whites stereotyped Natives as ferocious and savage fighters, they also stereotyped how thoroughly degraded Indians seemed in defeat. And last, many of these wars were indeed so violent that it is hard to imagine how mainstream mythology romanticized them or how participants and survivors lived together again.[72]

Turning to the first point, ending a war was inherently difficult for both sides; indeed, this observation is not particular to white/ Indian wars but is probably true of all wars. Even if a Native American leader decided to surrender, the military might be loath to accept it because when European Americans got the upper hand—as they generally did in the end—they wanted to inflict such crushing casualties that their opponents could never wage war again.[73] Agreeing to a surrender that left enough Native warriors alive to fight another day was more dangerous in the long term than decimating them in the short term.

For instance, it seems clear that Little Crow was willing to negotiate with Henry Sibley, though they were understandably wary of each other. A series of communications between the two is quoted in Heard's *History of the Sioux War*, beginning with Sibley's terse note written after the Battle of Birch Coulee: "If Little Crow has any proposition to make, let him send a half-breed to me, and he shall be protected in and out of camp."[74] To this Little Crow replied with a letter dated 7 September detailing the reasons he and his supporters had gone to war. Sibley sent him another brief, confrontational message: "LITTLE CROW,—You have murdered many of our people without any sufficient cause. Return me the prisoners under a flag of truce, and I will talk with you then like a man."[75]

This in turn precipitated a dictated response from Little Crow that was translated and written down in broken English by the Franco Dakota Antoine J. Campbell. In it Little Crow states that he had treated the 155 prisoners well but that he was still pondering their fate: "I want to know from you as a friend what way that il [sic] can make peace for my people—in regard to prisoners they fair with our children or our self jist as well as us."[76] But Sibley was not willing to consider surrender and sent another uncompromising letter on 12 September. After that the pacifist Dakotas took control of the captives and gathered them all at Camp Release, while Little Crow and his supporters fled.

Next, at war's end European Americans sometimes had a hard time feeling victorious because, they claimed, their Indian opponents looked so thoroughly defeated. However, these assertions of Indian passivity in defeat should be seen as either imperialist rationalizations of conquest or genocidal guilt. In the historical record Native Americans and other oppressed groups, such as African Americans, strongly and frequently resisted oppression and rebelled. But in the interpretive record, especially to European American soldiers, the Indian warriors really did seem battered and beaten people who should, perhaps, be pitied rather than hated.[77] Isaac Heard's *History* does not show sympathy but does describe the Dakota soldiers' degraded, virtually enslaved state: "The prisoners were linked together in pairs by chains forged to their ankles. As the proud but now crestfallen braves hobbled along, the soldiers would derisively salute them with '*Left!*' '*Left!*'"[78] A few white commentators, such as Sarah Wakefield, did express pity for the now-captive Dakotas. But Wakefield was unusual in this particular war, where the standard response of European American combatants and civilians was indeed suspicion and hatred, even if the Dakotas looked defeated.

A well-known incident indicating mob violence occurred when Sibley decided to move an initially combined convoy of prisoners to Mankato and their sixteen hundred or so dependents and other innocent parties, mostly women and children, to Fort Snelling. Gabriel Renville described in his memoirs what happened when the first group passed through New Ulm: "Both men and women, coming with stones, bricks, and pitchforks, and anything they could lay their hands on, and rushing through the ranks of the soldiers who were guarding them, attacked the chained prisoners in the wagons, and knocked many of them senseless."[79] Dakota soldiers were not the only ones to be hurt. Bypassing New Ulm, the innocent Dakotas bore the brunt of vigilante punishment too when they went through the town of Henderson, headed for Fort Snelling. Waziyatawin Angela Wilson records the oral history of her grandmother (Elsie Cavender), who told of an incident in which Elsie's own grandmother (Isabel Roberts, or Maza Okiye Win) marched: "Isabel Roberts . . . and her family were taken as captives down to Fort Snelling. . . . They passed through a lot of towns and they went through some where the people were real hostile to them. They would throw rocks, cans, sticks, and everything they could think of: potatoes, even rotten tomatoes and eggs."[80]

But the clearest case of generalizing about a group of defeated people concerns postwar prejudice against the Dakotas. Within the state the public clamored for the quickly convened military trials to find virtually all the accused Dakotas guilty of war crimes, to sentence them to hang, and to execute them rapidly.[81] Most white Minnesotans at the time seemed much more interested in revenge than in justice. They refused to acknowledge that large numbers of guilty Dakotas had already fled west into neighboring states or into Canada (along with many other

Dakotas who were not involved in the fighting but feared retaliation), and they took out their anger on those who remained. Bowing to pressure from General John Pope, the military tribunals recommended to President Lincoln that 303 of the almost 400 men tried be executed for various crimes including murder, rape, and theft.[82]

Lincoln and his cabinet were appalled at the haste with which the Dakotas had been convicted (over forty cases might be heard in a single day), at the flimsy accusations used to condemn, at the likelihood of self-recrimination in biased questioning, at the translation and other language problems, and at the number of outright errors. So they took steps to prevent further action until they could review the transcripts.[83] Despite mounting public opinion, Lincoln spent much more time trying to reach fair sentences than many Minnesotans thought he should. When he finally authorized only thirty-nine executions—a late reprieve for Tatemina (Round Wind) reduced the final number hanged to thirty-eight—his popularity plummeted in the state. However, even Lincoln did not either see or acknowledge a basic contradiction in the postwar treatment of combatants: since the Dakotas constituted a sovereign nation warring with the United States, the fighters should have been considered "legitimate belligerents" and "tried only on charges that they violated the customary rules of warfare, not for the civilian crimes of murder, rape, and robbery." Therefore "the commission tried the Dakota for the wrong crimes."[84]

The final point about white/Indian wars, according to Limerick, is that they were usually so violent that it is hard to imagine either how they could be romanticized in later American mythology or how their participants and survivors could coexist again. In terms of mythmaking, all kinds of print media—especially the wildly popular Indian captivity narratives and their progeny, cowboys and Indians stories—idealized European American conduct and demonized Indian behavior, thereby promoting propaganda. The captivity narratives by whites published right after the Conflict definitely tended to exaggerate the bravery of the European Americans and the brutality of the warring Dakotas and, by extension, virtually all Dakotas.

But in the 1890s, some thirty years after the war, a series of accounts, including many captivity narratives, appeared by European Americans and also Dakotas, sometimes sponsored by a local newspaper or by the Minnesota Historical Society. Quite a few actually came out in the society's journal, *Collections of the Minnesota Historical Society*. By this time communal animosity had begun to recede, and antiquarian zeal in the European American community fostered an interest in first-person accounts by participants of all backgrounds before they died. Among the Dakotas stories were more likely to be passed down orally before they appeared in print, if they ever did, though increasing numbers of Dakotas spoke and wrote English or wrote in Dakota. Widespread coexistence really was not an option for decades, since most Dakotas had left the state either forcibly or voluntarily. Even when Dakotas began to return some time later, living together was difficult. By then, however, more Native Americans had adopted originally European American practices, particularly Christianity, and so they were seen as less threatening and more assimilated than before.

Two of the core texts in my study illustrate, respectively, an impulse toward mythmaking and hatred and an impulse toward reconciliation and forgiveness. They are the only two novels that I include: *Indian Jim*, a dime novel by Edward S. Ellis, published in 1864; and *Betrayed*, an example of juvenile fiction by modern Sioux writer Virginia Driving Hawk Sneve, published in 1974. These works are at opposite ends of the verbal war fought to establish a particular interpretation of white/Indian relations. As the opening commentary of *Dakota Exile*, a 1995 documentary produced in Minnesota, states, "When the war ended the cultural war began."[85]

For Ellis, as the later chapter on his book will show, the Dakota War presented an opportunity to ridicule toleration and cultural sensitivity toward Indians. Although the Indian Jim of the title is prowhite and

Christianized, he disappears at the end of the story when a vengeful Dakota kills one of the main female characters. A little over a century later Sneve deliberately wrote *Betrayed* to present balanced and positive views of the Dakotas involved in the Conflict to the younger generation. At the same time she is careful not to demonize European Americans. In the late nineteenth and early twentieth centuries dime novels like *Indian Jim* sentimentalized events and purveyed propaganda, especially for a suggestible young adult readership. In a telling irony Sneve's late twentieth-century novel *Betrayed*, while it also fictionalized aspects of the Dakota Conflict, did so to foster conciliation, not provocation, among its juvenile readers.

By presenting "the war in words" as a series of individuals contesting their own versions of a war and shaping its legacy, I adapt a comment about Europeans' complex support of and resistance to the First World War, which fostered "a more subtle chronology and cartography" of events and their remembrances.[86] Similarly the Dakota War captivity narratives present wartime memories nuanced by time and space as commentators passionately defended their perspectives.

1

European Americans Narrating Captivity

Introduction

I never want to read any more stuf [*sic*] a bout that Indian outbreak, it is
simple terrible the way people write up those things. I remember well
after the outbreak the country was flooded with unscrupulous persons
that wrote a lot of sensational stuf it mattered not if it was true as not
just so they could sell thear books and the more lies they wrote the bet-
ter they could sell thear books. | Mary Schwandt Schmidt to Marion P.
Satterlee, 19 December 1915

Captivity narratives, particularly Indian captivity narratives, have been
part of the American psyche for centuries, and some scholars see them
as archetypal texts about the individual/imperial American experience,
exemplifying personal and national renewal. This thesis, of course,
is most powerfully articulated in Richard Slotkin's classic study of
the traditional captivity literature, *Regeneration through Violence: The
Mythology of the American Frontier* (1973).[1] Like other early critics, such
as Richard VanDerBeets and Roy Harvey Pearce, Slotkin sees "captivity narratives" as synonymous with "Indian captivity narratives," an
overlay that later analysts do not necessarily maintain.

Much captivity narrative scholarship up to the 1980s focused on a core
of seventeenth- to early nineteenth-century texts from the Northeast
and emphasized those by or about Puritans. This narrow sampling of
captivity stories fostered other European American, specifically Anglo,
colonial stereotypes, including barbaric Native Americans; glamor-
ous, heroic, or martyred white explorers and settlers; Anglo—rather
than other European—subjects; and historical amnesia regarding pre-
seventeenth-century contact between Europeans and Native Americans and regarding other early settlements away from the privileged
locus of New England.

But current scholarship complicates this definition. The 1990s and beyond have seen an explosion of book-length works as well as numerous articles on captivity, resulting in a whole field now called captivity narrative studies. Between 1992 and 2007 at least thirty books appeared on or pertaining to captivity narratives, including individual editions, anthologies of narratives, studies of individual captives, and critical and historical monographs.[2] Most of these books focus on Indian captivity narratives and on the experiences of non-Native hostages. Their collective contribution expands the corpus and the chronology of the genre by utilizing a variety of contemporary critical and historical approaches. Indeed, the most recent books show that the term "captivity narrative" is a particularly elastic one in American culture. *The War in Words* continues this emphasis on widening the literal and symbolic elements of captivity but does so within an underexamined set of texts about a single war.

Three 1992 publications indicate that captivity narratives were attracting the interest of a new generation of historians and literary critics. Nancy Armstrong and Leonard Tennenhouse's *The Imaginary Puritan: Literature, Intellectual Labor, and the Origins of Personal Life*, for example, was one of the earliest studies to recognize a link between captivity in Indian captivity narratives and captivation in seduction novels and to connect the British and American literary traditions in arguing that Mary Rowlandson's account influenced Samuel Richardson's novel *Pamela*. Both besieged female subjects affirm their identity through first-person narrative. The same year historians Colin Calloway and June Namias edited, respectively, an anthology of New England captivities and a scholarly edition of Mary Jemison's captivity narrative.

In 1993 two books provided the first comprehensive overviews of Indian captivity narratives' literary and cultural history: my own co-authored book, with James A. Levernier, *The Indian Captivity Narrative, 1550–1990*, and June Namias's *White Captives: Gender and Ethnicity on the American Frontier*. Both expanded the form's canon and chronology and paid particular attention to gender issues, including women as subjects and scribes. A year later, in 1994, John Demos's *The Unredeemed Captive* deconstructed John Williams's famous captivity narrative *The Redeemed Captive Returning to Zion* (1707) and privileged instead the submerged story (or stories) of his daughter Eunice. Known for most of her life by the Kahnawake names A'ongote or Gannenstenhawi, Eunice never wrote her own narrative, but many others told of her conversion to Catholicism and transculturation to Indian life. The book was nominated for a National Book Award, and it made captivity a mass-market, best-selling proposition, as it had been in previous centuries for certain primary texts.[3]

The focus of military historian Robert C. Doyle's *Voices from Captivity: Interpreting the American POW Narrative* (1994) is self-explanatory; its contribution lies in expanding the standard definition of "captive" to include soldiers held as prisoners-of-war, not just the civilian captives whose stories are better-known. The next three years saw the publication of three important monographs: Gary L. Ebersole's *Captured by Texts: Puritan and Postmodern Images of Captivity* (1995), Christopher Castiglia's *Bound and Determined: Captivity, Culture Crossing, and White Womanhood from Mary Rowlandson to Patty Hearst* (1996), and Michelle Burnham's *Captivity and Sentiment: Cultural Exchange in American Literature, 1682–1861* (1997). All three books use fiction, nonfiction, and other media such as film.

Ebersole examines a sizeable sample of representative captivities for the ways they have been used "as vehicles for reflection on larger social, religious, and ideological issues."[4] The two other books deal with an enlarged canon of different kinds of captivity narratives, including not only Indian captivity narratives but hostage accounts, slave narratives, and sentimental novels. Castiglia claims that despite the traditional interpretation of women being victimized by captivity, many were empowered by the act of writing or dictating their experience, an observation borne out by Sarah Wakefield, Martha Riggs, Helen

Tarble, and many other white and Native women who penned Dakota War accounts. Burnham's book examines captivity narratives as representing "cultural exchange." Although this exchange was meant to reinforce stable identity, in fact the written treatment of captivity or enslavement often destabilized and blurred identity in the eyes of both writer and reader. Nineteen-ninety-seven also marked the publication of June Namias's scholarly edition of Sarah Wakefield's narrative, signaling the significance of this pro-Indian, antigovernment text. It is, however, the only captivity narrative arising out of the Dakota Conflict to receive extended literary attention.

My own anthology, *Women's Indian Captivity Narratives*, came out in 1998. Women's contributions as authors and subjects of Indian captivity stories have long been recognized, but many of their texts were unobtainable in scholarly or full form or unavailable altogether. This collection recovered and published ten complete texts from the seventeenth to the early twentieth centuries, including Wakefield's. Another book that appeared in 1998, Jill Lepore's *The Name of War: King Philip's War and the Origins of American Identity*, uses many different texts, among them several key captivity accounts, to help illuminate King Philip's (Metacomet's) War of 1675 and trace its cultural influence into the nineteenth century. Lepore also shows how captivity texts, among others, reveal the horror and grief of war and allow their authors and readers to meditate on morality and identity. Issues of mourning, morality, identity, and self are also crucial aspects of many of the Dakota War narratives.

The publication in 1999 of *six* books on captivity narratives left no doubt that this was a hot scholarly field. Paul Baepler's anthology *White Slaves, African Masters* establishes that the hitherto underrepresented area of Barbary captivities formed one more component of the wider genre of captivity narratives. Another book dealing with "alternative" captivity is Nancy Schultz's edition of the two best-known convent captivity narratives. Almost invariably fictional and originating in nineteenth-century anti-Catholic prejudice, these tales detail the sufferings of young ingénues who joined convents as novitiates, only to be seduced by corrupt priests and tortured by sadistic nuns. A third book also widens the scope of captivity literature. James Hartman's *Providence Tales and the Birth of American Literature* argues that the Indian captivity narrative is a late development of a much larger hybrid genre, originating in England, that told stories of providential intervention in the world. Variations of the captivity narrative prototype similar to those in the three books just mentioned are a vital aspect of my examination of the Dakota War stories, which encompass Indian captivity narratives, imprisonment accounts, cultural captivation stories, and spiritual autobiographies, among other generic manifestations.

Anthropologist Pauline Turner Strong's *Captive Selves, Captivating Others: The Politics and Poetics of Colonial American Captivity Narratives* examines some accounts of Native Americans taken hostage by European Americans, as well as vice versa. Thus Strong recognizes that historically many Indians were captured and enslaved, a significant reversal of the basic captivity paradigm that had not at that time received as much attention as it warranted. Further, she discusses the ethnographic information that captivity narratives can reveal about indigenous culture, even if data are biased.[5]

Rebecca Blevins Faery's *Cartographies of Desire: Captivity, Race, and Sex in the Shaping of an American Nation*, also published in 1999, argues that two recurring cultural symbols, the white woman captured by Indians (Faery takes Mary Rowlandson) and the Indian captivated by white culture (Pocahontas is the prime example), have been vitally important "in constructing the geographic and ideological maps of the United States."[6] By devoting equal attention to an Anglo and to a Powhatan captive, Faery reinforces the point that both cultures experienced captivity in the dual roles of captors and captives. Barbara Mortimer examines the trope of captivity in her monograph *Hollywood's*

Frontier Captives: Cultural Anxiety and the Captivity Plot in American Film, which was the sixth book on captivity published in 1999. Although other texts refer to film versions of captivity narratives, Mortimer's analysis is the first to focus exclusively on this medium.

Two more book-length publications came out in 2000. Joe Snader's *Caught between Worlds: British Captivity Narratives in Fact and Fiction* shows that foreign—not only Indian—captivity formed a staple literary topic in eighteenth-century British fact and fiction. Snader pays particular attention to the transatlantic connections between the captivity narrative and the novel. The same year Gordon Sayre's anthology *American Captivity Narratives* made a strong link between Indian captivity narratives and slave narratives. From 2002 to 2004 historians, rather than literary critics, seemed to reclaim captivity narrative scholarship, though they use a range of interdisciplinary and cultural studies approaches for their analyses. In 2002 German American historian Don Heinrich Tolzmann produced a limited edition of two Dakota War accounts concerning German immigrant women. Titled *German Pioneer Accounts of the Great Sioux Uprising of 1862,* it focuses on historical and antiquarian, rather than literary, worth.

Two monographs in 2003 vary the standard, but by now much revised, paradigms of captivity, and both specifically involve historical aspects of Indian captivity narratives. They are William Henry Foster's *The Captors' Narrative: Catholic Women and Their Puritan Men on the Early American Frontier* and Evan Haefeli and Kevin Sweeney's *Captors and Captives: The 1704 French and Indian Raid on Deerfield.* The subjects of Foster's book are the Puritan men captured and taken to Canada between 1690 and 1760 and the French Canadian women who became their owners. Examining tales by the captive men and the captor women reveals interesting gender struggles in the eighteenth century and provides yet another challenge to the female/victim, male/victor stereotype. It also helps to correct the American nationalistic bias of excluding or downplaying Canadian texts and subjects. *Captors and*

Captives reconstructs the famous raid on Deerfield, using a variety of primary texts and participant stories. Haefeli and Sweeney aim to provide a definitive account of the attack, in which 50 Deerfield residents died and 112 were captured, by considering different perspectives as the events unfold chronologically.

The year 2004 saw the appearance of historian Linda Colley's *Captives: Britain, Empire, and the World, 1600–1850*, which uses what one review terms "an array of captivity narratives by everyday Britons captured by foreign powers to show the dizzying ethnic and cultural complexity of empire."[7] This lengthy book focuses on four contact zones within the British Empire: the Mediterranean, North America, India, and Afghanistan. Colley reiterates that captivity and its narratives are not, of course, a phenomenon restricted to the Americas, but she restricts her attention to the stories of captured Britons as support for her thesis, without treating them in specifically literary terms.

Two anthologies and a monograph appeared in 2006. Daniel E. Williams edited *Liberty's Captives: Narratives of Confinement in the Print Culture of the Early Republic*, which makes available seventeen little-known confinement narratives published between 1779 and 1818. Williams's introduction argues that such narratives reinforced the rhetoric of slavery and liberty so rampant during and after the American Revolution by merging and enacting self and nation. *Captive Histories: English, French, and Native Narratives of the 1704 Deerfield Raid*, edited by Evan Haefeli and Kevin Sweeney, makes available English, French, Abenaki, and Mohawk texts to provide different narrative perspectives on the 1704 Indian attack on Deerfield. Finally, Andrea Tinnemeyer's monograph *Identity Politics of the Captivity Narrative after 1848* examines the nineteenth-century captivity narrative's role in creating the U.S.-Mexican War in the American national imaginary.

The most recent books, appearing in 2007, are Lorrayne Carroll's *Rhetorical Drag: Gender Impersonation, Captivity, and the Writing of History* and Teresa A. Toulouse's *The Captive's Position: Female Narrative, Male*

Identity, and Royal Authority in Colonial New England. Other books are in the pipeline, as American culture continues to engage with factual and fictional captivity and as Native writers and critics play an increasing role in captivity narrative scholarship. Overall the trend to expand the definition and application of captivity continues unabated.[8]

1. Martha Riggs Morris and Sarah Wakefield
Captivity and Protest

When historian Marion Satterlee asked Mary Schwandt Schmidt to comment on his completed manuscript about the Dakota Conflict in 1915, she responded with a terse letter, partly extracted in the epigraph to part 1. Over fifty years after her captivity she still felt traumatized not only by the experience but by its exploitation in print. Although she had furnished some information for Satterlee's work beforehand, when she read it in print she objected to the graphic description of her sister's death and questioned his version of events. She also referred to a recent newspaper article that contained misinformation about her and concluded, "It is just as I say people don't know what they are talking a bout I think it is pretty late in the day to write a bout what happened 53 years ago."[1] Schwandt Schmidt understood that from the very beginning many European American commentators had cynically cashed in on the rhetorical and discursive uses of the Conflict, using it to make money and spread propaganda. They disregarded the truth (to the extent that it was knowable) and overrode the authority of participants (to the extent that they possessed it). In this regard Schwandt Schmidt and other participants became "historians of their own experience, reacting against and wanting to correct . . . distortions and misperceptions," similar to soldiers' first-person accounts during the First World War designed to bring a truer sense of warfare to the homefront.[2]

One reason that first-person captivity accounts sometimes vied with comprehensive histories that included multiple accounts is that they did not always adopt the standard anti-Indian propagandist line. When women wrote such stories, their gender and ethnic betrayal signaled a double transgression to mainstream American culture. Considered particularly vulnerable during Indian captivity, white women should not have forgotten their private roles and domestic duties afterward to criticize European American culture publicly. Anticipating Schwandt Schmidt, two other women who were intimately involved in the Conflict, Martha Riggs and Sarah Wakefield, tried to establish their subjectivity and authenticity in stories published soon after the war. These activist, pro-Dakota texts were not the norm, and many other white women provided conventional, racist accounts of victimization. But Riggs and Wakefield used the power of print to validate their viewpoints. Neither of the women wrote for publication before the war, but their intense experiences, sense of immediacy, strong beliefs, and raw talent turned them into superb protest writers soon after it.

Schwandt Schmidt, Riggs, and Wakefield, among other first-person narrators, "appeal to the status of the 'eye-witness/outcast' to establish their authority in writing 'true histories' [within] historico-political contexts."[3] I adapt this quotation from Ralph Bauer's study of the seventeenth-century Indian captivity narratives by Mary Rowlandson and Francisco Nunez Pineda y Bascunan, produced during "political friction between a colonial frontier society and a center of imperial administration."[4] The narrators of these two texts are authorized to speak and judge because they have suffered, and their experiences and texts mold a creole, not just an expatriate, identity. Correspondingly I believe that the recent immigrants to Minnesota in the nineteenth century felt authorized to speak and assert their identities against nonparticipant historians and the federal government in the Northeast, which must have seemed to them—consciously or unconsciously—like a colonial administration far removed from the realities of multiethnic frontier life.[5]

Martha Riggs was the second daughter of Presbyterian Stephen Riggs, longtime missionary to the Dakotas. He had originally joined the Dakota Mission under the auspices of the American Board of Commissioners for Foreign Missions (ABCFM) in 1837, the same year he married Mary Ann (Longley) Riggs. They imparted a love of evangelism to their family and worked in this field until they died. Six of the eight Riggs children chose mission work, and at least three, including Martha, worked directly with the Dakotas.[6] All were given Dakota names, Martha's being Hapistanna. She spent her childhood in various locales in what became the state of Minnesota, with brief spells elsewhere for formal schooling and other activities.

The entire family fled Hazelwood on the eve of war, but Stephen became an interpreter and chaplain to the troops while the rest of the family settled in St. Anthony, where Martha cared for her ailing mother until they moved again to Beloit, Wisconsin.[7] Some of the Riggs family's travels were by choice, since they and the ABCFM believed they could best reach converts through zealous itinerancy. But some travels were forced on them by their dangerous and isolated work. Like Martha, and her mother before her, many other missionaries strove for spiritual stability amid material change.[8]

In December 1866 Martha married fellow missionary Wyllys K. Morris, and they spent many years at the Good Will Mission that her father had established at the Sisseton Agency, Dakota Territory. She was a teacher and "general matron," and her husband was superintendent of the boarding school they founded.[9] Indeed, after the war Stephen Riggs served as superintendent of missions among the Sisseton Dakotas until 1883.[10] In 1891 the Morris family was on the move again, this time to another mission, at Omaha Agency, Nebraska, and four years later to Porcupine, South Dakota, to serve the Pine Ridge Reservation. By 1900 Martha was living in the town of Sisseton, South Dakota, surrounded by children and grandchildren, and she stayed there until her death in 1910. The best source of information on her life comes from the booklet *Our Martha*, a virtual hagiography that her sister Anna lovingly compiled shortly after Martha died.[11]

Anna draws attention to Martha's remarkable qualities: energy, diligence, courage, maturity, responsibility, generosity, piety, efficiency, and sympathy. She also recognizes her elder sister's verbal skills: "She wrote easily, and had a most unusual gift in correspondence. In this, as in many other things, she was her father's own daughter."[12] True to the nineteenth-century tradition of letter writing, both Stephen and Martha were faithful and prolific correspondents. Sometimes too each was moved to compose nonepistolary texts. Nowhere is Martha's rhetorical ability more evident than in her account of the family's escape from the Hazelwood mission, which appeared as a six-thousand-word open letter in the *Cincinnati Christian Herald* and the *Presbyter* in 1862, and which her father reprinted in his autobiography, *Mary and I: Forty Years with the Sioux*, almost twenty years later.

While the Indian captivity narrative might seem to involve only actual captivity, as its name certainly suggests, a generic oddity is that it also traditionally accommodates stories about Indian attacks or even fear of Indian raids causing dispersal (the captivity then involves being bound to the elements or to fright rather than to human captors). This is the case in the numerous reports on the Donner Party, for example, and it also applies to Martha Riggs's account.[13] Martha titled her piece "The Flight of the Missionaries" and dated it 26 September 1862. Although Martha's evangelistic fervor and seemingly liberal politics infuse this document, it avoids sensation and sentimentality. As Martha's mother wrote to her father soon after the piece appeared: "I think you will agree with me that it is a well written article. There are some parts very fine."[14] This story is in the tradition of the public protest letter, and it uses captivity for political purposes, specifically for public dissent. It also provides a nascent example of a female war correspondent's report, since Martha was a witness-participant within the forty-five-member missionary refugee party that left the Upper Sioux Reservation following reported attacks on the Lower Sioux Agency.[15]

The account opens dramatically but strategically with rumors of

Figure 3. Missionary escape party, 21 August 1862. Martha Riggs can be seen standing (*in the back, to the right*), wearing a pale bonnet and a cape and kneading bread dough. From the Collections of the Minnesota Historical Society. Used with permission.

war interspersed with references to pacifist Dakotas who provided enough warning for some European Americans to escape. Martha spends far more time on the nonmilitant Indians than on the militant ones. Rather than reinforce the negative stereotypes so prevalent in contemporary reports of alleged Indian atrocities, she provides a needed, though at the time unpopular, corrective. She does not interpret the serious events that befell her as traumas, but as hardships to be endured, maybe even enjoyed, as seen in this quotation: "Our day's march was slow but steady—only stopping when necessary to rest the teams; and although we considered ourselves in danger, we found it quite enjoyable, more particularly after *we* and the *grass* got dry, so that we could walk with ease."[16] Martha's self-fashioning as a spirit-filled person encouraged contemporary readers to trust her, while it disguised her radical vision of allowing everyone equal access to Christianity regardless of ethnicity.

Although the escape party was often drenched with rain, members took advantage of good spells of weather to rest and eat. At one of these stops Martha describes how they baked flatbread and "luxuriated on meat" from a cow they had killed.[17] Martha captures the occasion verbally but also mentions that it was captured visually: "Here our party was immortalized by a young artist—a Mr. Ebell—who had gone up into our region of country a few days previous to our flight, for the purpose of taking stereoscopic views."[18] Photographer Adrian Ebell's haunting image (engraved and somewhat ironically titled "The Breakfast on the Prairie" in his own *Harper's* account of the war) shows a group of men, women, and children lying or standing on the ground. A quick glance might indicate a picnic, but closer attention reveals that they are huddled too awkwardly for a social occasion, that they look disheveled, and that the only food evident is a large amount of dough being kneaded by Martha. While many people gaze into the camera grim and exhausted, it is typical of Martha that she is seen in action. If she couldn't do anything else, she could still bake bread.

As the party approached Fort Ridgely they realized the extent of the fighting and were advised to press on because the post was over-full and had been under attack only hours earlier. The group headed across the prairie once more, and Martha conveys their anxiety and tendency to stereotype and romanticize when endangered: "Every ear was intensely strained for the faintest noise, expecting momentarily to hear the unearthly war-whoop, and see dusky forms with gleaming tomahawks lifted."[19] But this fear of attack never materialized, and the longer they traveled without incident, the more secure they felt, and the more convinced they were that their escape was providential. When the Riggs family reached safety in Henderson, the first order of business, Martha lightheartedly reports, was to find a shoe store. She adds that some young people, including herself, had come to prefer walking to other forms of transport and to redefine paradise as a place with abundant water, clean clothes, plentiful food, and a comfortable bed!

Yet Martha's public letter does not end on this humorous note; it ends with an impassioned appeal that her readers not judge the warring Dakotas as typical. She points out how John Other Day, Lorenzo Lawrence, and other Christian Dakotas had risked their own lives to save dozens of captives. Not content to rest there, Martha's last comments establish that those Dakotas who rebelled had good reason to do so: "The Indians have not been without excuse for their evil deeds. Our own people have given them intoxicating drinks, taught them to swear, violated the rights of womanhood among them, robbed them of their dues, and then insulted them! What more would be necessary to cause one nation to rise against another? What *more*, I ask. And yet there are many who curse this people, and cry, 'Exterminate the fiends.' *Dare* we, as a nation, *thus* bring a curse upon ourselves and upon future generations."[20] Ultimately then she places much of the blame on unchristian whites, and she urges her readers to take communal responsibility. Although Martha's occasional effusiveness is a reminder that she was only twenty when she wrote this account, most of the time she comes across as a surprisingly mature correspondent and moral interpreter who ably articulated reformist arguments.

Throughout her mission career Martha was called upon to produce various kinds of texts. For example, she recorded the Dakota legend "Sweet Grass' Story," which was first published in 1876, and twenty-four years after "The Flight of the Missionaries" appeared she wrote the report on the Sisseton Mission effort included in the volume *The Dakota Mission: Past and Present* (1886).[21] Much of it is a paean of praise to her father for sustaining his evangelistic vision, but elsewhere she pays tribute to those Dakotas who remained Christians despite the traumas of war, describes the founding of boarding schools for Dakota boys and girls after the Conflict, and identifies several Native ministers who were trained in these reservation schools.

Martha Riggs exemplifies a second major wave of nineteenth-century Protestant missionaries to the Dakotas—the children of the original evangelists. Her parents and their contemporaries, such as Thomas S. Williamson, Samuel Pond and Gideon Pond, Alexander Huggins, and others, formed the first wave. The main catalyst for the earliest concerted mission initiative was the formation in 1810 of the American Board of Commissioners for Foreign Missions, the umbrella organization that fostered domestic and overseas mission work by Congregationalists, Presbyterians, Lutherans, and other evangelical Protestant denominations.

Although the ABCFM initially sent its missionaries to such far-flung places as India, Brazil, China, and Ceylon, some board members argued that it should make more of an effort to convert the Native American "heathens" at home. This endeavor gained strength from the Supreme Court's ruling that Indian peoples were "domestic dependent nations." The earliest ABCFM Indian missions were to the Cherokees, Choctaws, Osages, and Chickasaws, but in the 1830s the work expanded to the Ojibwes, Pawnees, Dakotas, and others. The ABCFM believed that its missionaries should have relatively brief tours of duty in a single locale. They should only stay long enough to convert a critical mass of Indians and train Native ministers, who would continue the work of Christianization and civilization; then they should move on.[22] While this was a reasonable aim, evangelism sometimes proceeded more slowly than the ABCFM wished, especially among tribes where literacy needed to be established before conversion. So European American missionaries might stay in situ longer than anticipated.

The first Protestant missionaries found themselves in unfamiliar territory culturally, politically, physically, psychologically, and spiritually. Many came with simplistic and idealistic notions of evangelism, along with negative stereotypes of their targeted converts. A study of missionary work among the Dakotas from 1835 to 1862 shows how at first missionaries saw their own culture as ethnocentric yet also believed they themselves were progressive and even egalitarian.[23] Over the years, however, some missionaries' preconceptions began to be modified, as

shown during and after the Conflict, when some defended Christianized Dakotas. These adaptations resulted from ongoing "bidirectional"
exchange, in which missionaries and Dakotas challenged each other
to interrogate identity and sometimes to integrate different ideas into
their sense of being.[24] For instance, missionary children brought up
with Dakotas, including Martha and her siblings, established friendships with their counterparts, and missionary sons sometimes married "assimilated" Dakotas and brought them into the family fold.[25]
Unlike her parents Martha was exposed to two cultures from birth,
Anglo and Dakota, and was arguably less ambivalent about the latter
than they were. Hence her unapologetic tone in "The Flight of the
Missionaries."

But many modern commentators remain deeply skeptical about
Christian evangelism because it developed alongside Western imperialism, and they highlight its generally harmful impact on Native
Americans. Osage/Cherokee theologian George E. Tinker believes
that all Christian missionaries to the Indians "were partners in genocide" despite their professed good intentions and (sometimes) surface
liberalism: "Disciplinary control, the imposition of European culture,
and even the imposition of European economic structures and technology actually became the gospel, even though it was necessarily a
gospel of bondage rather than one of liberation."[26] Florestine Kiyukanpi Renville and Elizabeth Cook-Lynn also express their suspicion
of conventional Christianity. Renville contrasts Christian hypocrisy
and self-righteousness with Dakota holistic spirituality.[27] And Cook-
Lynn, in one of many explorations of the subject, explains that her own
short story "A Visit from Reverend Tileston" shows the persistence of
Native spirituality, of what she calls "a native conscience," in the face
of Christian aggression.[28]

The overall failure of the mission effort—at least as originally con-
ceived—even extended to someone like Henry B. Whipple, the Episcopal bishop of Minnesota from 1859 to 1901, whom the Indians called

"Straight Tongue" for his frankness. Whipple became an ardent Indian rights activist, yet he was also an assimilationist who believed that conversion and "civilization" went hand-in-hand as Native Americans slowly adapted to Western culture. Humane and just methods of persuasion should be used, he maintained, but ultimately the Indians must conform and convert. Tinker characterizes Whipple as "a captive of his own culture and its implicit set of values" because ironically he reinforced the oppressive system he criticized.[29] A study of Whipple's missionary work with the Ojibwes reaches the same conclusion: that even committed "friends of the Indian" like himself were actually "cultural imperialists."[30]

Tinker, Renville, and Cook-Lynn draw on the theories of Vine Deloria Jr., the prominent Lakota author, activist, theologian, lawyer, and historian. In many writings, including the essays "The Missionary in a Cultural Trap" (1965), "Missionaries and the Religious Vacuum" (1969), "A Violated Covenant" (1971), and "Christianity and Indigenous Religion" (1987), Deloria reiterates the point that in trying to save individual Indians, missionaries risked destroying entire Indian societies.[31] Deloria's opening sentence to "Missionaries and the Religious Vacuum" forcefully conveys his thesis that "one of the major problems of the Indian people is the missionary."[32]

Some Native groups have redefined and revitalized Christianity by allying it with traditional spiritualities. But residual distrust of an originally white belief system has encouraged others to return to tribal religions, especially with the growth of Indian empowerment in the latter part of the twentieth century. Rose Bluestone, a Wahpekute/ Mdewakanton Dakota who told her life story in several interviews during the late 1980s, illustrates this point: "My parents' generation was forced to embrace Christianity; I was brought up as a Christian. Still, I always had my pipe. Now, when you go to the Dakotas, you should see the churches standing empty. Weeds are growing over them. The people are all turning back to the Way of the Pipe."[33]

Robert Berkhofer's approach in his classic study *Salvation and the Savage* (1972) accords with the Native scholars just quoted. This analysis of the Indian response to Protestant missionaries from 1787 to 1862 examines the complexities of conversion among various Native groups, including the Dakotas. Yet the missionaries' methods, regardless of denominational affiliation, were remarkably similar and extreme; they all agreed that "true Indian conversion meant nothing less than a total transformation of native existence."[34] When friction invariably arose, some Indians vented their anger as easily on missionaries as on soldiers and settlers. And when endangered, missionaries sometimes asserted an ethnically encoded identity as members of a common non-Native culture. During the Dakota Conflict, for example, Stephen Riggs sought government protection and played a significant role in postwar punishment, though at times he also stuck out his neck and defended individual Dakotas.

While considerable damage—cultural and otherwise—took place when the missionaries were white, the establishment of Native clergy tended to create more organic Christian communities based on traditional kinship and leadership values.[35] Like many ordained African Americans, these Native Americans reinterpreted the Bible and saw its message as radical and empowering despite the dominant culture's attempts to use it for social discipline. These points will receive further attention in part 2, "Native Americans Narrating Captivity," where I examine texts by several early Dakota converts such as Paul Mazakutemani and Lorenzo Lawrence, whose Christianity paved the way for other Natives, like John B. Renville, to formally train for the ministry.

An early missionary like Stephen Riggs found evangelism and cultural superiority inextricable, but his daughter Martha had been brought up among Dakotas and did not hold to Manifest Destiny as firmly as her father did. Another woman to whom Riggs was a kind of father figure went one step further than Martha. She was ex-captive Sarah

Figure 4. Sarah F. Wakefield, date unknown. Courtesy of the *St. Paul Pioneer Press* and the Minnesota Historical Society.

Wakefield, who wrote him three anguished but angry letters in spring 1863 at the same time that she sent a letter to Abraham Lincoln and began to draft her captivity story. Like a daughter, she sought Riggs's advice but also voiced her independence and rebelliousness. The letters privately reveal Wakefield's unorthodox Christianity and radical morality; they also function as the prelude to her publicly expressed convictions in the most controversial of all the Dakota Conflict captivity narratives, *Six Weeks in the Sioux Tepees: A Narrative of Indian Captivity*, first published in November 1863.

A brief examination of the three letters to Riggs and the one to Lincoln, all composed between 22 March and 25 April 1863, will better contextualize her published account and reveal her frame of mind as she was writing it.[36] Indeed, together her letters and narrative form a kind of intertextual continuum on the topic of her captivity. In the first letter, dated 22 March, she pointedly asked Riggs to tell her in detail how Chaska, her Dakota protector while in captivity, had come to be hanged. Only a day later she wrote to the president himself: "I am extremely sorry this thing happened as it injures me greatly in the community that I live. I exerted myself very much to save him and many have been so ungenrous [*sic*] as to say I was in love with him that I was his wife &c, all of which is absolutely false. He always treated me like a Brother and as such I respect his memory and curse his slanderers."[37]

Wakefield's letter to Riggs two weeks later, on 9 April, communicated her stunning decision to "procure a situation of some kind" and "accompany the Indians," though ultimately she stayed in Shakopee with her children. She had decided on this course of action, she said, because the Dakota women cared more about her welfare than her own community, which had shunned her for defending Chaska at his trial and called her "a 'Mono Maniac.'"[38] Encouraged by her husband to seek Riggs's advice, she confided to him, "I write to you freely as you are an elderly man, and a Minister in Gods Church, and I think you will advise me relative to my going with the Indians, as you would one of your Daughters did she ask you."[39]

On 25 April she opened her longest letter to Riggs with a bold doctrinal challenge: did he really believe that Christ came to save sinners like herself or to save only the righteous? Later in the letter she revealed another radical stance toward the imprisoned Dakotas she had visited: "I am very sensitive and impulsive and it did really make my Heart ache to see those poor fellows tied in Prison, it was so different from what they expected, and so different from our treatment by them: and although I know they were many of them guilty I did pity them and if I could have done it would have released every one of them."[40]

How must Riggs have felt about this impassioned woman who would have freed even the guilty? Certainly he would have considered her rashness to be inappropriate and extreme. Heartsick that she had deterred Chaska from fleeing because she believed his protection of her would outweigh his other wartime acts, Wakefield confessed in closing this last letter to Riggs that she felt like "his Murderer."[41] She was only slightly more circumspect about the imprisoned Dakotas in her postscript to the Lincoln letter: "I am in favor of the majority of the poor fellows being pardoned. *I can* not deem *them guilty as many persons,* as they were so *very kind* and *honorable* to *me* while I was with them."[42] The same passions and convictions expressed in these letters surfaced in her captivity narrative and affected its telling as protest literature.

Sarah (Brown) Wakefield was born in Providence, Rhode Island. She was living in Shakopee by 1855, as an early Anglo settler in what would soon become the state of Minnesota.[43] A year later she married another Eastern transplant, Dr. John Luman Wakefield, and by 1861 they had two children, James Orin and his baby sister, Lucy.[44] Through Agent Galbraith's influence John Wakefield became doctor for the Upper Sioux Agency. When Sarah first arrived there she felt displaced and depressed, but she soon adjusted to her new role as frontier wife and mother. The Wakefields managed to maintain a surprisingly comfortable, even luxurious lifestyle, with a well-equipped home and fashionable accoutrements.[45] On Sundays Sarah and her son sometimes rode to Riggs's mission church at Hazelwood.[46]

That first year relations between the whites and the Dakotas seemed stable. But at the beginning of August 1862, Wakefield says, the Dakotas began to demand provisions and harass agency employees. She comments, "All they cared for was food—it was not our lives; and if all these Indians had been properly fed and otherwise treated like human beings, how many, very many innocent lives might have been spared."[47] When news of the hostilities at the Lower Sioux Agency reached the Upper Agency, John Wakefield insisted that clerk George Gleason escort Sarah and the children on an already planned trip to visit friends back East. But en route to Fort Ridgely two Indians, whom Wakefield referred to as Chaska and Hapa (the correct spelling is Hepan), approached the party.[48]

Testifying on Chaska's behalf before the Sioux Trials Commission on the first day of hearings, Wakefield said that Hepan had shot Gleason but that when the clerk was dying Chaska "snapped his gun at him . . . to put him out of his misery."[49] In other words, she attempted to establish that Chaska was not technically or morally responsible for Gleason's death. She then pointed out that he had adopted a number of white customs and thus was "civilized," that he took pity on her, and that he actually saved her from death three times. Like her testimony, Wakefield's narrative is schizophrenic: it provides relatively objective information on people, events, and issues, but also highly subjective and sometimes wildly implausible rationalizations of her own and others' motivation and behavior.[50] Written so quickly after her traumatic experience, her captivity narrative performs its author's own instability and shaken sense of identity, encouraging readers to interpret the disparate data themselves.

At many points in her account Wakefield establishes that after some initial discomfort with the Dakotas, soon she felt so sympathetic toward them that she shared their anger at the government. This viewpoint had important ramifications for her treatment during captivity, since she claims that some Dakotas remembered her previous kindness and treated her differently from other hostages. Although Wakefield was not the only hostage to make this assertion, she specifically says in her letter to Lincoln that she had known Chaska's family for eight years. In particular Chaska became Wakefield's defender, especially since his brother-in-law Hepan initially wanted to kill her but then, after Chaska deterred him, to rape her. It seems likely that Chaska applied kinship ties to Sarah and her children and protected them as best he could. To counteract the danger from Hepan, the recently widowed Chaska apparently pretended that he wanted Wakefield as his own wife. Such a subterfuge caused immense problems during and after Wakefield's captivity because "it was constantly reported and many believed that I was his wife, and I dared not contradict it, but rather encouraged everyone to believe so, for I was in fear all the while that Hapa would find out we had deceived him."[51]

Wakefield maintains that other captives also misinterpreted and misjudged her behavior. Indeed, Mary Schwandt flatly stated in her account: "I remember Mrs. Dr. Wakefield and Mrs. Adams. They were painted and decorated and dressed in full Indian costume, and seemed proud of it. They were usually in good spirits, laughing and joking, and appeared to enjoy their new life. The rest of us disliked their conduct, and would have but little to do with them."[52] Wakefield admits to dressing like a Dakota woman and even agreeing to help kill other hostages, do traditional Dakota woman's work, and "be like a squaw."[53] However, she tries to rationalize her actions by saying that she was half crazy and thought submission was the only way to save her own and her children's lives. As evidence of her genuine trauma, she points out that within two months her hair had turned white and she had lost forty pounds.[54] But the other captives were not entirely wrong, for Wakefield certainly did not resist Dakota acculturation as thoroughly as many of them did. The debate really concerned her motives, with Wakefield saying that she did what she had to do in order to survive and her critics (which included General Sibley) saying that she sold out to the enemy.[55]

Stephen Riggs was among Sibley's entourage at Camp Release, and Wakefield mentions that when the two men asked her to identify her protector, they "made quite a hero of him for a short time."[56] Riggs was also the person to whom she was encouraged to disclose information "of a private nature," a euphemism for sexual abuse.[57] At one point the soldiers joked about lynching seven imprisoned Dakotas, including

Chaska, and Wakefield rashly threatened to kill anyone who did so. When Wakefield visited Chaska in prison at Camp Release, he blamed her for his conviction, and she blamed him for her social isolation. Before leaving to rejoin her husband Wakefield was relieved to hear that Chaska's sentence had been commuted to five years in prison. So she was distraught when later she learned in the press that he was one of the thirty-eight hanged prisoners. According to a letter that Riggs wrote to Wakefield, which she quotes in her captivity narrative, the error arose because Chaska (who was tried under the name We-Chank-Wash-ta-don-pee) responded when the name "Chaska" was called, instead of another prisoner called Chaskadon, who had killed and mutilated a pregnant woman.[58]

Presumably to avoid exactly such a mistake, each prisoner was identified during the trials not only by name but by number, and the presidential order carefully listed the thirty-nine condemned men in this way. In fact, Lincoln's secretary had dispatched a letter to Sibley asking him to ensure that there would be no mistake in sending the wrong man named Chaska to the gallows, partly because there were other men by that name, including one also known as Robert Hopkins, who was a close friend and convert of Stephen Riggs.[59] Unfortunately no one at Mankato had the trial records containing this crucial list of names, numbers, and cases; they had all been sent to Washington, as Lincoln requested.[60] We-Chank-Wash-ta-don-pee was number 3; Chaskadon was number 121.

Riggs was in the prison to oversee the executions and to help guard against such mix-ups.[61] Since he had met We-Chank-Wash-to-don-pee on several occasions, Wakefield felt that even under such tense and traumatic conditions, he should have realized when the wrong person replied and done something about it.[62] She states unequivocally, toward the end of her account, that she believes Chaska was killed either consciously or carelessly.[63] Riggs agrees in his autobiography that when the time came to separate the thirty-nine condemned men from the other prisoners at Mankato, there was some confusion about who was who. But he blames Joseph R. Brown, agent to the Dakotas from 1857 to 1860 and leader of scouting forces against the Dakotas during the Conflict, for the final selection: "To Joseph R. Brown, who, better than any other one man, knew all these condemned men—and he did not recognize all perfectly—was mainly committed the work of selecting those who were named to be executed. Extraordinary care was meant to be used; but after it was all over, when we came to compare their own stories and confessions, made a day or two before their death, with the papers of condemnation, the conviction was forced upon us that two mistakes had occurred."[64] On execution day, he says, the name "Chaska" was called, and We-Chank-Wash-ta-don-pee responded.

Presumably Riggs felt humbled if not humiliated when he saw his own letter quoted in Wakefield's captivity narrative and then read her angry response there: "Now I will never believe that all in authority at Mankato had forgotten what Chaska was condemned for, and I am sure, in my own mind, it was done intentionally. I dare not say by whom."[65] But in her letter to Lincoln sent months earlier Wakefield provided clear evidence that she thought Joseph Brown was to blame: "My Husband is very anxious this thing should be made public, as he thinks the mistake was intentional on the part of a certain 'Officer' at Mankato, who has many children in the Sioux tribe."[66] Since Brown was in charge of the Mankato jail, had been married to several Dakota women, and had children both in and out of wedlock in his frequent extramarital liaisons, Wakefield's allusion can only be to Brown.[67] And she is right that the confusion should not have occurred.

But if Chaska suffered injustice from European Americans while alive, they subjected him to indecency and inhumanity when dead. Not only were his body and the bodies of many—probably all—of the other hanged men rifled by souvenir hunters and later exhumed and removed by doctors for dissection, but one of his braids was cut as a "memento" to be sent to George Gleason's family.[68] On 26 December

1887, the twenty-five-year commemoration of the hangings, John F. Meagher of Mankato sent a letter to J. Fletcher Williams, secretary of the Minnesota Historical Society, along with an enclosure. Meagher explained that, unable to trace any of Gleason's relatives, he could not send the "relic of the time of the Sioux Execution" to them and instead had decided to give it to the Historical Society. Recalling events in which he had participated on the evening of 26 December 1862, he wrote: "We all felt keenly the injury he [Chaska] had don in murdering our old friend Gleason, in cold blood. I cut off the Rope that bound his hands and feet, and cut off one Brade of his hair. . . . I had the hair made into a Watch chain by a Lady friend in St. Paul. I wore it untill it was as you see about wore out, and now I send it to you, thinking that some day it might be of interest with the other mementoes of those terible times and that great hanging Event."[69]

The final atrocity and desecration concern Meagher's recollection of asking a "Lady friend" to fashion the hair into a watch chain, her agreement to do so, his use of it until it was almost worn out, and his belief that the Historical Society would deem it an appropriate donation.[70] It is true that ornaments and mementos woven of hair were fashionable among Victorians, but this was an entirely different matter. Much Victorian hairwork was connected with mourning and memorializing a beloved person. It was quite popular during the Civil War, when soldiers left locks of their own hair with their families to be made into mourning jewelry if they died. Indeed, from the 1850s to the early 1900s "hairwork became a drawing room pastime."[71] In Dakota culture long hair for men signified traditional identity. What better symbol of cultural appropriation than to take Chaska's braid and domesticate its significance by allowing it to be used for a white woman's genteel activity? It was at the very least a symbolic scalping. And what more permanent symbol of white dominance and revenge than to make this hair into a fob for a watch that marked the passage of time into what seemed like a white imperialist future?

The hypocrisy of her own culture was precisely the moral lesson that Wakefield's captivity taught her. In fact, Chaska's death led Wakefield to distrust conventional religion and received political belief. In Wakefield's third letter to Riggs she focuses on the insincerity and inconsistency of traditional Christianity as practiced by ministers and churchgoers. She adds that she "always attended Church and never forgot that there was a God" and that she wished to be baptized and to be treated charitably by the clergy and congregation.[72] We do not know exactly why Wakefield had not been baptized earlier, which would have been the norm for a woman of her social standing. Being a church member was required for socially prominent people, professionals, and community leaders, though nonchurch associations like freemasonry could substitute for churchgoing, as it did with John Wakefield.[73]

In her own way, in her letters and in her narrative, Sarah Wakefield was practicing the popular nineteenth-century religious trend of "liberal theology" or "empirical theology," and she was also anticipating the related twentieth-century movement of "liberation theology."[74] In her third letter to Riggs, Wakefield says that she had tried to follow Christian principles by treating the oppressed—here the Dakotas—as the majority of them had treated her. But when white society allowed politics and prejudice to prevail rather than an interest in the truth, she suffered a crisis of conscience. In this state she reacted particularly strongly against those in authority within the military and within the church.

As a result of her mistreatment after captivity Wakefield identified with the downtrodden Dakotas. Thus Wakefield's captivity narrative melds the moral, religious, and political to help her readers appreciate her position and to lay the groundwork for more idealized social interaction based on applied Christian values. But she did not have the missionary's moral authority, as Martha Riggs did; therefore most of Wakefield's contemporary readers probably focused more on the inherent prurience of her story than on her spiritual or social pronouncements.

After the war life went on for Sarah Wakefield, and like many other ex-captives, her moment in the public eye was brief. Although in the spring of 1863 she feared her husband would leave her, he did not (or at least not permanently).[75] The couple had two more children, Julia in 1866 and John in 1868, and faded from general view until John's sudden death of an overdose of opiates in February 1874. There were rumors that he may have committed suicide by taking too many drugs. A drinker, smoker, and bon vivant, John Wakefield died with outstanding debts that took up "$4,500 of an estate valued at $5,073."[76] In the end only $2,800 was awarded to his creditors, but this still left comparatively little for his widow and four children to live on. By 1876 the family had moved to St. Paul, where Wakefield gradually tried to reestablish herself by buying property, doing business, and taking a particular interest in her children's education.[77] She died aged sixty-nine on 27 May 1899 and was buried in a private ceremony.[78] The lack of a church service suggests that Wakefield's suspicion of organized religion, articulated so strongly in the 1860s, persisted throughout the rest of her life.

Like many ex-captives, Wakefield wrote and sold her story for various reasons. The first edition was published by the Atlas Printing Company of Minneapolis in November 1863 and the second, expanded one by the Argus Book and Printing Office of Shakopee sometime in 1864. Both apparently went through several reprintings, sometimes with a different title page, as was not uncommon with other captivity narratives. Probably these companies were technically printers, rather than publishers, which were merely typesetting a private manuscript for the author to sell cheaply and locally. The second edition was 18 percent longer than the original one, clarified its moral message, and specifically invited agents to sell the work.[79]

Wakefield's preface in both editions establishes three main motives for composition: to provide an accurate account for her children, to detail the life-saving help she received from Chaska, and to vindicate her behavior for people who did not know the full story and who might think she wrote primarily to make money.[80] Her first stated reason connotes the private sphere of domesticity for a middle-class Victorian white woman and identifies Wakefield in the role of mother. But her captivity narrative's rhetoric establishes that the primary audience is really white Minnesotans—whom she saw as racist—rather than her children. For example, at many points Wakefield directly addresses her readers with questions like this: "Now, my readers, what say you? Am I not indebted to those friendly Indians for my life and honor?"[81] Yet rhetorically Wakefield was in a very uncomfortable position, since vindicating herself and Chaska invariably required condemning settler society for prejudice and religious hypocrisy. Further, although her main reasons for writing were political and psychological, her request for agents to sell the book indicates that she must have hoped to make some money, as many ex-captives did who wrote up their accounts.

In her captivity narrative Wakefield confesses, "I am by nature a very cowardly woman."[82] But her letters and published account reveal a courageous woman who believed in her own moral worth and refused to adopt identity politics at the expense of human rights. These qualities certainly appeal to modern critics, who identify the radicalism of Wakefield's text. Indeed, all her writings form her powerful emotional resistance to "the binarisms—of white and Indian, civilized and savage, masculine and feminine, captivity and liberty—on which white, middle-class ideologies of class, race, and gender rested."[83]

2. Harriet Bishop McConkey and Isaac Heard
Captivity and Early Dakota War Histories

Apart from participants, other Minnesotans who had been only peripherally involved in the Conflict were willing and even eager to reinforce race, class, and gender binaries through the trope of captivity. In fact, a contest developed to move rhetorically beyond impressionistic first-person accounts like those of Martha Riggs and Sarah Wakefield and produce the first definitive history of the war essentially defined by stories of captivity. The main contenders were Harriet Bishop McConkey's *Dakota War Whoop; or, Indian Massacres and War in Minnesota* and Isaac Heard's *History of the Sioux War and Massacres of 1862 and 1863*, both published in 1863, and Charles Bryant and Abel Murch's *A History of the Great Massacre*, which appeared in 1864, the same year that McConkey and Heard put out revised editions.[1]

The 1863 and 1864 imprints of *Dakota War Whoop* were published locally, in St. Paul, the first by D. D. Merrill, a close friend of McConkey, but the second privately, by the author.[2] Encouraged by wider public interest in the Conflict via national magazine stories like Adrian Ebell's in *Harper's Magazine*, Isaac Heard placed the 1863 and 1864 editions of his volume with the publishing house of Harper and Brothers, considered one of the leading American presses by then. Meanwhile Bryant and Murch interested the Cincinnati publishers Rickey and Carroll in producing their volume in 1864. Perhaps also cashing in on the craze for Civil War material, these books competed for national as well as local publication and readership, in short for a share of the American book market's profits.[3]

McConkey and Heard went neck and neck to publish their respective works first, but they appeared at just about the same time. Harriet

Bishop McConkey (often known as Harriet E. Bishop, because after she divorced she successfully petitioned for her maiden name to be legally restored) ended her book with events in November 1863, so presumably it came out shortly afterward.[4] The *St. Paul Pioneer Press* promoted Isaac Heard's work on 20 September and 22 October and reviewed it in the 14 November edition; therefore it was obviously available by then.[5] Because the books were published so close together, it is not clear which technically came first, especially if their availability in different locations is factored in. Looking at Harriet McConkey before Isaac Heard provides interesting contrasts with Martha Riggs and Sarah Wakefield. In fact, these women form a trio of contesting early female responses to the Conflict. Also, the self-consciously literary *Dakota War Whoop* had a shorter shelf life than *History of the Sioux War* due to its many errors, so it makes sense to look at it first and then move to Heard's more substantial and enduring text.

Although Vermont native Harriet Bishop was a schoolteacher rather than a missionary when she arrived in Minnesota in 1847, she was responding to missionary Thomas Williamson's plea for female educators to go to frontier St. Paul. Williamson had sent a letter to William Slade, founder of the National Board of Popular Education, who had invited reformer Catharine Beecher to oversee selecting, training, and placing women teachers for the West. Beecher described "the Christian female teacher" as one who "will quietly take her station, collecting the ignorant children around her, inspiriting the principles of morality and awakening the hope of immortality."[6] Harriet Bishop was among Beecher's first intake of thirty-five trainees; she was the first to volunteer for a specific position out West; and she was zealous about bringing morality, literacy, and culture to the frontier.[7]

Bishop was thirty when she arrived in Minnesota, and she already possessed plenty of teaching experience apart from Beecher's month-long program: she had taken a teacher-training course in Fort Edward, New York; taught in the public schools; and become principal of the

Figure 5. Harriet E. Bishop McConkey. Undated oil on canvas, ca. 1880, by Andrew Falkenshield. From the Collections of the Minnesota Historical Society. Used with permission.

Moriah Academy.[8] She opened a school in St. Paul almost immediately in the only place she could find, a wretched cabin that had previously been a blacksmith's shop. Two weeks later she held Sunday school there. Although Bishop was the only Baptist in town at the time, her Sunday school classes formed the basis for what became the First Baptist Church of St. Paul.[9] But she quickly began raising funds for larger, purpose-built quarters that were completed in fall 1848.[10]

As a visible and vocal social reformer, and as a single woman before her unhappy marriage in 1858 and after her divorce nine years later, she held token celebrity status and used her position and organizational skills for various causes including temperance, indigence, and women's suffrage.[11] She was also active in a group called the Philecclesian Society in St. Paul, which met in 1857 and 1858 and put together several issues of a handwritten literary journal, *The Philecclesian Chronicle*.[12]

Evidently both McConkey and the society had literary aspirations. By 1851 McConkey was no longer in the classroom, but her pedagogical urge surfaced in a series of publications between 1857 and 1869. These years more or less coincided with her domestic duties as wife and stepmother, so she probably used the home base for her writing and hoped to boost the family income, as did many literary women in the nineteenth century.

McConkey's first volume was *Floral Home; or, First Years in Minnesota*, published in New York in 1857 as an autobiography cum travelogue cum promotional tract for Minnesota. It is interesting because it provides firsthand information about frontier Minnesota from a reformist woman's outlook but also reveals the prejudices of an upper-middle-class easterner. In the chapter called "Study of Indian Character," for example, McConkey negates romanticized views of Indian nobility to focus on negative ethnic stereotypes such as vengefulness, cowardice, and sexual promiscuity and concludes: "Instinct, more than reason, is the guide of the red man. He repudiates improvement, and despises manual effort. For ages has the heart been embedded in moral pollution."[13] The rest of the chapter applauds the sacrifices of missionaries like Thomas Williamson and suggests that progress among Native Americans can only occur if they convert to Christianity and adopt "civilized" habits. But whatever slight hope she had in 1857 for Indian improvement was practically destroyed in her mind when the Conflict erupted five years later.

McConkey seems to have had three major goals when she published *Dakota War Whoop* in 1863 and then expanded it from 304 pages to 429 pages in 1864: first, to make money; second, to write a comprehensive, credible, informative account; and third, to reinforce the widespread belief in Manifest Destiny. Two letters she sent to General Sibley asking him to endorse the second edition provide insight into the mechanics of producing and distributing the book and suggest its popularity, though she may have overstated this to appeal to Sibley.[14] On 19 October 1864 she wrote him that one hundred bookseller's agents had asked for copies of the book to sell. The bookseller thought that a brief introduction by Sibley would help sales, so she asked him to send one immediately if he was willing to do so. The next day she clarified her request: "An important point was an endorsement of its [the book's] corrections—a recommendation of the same & a statement as to the facility and ability of the Author for preparing it." Though concerned about taking up his time, she was "of course desirous to do all in my power to facilitate the Sale of my book, which the best judges think is destined for a wide one, & not to run out in one year."[15] The letters also mention other aspects of book production, such as including engravings and binding a few copies in gilt and morocco leather for a luxury market. At the end of the nineteenth century Return Holcombe, who was archiving the Sibley Papers at the Minnesota Historical Society, wrote and signed this memo underneath Bishop's first letter: "There are so many errors in Mrs. McConkey's book that Gen. Sibley refused to introduce it by writing a preface or recommending it in any manner."[16]

Perhaps the inaccuracy is not surprising, since McConkey cobbled the book together from various sources and genres. Her most important starting points were first-person accounts, primary documents such as letters and military reports, and work published in more ephemeral media including newspapers and magazines. These were necessary to lend authenticity to her work, as was the inclusion of captivity stories, many of them second- or thirdhand. George H. Spencer, an ex-captive, furnished detailed accounts of his experiences, as did Thomas Williamson, who, like Stephen Riggs, had fled his mission with an entourage in tow.[17]

McConkey overtly uses Spencer's input and voice at several points, for example in chapter 8, "Captivity and Release of George H. Spencer," and in chapter 20, "Cause of the War—What Is an Indian." Both are written in the first person, with the earlier chapter describing a captivity whose rigors supposedly justify the captive-participant using

racist stereotypes like this in the later chapter: "In the great chain of
nature the Indian is a connecting link between the wild beast and
the human species."[18] McConkey and other nonparticipant historians understood the "tyranny of the witness," namely the unarguable
moral status that the witness possesses merely by virtue of being a
witness-participant.[19]

All of chapter 16 in Dakota War Whoop is a letter on military maneuvers, dated 26 August 1862, from Charles Flandrau, commander of
volunteer forces at New Ulm and newly appointed commander of the
southwestern Minnesota frontier, to Minnesota governor Alexander
Ramsey. How McConkey obtained a copy of this letter (which is probably misdated) remains unclear, but it may already have been published
in a newspaper by the time she was drafting her book. Likewise, later
in her manuscript McConkey sees fit to reproduce the four-page letter
Minnesota senator Morton S. Wilkinson and Congressmen Aldrich
and Windom (not Windham, as McConkey spells it) had written to
President Lincoln, vehemently arguing against executive clemency for
the Dakotas. The letter is replete with accounts of captivity, atrocity,
and rape and doubtless circulated in the Minnesota popular press,
where McConkey picked it up, before the executions on 26 December
1862. Later, in chapters 70 to 76, McConkey reprints official military
reports, allegedly with Sibley's permission.[20]

Other individual accounts circulated in the Minnesota press immediately after the war. For example, the heart-wrenching story of
Merton Eastlick was well-known and easily available to Bishop. After
his father died in an attack, the starving eleven-year-old carried his
baby brother fifty miles or so (some accounts say ninety!) before being
reunited with his wounded mother. McConkey overlays the story with
extreme sentimentalism; indeed, she does not intend to provide an
objective account but to contrast "The Heroic Boy" of the chapter's
title with the brutal Dakotas. "Brave, darling boy! Did angels ever
before witness a deed like thine! History's page furnishes nothing

more noble, more deserving immortal fame! Thy name with the good and great shall live," she gushes.[21]

Since this story was so familiar, the fact that McConkey repeatedly misnames the boy Burton indicates her haste and carelessness. She intuitively knew that the generic roots of the captivity narrative lay in factual accounts and verifiable data like names, and of course the Eastlick story did have a factual basis (like Martha Riggs, Merton technically escaped Indian captivity only to be held captive by the elements). But in the end Merton/Burton is far more important to her as signifier than as biographical subject. The wrong name is just one indicator of essentially fictive elements she uses throughout her work.[22]

Another textual site indicating fictive as well as propagandistic tendencies occurs in chapter 3 of *Dakota War Whoop*, where McConkey describes the Acton incident. I have already given two versions of this triggering event in "Historical Perspectives on the Dakota War," using my own chronology and Big Eagle's summary from the participants themselves. It is imperative for McConkey to establish the attack's seeming irrationality to justify her later judgments of Indian character. Thus she presents the Indian youths as "reckless young warriors" who had gone out on an unsuccessful "scalp hunt" the previous day and were extremely drunk on "fire water."[23] They approached the Acton settlers for more whiskey and then attacked, intent on doing whatever "their evil hearts might devise," with "their demon thirst" infuriated by the sight of blood.[24] Although McConkey mentioned the late annuity payments and provisions in her previous chapter, she portrays the Dakotas as hotheaded and impatient. Nothing the government did or didn't do warranted taking matters into their own hands, as far as she was concerned, and in this she voiced a prevailing view.

Several other textual characteristics suggest that McConkey may have been familiar with published captivity narratives and used some of their strategies. Mary Rowlandson's famous captivity account of 1682, which was regularly reprinted and widely distributed throughout the nineteenth century, established certain generic expectations. These included a graphic description of the initial attack(s) focusing on injured or dead male protectors and vulnerable women and children. Rowlandson's narrative was well-known and often republished in the East, where McConkey lived until she was thirty, so she may well have read it. Even if she was not directly influenced by Rowlandson, she certainly echoes the earlier text in an interesting example of intertextuality. Here is Rowlandson in the early pages of her account:

> No sooner were we out of the House, but my Brother-in-Law (being before wounded (in defending the House) in or near the Throat) fell down dead, whereat the *Indians* scornfully shouted, and hallowed, and were presently upon him, stripping off his Clothes. The Bullets flying thick, one went thorow my Side, and the same (as would seem) thorow the Bowels and Hand of my dear Child in my Arms. . . . My elder Sister being yet in the House, and seeing those woful Sights, the Infidels haling Mothers one way, and Children another, and some wallowing in their Blood, and her elder son telling her that (her Son) *William* was dead, and my self was wounded; she said, And *Lord, let me die with them*: Which was no sooner said, but she was struck with a Bullet, and fell down dead over the Threshold.[25]

Here, almost two hundred years later, is McConkey, imaginatively re-creating the psychological and physical distress, since she was not a participant in an Indian attack, as Rowlandson had been:

> In every direction is seen men, women and children with streaming hair, *en dishabille*, or garments rent and torn, perhaps bloodstained, in wild confusion flying from the theatre of actual danger. . . . Mothers go one way, children another, while perhaps the husband and father hides himself from sheer fright, or becomes powerless for action from the same cause. . . . One mother has

dropped her darling infant by the wayside, and being hotly pursued, could not stop to recover it. A child has seen its parents, perhaps, both fall beneath a murderous bullet or tomahawk, and barely escape with life.[26]

Both accounts are characterized by chaos, bloodshed, nakedness, and above all by women being separated from loved ones, especially their children. Both also contain the standard stereotypes of savage Indians and victimized captives. The major difference between the two concerns Rowlandson's piety, which has been replaced, two hundred years later, by McConkey's sentimentality. This is typical of changes in the late eighteenth- and nineteenth-century captivity literature.

Another source for McConkey's use of graphic violence involved the popular anthologies of Indian captivity published throughout the eighteenth and nineteenth centuries. They include the infamous *Manheim* narratives (1793), *Horrid Indian Cruelties* (1799), *Indian Anecdotes and Barbarities* (1837), *Indian Atrocities* (1846), and John Frost's *Heroic Women of the West* (1854).[27] Most of these collections were rabidly anti-Indian and largely if not wholly fictional. Especially throughout the first half of her book McConkey frequently catalogs gruesome torture, sexual abuse, and mutilation, such as disembowelment, decapitation, crucifixion, skinning alive, and rape.

Historically considerable doubt exists about the extent of Indian violence during the Conflict, but it was useful for the military and the government to exaggerate the brutality and reinforce calls for Indian dispossession.[28] In this they indulged in "propaganda discourse."[29] And most of the literary accounts reiterated the standard propagandist line by inserting canned (sometimes plagiarized) descriptions when they did not actually invent them. The other cumulative Dakota Conflict histories, by Heard and by Bryant and Murch, also describe graphic violence.

Thus initial true reports and newspaper stories based on eyewitness accounts "helped to make the information seem irrefutable," as did later reports from commissions of inquiry on enemy atrocities.[30] These informational schemas reinforced each other and were typical of many wars in America and elsewhere. Indeed, an analysis of Native American identity in the nineteenth-century white press concludes, "This emphasis on violence ensured that a major theme of Indian news would be inflammatory and consciously anti-Indian, the press solving the 'Indian problem' by advocating and justifying white revenge and genocide."[31]

Though McConkey used a range of other documents when putting *Dakota War Whoop* together, she still struggled to impose her didactic, belletristic voice on the entire text. That voice is prone to emotional outbursts, as in the Merton Eastlick section, and judgmental commentary, as in the descriptions of alleged torture. The autobiographical aspects of Morris's and especially Wakefield's texts show "the gendered signature," namely the ways that the "gendered self, has shaped the *generation* of the text."[32] Not writing autobiographically, McConkey tries to evade gender identification and adopt the role of universal chronicler to her community. However, this was not possible: the male authors assumed precedence over her, and even though Bryant and Murch's tome was as provocative as hers, Heard's was somewhat more balanced.

Despite *Dakota War Whoop*'s disappointing reception, McConkey continued her literary endeavors. An 1864 imprint titled *The Poets and Poetry of Minnesota* included six poems by her, and she published a long poem in 1867, *Minnesota; Then and Now*, which provides a poetic overview of the state's evolution, focusing on moral uplift.[33] She had not changed her mind about the dynamics of the Conflict, and she wrote this about it in her lengthy poem:

> And, scattered o'er the prairie, oft bleaching bones are seen,
> Reminders of the slaughter of those inhuman fiends.

No more the savage war-whoop is ringing on the air,
No more the horrid scalp-dances debase this region fair,
Uprisen from these ashes, now phenix-like, we see
A strong, God-fearing people dwell in security.[34]

After 1876 the *St. Paul City Directory* listed McConkey as an author and lecturer, and she apparently kept diaries, which have been lost.[35] She died in 1883. A biographical sketch of her at the end of the nineteenth century concludes, "To the time of her death, she was ever active and energetic in educational and Christian work."[36]

Isaac Heard was born in New York State in 1834, went to college, studied law, and arrived in St. Paul in 1851. He clerked at several law offices and then, according to a collection of profiles on early St. Paul settlers, his "talents and ambition" led him to serve as city attorney in 1856 and from 1865 to 1867, to serve as county attorney from 1857 to 1863, and to join the state senate in 1871.[37] Obviously by the time he served in Sibley's army he was already well-established as a lawyer and well-qualified to be a member of the Sioux Trials Commission. His performance as recorder (some sources say as judge advocate) only enhanced his standing in Minnesota and gave him name recognition when he published his history.

Heard first attempted to establish his authority—as many writers of Indian captivities did—by writing a preface to his book. There he gives his credentials: he was a longtime resident of Minnesota; had fought during the Conflict; had acted as recorder, obtaining firsthand information from "Indians, half-breeds, traders, white captives, fugitives from massacres, and others"; and had read supplementary documents, including newspaper articles and "public treatises."[38] From all this data he had tried "to form a connected and reliable history" despite his admitted haste in drafting the book, and contemporaneous reviews generally agree that he succeeded.[39]

Harper's Magazine, owned by the publishing company that brought out *History of the Sioux War,* praises him for writing this "strictly authentic narrative" and for telling readers "the straight story."[40] The pro-Indian reviewer in the Boston-based *North American Review* opens by saying the book should have been titled "The Sioux Massacres" to indicate "massacres perpetrated on the Sioux as well as by them."[41] Yet he too applauds Heard's "clear and vigorous style" and congratulates him for his relatively restrained commentary.[42] However, much of the review passionately defends the Dakotas and condemns the trials (and Heard's involvement in them) as a travesty of justice.[43]

Most interesting and significant of all, Stephen Riggs published a review-letter in the *St. Paul Press* on 17 December 1863, commending Heard for bringing together so many scattered materials and taking such "great care to be correct in his statements."[44] Yet despite Heard's thoroughness, Riggs remarks that he tends to see things simplistically and overlooks warranted ambiguity or multiple interpretation. In some places Riggs actually corrects mistakes made by Heard. One of the opening epigraphs to the earlier "Historical Perspectives on the Dakota War" comes from Riggs's review, and it clearly shows that he did not believe that Heard—or anyone probably—could produce an authoritative history because the Conflict was so complicated. A definitive text that was truer to historical memory would be contradictory and incoherent. Thus for Riggs any written history that *was* coherent would necessarily be incomplete because the alternative would be unreadable. Readers are prone to trust an author like Heard who writes authoritatively, Riggs suggests, but his approach "may, and sometimes does, work against the interests of truth and history."[45]

In fact, Heard opens chapter 1 by presenting the Conflict as a leading scene "in the bloody drama which attends the advance of the white race across the continent."[46] He dramatizes the contributions of players like Godfrey and Little Crow, sees the war as the climax to this story, and presents the executions and ongoing battles with the Sioux as the resolution to a plot "full of thrilling interest."[47] He even titles this chapter

"The Scene and the Actors." Though he is not the only historian to use the rhetoric of drama (McConkey and Nix do so too, for example), it is most dominant in Heard's performative methodology. Despite the insertion of first-person accounts, military information, created dialogue, letters, and minibiographies that sometimes delay or repeat events, Heard does not lose his organizational grip. For example, he devotes chapters 14 and 15, respectively, to the captivity narratives of Samuel Brown, the son of Joseph and Susan Brown, and of Josephine Huggins, the wife of a missionary who was killed at the Lac Qui Parle mission, but afterward he returns to the main narrative thread.

Heard also uses brief biographies of important figures such as Joseph Godfrey (Otakle). "Godfrey's Story" is the title of chapter 13, which is told in the first person.[48] But Heard first introduces him in chapter 1, where he says the book will show "the mysterious part enacted by the negro Godfrey."[49] Indeed, Godfrey appears throughout the text, for example, in the trials section, where his evidence saves himself but convicts many Dakotas, and in the section providing biographical information on the men in Abraham Lincoln's final execution list. Heard is captivated but puzzled by Godfrey, whose motives and credibility he cannot fully explain. He believes that his readers will also be interested in this ambivalent, Iago-like figure and makes him a fit subject for literary presentation.

Charged with murder, Godfrey was the first person tried by the military tribunal. Several witnesses testified that he willingly took part in battles and atrocities, and Heard himself corroborates this belief at one point in his text.[50] Nevertheless Godfrey so manipulated the court by his speech and performance that they recommended commuting his death sentence. Heard describes the scene at Godfrey's trial: "He had such an honest look, and spoke with such a truthful tone, that the court, though prejudiced against him in the beginning, were now unanimously inclined to believe that there were possibilities as to his sincerity. His language was broken, and he communicated his ideas with some little difficulty. This was an advantage in his favor, for it interested the sympathetic attention of the listener, and it was a pleasure to listen to his hesitating speech. His voice was one of the softest that I ever listened to."[51]

Moreover, Godfrey was phenomenally successful at implicating others, "his testimony being substantiated by the subsequent admission of the Indians themselves."[52] Since many Dakotas spoke little or no English, these admissions were often also obtained by Godfrey, who "would soon force the Indian, by a series of questions in his own language [i.e., Dakota], into an admission of the truth. He seemed a 'providence' specially designed as an instrument of justice."[53] That Heard designates Godfrey's role as providential harks back to the Puritan rationalizations of clashes between colonists and Native Americans so often dramatized in Indian captivity narratives like Rowlandson's. It also suggests, as Heard states elsewhere, "civilization's irresistible march."[54]

Contrasting Heard's treatment of the Merton Eastlick story with McConkey's illuminates differences in the cultural work each history was trying to perform by its uses of captivity. Heard places this case study within the larger context of the Lake Shetek incident. On 20 August 1862 Sisseton Dakota chief White Lodge (Wakeyeska) and others, including Lean Grizzly Bear (Matata-ma-hucha), attacked a mostly German settlement of about fifty at Lake Shetek in southwestern Minnesota. Some settlers died in the attack, others escaped, and ten were captured: Julia Wright and her two children; Martha Duley and her three children, one of whom died in captivity; and three young girls: Lillie Everett, and Thomas Ireland's two daughters.

White Lodge, along with his followers and prisoners, traveled to the Missouri River in present-day Emmaus County, North Dakota. There, seeing a passing canoe with Major Charles Galpin and his Dakota wife, one of the captive women shouted for help. Galpin's wife recognized that White Lodge was trying to trap them and told her

Figure 6. Lake Shetek captives after release. Photo courtesy of the South Dakota State Historical Society–State Archives.

husband not to stop. But the captive's message got out, and a group of young men from the Sans Arc Band of the Cheyenne River Sioux Tribe (Teton Lakotas) eventually rescued and returned the captives as a humanitarian gesture and as evidence that they disapproved of the Dakotas' hostage taking. For the apparent foolhardiness of their mission their own people called these Lakota youths the Fool Soldiers or the Crazy Band.[55]

In his chapter on attacks and captivities removed from the main war arenas, including Lake Shetek, Heard uses information from newspapers and from first-person testimony at trials such as Alomina Hurd's.[56] Like McConkey, Heard also misnames Merton Eastlick and repeats other inaccuracies, but his description of Merton's escape is brief and understated: "Mrs. Estlick's [sic] son Burton, not ten years of age, and his little brother, aged five years, having become separated from their mother, arrived safely at the settlements days after the attack. Burton alternately led and carried the little fellow a distance of eighty miles. Such instances of heroic fortitude were not common."[57] Heard's relative objectivity contrasts with Bishop's emotionally charged tone. Yet in this chapter and elsewhere in his book Heard is not beyond repeating examples of supposed atrocities, including the gang rapes of several girls and young women, mutilations, and arrows shot at "defenseless women and children."[58] As with the Eastlick anecdote, Heard generally leaves readers to draw their own conclusions, whereas McConkey uses heightened and lengthy descriptions with more authorial manipulation and intrusion.

Both of these full-length histories betray a discursive double vision regarding narrative technique that is also evident to a greater or lesser extent in other captivity narratives about the war. On the one hand, many European American authors use pejorative stereotypes to demonize the Dakotas, as their readers fully expected them to do. On the other hand, historical reality forces them to accommodate information about Christian and nonviolent Indians. Conversely, while praising European American culture as civilized—again, as their readers anticipated—these authors sometimes reveal what they characterize as isolated white atrocities. Heard mentions in passing, for example, that some white soldiers used an Indian corpse for target practice and even scalped Indians.[59] (Significantly, in a private letter to his wife dated 23 September 1862, Stephen Riggs admits: "I confess I have been very much ashamed of our men today. They scalped most of the Indians and manifested much savageism [sic] in reference to them."[60])

Perfunctory public comments do not indicate the genuine historical ambiguity that Riggs wished for. Instead such statements provide an expected narrative nod to a few praiseworthy Indians and pro-Indian activists but reinforce white culture, with only passing reference to lapses supposedly resulting from combat fatigue. In other words, contemporary readers tolerated examples of one or two "progressive" Indians amid a much greater focus on Native barbarity, and tut-tutted about a few rogue whites, but did not alter their basic view that traditionalist American Indians were brutish and inferior, while white Americans were civilized and superior.

These contradictory elements are certainly present in Heard's book. For example, Heard states that at the beginning of the Conflict "former friendship and kindness availed nothing" when Dakotas attacked and killed settlers, and yet only a few pages later he relates how John Other Day, "a civilized Indian," warned settlers of the impending hostilities and escorted some to safety.[61] In an earlier chapter, "Causes of the Outbreak," Heard mentions exploitation of the Dakotas by traders and others; however, he opens the same chapter by stating that "the Indians were predisposed to hostility toward the whites."[62] Likewise, at the end of *History of the Sioux War* Heard makes six recommendations for improved relations between Indians and whites. After this final chapter he appends Bishop Whipple's famous address, "An Appeal for the Red Man"—already extensively published in different outlets—and a letter from George Bunga, who was of African American and Ojibwe ancestry, asking for clear and ethical dealings with the Red Lake Ojibwes. Does ending his history this way mean that Heard was pro-Indian himself? Certainly not. He gives the appearance of fairness, but ultimately his message is that more equitable dealings with the defeated Indians in Minnesota will hasten the peace process so that the state can once again be "the resort of the emigrant from every clime"—the European emigrant, of course.[63]

After the Conflict Heard became even more prominent as a lawyer and participated in many high-profile law cases, but in 1893 he had a nervous breakdown; returned to Goshen, New York; and lived as an invalid until his death in 1913.[64] He was buried in St. Paul, indicating the importance of his Minnesota years, though it is not clear why ill health had required him to leave the state two decades earlier. One obituary described Heard as "a classical student" with "marked literary ability" whose history, a half century later, was still considered "the standard and accurate story of that struggle."[65]

3. Edward S. Ellis
Captivity and the Dime Novel Tradition

For Isaac Heard to characterize the Conflict's events as both state and national drama indicates how quickly it moved into the contemporary cultural imagination. Indeed, the Dakota War and the Civil War signified, on a micro- and a macrolevel respectively, the country's multiple engagements with race in 1862. Equally important as the conflicts themselves were the stories told about them in histories and captivity narratives, among other genres. But those stories were not confined to nonfiction. As early as 1864, when Edward S. Ellis published the dime novel *Indian Jim: A Tale of the Minnesota Massacre*, the Dakota War had already become the stuff of full-fledged fiction.[1] Dime novels themselves were a recent but already popular phenomenon by then: they were small (four by six inches), short (about one hundred pages), cheap (ten cents, of course), and paper bound.

In 1860 the firm of Beadle and Adams published *Malaeska: The Indian Wife of the White Hunter*, an Indian captivity narrative by Ann Stephens, as the first title in its new series "Beadle's Dime Novels."[2] From then until dimes dwindled in the early twentieth century, Indian captivity narratives remained one of several staple genres that authors used. "Beadle's Dime Novels" was an instant success, and the company brought out a new title about once every two weeks for the next fourteen years, until it replaced the original series with "Beadle's New Dime Novels." Beadle enjoyed such success with its first run of dime novels that several other publishing houses began publishing their own series, so that ultimately the expanding market in popular fiction turned "dime novels" into a generic term referring to all cheap fiction with paper covers.[3]

Only a few months after the success of *Malaeska* in 1860, Beadle published Edward S. Ellis's first book, *Seth Jones; or, the Captives of the Frontier*, as number 4 in the "Dime Novel" series. Twenty-year-old Edward Ellis was the schoolteacher son of the famous hunter Sylvester Ellis, and his extensively marketed book launched him on a successful and lucrative writing career lasting until his death in 1916.[4] Ellis contracted with Beadle to write four novels a year, and in 1864 *Indian Jim: A Tale of the Minnesota Massacre* appeared. At the time nothing distinguished it from the other captivity narrative dimes, except that it did not appear to have the best-selling potential of Ellis's earlier efforts *Seth Jones*, *Bill Biddon*, and *Nathan Todd*. However, by then Ellis had established himself "as the new novelist of the frontier"—a worthy successor to Fenimore Cooper—and Minnesota was just another frontier he chose to tackle.[5]

It is not clear how Ellis became interested in the Dakota Conflict. But the opening up of new territories established after the Mexican War, the discovery of gold in California, and the Dakota War itself helped to reestablish "frontier conflict with Native Americans as a central topic in the national imagination."[6] (In the 1930s an article appeared in the newspaper *Southern Minnesotan* on Al DeLong, an eighty-nine-year-old Dakota War scout whose life, according to a byline, "Rivals [a] Dime Novel." Thus the Dakota Conflict was seen even sixty years later as a worthy subject for dime novels.[7]) Ellis may have been influenced by other writers who recognized the war's potential for profit making and propaganda in the publishing world. He certainly could have learned a great deal from extensive press coverage in 1862, and he might even have read the 1863 editions of McConkey's history or, more likely, Heard's. However Ellis came across his information, details in *Indian Jim* indicate that he used historical persons and events to authenticate his novel and to provide the appearance of novelty and currency. For while many dimes seemed almost interchangeable in terms of "scene, character, and action," the best also possessed unusual and often marketable variations of the basic pattern.[8] Thus good dime novels might simultaneously provide their readers with a formulaic comfort zone and also use new source material and exhibit literary skill.

Because *Indian Jim* is not well-known, a brief overview of the plot is necessary. The book opens in August 1862 with two cousins, Marian Allondale and Adolphus Halleck, on a steamer headed up the Minnesota River from St. Paul. They are going to stay with family friends, the Brainerds, who moved to Minnesota in 1856 to begin life anew after a business failure. Marian and Adolphus are informally engaged, but they behave more like friends than lovers. An artist, Adolphus possesses overly romantic notions about Indians, while Marian exhibits stereotypically negative views. In one of several debates on the subject Adolphus characterizes Native Americans as "high-souled, brave, and chivalrous," but Marian responds that they are "treacherous, merciless, [and] repulsive," though she admits that "the *Christian* Indians are somewhat different."[9]

Despite the fact that Adolphus's romanticism blinds him, Ellis is careful to tell readers that deep down he possesses "the sterling qualities of the true gentleman."[10] This is to validate the amount of time the plot devotes to him and to make his final transformation more credible. The Brainerd family consists of both parents, as well as two unmarried children: twenty-one-year-old Will, a college graduate and wounded Civil War veteran, and seventeen-year-old Maggie, a beautiful and religious young woman. Predictably, during the course of the story Marian is attracted by the "modest and manly" Will and marries him at the end, whereas Maggie is attracted by the possibilities of converting the irreligious and irresponsible Adolphus.[11] He in turn reacts to a sensibility related to but different from his own—the spiritual rather than the artistic.

As war breaks out the family has to leave their homestead, but a Christian Dakota, the Indian Jim of the title, aids them in their flight and serves as a physical and moral guide. He is presented as a reformed character: an Indian who before conversion had been violent and alcoholic but who underwent an amazing transformation after missionaries converted him to Christianity. Adolphus's romanticism, indecisiveness, and inability to interpret events correctly are constantly challenged, especially when Dakotas capture Marian and Maggie. Finally, when Maggie dies at the hands of a vengeful Indian, Adolphus understands the error of his ways and prepares to enter the ministry. This rather abrupt plot resolution is typical of dime Westerns, most of which were one hundred pages long. True to form, *Indian Jim* is exactly one hundred pages, so Ellis may have rushed his ending to meet the formula length requirement.

The two most important characters in the book are Adolphus Halleck and Indian Jim. Ellis draws on nineteenth-century stereotypes of the impractical, illusion-filled artist and the "good" Indian, yet he also complicates both characters somewhat by placing them in situations that raise nuanced moral questions. Through these opposing characters Ellis continues a dialogue initiated by Fenimore Cooper on reading the landscape, reading human nature, and reading books.[12] In the presence of so much fragmented information, the writers ask, what interpretive guide should be used? While Adolphus is the most important character because he changes so fundamentally (perhaps unconvincingly), the text also invites readers to examine their own methods of constructing politics, people, religion, and region. However, ultimately Ellis issues not so much an invitation as an imperative to use the Bible as the single guidebook in life.

At the beginning Adolphus views the Indians in idealized terms, as figures in a wild landscape, and he privileges his role as artist and scholar—that is, he "sees" things artistically but turns a blind eye to whatever does not fit his predetermined views. He is removed from reality because he is too busy either reading about it or representing it in his art. For instance, at several points he withholds or ignores

crucial information because it would reinforce the negative characteristics of the Sioux that he refuses to acknowledge. Sometimes his
bravado is completely misplaced, as when, fleeing from the house with
Will Brainerd and Indian Jim, he confidently but incorrectly asserts
that the approaching Indians pose no threat because he has "read
enough books to know something about them."[13] At other times he
begins sketching at ethically suspect points, such as when he stops to
draw a dead Indian instead of conducting both Marian and himself to
safety after an attack. Seeing a neighboring house on fire, Adolphus
wonders whether the children have been playing with matches, to
which Will responds, "No sane man can doubt who are the authors
of that deed."[14]

Finally, in two heavy-handed tropes Will lectures his friend on reality versus fancy—"It's time, 'Dolph, you gave up those nonsensical
ideas, and came to look upon the American Indian as he *is*, and not
as your fancy has *painted* him!"—and then, a little later, on plain sight
and common sense regarding Indians versus misplaced romanticized
views—"You'll have to provide yourself with a microscope, 'Dolph, if
you wish to discover these phenomena; for, you see, they are not visible
to the naked eye."[15] A little earlier Adolphus had trouble interpreting
information viewed through a telescope; now Will tells him he needs
a microscope. But in fact Halleck does not need an artificial means of
focusing judgment; he needs a sound moral guide to interpret life's
disparate data.

Although Ellis introduces Halleck as someone influenced by the
nineteenth-century American romantic painter Albert Bierstadt, he
may have decided to make his main male character an artist primarily
to underscore his flawed *vision*.[16] In other words, Halleck's being an
artist may be just an excuse for a kind of character pun on sight and
insight and for the innate romanticism of creative people like artists. By
the end of the book Adolphus Halleck has abandoned one-dimensional
artistic representation for deep spiritual truths, or faith in art for faith

in God. Just as the missionaries converted Indian Jim, Maggie, who is a missionary at heart, converts Halleck in the final pages of the book and guides him to salvation.

Indian Jim, who is sometimes called Christian Jim, performs a number of functions in the book. At one level Ellis cannot move beyond stereotypical characteristics; for example, he suggests that like many nonwhites in popular fiction—Indians and African Americans alike—Jim is inarticulate. In fact, Jim's first words, "Good ebening," sound more black than Indian, as if Ellis is using a generically "ethnic" linguistic marker.[17] But two things differentiate Jim from other Dakotas: his ability to read signs and his Christianity. Late in the novel, in a remarkable authorial comment, Ellis writes that Adolphus and Will "were hourly in danger of attack and massacre; but under the good providence of God, the skill of Christian Jim saved them. He detected 'signs' constantly, and, by timely foresight and precaution, avoided discovery."[18] At several points the narrative conspicuously uses the word "signs" to describe Jim's and the settlers' as well as the Dakotas' attempts to read what is going on.[19]

But Jim's success in negotiating danger is based not only on sound knowledge of the land but also on the bedrock of Christianity; it is typological. On first hearing Maggie describe Jim positively, Adolphus believes that she is reinforcing his romantic view of Indians. However, she corrects him: "It is not the Indian that is thus, but the *Christian*."[20] As Will and Adolphus wonder whether the rest of the Brainerd family is safe, Jim solemnly reminds them, "Dey are in the Great Father's hands!" and still later he again tells them to trust in God.[21] Yet he has to disappear from the novel because Maggie's death makes her into the major Christian sacrificial symbol. In contrast to Jim, her last words to Adolphus are not just articulate but eloquent: "Yes; seek me—meet me—."[22] Indeed, she is called "the sainted Maggie" in the novel's concluding paragraph.[23]

Two other aspects of this dime novel, its literary and historical allusions, suggest more technical skill than is evident in many other examples of the form. Sometimes Ellis is self-consciously literary, for example when he describes Adolphus as having admired the Indians ever since he "pored over the enchanting pages of the Leatherstocking Tales" or when he refers to Longfellow's *Hiawatha* or to the humorist Artemus Ward.[24] Yet there are also subtler examples of intertextuality that may indicate Ellis's influences and reading. For instance, while Maggie's last words fall into a nineteenth-century sentimental tradition of saintly characters' dying prophetic utterances, they do seem to recall one of the most famous examples of this phenomenon, little Eva St. Clare's transcendent death in *Uncle Tom's Cabin*, published in 1852. Eva's dying words, "O! love,—joy—,peace!" as well as the emotional response of those around her to her death, mark the way that radical Christianity impresses itself on the heart through martyrdom. Both novels too suggest how sentimental fiction operated ideologically by disrupting the male-centered, action plots of dime novels and fictionalized slave narratives like *Uncle Tom's Cabin*.[25]

Also, after dinner on the evening that Marian and Adolphus arrive at the Brainerd house, the moonlit atmosphere is described as "a fairy veil thrown over the rugged, disproportional outlines, softening down the harsh expression, smoothing out the wrinkles of time, and giving a mellow beauty to the plain and homely."[26] The full quotation is several pages longer and is reminiscent of Hawthorne's famous definition of romance in the Custom House section of *The Scarlet Letter* (1850). These earlier novels, by Stowe and Hawthorne, were best-selling romances that must have been familiar to the bookish Ellis. Perhaps he was trying to legitimate his own writing by such apparent allusions and by establishing *Indian Jim* within the same genre. Certainly many fictional captivity narratives—dime novels or not—fall into the wider genre of romance.

The historical references to the Dakota Conflict, however, help to place the novel in the dime Western and historical romance traditions.

While many of the references are fleeting, Ellis inserts them fairly naturally and convincingly within the fabric of the narrative. For example, in discussing Christianized Dakotas Marian refers to the missionaries Dr. (Thomas) Williamson and Mr. (Stephen) Riggs, and later Will mentions a converted Dakota named Paul, presumably an allusion to Paul Mazakutemani. References are also made to other Indians, such as Little Crow, Wacouta, and Cut Nose.[27] In line with the dime Western's sensationalism, as well as the reports of Indian atrocities during the war, Ellis describes a number of settlers killed brutally.[28] Although Ellis is more restrained than McConkey, Heard, and Bryant and Murch in their accounts, his use of graphic violence also fits with the anti-Indian propagandist cultural work that dime novels often performed. In this they both reflected and reinforced prevailing (white) cultural norms.

After 1864 Ellis continued publishing at an extraordinary rate, sometimes under his own name and sometimes under several dozen pseudonyms.[29] Later in his career he wrote nonfiction as well as fiction, and he returned to the topic of the Dakota Conflict several more times, though in increasingly diluted form and with fewer references to captivity. For example, in the five-hundred-page historical overview called *The Indian Wars of the United States*, published in 1892, he discusses wars from 1607 to 1891 as a means to justify white superiority.[30] He spends almost twenty pages on the Conflict alone and credits Heard's *History of the Sioux War* as the source for much of his information, which may also signal that he used Heard much earlier, when writing *Indian Jim*. Although Ellis is surprisingly candid in admitting that the Conflict's causes were based on widespread exploitation and greed by agents, traders, settlers, and the government, he still sees the American Indian overall as "more animal than intellectual."[31]

In 1900 Ellis published *Red Plume*, a lengthy novel that takes place at the beginning of the Dakota War.[32] Ellis rehashes some names and character types from *Indian Jim* (for example, an impractical character named Adolphus Pipkins, known as 'Dolph, who is a more lightweight reincarnation of Adolphus Halleck), though there are some notable differences, such as the historically unlikely presence, for 1860s Minnesota, of Quakers on the frontier. The Red Plume of the title is the stereotypically "good Indian" amid many "bad" ones. But it is the book's concluding sentence that indicates the hoped-for erasure of all Indians—even those sympathetic to whites—that mainstream culture desired: "Red Plume and Otter moved further west before the advancing tide of civilization, and all subsequent record of them has been lost."[33]

Then in 1908, only a few years before he died, Ellis reissued *Indian Jim* and also published another dime-length novel, this time for a young adult readership, *The Story of Red Feather*.[34] At this point the Dakota War could either be recycled (the reissued *Indian Jim*) or treated generically as symptomatic of any Indian war (the new book, *Red Feather*). While *Indian Jim* draws substantially on historical aspects of the Dakota War, the links are much weaker in *The Story of Red Feather*, where the setting is 1860s Minnesota and the title character is partly based on Little Crow. Although the novel takes place during what seems to be the Dakota War, Ellis does not state this in so many words. Two children rescue Red Feather as he gets stuck in a cabin window and swells up; then they hold him captive while subjecting him to pious and ideological lectures about the inevitability of Manifest Destiny.[35] When he finally agrees to reform, the underpinnings of this ludicrous plot are clear: they are to show the propagandist uses of juvenile literature to reinforce the status quo.

What may have made *Malaeska*, *Indian Jim*, and the Western dime novels that followed so enormously popular was that they combined and transformed two very popular narrative types, the captivity narrative (or more broadly the frontier tale) and the "sentimental" tale.[36] Such stories had significant appeal across class and even gender barriers.

The forging of captivity, sensation, and sentiment was already evident in fact-based accounts of the Conflict, like Wakefield's and Bishop's, as was the tendency to merge genres. But it was the dime novels that further experimented with genre and that carried this material to a particularly broad reading public.

4. Mary Schwandt Schmidt and Jacob Nix
Captivity and German Americans

The fate of Mary Schwandt in person and in print marks a transitional point in the production of Dakota Conflict captivity narratives. The earliest version of her story came out in Bryant and Murch's *A History of the Great Massacre by the Sioux Indians in Minnesota* (1864), where it was regularized (in terms of punctuation and spelling) and at least partly editorialized.[1] But 1894 saw the appearance of a changed version sponsored by the Minnesota Historical Society, collected by society employee Return Holcombe, printed in *Collections of the Minnesota Historical Society*, but first published with the society's permission in the *St. Paul Pioneer Press*.

These publications represented the state and local media's wish to preserve and present firsthand accounts, particularly by under-represented and/or previously muted groups such as non-Anglo whites—Germans, for example—and Dakotas. But also, by the 1890s newspapers and historical publications were competing for hitherto unheard stories about the war to boost readership and reach the huge number of newcomers to Minnesota since 1862. For example, federal census statistics for 1860 indicate that Minnesota's population then was 172,072, whereas by 1890 it had risen to 1,301,826. And since the largest bloc of new immigrants were Germans, that too may help explain greater interest in the 1890s for publishing German accounts.[2]

Additionally antiquarians wanted to document early Minnesota history and recover information about the Conflict, particularly as the non-Anglo ethnic minorities were no longer seen as so threatening to mainstream American identity. They also naively believed that residual hostility and self-serving subjectivity had completely evaporated by then. Even today the experiences of early German settlers in Minnesota are inadequately represented in historical and literary analyses, including captivity narrative studies, despite the fact that German Americans are the largest ethnic group in the state.[3] For instance, the 2002 essay collection *Germans and Indians: Fantasies, Encounters, Projections* contains only 5 pages on Minnesota out of 350 total.[4] Thus, analyzing the stories of German immigrants like Schwandt, Jacob Nix, and Benedict Juni helps remedy the complaint of German American scholars that "the monolingual Anglo-Americans" have traditionally downplayed these contributions locally and nationally.[5]

After 1894 Schwandt Schmidt retold her story many times, trying to wrest control of it, protect her place in local history, pass on family remembrances to her children, and maybe prepare it for book publication, though there is no evidence it actually came out.[6] Her narrative transformations moved from victimization to empowerment, from anger to acceptance, as evidenced by the account of 1864 and the mostly unmediated versions of 1894 and later. Schwandt Schmidt thus illustrates a compelling truth about war and memory: "How wars are remembered can be just as important as how they were fought and first described."[7] If Schwandt Schmidt could not prevent other historians, such as Marion Satterlee, coming up with their own interpretations—as seen in the epigraph to part 1—she could combat them with her own words in print and voice in person.

While the 1864 version presented Schwandt as an unwilling captive throughout the Conflict, the 1894 one placed her within a familiar narrative prototype. Schwandt's adoption during captivity by the kindly Dakota woman Snana (Maggie Good Thunder, later Maggie Brass) provided a Minnesota version of John Smith's rescue by Pocahontas, which had long been part of the national mythology. Under the auspices of editor/journalist/historian Return I. Holcombe, who had became interested in Dakota War history, Schwandt Schmidt's 1894 story appeared in the *Pioneer Press* and then in *Collections of the Minnesota Historical Society*. Holcombe also arranged for captivities by Jannette DeCamp Sweet, Nancy McClure Huggan, Big Eagle, and Maggie Brass herself to be published in the society's *Collections* over the next few years. Accordingly, in the 1898–1900 volume Brass provided an account that corroborated Schwandt Schmidt's, that considered the war from a Dakota woman's standpoint, and that reinforced her position as Minnesota's Pocahontas.[8]

At her death in 1939 Mary Schwandt Schmidt left hundreds of pages of documents, now lodged at the Minnesota Historical Society, including holograph manuscript or typescript versions of her story dated internally or externally about 1913, 1915, 1929, and 1935, as well as many letters from Maggie Brass; a list of talks she gave from 1910 to 1920; a family history; and photographs of herself, her husband, Maggie Brass, and other ex-captives.[9] This material provides fascinating contextual information on the published accounts of her own story and on others involved in the Conflict. Schwandt Schmidt was obviously someone with an urge to read, record, and revise her experiences, depending on audience and timeframe, once she broke her thirty-year silence in 1894. Not surprisingly the later versions show Schwandt Schmidt reaching back into memory but also reinterpreting events from the vantage point of her later experiences as a wife, mother, and patriot.

As Schwandt Schmidt tells in unpublished as well as published accounts, she was born in Germany (Prussia, technically, since Germany was not politically unified until after 1871) in 1848 and came to Canada with her parents in 1856. They were part of a third major immigrant wave (1848–66) to North America, mostly comprising political refugees who were well-educated professionals.[10] The Schwandt family moved to Wisconsin in 1859 and then to Flora Township, Renville County, Minnesota, in May 1862. They thus followed a pattern typical of many early German migrants to Minnesota, who did not come directly from Europe but from German settlements in Ohio, Wisconsin, and Missouri, for example, where land was becoming more limited and expensive.[11] Most of these Minnesota German immigrants, like Mary's parents, were "pioneer farmers" who lived American-style "on scattered homesteads or farmsteads" rather than European-style in agricultural villages.[12]

The Schwandts were not poor: Mary says they had between four hundred and two thousand dollars when they arrived in Minnesota.[13] Interaction between the Germans and the Dakotas was strained even before the war because the newcomers generally did not value sharing outside their own community and were culturally and spiritually clannish.[14] In fact, Flora Township, where the Schwandts lived, had been part of the Sioux reservation until 1858, when it was ceded by treaty. Of course English settlers could be bigots too, but the Germans, especially those from New Ulm, had a particularly bad reputation among the Dakotas and were sometimes called "iasica," or "'bad speakers,' a derogatory term that placed them outside of the Dakota world where humans were bound by ties of kinship and reciprocity."[15] And certainly the poor relations may explain why the Germans came in for particular violence during the war, along with the fact that large numbers of Germans settled close to the Lower Sioux Reservation and thus were more vulnerable to attack because of their geographic proximity.[16] Fraught German/Dakota interactions also hint at the special poignancy attached to Maggie Brass's adopting a member of this marginalized group.

In June 1862 Mary went to stay with Valencia and Joseph Reynolds at what was called the Half-way House, a stopping place between the Upper and Lower Sioux Agencies, eight miles from her parents' claim. She was not considered a domestic but moved there to attend a school that was supposed to open that fall and to do light housework for her keep. She says she was called "the errand girl."[17] Thus she was separated from the rest of her family when war broke out a few months later. At her family's homestead everyone was killed but her younger brother August, who was severely injured but survived. Mr.

and Mrs. Reynolds escaped to safety, but Mattie Williams (a visiting niece of the Reynoldses), Mary Anderson (a Swedish serving girl), and Mary Schwandt were captured en route to New Ulm. Mary Anderson was badly wounded and died in captivity a few days later. All three girls were sexually harassed if not actually raped shortly after being taken. In the 1864 version of her story, in Bryant and Murch's history, Schwandt says she was raped, but she does not refer to this in any other documents, and the information may reflect Bryant and Murch's editorial intrusion, an issue that I will address shortly. After several days Schwandt was sold to Wamnuka (Barleycorn) and her daughter, Maggie, in exchange for a pony. They adopted and protected her, then took her to Camp Release as the war wound down.

The mother-and-child relationship between Snana and Schwandt, which dominated the stories of both women from the turn of the century onward, is almost entirely absent in the 1864 version within Bryant and Murch's lengthy history. A little information on these male editors will indicate their general aims and specific approaches to texts like Schwandt's. Lawyer Charles S. Bryant was born in New York State in 1808, studied classics in Indiana, became a law student in Ohio, and was admitted to the bar there in 1838. He and his family moved to Minnesota in 1859 and eventually settled in St. Paul, where he carried on a successful law practice.[18] Bryant was involved in the Conflict after hostilities ended as a recorder of claimants' testimony before the Board of Commissioners, established to settle property damages against the Dakotas.[19] In connection with this work, he says, he "was compelled to listen to tales of horror of a character entirely too dreadful to be concealed," which could not, however, find their way into the officially abridged evidence about property loss alone.[20] Naturally Bryant cloaks this patent sensationalism with the moral imperative of revelation to reassure voyeuristic readers. Historically the violence within many captivity narratives had been similarly justified and sometimes completely fabricated.

In the preface to *A History of the Great Massacre*—whose title alone is inflammatory—Bryant says that he was unable to complete the history on his own in a timely manner and so requested Abel Murch's assistance in the first nine chapters and in preparing some of the personal narratives, probably those comprising chapters 13 to 20.[21] In terms of writing skill, Bryant would have been quite capable of undertaking the work, since an entry on him in *The Poets and Poetry of Minnesota* (1864) states that he had composed "a great amount of literary matter," both published and unpublished.[22] Abel Murch was a carpenter who had been employed at the Upper Sioux Agency and who fought with the Renville Rangers; earlier in life he had been a cabinetmaker and book agent. His participation as a soldier during the war effort and presumably his contacts as a book agent added to the salability of the book, which one contemporary called a "popular work."[23]

While Bryant and Murch state that they aimed to produce relevant "facts . . . in a connected form, and in the plainest possible manner," and while they certainly do include many first-person survivors' accounts and other documents, their true racist agenda can best be seen in their front-page epigraph and in consistent editorial intrusions throughout their 504-page tome.[24] The epigraph from the ancient Iranian poet Ferdousi (940?–1020 CE) reads, "For that which is unclean by nature thou canst entertain no hope; no washing will turn the Gipsy white."[25] It is obviously a message that Indian assimilation will not work any better than attempts at racial merging in ancient times. And Bryant and Murch's judgmental intrusions throughout are well-represented by the telling conclusion to their book: "Natural enmity to the white man is the ruling passion of savage races. With the Indian, Little Crow will be remembered as a hero; by the white race, he will be regarded as a monster in human proportions. May his fate be a warning to all conspirators against civilization and progress, whether among civilized or savage races!"[26] Predictably this prejudice affects their presentation of Schwandt's story.

The initial version of Schwandt's story appears as one of many first-person testimonies and captivity narratives in this history, and the mostly simple sentences and straightforward chronological organization suggest its origin in a verbal account or a written deposition. Schwandt did indeed present testimony in 1863 before the Sioux Claims Commission. However, within the book several markers indicate bias and editorialization, though whether from the editors or the subject or both is not clear. For example, Schwandt describes, after her capture, the "loathsome attentions" of several Dakota "fiends," who "took me out by force, to an unoccupied tepee, near the house, and perpetrated the most horrible and nameless outrages upon my person. These outrages were repeated, at different times during my captivity."[27] Some of the later manuscript versions do use such racist rhetoric, but others do not. None refers so specifically to rape.

At this point a textual comment that is set off typographically from the narrative by a paragraph break and square brackets reads, "The details of this poor girl's awful treatment, in our possession, are too revolting for publication.—EDITORS."[28] This is the most obvious reference to rape, and it seems to be corroborated by another captive, Jannette DeCamp Sweet, who states in her narrative, "Mary Swandt [sic] had fled to me for protection from their indecent assaults."[29] Whether or not Schwandt was really raped is still open to question. But it is true that Schwandt and Mattie Williams testified at the Trials Commission against Williams's captor, Tazoo, whom they both accused of raping Williams; indeed, in his own testimony Tazoo admitted doing so.[30]

The rape issue is obviously compounded because even today women who are raped do not necessarily admit to it, fearing social stigma, and women who are not raped but who are afraid of or undergo harassment—especially white women by men of color—may interpret and articulate the experience as rape or may keep silent when others do so on their behalf. There is also the issue of traumatic or selective amnesia to consider. Some women simply cannot or do not remember. One of the reasons that women's captivity narratives were so popular from the seventeenth century on was owing to the strong propagandist and prurient element of female sexual victimization.[31] Inflammatory claims of rape during the Dakota Conflict were widespread in the popular press, and while a few may have been true, the vast majority were not. The relationship between real rape atrocities and mythicized—often propagandist—ones is complex, and owing to the power of the created accounts, sometimes the real events become weaker with personal and communal memory loss.[32]

The other example of possible textual interference comes in such loaded references to Maggie and Andrew Good Thunder as "I was forced to call them father and mother," "They took off the squaw dress they had compelled me to wear," and "They made me carry water and make bread."[33] In October 1915, when Schwandt Schmidt delivered an address before the Colonial Dames of America in Minnesota, within another of her many captivity accounts, she admits, "When I parted with Snana at Camp Release I guess I was very ungrateful, but I was glad to get away from the Indians," and this comment sheds some light on the tone and information published in Bryant and Murch.[34] Yet elsewhere in this 1915 talk Schwandt Schmidt says that after their initial captivity she and the other two girls hid in an attic for three days on the advice of the Dakota named Wacouta, then went to Little Crow's village, where she was soon adopted by Snana. There is no reference to her own rape or sexual abuse. However, she infers that Mattie Williams was raped when she says that the Indian who had first captured Mattie claimed her in Little Crow's village: "Well, what could she do? She had to go with him. He took her to his tepee, where he had a squaw and family."[35]

In her manuscript "Recollections of My Captivity among the Sioux," which internal evidence dates about 1929, Schwandt Schmidt reconstructs the train of events leading to the 1894 account published in a state newspaper and then preserved beyond the ephemeral medium of

Figure 7. Mary E. Schwandt Schmidt and Maggie Brass (Snana) in 1899, Shepherd Photo Studio. From the Collections of the Minnesota Historical Society. Used with permission.

newsprint in the Minnesota Historical Society's journal. The man who interviewed her was probably Return Holcombe, though she does not identify him by name. Schwandt Schmidt says she is writing for her son and daughter, and because she speaks here with the authority of a parent passing on family history, I am privileging information in this account: "At one time the Pioneer Press a St. Paul daily news paper sent a man to our home to see if I would give them my experience when living with the indians. I hesitated . . . as I never wanted to talk a bout that terrible time, but the man said it would be a sin for me not to tell my story and let this generation know what the early settlers had to go through all the hardships and at last loose thear lives besides and said he it belonged to the History of Minnesota."[36]

The story appeared in the Sunday newspaper, and the matron at the Santee, Nebraska, Indian Agency School, where Snana (then called Maggie Brass) was living, "embraced Snana saying my dear I never knew or dreamt you was such a wonder full woman as you have turned out to be, here, read this and see what this woman says about you, what you have done for her when in great need of help."[37] By the following Friday Schwandt Schmidt had received a letter from Brass, which led to regular reunions after three decades, public recognition for Brass, and whatever occasional financial support Schwandt Schmidt could offer to her.[38]

What did Schwandt Schmidt say in the *Pioneer Press* that so touched the matron? This second version is twice as long as the earlier one; is better organized; and has a much stronger narrative, descriptive, reflective, and retrospective feel. Perhaps the most significant change, apart from added details, concerns the emotionalism of Schwandt Schmidt's recollections: for example, of saying goodbye to her parents and siblings (temporarily, she thought, to take up her position in the Reynolds house, but permanently, as it transpired), of seeing Mary Anderson die, of being threatened by Little Crow, and of being adopted by Snana.

Indeed, the narrative segues from Schwandt Schmidt's initial admission of hatred toward some Dakotas to her love and gratitude toward Brass, "one of the handsomest Indian women I ever saw, and one of the best."[39] Repeatedly Schwandt Schmidt emphasizes Brass's maternalism to her: "Maggie could not have treated me more tenderly if I had been her daughter. Often and often she preserved me from danger, and sometimes, I think, she saved my life"; and, on Brass's defending her against some drunks, "Maggie sprang up as swiftly as a tigress defending her young"; and, "Wherever you are, Maggie, I want you to know that the little captive girl you so often befriended and shielded from harm loves you still for your kindness and care."[40]

What Schwandt Schmidt (and perhaps her editor) seems to be doing here is shaping her narrative according to what Devon Mihesuah calls "the artificially idealistic" rather than "the extremely pejorative" stereotype of Native Americans.[41] Analyzing literary stereotypes of Native women, Rayna Green uses the term "the Pocahontas perplex" to indicate the phenomenon of an Indian woman seeming to privilege white culture above her own by rescuing a European from harm.[42] John Smith's most detailed recounting of his supposed rescue by Pocahontas in the *The Generall History of Virginia* of 1624 assumes romantic overtones, with a male captive and a female rescuer, even though historically Pocahontas was still a child and Smith was a middle-aged man. But another modification of the Pocahontas story involves an Indian mother figure and usually a white woman and/or child that she helps. Both these positive Indian female stereotypes (lover and mother) are seen in countless captivity narratives. Unusually, in the case of Schwandt and Brass, the mother-child relationship existed not only in 1862 but later, in their postcaptivity life, where it had a basis in reality beyond romantic rhetoric.

Following the republication of her captivity narrative in 1894 in the *Pioneer Press* and *Collections of the Minnesota Historical Society*, Schwandt Schmidt took to heart the imperative that she needed to make her story better known; indeed, that she was morally required to do so. The list of talks she gave between 1910 and 1920 logs addresses to schools, missionary meetings, and churches and to such groups as the Daughters of the American Revolution and the Colonial Dames. Sometimes she spoke before as many as several hundred people.[43]

She was also determined to raise funds for a monument to her family at the site where they died. The State of Minnesota eventually appropriated two hundred dollars for it, and it was dedicated in her presence on 18 August 1915, exactly fifty-three years after the Conflict formally began. The address given on that occasion by Minnesota Historical Society archaeologist Warren Upham clearly shows the pacifying power of the Schwandt/Snana story amid residual racist rhetoric:

In the dedication of this monument telling of the awful tragedy of race hatred and massacre which befell a German family of pioneers here fifty-three years ago, let us not forget the bright flower of a lifelong friendship which bloomed about their graves, gladdening the life of the rescued survivor of that family and the life of the kind Dakota woman, Snana, her rescuer.

The Historical Society of this State, in its published volumes, preserves to all coming time the narratives of Mary Schwandt and of Snana. Children of parents and of races who met then in mortal conflict, the one a captive German girl, the other a bereaved Dakota mother, they loved each other with affection that may be compared with that of David and Jonathan nearly three thousand years ago.

Can we learn something from this? Does it even shed forth a ray of hope that when the present direful world war shall be ended with treaties of peace, it may be the beginning of trust and helpfulness, of mutual respect and friendship, between all the now warring nations?

"Till the war drums throb no longer, and the battle flags are furled,
In the Parliament of man, the Federation of the World."[44]

Upham took a single experience from the Conflict, made it representative of harmony between European American and Native American nations, imbued it with typological significance through the references to David and Jonathan, and then gave it worldwide meaning in the context of the First World War. However, the inscription on the monument itself, which signifies the permanent written interpretation versus the temporary spoken one, is uncompromising in its pejorative language: "Erected by the State of Minnesota, In Memory of Martyrs for Civilization [list of the names of the Schwandt family] Murdered by Sioux Indians [date of death and date of the monument's dedication]."

Figure 8. Jacob Nix. From the Collection of the Brown County Historical Society, New Ulm, Minnesota. Used with permission.

Perhaps Schwandt Schmidt had been moved to memorialize her family after seeing, about seven years earlier, Maggie Brass's name engraved on the monument for the "Friendly Indians" at Morton, Minnesota. It was the sixth name but could only be added after her death in 1908.[45]

The eyewitness accounts of a fourteen-year-old girl and a middle-aged military man, Jacob Nix, both represent the Conflict's impact on German American immigrants in Minnesota. While Schwandt's story received attention early on in Bryant and Murch's history, as did a disproportionate number of the women's captivity narratives, Nix waited until the twenty-fifth commemoration of the Conflict, in

1887, to publish his book version in German. Printed in Milwaukee, it circulated in New Ulm and perhaps also more widely within the Midwestern German American community. It was not fully translated and nationally available until 1994, when it appeared as an imprint from the Max Kade German-American Center and Indiana German Heritage Society.[46]

Jacob Nix, who commanded the volunteer troops at New Ulm that successfully fended off the first Indian attack, was born in Bingen am Rhein in 1822. He fought during the German Revolution of 1848, in which the middle classes tried to remove power from the ruling aristocracy. When the uprising failed he was arrested, accused of treason, and sentenced to death. He escaped to Holland and then came to the United States, arriving in New York and moving to Cleveland after a year. Like many other 48ers—as German revolutionary soldiers were called—Nix became active in the German American Turner societies, which were utopian experiments in socialism and communal living.[47] He and his compatriots tended to be "middle-class liberals, radicals, and republicans of wide talents and varied backgrounds" who "provided an unusual intellectual, political, and cultural leadership in the United States at a time when the German settler, and the immigrant in general, were under attack by nativists."[48]

In 1855 Nix and Wilhelm Pfaender, cofounder of the first American Turner society, proposed establishing a public ownership settlement of "workers and freethinkers in the Northwest where soil and lumber were abundant."[49] This group joined with a Chicago German immigrant society that had founded New Ulm in 1854, and Nix and his family arrived there in 1858. At this time the New Ulm population of 440 was 80 percent German.[50] By 1859, when the socialist ideal in New Ulm had proved unworkable, the community underwent a dramatic social change, from "talented ethnic leaders to an Americanized status elite."[51] Nix's account recognizes the contributions of New Ulm's German inhabitants to state and national affairs and uses the captivity narrative not just for anti-Indian propaganda but for anti-Anglo propaganda too. Nix responds to the nativist interpretation of the Conflict by presenting himself and the New Ulm settlers as new patriots. Since his original audience was German Americans, he felt he was merely reinforcing their ethnic pride and righting the record for posterity, though he did so from a decidedly New Ulm–centric viewpoint.

On 18 August 1862 refugees from the attacks at the Upper and Lower Agencies began to arrive at New Ulm, which had been depleted of many able-bodied men owing to Civil War enlistments. According to Nix, by 1862 the town had two hundred buildings and over nine hundred citizens.[52] Because of Nix's previous military experience, Sheriff Charles Roos appointed him commandant of New Ulm's volunteer forces. It was this group that successfully defended the town against the first Dakota attack on 19 August before the main body of state militia arrived. When the Indians regrouped for another assault on 23 August, the troops under Flandrau had come, and the combined forces kept control of New Ulm once again. By then Nix had relinquished his command, and he resented Flandrau's tardy arrival and tendency to take full credit for defending the town.

In his foreword Nix makes several points that underpin the rest of his account. First, he says he is answering friends' requests for "an accurate account of the Sioux Uprising."[53] Similar comments within Indian captivity narratives had been used from earliest times as a traditional explanation for making the private public and setting the record straight. The seventeenth- and eighteenth-century women's captivity narratives, in particular, often camouflaged their authors' decision to move beyond the domestic sphere and seek publication by claiming that they were only giving in to public pressure. Although Nix concedes that several histories had already appeared—including, of course, those by McConkey, Heard, and Bryant and Murch—he states that "none of them provide a correct and reliable history of those days of horror; especially the English-language works are full of errors and distortions."[54] Nix's remark is self-serving but generally correct. He also claims authority because he was "an eyewitness" during the entire Conflict and had access to "the most reliable sources." For these reasons, he says, his work "consists of history, rather than myth."[55]

Naturally Nix's text has its own blind spots, but it does include his extended participation as a soldier, from 1862 onward, in several Indian campaigns. Having recovered from wounds received at New Ulm, Nix enlisted in the First Mounted Rangers and became captain of the Second Minnesota Cavalry. He served until 1865, after which he returned to New Ulm and went into business for a decade, apparently without much success. After the city petitioned that he be granted a war pension in 1874, he became interested in local politics, and he was elected to the office of assessor and then town clerk until his retirement in 1886.[56] Thus when he published *The Sioux Uprising in 1862* Nix had recently retired and was a well-known community figure.

Nix's most important literary contributions are to furnish a different perspective and to include fuller information than the earlier Anglo histories, which had downplayed the German military help during the war. A glance at McConkey's, Heard's, and Bryant and Murch's texts underscores Nix's concern about inaccuracy and bias. McConkey was particularly scandalized because New Ulm had been founded by the Turners, whom she calls "a class of infidel Germans" who were "strong in wickedness" and spent the Sabbath "drinking and dancing."[57] She even states that a day or so before the town was attacked, some inhabitants burned an effigy of Christ, a detail that Nix addresses and contradicts as a particularly outrageous fabrication.[58] She does not mention Nix and characterizes the Germans as unable or unwilling to defend themselves. According to McConkey, only an advance party from Flandrau's forces kept the Dakotas at bay until the commander himself arrived, and even they were unable "to rally the panic-stricken citizens" in the interim.[59] McConkey's prejudices smack of the mid-nineteenth-century Know-Nothing Movement, whose nativist propaganda specifically targeted German immigrants.[60]

While Heard's tone in *History of the Sioux War* is more objective than Bishop's, he too gives credit to the advance guard from Flandrau for saving the town after the first attack, and he too omits any mention of Jacob Nix. Heard characterizes the townsfolk as being "in a state of utter frenzy," with "no organization for defense," and "huddled together like a flock of frightened sheep."[61] Once again Heard's history paints a picture of disorganized and panicked Germans awaiting the superior state forces to rescue them from their own inadequacies, as well as from the Indians.

Bryant and Murch's *A History of the Great Massacre* is the least biased of the three Anglo histories in its treatment of the New Ulm sieges. It characterizes the settlement as a "beautiful and enterprising German town," but it does not mention Nix either, and it too emphasizes Flandrau's volunteer forces and the second defense of New Ulm.[62] Forty years later Lucius F. Hubbard and Return I. Holcombe, who compiled their own account of the war within their compendious 1908 history, *Minnesota in Three Centuries*, said that these same three early general histories, "which were written and published not long after the outbreak, and each of which is, in the main, an excellent account of the Indian uprising and the incidents connected therewith, all contain many incorrect statements."[63] No wonder Nix felt impelled to provide his own version.

In fact, the publication of Charles Flandrau's own autobiography/ military report in 1891, *Minnesota in the Civil and Indian Wars*, excludes the First Battle of New Ulm altogether and therefore any mention of Nix as its commandant. It also ignores the German-oriented history by Alexander Berghold, a contemporary bestseller providing a fuller account of the New Ulm attacks, which Flandrau would have known and could have used. However, it is also true that Flandrau's volume primarily recorded military battles, like the Civil War books being churned out at the time, and that he was mostly concerned with the deeds of military men compiled from military records, not civilians like Nix, despite his heroism.[64] A review of some of the Anglo and German histories in William Watts Folwell's 1924 *A History of Minnesota* concludes that Nix's and Berghold's accounts of the first New Ulm battle are the correct ones.[65]

Nix aims to even up the German/Anglo accounts by making a particularly bold claim: that successfully defending New Ulm in the first battle was essentially the key to winning the entire war. He says this at several points in the narrative to prove the bravery of the townspeople and the strategic importance of the town itself, at the head of the Minnesota River Valley.[66] If the Dakotas had got a foothold in New Ulm, he believes, they could have made much greater headway. In a chapter titled "Honor to Whom Honor Is Due!" Nix reiterates: "The main battle for the defense of the settlers in the Minnesota Valley was fought in New Ulm on the 19th of August 1862. This battle, the outcome of which gave notice to the Indians: 'This far and no further,' was almost exclusively fought by Germans."[67]

While Nix disapproves of the English histories for their subjectivity and partiality, his own anti-Anglo, anti-Indian agendas constantly push through his narrative texture. Sometimes the U.S. government and the English are the special focus of his condemnation, as when he says that official agents ignored the warning signs of an Indian rebellion "with unpardonable carelessness" and that Englishmen—unlike Frenchmen—took Native women without marrying them so that mixed-blood children were brought up as Indians and became vehemently antiwhite because of their fathers' neglect.[68]

However, he displays his strongest prejudice toward the Dakotas in general and uses such extreme racist rhetoric at times that it sounds like a parody. This is especially evident in racial slurs like "red brutes," "murderous firebugs," and "red cut-throats."[69] For Nix the combination of arrogant Anglos and savage Natives made the Dakota Conflict so explosive and damaging that while he condemned the English for

contributing to (even causing) the situation, he was particularly vehement in defending the convictions of almost four hundred Indians
sentenced to hang for war crimes. Not to hang them, it seemed to Nix,
was as erroneous as believing that the idealized portraits of Native
Americans in Fenimore Cooper's novels, which Nix discusses in his
text, came from "truth and reality" when instead they came from the
imagination.[70]

Nix's text functions as a captivity narrative in several ways. First,
it tells of an entire town held hostage during two attacks by Native
Americans. Not only were the townspeople besieged, but those who
had fled to New Ulm for safety were also confined under duress.
Second, it shows how a marginalized ethnic group could be culturally diminished by the majority until its constituents spoke out and
resisted the official version of events. Not to strain the trope, the
dominant Anglo culture held the nonassimilated group hostage to
prevailing cultural norms.

Third, it contains several places where Nix has absorbed the rhetoric
of captivity and applied it in a new context. I am thinking here of the
two textual sites where he refers to the Indians themselves as captives after the Conflict. Accusing the U.S. government of deliberately
providing the conditions under which the Dakotas would rebel, Nix
criticizes the familiar pattern of Indian massacres, white recrimina-
tions, and round-ups of the guilty, only to "bring the captives to newly
erected reservations."[71] Nix discusses how after the war the soldiers
involved in defending New Ulm and the Minnesota River Valley considered lynching the imprisoned Indians but were thwarted from doing
so. Four times in the space of a page, Nix refers to these Indians as
"male captives" and as "captive Indians," apparently using the rhetoric
ironically, recognizing that the European Americans previously held
captive by the Dakotas had by then been either killed or freed.[72] Also,
by choosing this term rather than "imprisoned" or "incarcerated," Nix
underscores the archetypal power of the captor/captive, empowered/

disempowered dynamic. The warring Dakotas, who temporarily held the power to take captives, were now themselves dispossessed.

Publication and local distribution of Nix's history in 1887 consolidated his position as a respected community leader who spoke his mind and advocated freedom of thought—remnants of the Turner ideals he held when he first came to Minnesota. An account of his contributions, published locally in 1947, called *The Sioux Uprising in Minnesota, 1862* an "amazing saga" that would interest New Ulmers and that "should be preserved for future generations."[73]

5. Jannette DeCamp Sweet, Helen Carrothers Tarble, Lillian Everett Keeney, and Urania White
Captivity and the Antiquarian Impulse

To understand the circumstances by which the next text, Jannette DeCamp Sweet's "Narrative," came to be published in the *Pioneer Press* in 1894 and then in *Collections of the Minnesota Historical Society*, it is necessary to review information on the Minnesota Historical Society itself and Return Holcombe's relation to it. For Holcombe was involved in the publication of a trio of related women's captivity narratives in the 1894 *Collections*: the first by Jannette DeCamp Sweet, the second by Nancy McClure Huggan, and the third by Mary Schwandt Schmidt.[1]

The Minnesota Historical Society was founded in 1849, nine years before the Minnesota Territory became a state. It remains Minnesota's oldest institution, and since statehood it has benefited almost continuously from legislative appropriations contributing to its total budget. The initial idea for the society came from the territorial secretary, Charles K. Smith, and at the first annual meeting address in 1850 the Reverend Edward D. Neill exhorted members, "Write your history as you go along, and you will confer a favor upon the future inhabitants of Minnesota."[2] The imperative to preserve history, usually from a Eurocentric viewpoint, played a particularly important part during and after the Conflict. The membership group of the Historical Society that was established at the time of founding provided specific institutional support and enabled information to be more widely disseminated. For example, as early as 1851 the society raised funds for the Smithsonian to publish *Grammar and Dictionary of the Dakota Language* by Stephen Riggs, the Pond brothers, and Thomas Williamson.[3]

The Minnesota Historical Society's next phase of development spanned the appointment of J. Fletcher Williams as secretary from 1867 to 1893, a man passionately committed to collecting and preserving the library collections, not just providing a venue for history buffs to meet.[4] From 1893 to 1895 William R. Marshall (who added introductory notes to all three women's narratives in the 1894 *Collections*) assumed temporary control. He was a soldier who had served briefly on the Sioux Trials Commission and was the editor of the *St. Paul Pioneer Press* both before and after the Dakota War. Marshall then handed the reins to the geologist and historian Warren Upham, whose primary interests concerned writing on Minnesota history, increasing the library, and boosting state funds. Upham served as secretary from 1895 to 1933.[5] Thus, at the time that the Sweet/McClure/Schwandt accounts were published in volume 6 of the *Collections*, the society was primarily dedicated to collecting, preserving, and publishing Minnesotiana and was beginning to recognize the importance of Dakota versions of the Conflict.

Return I. Holcombe was born in Ohio in 1845 and served in the Tenth Missouri Regiment during the Civil War. Afterward he became a printer, newspaper editor, and antiquarian. He moved to St. Paul in 1890 and started work on a history of the city, which prompted the Minnesota Historical Society to employ him as an assistant on several projects from 1893 to 1894, most notably arranging and archiving General Sibley's letters and papers.[6] But Holcombe also became fascinated with the Dakota War and, thirty years after the fact, seemed eager to record captivity narratives and present different viewpoints on the hostilities in other narrative genres. Accordingly the same issue of the *Collections of the Minnesota Historical Society* in which Jannette DeCamp Sweet's story appeared also included works by Nancy Huggan, Mary Schwandt, and Big Eagle (Wamditanka). Other Dakota War accounts that Holcombe collected came out in subsequent volumes of the *Collections*. Later, with Lucius F. Hubbard, Holcombe authored volume

3 of the history *Minnesota in Three Centuries* (1908), which includes a relatively objective and unsensational account of the Dakota War.[7] So perhaps Warren Upham was not merely eulogizing when he stated in his obituary on Holcombe, "Among all whom I have known in historical work, he was the most careful, anxious, and persistent to attain accuracy and truth."[8]

It was William Marshall, as interim Minnesota Historical Society secretary, who solicited a manuscript from Jannette DeCamp Sweet via Return Holcombe. Extracts of this account were first published in the *St. Paul Pioneer Press*. After reading this version Sweet commented in a letter to Marshall: "I think Mr. Holcombe did well in abridging the manuscript. Of course it breaks the continuity of the narrative."[9] Indeed, the journalist's introduction in the newspaper story stresses that it contains only portions of Sweet's narrative and that the full version would appear within a forthcoming *Collections* volume. The newspaper story also uses section breaks and titles that are missing in the later volume. In a letter written earlier in July, Sweet had provided some genealogical information to William H. Grant, of St. Paul, and Secretary Marshall had handwritten at the top of this typescript, "If Mr. Holcombe wishes to use these facts, it will be all right to do so."[10]

The data indicate that Sweet's first husband, Joseph W. DeCamp, was descended from an eighteenth-century French nobleman who settled in New York. Later some of his descendents moved to Ohio, where Joseph was born. Jannette and Joseph married in Ohio, then settled in Shakopee, Minnesota, in 1855. Like John Wakefield, Joseph DeCamp received a political appointment following Thomas Galbraith's selection as Indian agent for Minnesota. The DeCamps moved to the Lower Sioux Agency in 1861 so Joseph could run the sawmill there, and Jannette says that soon she was accustomed to living in "friendly intimacy" with the mostly "kind and peaceable" Dakotas.[11] On 18 August, when the Lower Agency was attacked, Jannette was there with her three young sons because Joseph had gone to St. Paul on business.

Hearing of the troubles, he quickly returned, but he died after being wounded at the Battle of Birch Coulee.

Sweet's letter of 10 July 1894 and the introduction to her captivity narrative emphasize the pain of trying to recoup war recollections. The letter refers to "those weeks of anguish" whose memory "is too awful to record," while the narrative explains, "It is a part of my life which I would much rather forget than remember, and which, after so many years' time, I can now dwell upon but with feelings of the utmost horror."[12] In some captivity narratives assertions like these encouraged audiences to expect private revelations. But Sweet's reluctance to speak within the dual media of a personal letter and a historical account (rather than a commercial book publication) confirms the authenticity of her response.

Like Mary Schwandt Schmidt, Lillian Everett Keeney, and to some extent Nancy Huggan, Sweet relates traumatic events she had previously suppressed or could recall only imperfectly. None of these women volunteered their stories; all were solicited long after the fact.[13] The women responded as a public duty in 1894, and most of them left it at that. Only Schwandt Schmidt moved beyond her initial discomfort and kept on retelling her story regularly when she and her rescuer became minor celebrities in Minnesota.

Sweet's account reiterates familiar information, for example that the Dakotas were starving in 1862 and that they were intensely interested in the Civil War because a permanent change in the fortunes of the North might benefit them. She also states that her family's wish to help Dakotas before the war by sharing food undoubtedly "became the means of our preservation from horrid tortures and a lingering death," since several Dakotas came to their aid, including Wacouta, Wabasha, and Lorenzo Lawrence.[14] As further evidence of Jannette and Joseph's sympathy, Sweet says that the Dakotas named her husband Chan-ba-su-da-su-da-cha, or "the friendly man," and that she could speak and understand Dakota.[15]

Although Sweet expresses her regret that words cannot adequately describe events or convey emotions, her narrative is particularly sharp and detailed in places. These textual sites may indicate hypermnesia—the opposite of amnesia—in which the mind compulsively sees and reexperiences traumatic incidents in sharp relief. Sometimes they intrude unpredictably into the consciousness of survivors. Sweet even speaks in these terms. For instance, when she provides a minutely detailed description of Wabasha sitting on his horse in full battle dress, she states that, "Every detail seemed to strike me as if photographed," and she likens him to the subjects of George Catlin's paintings.[16] Later, trying to portray what she ironically terms "the gay cavalcade" of hundreds of Dakotas loaded with plunder, she says it was "a scene which, once looked upon, could never be forgotten."[17] When Lorenzo Lawrence leads Sweet and her three young children to safety after their captivity and she passes by her old house, she insists on stopping to recover some papers and account books and effectively describes the ruin and chaos: "Everything which could not be taken away was torn up and thrown about, feather beds emptied, furniture hacked to pieces and otherwise destroyed."[18]

Sweet's captivity narrative contains very few examples of the impulse to demonize Indians, though she expresses scorn for Godfrey and claims that apart from Cut Nose, he "always stands out most prominently in my memory."[19] But it does exemplify a standard sentimental trope in the women's captivity literature: the captive woman as mother and the impact of the experience on her children. When Reverend Joshua Sweet met Jannette DeCamp (as she was then) on her safe arrival at Fort Ridgely, he broke the sad news to her that Joseph had been killed. As she recalls her reaction, it is not in terms of her own loss of a husband but of her children's loss of a father: "Every hope seemed blotted out from the horizon of my existence, and life and liberty bought at such a price seemed worthless as I looked at the future of my fatherless children, without a home and many hundred miles from my people."[20] But they were not fatherless for long, as she married Joshua Sweet in 1866 and reunified the family by providing a second father for her sons. Similar stories of family disintegration and reintegration can be found in countless women's captivity narratives from the seventeenth century on.

However, Sweet's narrative does not end with this newly bonded family. It concludes with her thanking Lorenzo Lawrence by name and acknowledging many other unnamed Natives who aided captives and thereby jeopardized their own safety. Indeed, a good deal of Lawrence's own narrative, which will be examined in part 2, on Dakota texts, discusses Jannette DeCamp and the other captives Lawrence rescued. These Indians, Sweet stated, deserve "the highest praise for their devotion."[21] And in her final sentence she says to all who befriended her so many years before, "I tender my heartfelt thanks, and, in the language of Wabasha, 'I shake hands.'"[22] Unusually then, despite Sweet's traumatic experiences, her last words are conciliatory, not confrontational.

While the three accounts by Sweet, Huggan, and Schwandt Schmidt that appeared in the same issue of *Collections of the Minnesota Historical Society* can be read independently, they were meant to be read consecutively: each gets progressively shorter (twenty-six, twenty-two, and thirteen pages); each relies on previously mentioned information; and Schwandt Schmidt—in the last and shortest text—remarks that since Sweet has described the events of the first four days of captivity so clearly, "it seems unnecessary that I should repeat them; and, indeed, it is a relief to avoid the subject."[23] But whether Mary Schwandt Schmidt or Return Holcombe cut short the account is not known for sure. Evidently the editors of the *Collections* assumed that readers would move through all the captivity narratives in turn and would retain some of the information they had just read.

Helen Mar Carrothers McNanny Tarble's story exists in three main texts, all told in the first person: the fourteen-page account in Bryant and Murch's *History* (1863), a newspaper story published thirty years later in the *St. Paul Pioneer Press* (1894), and a separately published book (1904).[24] Bryant and Murch's voluminous *History of the Great Massacre of the Sioux Indians*—containing the earliest of Tarble's stories—has a three-part structure: chapters 1 to 12 cover the course of the war; chapters 13 to 20 include discrete narratives, most of them by ex-captives; and chapters 21 to 25 explain the postwar situation, right up to the book's publication in 1863. Thus the individual narratives are sandwiched in between more general information, and they are there to display the human face of war. Tarble's captivity narrative is not a transcription of oral testimony; she was asked to write down what she calls her "simple story of my adventures among the Sioux Indians."[25] Echoing the rationale that many women in earlier times gave for writing their narratives, Tarble says that friends had prompted her to do so. Presumably Bryant and Murch did too, and she seems to have had a larger, more impersonal audience in mind than a close circle of friends, as seen in her generic comment, "The reader may imagine my joy at reaching Fort Ridgely."[26]

This version focuses on Tarble's wartime experiences and contains many details about the unpredictability of the captives' fate; the constant search for food and shelter; the pain of seeing looted material that had belonged to family and friends; the vulnerability of women concerning sexual abuse; and the determined individual's initiative in seizing the opportunity to escape. Tarble's account does not appear to be edited beyond the parenthetical comment at the beginning: "We give the personal narrative of Mrs. Carrothers in her own words."[27] There is little judgmental commentary within the text, and the overall impression is that this captive escaped her harrowing experience relatively unscathed.

As I indicated earlier in this chapter, the Minnesota Historical Society and the *Pioneer Press* played an important role in collecting and publishing survivor narratives in 1894. In fact, the second version of Tarble's story appeared in the pages of the *Pioneer Press* on 15 November 1894. Tarble's visit to her daughter in Minneapolis may have prompted her to produce this text before she returned home to Tacoma, Washington. While some of the captivity narratives collected in the 1894 *Collections of the Minnesota Historical Society* had first appeared in the *Pioneer Press*, Tarble's had not. Why? We do not know for sure. But the reason may simply be that more accounts could appear in the daily paper because of its constant demand for newsworthy material than could be reprinted in the *Collections*. The story Tarble told for the *Pioneer Press* is almost 30 percent longer than the Bryant and Murch one, it provides more details and anecdotes, and it situates Tarble's wartime experiences within the context of her earlier and later life.

Ten years later, perhaps to capitalize on the fortieth anniversary of the Dakota War, in 1904, Tarble published a book-length version of her captivity, the sixty-five-page *Story of My Capture and Escape*. Its lengthy subtitle, *With Historical Notes, Descriptions of Pioneer Life, and Sketches and Incidents of the Great Outbreak of the Sioux or Dakota Indians as I Saw Them*, aptly describes the historical and ethnographic information that lengthened her basic narrative. Therefore, like many Indian captivity narratives, particularly those by women, Tarble's own story is sandwiched between general data at the beginning and the end of the book. Often such a structure betrays editorial intervention despite a first-person claim of total authorship and experiential authenticity. In Tarble's case either she or someone else appropriated the introductory and concluding material largely from Bryant and Murch, without indicating the source. Even without referencing this source, readers can tell that the tone and information in the opening and closing sections are completely different from the central portion. In fact, Tarble actually signs off on page 50, before the final sections subtitled "Character of the Red Men's Rebellion," "Incidents of the Indian Uprising," "Fort Ridgely and Its Gallant Defense," and "The Hanging of Thirty-Eight Indians at Mankato," comprising the last sixteen pages.

The opening section of Tarble's 1904 story, called "Early Indian History of Minnesota," discusses initial contact between Europeans and Dakotas, as well as long- and short-term causes of the Conflict. Yet this section's primary function seems to be proving the Indians' innate savagery. Thus the first sentence makes the outrageous generalization that the war was "the most appalling exhibition of Indian treachery and ferocity ever perpetrated" and that more whites were killed in it than in any other European/Indian warfare in the nation's history.[28] The narrator continues to provide information on Father Louis Hennepin's explorations in the seventeenth century and on later expeditions and treaties, taking data in the same order as they appear in the first two chapters of Bryant and Murch's *History*.

Sometimes information is lifted verbatim or in thinly disguised paraphrase, as in the following example: "The taking from the general fund of the tribe the money necessary to the carrying out of the civilization scheme was very distasteful to the 'blanket Indians,' and they inveighed bitterly against it" (Bryant and Murch), and "The taking from the general fund of the tribe the money necessary to carry out the civilization scheme was always a source of irritation to the 'blanket' Indians. This was one of their greatest grievances and they bitterly denounced it" (Tarble).[29]

After discussing various treaties and the establishment of the Upper and Lower Sioux Agencies, the narrator of the historical introduction speaks of the tensions within the Dakota bands caused by those wishing to retain their traditional culture and those willing to assimilate. Like so many other European Americans writing on the Dakota Conflict, Tarble nevertheless generalizes about all the Indians with such comments as "The heedless, thriftless and shiftless habits of the Sioux are well known," "They were cunning, deceitful and treacherous," and "The massacre was merely an expression and demonstration of the savagery and barbarism existing in every Sioux Indian," and such racist tags as "red demons" and "tiger-like dispositions."[30] This same stereotypically judgmental tone returns in the final pages and at some points even in the central part of the narrative proper, predictably following descriptions of attacks or atrocities. There, though, the racism is diluted by other facts concerning Tarble's first few years in Minnesota, when, as a child bride of thirteen recently arrived from Wisconsin and living in an isolated cabin with her much older husband, the nearby Dakotas were her only friends.

In the narrative itself, which carries the section title "My Experience during the Outbreak," Tarble tells how she was born in Wisconsin in 1843 and married James Carrothers, a man double her age, in 1856. It was quite normal for a frontier working-class girl barely in her teens to get married. The classic study *Women's Diaries of the Westward Journey* states, "Marriages on the frontier were often made before a girl was half through her adolescent years," and it quotes a fifteen-year-old bride's diary stating that the young men thought it odd if a girl remained unmarried at sixteen.[31] This practice makes sense because the young were best able to withstand the long cross-country journey and the rigors of frontier life.[32]

The couple's travels took them mainly to where there was carpentry work for James Carrothers. Passing through Mankato they heard about employment at the Redwood Agency, so they took a claim in Renville County. Tarble describes her shock at first seeing Indians, perhaps to appeal to the prejudices of the "present generation," which, she says, scarcely "know or imagine what the first pioneers had to endure."[33] Yet she also defends her response by reminding readers that she was "a child wife" many miles from home.[34] Her initial reaction also contrasts with her later friendships among the Dakotas and even her partial acculturation to their ways.

Tarble indicates the hardships of isolation, hunger, and sheer drudgery, but she is proud that she "worked and tugged, lifted and hewed, and did much of the work" needed to build the family's first house.[35] This is no Sarah Wakefield or Harriet Bishop McConkey; Tarble is used to the gender equity of manual labor. At the same time that Tarble recalls her work as a young wife, she also injects into the narrative information about her husband's frequent absences at the Lower Agency, for days and even weeks on end. Her loneliness helps explain for her white Minnesota readers (the narrative was published in St. Paul, presumably for a state audience) why she became friends with the nearby Dakotas. "Naturally," she states, "I began to drop into their ways and learned their language," and therefore she believes they almost felt she "belonged to them."[36] As a teenager she would have been not just impressionable but more linguistically adept and culturally flexible than an adult.

Two Native women attended her when she gave birth to her first child at fifteen, and a Dakota shaman instructed her in traditional remedies, furnishing knowledge that allowed her to treat illnesses successfully throughout her life, including those unresponsive to Western medicine. This shaman is believed to be a man named Parent Hawk.[37] Even when other settlers such as her brother-in-law and family moved nearby, she maintained close—even kinship—contact with the Dakotas. "We were very happy and knew no fear," she says, using the inclusive pronoun "we," whether consciously or unconsciously, for herself and her Native friends.[38] Her comment is honest, nostalgic, and strategic, in light of the subsequent irreparable sundering of those ties evident in the narrative soon after.

Tarble's account contrasts in several ways with that of her sister captive, Urania White, who also chose to tell her story decades after the events occurred. First, Tarble's acculturation to Dakota life and her contacts among the local bands initially assured her that she and her family would be safe. Recalling the news of the warehouse break-ins at the Upper Agency two weeks before the war began, she says that she was not frightened because she was "practically an adopted child of the Sioux and had the special protection of their great medicine man."[39] Even when it became clear that her privileged position would not give her complete immunity, she conversed with the Indians in Dakota to buy time and gauge the situation better. Like White, Wakefield, and several other women captives, Tarble was reminded that crying women would be harshly treated, but unlike the other two, her acculturation allowed her to respond with little cultural strain. In fact, she tried to reassure the "very nervous and alarmed" Urania White, a newcomer to the area, and persuade her to conform too.[40] But most of all, Tarble's knowledge of Dakota culture and of the land, plus her own resilience and determination, provided the conditions for her successful escape.

Tarble describes some of the same atrocities as Urania White, for example the killing of Mrs. Henderson and her children, but she does not dwell on their immediate psychological impact as White does. Regarding the burning of Mrs. Henderson, Tarble recognizes a revenge motive for the Dakotas' behavior. She explains that Mr. Henderson had constantly ridiculed the Indian shaman who was Tarble's mentor and even refused his help when he offered to treat Mrs. Henderson because the agency doctor despaired of her recovery. Tarble felt that "the old medicine man" instigated the violence to avenge Mr. Henderson's "insults and abuse" toward him.[41]

Tarble believes that traditional Indian healing is in many ways superior to Western medicine. The shamans, she says, "better understood—or at least better heeded—certain natural laws," and decades later she tells her readers that she believes even more strongly in their teachings.[42] After all, she saved the lives of herself and her children when, not having eaten for days, they were given too much food, too quickly, at Fort Ridgely and became deathly ill. Her self-satisfaction is obvious as she describes how the fort doctor "pooh-poohed" her efforts and told the commanding officer that her daughter, Althea, would die, but how only a week later the child had completely recovered.[43] Earlier, when Tarble first introduces the Native healer into her story, she acknowledges that his wisdom enabled her to help many others after conventional remedies proved useless. But she also concedes that while these treatments helped physical problems, nothing could combat her "fearful mental strain" following the Conflict, save the passage of time.[44]

In contrast to Urania White, who remained a captive for the duration of the war, Tarble's earlier resilience and physical stamina enabled her to escape with her two children after a Dakota woman provided them the opportunity to do so. White and Tarble exemplify two classic symbols of hostage women evident throughout the captivity literature: White is woman as victim, while Tarble is woman as victor.[45] Previously Tarble had stated that several Indian men claimed her, presumably for her toughness and her acculturation to Dakota life, and that Little Crow had ordered her killed because she caused such discord among his soldiers.[46]

A Dakota woman then took her to a field and told her to remove her dress, but she refused unless the woman provided other clothing. An ensuing storm allowed Tarble and her children to make their escape and carefully conceal any traces of their steps. Although they endured rain, thirst, hunger, mosquito bites, and eventually exhaustion, they persisted. Perhaps the most telling symbol of Tarble's will to survive occurs when she finds a boat at the scene of the battle at Redwood Ferry, fought some weeks earlier. Surrounded by death, including a corpse in the boat itself, she first dumps the body and then uses a teacup to bail out water as she and her children cross to the other shore in the leaking craft. The teacup, a signifier of leisure and gentility taken from a ransacked house, instead becomes the means of survival. Once ashore she recognizes where she is and soon reaches Fort Ridgely three days before the siege is lifted, thus enduring a further three days of captivity at the fort.

Tarble's account contains examples of the many instances of intertextuality among the Dakota War narratives. For example, several soldiers and Joseph DeCamp came out to meet Tarble as she approached the fort.

Figure 9. Mary E. Schwandt Schmidt (*left*), Urania S. White (*center*), and Helen M. Carrothers (*right*), 11 September 1907. From the Collections of the Minnesota Historical Society. Used with permission.

DeCamp rushed up to her, mistakenly thinking she and her children were his own family. Tarble also mentions Valencia Reynolds, Mary Schwandt's employer, who was another refugee at Fort Ridgely. In a rare instance of humor Tarble describes how during the siege at the fort she and Mrs. Reynolds roughed up and seized what they believed was an Indian intruder. In fact, it was only another woman in a hoop skirt, trying to find shelter by entering through a window. Each party mistakenly believed the other was hostile.

Women who returned from captivity often had adjustment problems, particularly married women whose husbands suspected rape or consensual sex with Indian men. Throughout her account Tarble hints that her spouse was insensitive to his young wife's needs. For instance, she recalls how terrified she was on first meeting Indians long before the Conflict but comments, "My husband seemed to have little patience with my fears."[47] After her first confinement he left her alone only a day after she and her newborn had tipped out of a sled into freezing water, and she feared that they would both get sick. Immediately after the war she and her children returned to Wisconsin. In spring 1863 the Carrothers family moved to St. Paul and St. Peter, but then the couple split up. In Tarble's words, "After my capture by the Indians there was discord between me and my husband, and at St. Peter we 'agreed to disagree.'"[48] She does not reveal what they quarreled about: perhaps his insensitivity to what she had been through or her behavior while in captivity or both.

After the war Tarble worked for Mr. and Mrs. Reynolds until she remarried. Again, in a pattern discernible throughout a number of captivity narratives, her mental insecurity is mirrored by her physical dislocation as she moved within Minnesota and on to North Dakota, Montana, Oregon, and Washington, losing her second husband, supporting her new young family as a single parent, and finally returning to Minnesota and marrying L. H. Tarble in 1897. As the first-person narrative proper ends, Tarble rationalizes her story by expressing the hope that it will show the hardships of the early European immigrants to a new generation of Minnesotans.

But *The Story of My Capture and Escape* does not end on this note. The final section, covering the Conflict's major incidents and concluding with the Dakota removal to Crow Creek in 1863, shows, first, how the Natives had despoiled the recently formed state, and, second, how the Conflict's national significance had been lost in the country's single-minded focus on the Civil War. Underpinning both rationalizations is the trope of violation. It is clearest in the sexually charged description that "thus situated, thus lovely in her virgin growth, Minnesota had but one dark spot on her fair bosom," namely "the dusky savages."[49]

This quotation provides a classic instance of the male gaze and the male touch, as seen in studies of the rhetoric of exploration and colonialism, particularly those by Annette Kolodny.[50] So it is hard to avoid the conclusion that either a male editor added these flourishes or, more likely, that Tarble lifted information from another text, as she did with the introductory material. The trope also operates in the sense that Minnesota history has been violated or at least subdued by stronger American historical imperatives and priorities. The metaphors are particularly compelling owing to the widespread claims of Indian rape during the war forty years earlier. The contemporaneous rumors of rape and the later supposed land and historical abuse constitute a kind of rhetorical rape in which violator and violated, signifier and signified, are unstable.

A final noteworthy aspect of Tarble's captivity narrative also concerns word choice, this time near the end. After the mass hanging at Mankato the text describes how the remaining male prisoners were sent to Davenport, Iowa, and "placed in confinement." Several Dakota women accompanied them and "shared their captivity," Tarble continues.[51] Doubtless Tarble saw the Dakotas' fate as a particularly ironic role reversal in which the captors themselves had become the captives. Perhaps too she believed this was punishment enough for what she perceived as a betrayal of cordial prewar relations between whites and Dakotas. Since many European Americans similarly claimed an earlier sympathetic relationship between the cultures, both they and Tarble could only resort to the racist stereotypes of innate savagery to explain the Natives' later behavior.

In the experiences of two of the remaining authors discussed in this section, Lillian Everett in this chapter and Benedict Juni in the next, we see the impact of war and captivity on another constituency, namely young children. Gender as well as specific experiences inflect their accounts. Lillian Everett was about six when she was captured

Figure 10. Lillie Everett, 1862. Photo by E. P. Masterson, Port Jervis, New York. Nebraska State Historical Society Photograph Collections. Used with permission.

during the violent Lake Shetek attack; later she remembered very little of what had happened, and what she did recall was traumatic and nightmarish. Benedict Juni, however, was ten when he was taken near New Ulm; decades later he retold (maybe created) events in detail but recast them as every white boy's wilderness adventure fantasy.

In 1894, while preparing an unpublished manuscript called "Early History of Lake Shetek Country," Dr. Harper Workman of Sleepy Eye, Minnesota, contacted survivors of the Lake Shetek incident. Workman provided another instance of the boom in Dakota Conflict information-gathering thirty years after the war itself. One of the people he wrote to was Lillian Everett Keeney, then living in California, to whom he sent a series of questions. She responded in a letter, copied in Workman's typescript, to which he added "Confidential" and "I promised Mrs. Keeney that this letter would not be published."[52] The generic medium of the personal letter encouraged Keeney to provide intimate and authentic information that she really did not want to be made public. After all—like the other Lake Shetek survivors—she would have had ample opportunity to tell her story before if she had wished.

Because the letter has never been published, I quote from it extensively below. At the beginning of her correspondence she muses, "Doubtless you will think it strange that I am able to answer so few of your questions but my health and nerves were so shattered by what I had undergone that the subject was avoided as much as possible for many years, and as I grew older neither my father or myself could speak of it at any length, so it has become a kind of a dream to me and hardly seems my own experience."[53] She continues to address questions Workman posed about other survivors of the Lake Shetek attack but says she does not know much about them. She does, however, acknowledge the kindness and help of Julia Wright during their shared captivity.

The letter then describes colloquially and incompletely what she does remember. Its detached tone may indicate that she has finally come to terms with her past, that she no longer has any interest in it, or that she can speak of it only in these emotionally controlled terms: "I was left beside my dead mother all night as I was wounded and had fainted and they probably thought I was dead, early the next morning two Indians came back on my uncles horses and after going through the pockets of the dead took me with them leaving my baby brother who was wounded but still alive and a little girl (I think Mrs Irelands) who did not seem to be wounded."[54] Matter-of-factly she adds, "I suppose these children starved to death, we never were certain of the fate

of the baby as they did not find his body when burying the others."[55]
The family members who were buried included Lillie's mother and
another brother, so that the only survivors from the Everett family
were herself and her father.

She then concedes that although the captives were not allowed to
congregate, she did not "think the young children were very badly
treated."[56] She was first taken in by an Indian woman who wanted
to get rid of her and who abused her. Two older Dakota women who
had worked for Lillie's mother found, revived, and cared for her. After
this beating often she was too weak to walk unaided, so they carried
her. She singles out for thanks an Indian woman whom she calls "Old
Scalpy," because she had been scalped herself: "She was very kind
to me taking the best care of me she could as I was sick a great deal
after this."[57] Toward the end of the letter she provides some more
information on her father and then apologizes again: "I am sorry I
am not able to give you more information but it is something which
I have always tried to forget."[58] Following are some of the things that
little Lillie Everett did not know when she was taken and chose not
to uncover later on.

As described earlier, the 1862 Lake Shetek attack—almost invariably called the Lake Shetek Massacre in white histories—took place
in western Minnesota and received widespread press coverage. About
a dozen settler families lived there at a fairly basic subsistence level,
though some had been in place for as long as four years. While there is
disagreement about exactly which Indian bands were involved, apparently those of White Lodge, Lean Grizzly Bear, and Sleepy Eyes began
to loot cabins and kill white men on 20 August. An old Dakota whom
the settlers called Pawn and whom they knew from frequent visits to
the area lured them into a nearby marsh with tall reeds. But it was an
ambush, and because the settlers were poorly armed and unprepared,
about a dozen died in what came to be known as Slaughter Slough.

Twenty or so escaped from the slough or sometime during captivity, but White Lodge took a group of women and children hostage and held them for several months until the Fool Soldiers rescued them. While most of the captives were handed over to the authorities in September 1862 at Camp Release, White Lodge's band had never merged with the main body of Dakotas, so it took longer for the hostages he had taken to be recovered.[59] Certain incidents during the Dakota Conflict captured the contemporary imaginary, and the attack at Lake Shetek was one of them; the battles at Fort Ridgely, New Ulm, and Birch Coulee and the freeing of captives at Camp Release were some of the others.

Lake Shetek occupies a particularly sensitive place in European American historical memory for the following reasons: the settlers were initially so defenseless and outnumbered; the death rate within specific families such as the Duleys, the Irelands, and the Eastlicks was especially high; although close to half the residents escaped captivity, many endured terrible hardships, such as the Eastlick family; and several women and children captured by White Lodge and others were abused.[60] William Duley's role at the Mankato hangings is also particularly significant. Duley himself was wounded but escaped during the assault. However, three of his children died, and his wife was injured and apparently raped, though eventually she came back alive along with two of the children who had been in captivity with her. For his losses—his wife and children had not yet been released and were still missing, presumed dead, in December 1862—the authorities gave William Duley the dubious honor of cutting the trip rope that allowed all thirty-eight condemned Indians to be hanged simultaneously. It was a dramatic representation of revenge.

The reuniting of Lillie Everett and her father also captured the popular imagination. She does not describe it in her letter (she was probably too young to remember), but the *Mankato Weekly Record* quotes a journalist from the *Fort Dodge (Iowa) Republican* who was present: "The child took the hand of her father and he pressed her to his bosom; but not a word was spoken by either. The joy of meeting the sole remnant of his family was so saddened by the recollection—so vividly forced upon his mind by the presence of his child—of the fate of his dearly loved wife and darling boys, that the strong man was overcome with emotion. He wept like a child."[61]

After the war William Everett returned to Wisconsin until 1867; he had lived there before moving to Lake Shetek in 1859. He moved back to Minnesota a few years later and then to Oakland, California, where he died in 1892, never having recovered from his wounds, according to Lillian's letter. Lillian Everett lived on the West Coast after 1883 and married twice. Harper Workman notes in his manuscript that at some point after 1911 she visited Lake Shetek for the first time since the Conflict, but "she could not remember ever having seen the Lake before."[62] Time and trauma had erased that memory.

Although Urania White's captivity narrative appeared in the 1901 volume of *Collections of the Minnesota Historical Society*, internal evidence dates it to 1898 (a note after the title saying that the account was read at the monthly meeting of the Historical Society's Executive Council on 14 November 1896 is probably a misprint for 1898). At thirty-one pages it is longer than some of the other Dakota Conflict narratives that appeared in the society's journal. The text has a strong narrative flow, a real descriptive flair, and a clear organization identified by subheadings; in other words, it is a finished piece of writing.

Particularly noteworthy and distinctive is the information White gives on her fragile psychological state during and after her ordeal and on Native customs she observed while living with the Dakotas. The combination of private revelations of psychological duress, minute observation, and ethnographic data makes for compelling reading, and in this sense White writes with a better sense of audience interest and need than some of the other captive authors. As with many hostages throughout history, White was in the public eye briefly when she was released and perhaps later when she published her experiences, but little is known about her otherwise, except for what she tells readers in her text.

Like most of the other European American writers discussed in this section, White came to Minnesota from elsewhere. She was born in New York State in 1825 and married Nathan White in 1845. Two years later they moved to Wisconsin and stayed there for fifteen years. But in the spring of 1862 they were on the move once again, this time to Minnesota, "looking hopefully forward to better times," as she says in her narrative.[63] The implication is that they had gone through some bad experiences in Wisconsin and had therefore decided to head elsewhere. Numerous Indian captivity narratives describe the white characters as living in a bucolic natural environment before the attack; indeed, the term "settlers" indicates that they had found a place to put down roots. Such is the case in the first few pages of White's account, where White mentions the huge trees, bluffs, stream, valley, and wild flowers on her property. Although she heard rumors of war on 18 August, she discounted them until her daughter urged the family to flee (minus White's husband, who was elsewhere on business). During the attack her eldest son was killed and scalped; her twelve-year-old son, Millard, escaped; but she, her daughter, Julia, and her baby boy were captured.

White's document shares with only a handful of other Indian captivity narratives within the entire generic corpus an effective articulation of psychological trauma and distress.[64] For example, after the terrifying attack and attempted flight, in which nine people died and eleven were captured, and after White witnessed the death of her neighbor Mrs. Henderson and two little children (thrown to the ground, covered with a feather mattress, and set alight), she says, "My courage sank as I wondered in a dazed, half insane manner, what would be our fate."[65] Through the aid of the Indian couple who adopted her—of whom she observes, "I cherish with kindest feelings the friendship of my Indian father and mother"—White tried to come to terms with new realities and different cultural norms, such as stifling tears and concealing depression because prisoners were told that those who cried would be killed first.[66]

Yet sometimes she veered between horror and hilarity, as people in extremis sometimes do. For example, she describes the incongruity of seeing Indian children wearing rich looted fabrics and then the sudden realization that the plunder came from her neighbors and friends: "When the laugh died on our lips, the terrible thought crowded into our minds, Where did these things come from? What tales could they tell if power were given them to speak? Where are the butchered and mutilated forms that once wore them? My heart was crushed, my brain reeled, and I grew faint and sick."[67]

A little later White consciously analyzes and explains that had she given in to a true realization of her situation, she would have gone mad and probably would have been killed for such demented behavior. Therefore she distracted herself by looking at the seemingly unimportant things that her captors did. She recalls a particularly chilling incident when she almost lost her grip on reality: "I said to one of my neighbor captives, when we were first made prisoners, that I felt just like singing, so near did I in my excitement border on insanity. I have thought since many times that, had I given up to the impulse and sung, it would have been a wild song and I should have certainly crossed the border of insanity and entered its confines."[68]

White also discusses the excruciating mental torture brought about by her own and her two children's abrupt change in cultural status. Early on, for example, families were separated, and individuals were left to agonize over where the others were and what was happening to them.[69] After stating that sometimes she felt so distraught that she could not eat because when she tried to swallow she choked, White adds, "No bodily suffering, however great, is so keen as mental torture."[70] Later a crisis arises when an Indian threatens to rape White's teenage daughter, Julia. She asks a man called Black Robinson to intervene, but before she knows whether or not he has succeeded, she speaks of being left "to worry over the great danger that threatened" Julia.[71]

White also describes being inside a tepee and unwillingly witnessing a warriors' ritual that involved chanting and beating the ground with sticks: "The horrors of this experience I can never forget. It seemed as though my reason would be dethroned under this terrible, monotonous chant."[72] And then there were the cruel times when she dreamed of more Indian attacks or of having escaped to safety only to wake and discover that she was still imprisoned.[73] At Camp Release White conveys the various reactions among the newly freed hostages, such as joyful tears, hysterical laughter, obsessive chatter, hand clapping, and dancing, though she says that she herself was silent and reflective. Perhaps it took a thirty-year interval for White to retrieve these memories, confront them, and describe them so graphically.

Skillfully interwoven among such carefully observed psychological details are data about Dakota culture. White seems to want to record information about her own private ordeal as well as information about Dakota traditions that by the late nineteenth century had been compromised and changed for many Natives. But there may be another underlying reason why White combines these two discursive strands. Critical theorist Yael Ben-zvi suggests that there are three types of "authenticity" that help define the Indian captivity narrative: historical, literary, and ethnographic.[74] A verifiable historical event (in this case an experience during the Dakota Conflict), filtered through a particular literary genre (the captivity narrative), could gain additional credibility from the inclusion of ethnographic data.

In White's narrative, for example, the information she provides on Indian customs "translated lived experience into explicitly authoritative knowledge and enhanced the internal logic of the text's claim for authenticity."[75] This marriage of the captive survivor and the sociologist is also evident in the 1904 narrative by Helen Tarble, who was captured and held with Urania White. White's narrative refers to Dakota food and cooking practices (including a dog feast), jewelry (noting that the Indians took the wheels from plundered clocks and wore the large ones for earrings and the small ones for bangles), clothing, tobacco, ability to pack up and move quickly, burial practices, face and hair ornamentation, as well as manner of eating, washing, dancing, and carrying babies. Indeed, White comments late in her account that the Dakotas "had rules of etiquette which they strictly observed" and that they often scolded her for her many lapses.[76] But White mentions most of this data in the central part of her narrative, in the sections primarily concerned with her captivity.

The five-week ordeal is framed by initial information on her family background and family members and subsequent details on the family's wanderings close to their ruined homestead; next to St. Peter; then on to St. Paul; to their old home in Wisconsin, where relatives and friends gave then a warm welcome; and finally back to Minnesota, to try their fortunes once more in the spring of 1863. She therefore sees her captivity as a brief but horrific interlude between her family's first unsuccessful attempt to put down roots in Minnesota and their ultimate ability to do so when they returned.

6. Benedict Juni
Captivity and the Boy's Adventure Story

The final captivity narrative in this section, by Benedict Juni, does not fall in the same category as any of the other accounts. Juni was ten years old when taken, and he viewed his stay with the Dakotas as more of a boy's wilderness adventure than a harsh captivity. His later recounting of his experiences, although pejoratively titled *Held in Captivity*, retains his sense of curiosity and optimism, inflected by his age and gender. Older than the traumatized child Lillian Everett but younger than the resourceful teenage mother Helen Tarble, Benedict Juni positively *enjoyed* living with the Dakotas, even under wartime conditions. If his story weren't true, it could have been the basis for a different kind of dime novel than *Indian Jim*, one that catalogs the character-building and exciting adventures of a latter-day Tom Sawyer or Huck Finn.

Mark Twain himself saw the possibilities of placing these ever-youthful characters within an Indian captivity when he wrote *Huck Finn and Tom Sawyer among the Indians*. Twain wrote fifteen thousand words of this manuscript, begun in 1885 as a sequel to *The Adventures of Huckleberry Finn*, then stopped in midsentence and never completed it.[1] The story follows Tom, Huck, and, incredibly, Jim as they join a westering family on the Platte River. A group of Sioux first befriends the group and then suddenly kills the parents and older boys but captures two girls and Jim. Huck, Tom, and a mountain man (!) follow the Indians and prepare to rescue the girls by attacking the camp; however, the manuscript ends at this point. It seems obvious that Twain was extending the famous conclusion to *The Adventures of Huckleberry*

Figure 11. Benedict Juni. From the Collection of the Brown County Historical Society, New Ulm, Minnesota. Used with permission.

Finn, where Huck claims that he can only be comfortable following a westward course toward Indian country: "But I reckon I got to light out for the Territory ahead of the rest."[2] The plot of the unfinished novel appropriates stereotypical captivity tropes, including an Indian attack, the death of family members, the capture not just of two girls but of an ex-slave, and a rescue attempt, all cast, like many fictional captivity narratives, within a picaresque model involving a series of adventures.

But if Twain's truncated manuscript indicates that Twain was unable to resolve the plot of his novel, Benedict Juni's Dakota War escapades, seen through the lens of his later years, provide a valid conclusion to and commentary on his actual experiences.[3] And that conclusion was conciliatory toward the Dakotas. Juni's *Held in Captivity* was published posthumously as a twenty-two-page pamphlet in 1926, appended by a one-page summary his wife wrote about her captivity experiences.[4] Earlier, shorter versions had appeared in a local newspaper before 1908 and within *History of Brown County Minnesota* in 1916, the latter apparently standardized by the volume's editor.[5] Juni's obituary says that his story was so well-known in the area that it was something New Ulm residents "never tired of hearing rehearsed."[6] Written or spoken by himself or others, Juni's experiences had passed into local lore, then, before formal publication.

Juni was born in Switzerland in 1852 and emigrated to Minnesota in 1856. His family first settled in Mankato and then moved near present-day Morton in 1860.[7] In the opening paragraphs of his narrative Juni establishes that his family was in almost daily contact with Natives and that they all learned to speak Dakota. Like several other narrators, such as Wakefield, Sweet, and Tarble, Juni also claims that his family treated the Indians in a fair and friendly fashion before the war. As a mark of reciprocal respect, Juni relates, several Indians warned his father of an impending attack and gave him a new gun to defend himself. Partly owing to the help of other Dakotas, all of Juni's family, except a married sister who chose death over captivity, eventually reached Fort Ridgely.

Juni was separated from the rest because his father sent him to warn neighbors of the danger. Trying to rejoin his parents, Juni saw a dead ferry man and understood that he too was at risk, yet he continually presents himself within his narrative in a self-deprecating, even humorous way. He is neither a heroic rescuer nor a passive victim. Instead he is a naive though somewhat sobered observer who describes death and destruction in a detached tone; at one point he actually mentions his "cool, common sense" under duress.[8] This discursive strategy reflects his boyish inability to comprehend exactly what was going on at the time.

For example, when Juni's captors took him back to his ransacked house, he went up to a neighbor, John Zimmerman, who was "in such a position that I believed he was taking a nap in the shade."[9] As he tried to rouse Zimmerman the Indians smiled. Only then did Juni realize that Zimmerman, as well as Zimmerman's father and younger brother, nearby, was dead. Right after, Juni recalls staying calm, trying to take the family Bible to read because he thought he might be bored while in captivity, and being surprised when told to leave it because it might be an encumbrance. In fact, during much of his seven-week sojourn with the Dakotas Juni spent his time working or playing like other Native children, though latterly he met and interacted with other captives.

Juni established a reputation among the Dakotas as a skillful cattle drover, and they required him to take many teams across the river. He also claims that they regarded him as "quite a prodigy" because he could read and they thought he could write.[10] Partly owing to his adaptability and adeptness, his several captors also became his protectors, and he had specific duties within their households, such as getting water and fuel, feeding and watering the horses and oxen, and obtaining tobacco. He was well-treated and well-fed; he actually says that he "had never lived so well as far as food was concerned."[11] Even though he lost some weight at Camp Release, his friends and relatives still greeted him on his return by saying how fat he was. He possessed both a formal Dakota name (Ta-han-sha) and a nickname (Pa-ska, meaning "white head," for his long, blond hair), and he also wore Dakota dress.

Like Huck Finn, Juni cannot and does not avoid noting violence, but he does not dwell on it. Rather, he constantly returns to the positive aspects of his experience while with the Dakotas. For example, when two girls from his first captor's family came to visit him some distance away, he says that their kindness exemplified a "more practical Christianity than many of our so-called Christians of the white race."[12] And, he continues, such instances support his major narrative aim that readers judge Natives more positively and stop using "vile epithets to hurl against" them. He even admits, "I often long to meet the friends of those days when friends were few but thoroughly appreciated."[13]

As an example of a cultural encounter different from the stereotypical white/Indian war confrontation, Juni describes keeping company with a Dakota girl his age. Though he could have spoken with her, they did not usually talk when they met; instead they silently pored over an album containing tintype pictures and copies of *Harper's Magazine* filled with war illustrations. The irony of these two cultural representatives peacefully viewing war pictures presumably resonated with Juni's early twentieth-century readers. His description is direct and detailed without emotive commentary. Recalling this memory leads Juni to observe that Indians were better parents than whites and were morally superior in other ways.[14] Thus, when told that he must return to white culture at war's end, Juni was unhappy because he had become attached to his new family and his new life. "I had despaired of ever getting back to civilization and was contented with my condition," he says.[15]

Within his narrative the primary identity Juni establishes is that of a curious and honest boy. For instance, he describes with a certain amount of relish every white boy's dream of burning down the schoolhouse and sacking the church, and in the destruction of those symbols of civilization and constraint, his story once again echoes aspects of *The Adventures of Huckleberry Finn*. While the Indians were camped at Hazelwood, half a dozen white captive boys, including Juni, occupied the building that had doubled as a school and chapel at the mission. They ransacked the desks, scattered the books, rang the large bell in the belfry, and shattered the windows. The next day they took rod iron from a workshop in another building and made spears that they hurled against fence posts. Finally, that same evening the boys built "a monstrous bonfire" and burned the Riggs and Williamson houses, among others.[16] Juni is careful to note that his master disapproved of this behavior when told of it. Other captives viewing the conflagration, like John and Mary Renville, assumed that Indians had set it.[17]

Three of the gang members stuck together even when they arrived at an encampment close to Camp Release, but conditions there were so primitive and so much worse than when they were (real) captives that they made "a break for liberty."[18] The other boys escaped successfully and met Sibley's forces, but an Indian wishing to be seen as a liberator recaptured Juni and returned him. Obviously the tropes of captivity and liberty in this incident entwine themselves ironically. As an Indian captive Juni was freer than when he was freed at Camp Release; accordingly he tried to escape his unfree state there, only to be forcibly captured and made to return to what most ex-captives saw as freedom.

More than the other hostages, Juni admits to some cultural confusion, as when he notes, admittedly tongue-in-cheek, that he was becoming Dakota and fully expected to accompany the Indians at the Battle of Wood Lake. However, he was too young to fight, and the Dakotas understood that his mere presence there would place him in a moral bind. After the Indian defeat his captor decided to turn him in rather than subject him to cold and hunger on the move northwest. Also, since they would have to leave the cattle behind, Juni's help as a drover was not needed anymore. Juni's captivity experience trained him in cultural comparisons. He was not the only one for whom this was true: Sarah Wakefield, for example, states that conditions at Camp Release were much worse than during her captivity, and she judges Chaska more positively than many other whites. But there was less at stake for Juni in making similar positive comments about his life with the Dakotas.

First, Juni was a child, not an adult, when captured, and second, he told his tale (and it was a tale) decades later, not immediately afterward, like Wakefield. Third, he was well-treated and, as a male, had far more freedom while captured than girls and women. Finally, the dominantly humorous tone he adopts as an adult narrator enables him to inject pro-Dakota information without much risk of alienating his readers. As evidence of Juni's comic vision, he tells how he became lice-ridden at Camp Release and how his father had to delouse him when they met. Then he adds, "I have shown you so many beams of sunshine that you will pardon me if I have called your attention to a dark shadow."[19] Forget captivity, forget war, forget death and destruction—he claims that one of his darkest memories is of his father harshly scrubbing him to get rid of the vermin! Again, it is hard to ignore the parallel with Huck Finn, for whom the strictures of conventional white society were so onerous.

Like Huck too, Juni is a careful observer, especially of human behavior and cultural norms. At the beginning of his captivity, for example, he describes young Native men armed with new shotguns, gunpowder, and balls, throwing looted tin pans into the river, letting them float downstream a bit, and then shooting at them. He is quick to add that the men were not doing this for sport "but to learn the range and bearing of their new weapons."[20] Elsewhere, like so many other ex-captives, Juni provides information on Dakota words and customs, and he also reveals that even as a youngster he realized that factions existed among the Indians, primarily among the war and the peace parties.[21]

Juni ends his narrative abruptly and humorously by recalling his welcome at Fort Ridgely. There, on his first night, he sat down at the officers' mess for a meal served on china at a linen-covered table. The formality of the occasion suggested that a feast would follow, but Juni was disgusted when the first dish turned out to be the boring but digestible fare he ate at Camp Release: boiled rice and sugar.[22] Unlike some of the other captives, Juni was not scarred for life as a result of his ordeal, and he ends his story on an optimistic note. Juni's later life suggests a well-balanced individual who was a naturalist, educator, and soldier and who continued to live in the same area around New Ulm where he had been captured. His obituary stresses his educational service in the local public schools and states that he followed the vocation of teacher for thirty-four years.[23]

Historians acknowledge "the immense need for self-expression that warfare has always aroused."[24] Accordingly, part 1 of *The War in Words* has examined the discursive strategies European Americans employed concerning the Dakota War and has shown their uses and modifications of the captivity narrative tradition. Some people, like Lillian Everett Keeney, could barely verbalize their experiences, while others devised methods to express the essentially inexpressible. A few, including Benedict Juni, dealt with events that they themselves did not identify as traumatic even if other people did. In each case, however, opening the linguistic floodgates allowed the authors to reclaim and reinterpret experience. Kiowa author N. Scott Momaday believes that "the dichotomy that most closely informs the history of Indian-white relations is realized in language."[25] Therefore part 2 of this book shows how Native Americans involved in the Dakota Conflict voiced their own experiences of confinement and captivity.

Native Americans Narrating Captivity

Introduction

When there is a long matter to state, and a single man designated to state it, there will be probably many things left out, as the memory is uncertain. | Big Eagle (Wamditanka), "Evidence taken by the Indian Peace Commission . . . June 15, 1868"

Listen: imagination is all we have as defense against capture and its inevitable changes. . . . The best weapons are the stories and every time the story is retold, something changes. | Sherman Alexie, "Captivity" (1993)

In the stories we tell, we translate lived experience into narrative; conversely, we rely on narratives to live our lives, make sense of our worlds, engage in production, relate to others, and construct and assert our identities. Is language then, as Nietzsche suggested, a prison-house, narrative captivity? Or is language intrinsically liberating? . . . Or are the moves dialectical? | Scott Lyons, "A Captivity Narrative: Indians, Mixedbloods, and 'White' Academe" (1998)

In 1985 African American literary critics Charles T. Davis and Henry Louis Gates published what was then a groundbreaking examination of the slave narrative.[1] Davis and Gates, however, pointedly titled their book *The Slave's Narrative* to emphasize that the term "slave narrative" rhetorically perpetuates the enslaved person's lost control over his or her own body. Whereas the phrase "slave narrative" further objectifies the person (as an adjective) and privileges the narrative (as a noun), Davis and Gates's preferred term, the "slave's narrative," returns to the slave his or her own self, subjectivity, story, history. By rejecting the traditional term but replacing it with a seemingly cognate but actually opposite one, Davis and Gates challenge the rhetoric of mainstream discourse. Yet despite their persuasive example, and despite increased cultural sensitivity, the genre is still called "the slave narrative." Continuing to operate mostly within the (white) academy, the term is tenacious.[2]

The rhetorical issues surrounding "the Indian captivity narrative" reverse the difficulties that Davis and Gates had with "the slave narrative." For Native scholars "the Indian captivity narrative" is problematic because, contrary to its apparent meaning, the genre traditionally concerns non-Indians captured by Indians. For black scholars "the slave narrative" is linguistically suspect and also controversial since early factual accounts by African Americans were doubted contemporaneously and since white fiction writers so quickly adopted the form, most famously in Harriet Beecher Stowe's *Uncle Tom's Cabin*. Thus the authenticity of both Native Americans' and African Americans' experiences frequently suffers from appropriation, from linguistic labeling, and from blurring of fact and fiction.

But "authenticity" is a complex concept and is not necessarily the same as Western notions of "truth" among historians, anthropologists, and literary critics. Elizabeth Cook-Lynn's essay "Postcolonial Scholarship Defames the Native Voice: Academic Genocide?" explores white and Indigenous criteria for veracity, authenticity, and representation. It focuses on the famous memoir *I Rigoberta Menchu: An Indian Woman in Guatemala* (1984), which has been called "the most important self-told native text of our time."[3] Yet certain mainstream scholars have criticized Menchu's Nobel Prize–winning work for factual inaccuracy, misrepresentation, and even fraud.[4]

Cook-Lynn responds: "Those anthropologists and ethnographers who 'seek truth' through scientific methodology demand that 'memoirs' be factual and truthful, while others who understand the act of remembering in a variety of different ways find the works useful as a way of 'knowing,' rather than a way of 'truth.' This controversy may be nothing more or less than a recognition of the different functions of genre in different disciplines," or it may be "a political challenge rather than a scholarly one."[5] Indian autobiographies—the larger genre that subsumes first-person captivity narratives by Indigenous people—often "'talk back' to Euroamerican society with its own literary strategies," observes Penelope Kelsey.[6]

Responding to this kind of challenge, some contemporary Native American writers and critics now embrace the term "Indian captivity narrative" for its self-evident meaning. Namely, the Indian captivity narrative, even if it is not included within the wider captivity narrative rubric, can indeed concern stories that Indians tell about their own confinements, whether confined *by* European Americans or other Indians, or *to* European Americans or other Indians. By reappropriating and realigning the term—often ironically—Native authors and theorists move toward a discourse of decolonization and encourage others to do the same.[7]

For instance, at the 2004 American Literature Association Conference, the Association for the Study of American Indian Literatures organized a panel titled "Indians Re-Visioning the Captivity Narrative." This was a radical move, considering that Indian captivity narratives had long been considered part of a white literary tradition that tended to stereotype and demonize Native Americans. The first paper, which I gave and which parts of this chapter expand, considered broad definitions of the captivity narrative as applied to Virginia Driving Hawk Sneve's *Betrayed*. As I explain later, Sneve's work operates as a kind of counter captivity narrative because it thwarts, appropriates, and modifies elements of the conventionally Western genre. It avoids ethnic stereotyping of whites and Natives, drawing on its author's bicultural heritage, and it shows, as the historical record bears out, that both groups experienced captivity.[8]

But the second and third papers reexamined and deconstructed Mary Rowlandson's seventeenth-century captivity narrative, which functions as a generic icon for many European American scholars. Betty Donohue's (Cherokee) paper looked at the Indian voices embedded in Rowlandson's account, which are recoverable despite Rowlandson's attempts to mute, misinterpret, or demonize them. And Theresa Gregor's examination of Louise Erdrich's poem "Captivity" (1984) and Sherman Alexie's prose-poem of the same name (1993) showed that while Rowlandson becomes a kind of "apparitional presence" in the poem by Erdrich, she has the same or lesser standing as the Native narrator in the "interstitial narrative" by Alexie. All three panelists acknowledged the captivity narrative as a trope in the Indian texts.[9]

Significantly, at the 2004 Mystic Lake symposium on Native American literatures another session treated the same kind of topic, this one called "Capturing Captivity: Retaking American Indian Captivity."[10] These two panels at national conventions mark a real change, because they represent a further adaptation of the "moveable" captivity narrative form and because they show Indians themselves using captivity narratives as rhetorical empowerment. In this way a Native consciousness—or self-consciousness—about Indian captivity narratives is beginning to "affect the Indian imaginary."[11]

Erdrich and Alexie are not the only contemporary American Indian writers to acknowledge the captivity narrative's archetypal significance and use or otherwise engage with it.[12] Gerald Vizenor in particular has played with the notion of words and terms as both restricting and liberating and has used the rhetoric of captivity in many contexts. In a recent book, *Fugitive Poses* (1998), he explains how the image of the Indian in Rowlandson parallels the image of the alien in UFO abduction stories: "The aliens and *indians* [sic] are simulations of the other in stories and narratives. The abductees and captives are pioneers in their stories, and they encounter the other in adverse dimensions."[13]

Vizenor is particularly fascinated by the ironies of Ishi, reportedly the last survivor of the Yahi (a subgroup of the Yana), who in 1911 appeared in the town of Oroville, California, alone and starving. Anthropologists Alfred Kroeber and Theodore Waterman removed him from jail to the Museum of Anthropology (San Francisco), where he died of tuberculosis in 1916.[14] Ishi's brief spell in prison and his life in the restricted environment of the Museum of Anthropology certainly constitute captivity. Several of Vizenor's works explore Ishi as white culture's ultimate "Wild Man" and constructed Indian but Native culture's ultimate resistance hero, who shared what he wished about his culture and language but never revealed his true name. Indeed, it was Kroeber who came up with "Ishi," which means "man" in Yana, when pressured by rabid reporters to name the Indian.

College teacher Scott Lyons (Ojibwe) adapts the captivity narrative trope in his essay "A Captivity Narrative: Indians, Mixedbloods, and 'White' Academe" by invoking "the signifier as an ironic metaphor multiplicitous in its meanings, as stories open to revision," and by examining the verbal captivity of Indian students in academe.[15] Captivity also undergirds Leslie Marmon Silko's (Pueblo/Laguna) haunting novel about war and identity, *Ceremony* (1977), as well as other poems in Erdrich's *Jacklight* collection apart from "Captivity," especially in the sections "Runaways" and "Hunters." Beth Brant's (Mohawk) moving 1984 short story titled "A Long Story" counterpoints two Native mothers, one in 1890 and another in 1978, whose children have been taken away/captured/removed by the American government, though for different reasons. And of course Janet Campbell Hale (Coeur d'Alene) also confronts captivity in the title, content, and thematics of her 1995 novel, *The Jailing of Cecelia Capture*.

Dakotas too have theorized captivity. Waziyatawin Angela Wilson, in an oral history project, quotes her grandmother telling how family members "were taken as captives down to Fort Snelling" by the U.S. government and then adds that her grandmother "titled this portion of the United States–Dakota Conflict 'Death March,' consciously drawing on the similarities between the removal of Dakota . . . with the Bataan Death March in World War II."[16] Rose Bluestone's (Wahpekute and Mdewakanton Dakota) autobiographical "From My Grandmother I Learned about Sadness" narrates a similar story of her grandmother witnessing her great-grandfather's hanging at Mankato, of the family's detention at Fort Snelling and in a stockade at Fort Thompson, and of their confines at the Santee Agency.[17] And the oral history of Floyd Red Crow Westerman also tells of confinement and captivity.

It opens with this powerful statement: "I am a descendent of those who were hung in the greatest mass execution in American history at Mankato, Minnesota."[18]

I believe that the Dakota Conflict captivity narratives examined in this section, whether spoken and/or written by the Native subjects themselves, present "a hybridized, multidirectional, and multigeneric discursive mode" that sometimes subversively "redefines the boundaries of Euramerican discourse."[19] Or, as Penelope Kelsey observes about the twentieth-century Native autobiographers whose work she examines, "As a result of their engagement with multiple cultural worldviews, the identities that these narrators create for themselves alternately borrow different gender, class, and racial structures from the two or more traditions."[20] However, it is important to understand that the Native authors or subjects produced texts that were as diverse generically and politically as the non-Native ones discussed previously. All the authors or speakers in this book found that the war challenged them by reinforcing identity in some cases but disrupting or reshaping it in others. And naturally all used language to tell their stories, though the original accounts were often translated, mediated, or generically resituated, sometimes by the subjects themselves and sometimes by others, as in oral texts or testimony written down by another hand.

As is well-recognized, the issue of editorial intervention in Native texts is particularly problematical, and a number of theorists have explored its implications. Western intermediaries like anthropologists, journalists, and historians have always "shaped the material they received, sometimes to a large extent, sometimes very little, some by questioning, nearly all by editing, many by merely suggesting that an individual could tell his life at all. Even where the Indian wrote of his own volition, without the aid of an editor—and there are many such autobiographies—one could argue that white society plays the role of collaborator. It is the white society which provided the pen and letters, the questions and the occasion for written autobiography."[21]

Regarding oral history, Serle L. Chapman (Cheyenne) also insists that "the cultural points of references of the interviewee and the interviewer are critical."[22]

Gretchen Bataille and Kathleen Mullen Sands agree that almost all Indian autobiography is collaborative in one way or another, and they examine the two processes, oral and written, that result in Indian autobiographies being published. They further divide oral autobiography into "ethnographic" and "as-told-to" types, though neither the oral/written nor the ethnographic/as-told-to distinction is absolute. Ethnographic autobiography (exemplified here by Good Star Woman) is "a personal document" that a collector edits for its ethnographic, not literary, worth.[23] The as-told-to autobiography, which evolved from the ethnographic one, tends to present a longer life story; use literary strategies such as emotional response, dialogue, point of view, and flexible sequence and structure; and exhibit a clearer sense of audience.[24] Big Eagle's story falls into this category.

In addition to these two forms of originally oral autobiography are two written forms: the Indian-written life story and the consciously literary autobiography that is virtually identical to mainstream American autobiography. The first may be edited before publication, but the key is that an Indian wrote it down first.[25] The accounts by Paul Mazakutemani, Maggie Brass, and Nancy Huggan are good examples of the first type; probably none of the Dakota War texts I have chosen falls squarely into the second category of belletristic autobiography.

Further, the date of composition and the circumstances under which the information was told, published, revised, and/or republished were often connected with the subject's political and personal allegiances regarding the Conflict. The closer the texts were to 1862, the more likely that the Indian writers or tellers whose work appeared in print either were, or said they were, accommodationists. Only later, with the passage of time, might Dakotas be more willing to speak frankly and the majority press be more willing to publish responses dissenting

from the prevailing mainstream ideology. However, even today the
Dakota community is disunited over whether to make originally private
and frequently painful accounts of the Dakota Conflict more public,
either for other Dakotas or for a wider readership. This may have to
do with Dakota cultural practices of privacy, as well as the familiar
fact that in 1862 Dakotas themselves were divided over whether to
support the U.S. government against those who rose up against it.
Sometimes family members turned against each other over this very
issue. Retelling the story of Solomon Two Stars, who felt compelled
to shoot his own nephew, Florestine Kiyukanpi Renville concludes,
"I believe the oppression here by whites was so intense that it sometimes meant choosing one's own safety and remaining alive instead
of helping relatives."[26]

For Dakotas the notion of a civil war operated essentially on three
levels: intratribal war, state war, and national war. Big Eagle understood all too well the divisive power of these swirling issues in his
assessment of prewar loyalties: "Then a little while before the outbreak
there was trouble among the Indians themselves. . . . There was a
white man's party and an Indian party. We had politics among us and
there was much feeling."[27] The following narratives show how these
profound disagreements affected the Dakotas' treatment of each other
and of non-Natives during and after the Conflict. They also drama-
tize the war of words that determined the Conflict's oral and written
representations.

In the lead-up to war traditionalists sometimes targeted assimilation-
ists by exiling them from their communities and relatives, mocking
them for adopting Western ways, and destroying their crops. If non-
Natives such as missionaries made moves to protect the conciliatory
Indians, it further intensified the inter- and intratribal differences.
Therefore traditionalists forced progovernment Dakotas to choose
between warring against their own people and warring against a perceived common enemy, the encroaching Europeans. Those Dakotas

with the greatest exposure to white culture, for example the ones affiliated with the ABCFM missions, were usually the most vocal opponents of the war and the most likely to help European Americans.[28] In this book the narratives by Paul Mazakutemani, Lorenzo Lawrence, Cecelia Campbell Stay, and Maggie Brass, among others, represent an accommodationist viewpoint.

Prominent in the progovernment lobby were many people from a European American/Native American background who found themselves in a particularly difficult position during the Conflict because European Americans and Dakotas vied for their loyalty. The narratives by bicultural authors signify a range of responses illustrating their liminal status and their ability to negotiate or exploit both sides of the ethnic divide. As cultural intermediaries they might straddle borders and use them as "pathways that link peoples rather than barriers that separate them."[29] Coming from two or more ethnic, cultural, and linguistic backgrounds, some mixed-blood Dakotas were skilled brokers between two often conflicting societies, while others identified with a single culture.[30] Although none fashioned themselves as the "tragic mulattos" of so much nineteenth-century fiction, it is clear that people of mixed race were culturally vulnerable. First, the prowar Dakotas captured them, killed them, or coerced them to readopt a range of traditional tribal practices and held many of them captive during the war. Second, some non-Natives were quick to assume that those from a blended racial background would invariably support the war.

The following quotation shows just how complex the makeup of this white/Dakota community was: "Some were the children, grandchildren, or even great-great-grandchildren of French voyageurs and Dakota women and can be called Franco-Dakota people. Others had English or Scottish ancestors and can be characterized as Anglo-Dakota people. In 1862 their numbers were significant, comprising roughly 15 percent of the Dakota reservation population. Some of the mixed-bloods identified closely with the tribal group and had substantial influence in Dakota councils. Many of the others who became entangled in the conflict were made captives by the Indian warriors."[31] And some ethnically blended people were not just of white/Native background, but of black/white/Native ancestry, further complicating their identity and loyalty. The following chapters reveal how all these Dakotas remembered and retold various forms of captivity and confinement.

7. Samuel J. Brown and Joseph Godfrey
Captivity and Credit

The captivity narratives of Samuel J. Brown and Joseph Godfrey (Otakle), both of whom came from mixed-race backgrounds, are the earliest of my chosen texts in part 2 regarding original composition. Not surprisingly they illustrate conflicting cultural identities and agendas that affected the presentations of captivity and confinement. Specifically Brown and Godfrey framed their accounts to conform simultaneously to white readers' expectations of mainstream captivity narratives but also to convey the quandaries of the first-person narrators. The narratives originally appeared in Heard's *History of the Sioux War*, having been obtained from oral testimony and interviews.

But Brown's account had greater long-term visibility than Godfrey's because it was rewritten, augmented, and reoriented by Brown himself and by others. The three versions of Brown's story used here come from Heard (1864); from Brown's own text *In Captivity* (1897, 1900); and from *Stirring Adventures of the Joseph R. Brown Family* (1933, 1947), by Samuel's nephew George Allanson. They occur at key points in Brown's biography or reputation: first as a teenage witness-participant; then as a middle-aged businessman, journalist, and missionary with a white primary identity; and finally as a family member whose exploits are proudly placed by others within a larger and longer generational framework.

Both Brown and Godfrey used their stories to credit or validate their own actions and attitudes. In this way they adapted a standard use of the captivity narrative: helping to authorize a captive's behavior during and after captivity. This impulse recognizes that in war a

Figure 12. Samuel J. Brown, February 1866. From the Collections of the Minnesota Historical Society. Used with permission.

prisoner "is doubly unfree, since he is not set loose from his former allegiance, or so he is told, by his captivity. If he is forced to face his captors, bound or at gunpoint, he must also look over his shoulder to the authorities of his own state."[1] One of the best-known examples of such cultural work occurs in Mary Rowlandson's account, where she feels it necessary to insist that she was not violated. Despite being held by Indians "that feared neither God, nor Man, nor the Devil," she assures her audience that "not one of them ever offered the least abuse of unchastity to me, in word or action. Though some are ready to say, I speak it for my own credit; but I speak it in the presence of God, and to his Glory."[2] Contrary to female captives like Rowlandson, Brown and Godfrey did not need to reassure readers of their sexual purity; instead they wanted to establish other kinds of credit and credibility with their mostly white readers.

Samuel J. Brown was born in 1845, one of the many children of

Susan Frenier Brown and her influential but controversial husband, Major Joseph R. Brown. Susan Brown came from a Franco Dakota background; she was a half-sister of Gabriel Renville and was related through him to Little Crow himself.[3] A sometime land speculator, frontiersman, and newspaperman, Joseph Brown became agent to the Dakotas in 1857. He was in the forefront of various measures to make them self-sufficient, including farming, yet he was also mindful of traditional Sioux culture, and he recognized and invoked his many Dakota kinship ties.[4] However, whether he did so out of cultural respect or out of profit and pleasure-seeking is unclear (he was a notorious womanizer and had children with women other than his Dakota and Ojibwe wives). Samuel received a formal education and then studied for the ministry at Seabury Divinity School, but he was on vacation at his parents' well-appointed home near the Upper Sioux Agency when war broke out.

Isaac Heard includes Brown's story as one of three first-person captivity narratives in the middle of *History of the Sioux War*, sandwiched between those of Joseph Godfrey and Sophia Huggins. In terms of gender and ethnic representation, they make an interesting trio. Heard predisposes readers to be favorable toward the Browns in his introductory descriptive paragraph. He stresses the family members' status in the white community by identifying them as "Major Joseph R. Brown's wife and children"; he says that they live in "a very fine stone house, elegantly furnished," to show their wealth and sophistication; and he describes Samuel as "a remarkably intelligent boy" whose story is therefore trustworthy.[5] Joseph Brown's powerful position may well have encouraged Heard to flatter him by favorable descriptions of his family.

Indeed, Samuel Brown's six-page account, which follows Heard's introduction, is most concerned with basic chronological information and a few telling details, rather than lengthy description or judgmental commentary. It certainly has the feel of eyewitness testimony fashioned into a rough narrative, which is exactly how Heard characterizes it:

"Samuel Brown . . . narrated to the writer the following particulars connected with the affair."[6] Brown begins by saying that on 18 August, while he was at the Yellow Medicine Agency, an Indian warned him that Dakotas were killing whites at the Redwood Agency. Because Joseph Brown was away, Susan Brown had to negotiate the family's safety. In this first account Samuel sets up a narrative strategy that becomes even stronger in the later version: his mother's reactions form the touchstone for the group's response. Her quick wits were soon needed since, only a few miles away from home while trying to reach Fort Ridgely, they and their neighbors were captured by Cut Nose, Shakopee, Dowannie, and others.

Samuel conveys the tension as Susan identified herself and bargained with the three warriors. When Dowannie said he would kill the entire party, an Indian intervened whom Susan had helped in the past. Having ensured her family's safety, she then defended the white men accompanying her and finally prevailed. For a while John Moore and his relatives sheltered the Browns, but then the two eldest Brown sons, Angus and Samuel, took a message to Little Crow from Susan. Once under Little Crow's protection the Browns bided their time until their relative Joseph Akipa Renville arrived. As Samuel says in ending his story, "From that time until our deliverance we remained with our relatives, and were well treated by them."[7] Thus the narrative time frame covers only Samuel's six-week captivity.

Samuel handles other unpleasant events matter-of-factly, probably owing to his youth, sense of immediacy, and eyewitness status (his later retelling reflects the different personal and cultural moment and may indicate the increased control he was able to exercise over his story's publication). After being captured, for example, he saw "three men and a woman on the road terribly hacked up. This party [i.e., his captors] had committed the murders. The men had been mowing together; their scythes and pitchforks lay near." A little later he states that Cut Nose "went to a wagon, and told a Scotch girl who was in it that he wanted her for his wife, and to get out and follow him. She refused, and then he drew his knife and flourished it over her, and she got out and went away with him."[8] Despite the implication of rape Samuel does not moralize or add further information. In fact, the only narrative commentary he makes elsewhere in this version concerns the kindness of Little Crow and his other Indian relatives and friends.

Samuel Brown's life changed considerably between the captivity narrative in Heard's book and the account he wrote and published thirty-four years later. He did not return to his theological studies after being freed at Camp Release. Instead he joined the newly organized Scout Force of Sissetons and Wahpetons. These men either had not been charged or had been acquitted, and they were made responsible for capturing fellow Dakotas who were still at large.[9] Here is how the scouts operated, according to information on the Sisseton-Wahpeton Lake Traverse Reservation Web site: "On the western side of the Lake Traverse Reservation, the Army established Fort Wadsworth, later re-named Fort Sisseton, where the Sisseton Wahpeton leaders, under force of Army Cannon, were ordered to establish up to 30 scout camps where they were to detect any of the other Dakota people who had escaped from Minnesota and were trying to return to Minnesota. General Sibley's orders were very clear, as he ordered them to TAKE NO PRISONERS, and should they fail in regard to this order, they and their families themselves would be killed by the Army."[10]

This practice has an even wider and more sinister aspect in European American/Indian relations, as indicated in the following comment: "Numerous unthinkably barbarous customs the whites intimidated the Indian into adopting, including their own employment as black and Indian slave hunters, and as mercenaries to fight the whites' wars."[11] And Florestine Kiyukanpi Renville poignantly recalls how she used to feel ashamed of her great-grandfather, Gabriel Renville, because he led the scouts.[12] Later she came to understand the complex war and the terrible decisions it forced Dakota families to make.

From 1862 until 1866 Samuel served in various scout positions at Fort Wadsworth under his father's command, and after Joseph Brown resigned Samuel became acting military agent for a while. But on 19 April 1866 he rode to another scout camp to warn of an impending Indian attack. When he arrived and realized it was a false alarm, he immediately rode back that night in severe weather to alert his commanding officer. This heroic action, remembered in Minnesota as its own version of the ride of Paul Revere, left Brown crippled and unable to continue in the military. So he returned to Browns Valley, where he became postmaster and ran various businesses. In the 1870s he joined the editorial staff of the *Daybreak*, a newspaper dedicated to assimilationist Indian interests, took charge of the government school at Crow Creek for a while, and worked as a lay missionary.

The *Mankato Weekly Review* first published *In Captivity* from March to May 1897. Brown says in a prefatory note that he "gleaned" the material from diaries that he and other relatives kept at the time and that he originally prepared it for the Minnesota Historical Society at Governor Marshall's request.[13] This occurred during the 1890s, when Marshall briefly became secretary of the society and asked many participants to submit data on the Conflict, as discussed in the previous section on European American texts. The *Mankato Review* then published the story as a separate pamphlet that the U.S. Senate republished in 1900. The booklet's many subheadings suggest its origin as a newspaper story needing to be divided into manageable paragraphs with topic titles. Brown provides much more explanation about the war's causes and consequences, extends the chronological information to 1866, increases the role of Susan Brown, stresses the innocence of the Upper Sioux bands of Sissetons and Wahpetons, and adds descriptive details and moral judgments that enlarge the Heard version sixfold. As Sissetons, the Brown family stood to benefit legally and financially from a clearer differentiation between the Upper and Lower Sioux bands' involvement in the war.[14]

Brown's first section gives a brief history of the eastern Sioux. It acknowledges the problems of delayed food distribution and annuity payments and explains that almost the entire prowar lobby came from the Lower Agency. However, much of the narrative proper focuses on aspects that a primarily white readership would expect and even relish, such as Susan Brown's assertiveness toward the hostile Dakotas; the warriors' cruelty; the captives' sufferings; Little Crow's motivation; and Samuel's postwar role as interpreter and scout, including his heroic ride.

For instance, when the family is first captured, Samuel conveys his mother's words and actions as he does at many other textual sites: "She knew that to save us she must speak and make herself known. She must do so quickly or we would be killed. So she stood up in the wagon, and, waving her shawl, she cried in a loud voice that she was a Sisseton, a relative of Waanatan, Scarlet Plume, Sweetcorn, Ah kee pah, and the friend of Standing Buffalo; that she had come down this way for protection and hoped to get it."[15] Samuel also reveals his racism in describing the Dakotas Susan confronts as "perfect man-eaters in appearance" who needed to be restrained because if they began "killing and scalping in her presence their savage natures would become uncontrollable and we would all meet the same fate."[16] Using such prose was of course standard at the time and also helped Brown to reinforce his own white, "civilized" identity. A little later Samuel describes Susan's disapproval of Dowannie's scare tactics in dashing toward the party with his gun cocked. Increased use of dialogue—some of it surely fabricated after such a long time lag—also heightens the drama between Susan and the Dakota rebels.

Eventually, after Susan applied to Little Crow for protection, the family moved to his quarters as prisoners until they joined their other relatives. The account suggests that Susan became Little Crow's confidant initially, as he revealed how the war began, how the military strategy evolved, and how the insurgents dealt with increasing losses.[17]

Although Little Crow told her that young hotheads had started a war that he initially opposed, "he joined them in their madness against his better judgment, but now did not regret it, and was never more earnest in his life."[18] Samuel, however, did not interpret Little Crow's admission as a spontaneous confession but as a calculated move to gain support from the Upper Reservation Dakotas through Susan's influence. If this was indeed Little Crow's plan, it failed, because the prowhite faction gained more, rather than less, control.

In Captivity also describes violence more graphically than the earlier version, some of it signaled by inflammatory headings like "Savage Brutality," "Our Scalps Demanded," and "Killed a Whole Family—Hellish Brutality." Two examples involving Cut Nose contrast with the earlier versions of the same episodes. Brown now spends one paragraph on the incident in which Cut Nose killed four people mowing and says that two of them had their farming tools stuck into their bodies. He then fills another paragraph with racist rhetoric to describe "the Fiend Cut Nose."[19] Additionally he expands, dramatizes, and sentimentalizes the episode involving the Scots girl, identifying her not by ethnicity but by beauty and saying that she only submitted because she thought she would be scalped. It is hard to know whether these details were true or whether Brown added them to vilify Cut Nose.

Heard's account ends logically with the Brown group's release from captivity, but In Captivity contains an interesting reverse captivity, with Brown essentially as captor and the Dakotas as captives, and it concludes with Brown's famous ride in 1866. After his own release Brown details his position as scout and interpreter in helping to confine the Dakota men who had not fled but were camped with their families near the Upper Sioux Agency. He rationalizes the military's actions in bringing about the men's arrest and custody by tricking them into thinking that the annuity payments would finally be disbursed, by telling them that they and their families should report to the warehouse, by separating the men from the women and children, and by disarming the men so that they could be taken without resistance. "In this way," Brown boasts, "we succeeded in arresting and safely detaining in custody 234 of Little Crow's fiercest warriors."[20]

Was he really unaware of the irony and inaccuracy of this statement, since many of the "fiercest warriors" had already left the state and many of those he helped to capture were innocent?[21] Denying or at least downplaying his Dakota heritage consolidated his identity as a white man and reflected the influence of his father. He further reinforces that role at the end of the text by detailing his heroic night ride and concluding that although he was physically wrecked afterward, he had done his duty. That ride formed the basis of several accounts, variously titled "Night Ride of Samuel J. Brown" (1900), "Samuel Brown's Night Ride" (1900), and "Sam Brown's Ride to Save St. Paul" (1913). The last one was written by Ludvig S. Dale, published in the Boy Scouts magazine *Boys' Life*, and illustrated by a young Norman Rockwell.[22]

Samuel Brown died in Browns Valley in 1925. One obituary commented, "A pathetic feature of the funeral service were the Indians who hovered on the outskirts of the crowd—true mourners for one always ready to help them in their perplexities."[23] But if Dakotas paid their respects because he was kin, Brown did not identify with that side of his heritage as an adult. His narrative *In Captivity* "revealed a man who thought and wrote as a non-Indian vehemently opposed to the Dakota warriors."[24] Waziyatawin Angela Wilson puts it even more forcibly: "Samuel Brown, thoroughly indoctrinated with racist ideology that condemned the 'savage Indian,' betrayed his Dakota people."[25] Including this and similar prowhite accounts within the present section, "Native Americans Narrating Captivity," reinforces the fact that some people of mixed ancestry, especially among the elite, accepted and were accepted by European American society for class or cultural reasons despite their Native roots.

In 1933 George G. Allanson wrote the twenty-page booklet *Stirring*

Adventures of the Joseph R. Brown Family, published by the *Sacred Heart (Minnesota) News* and submitted to a Minnesota Tourism Bureau contest on the Dakota Conflict of 1862. Then in 1947 the *Wheaton (Minnesota) Gazette* republished it in article and afterward in booklet form. Only fifteen years away from the war's centenary the editorial prefacing the 1947 pamphlet quotes a local history that blames the government for kindling the war: "The officials at Washington and their representatives on the reservation were solely responsible for the great massacre."[26] When Allanson's narrative begins, it is clear that his mother—Samuel's sister Ellen—as well as other relatives had furnished supplementary information for the publication, although he sticks to *In Captivity*'s basic organization, content, and even wording.

To give one example, Allanson provides specifics on the Browns' magnificent nineteen-room, three-and-a-half-story stone house, filled with New York furnishings before the war, and he details the incident in which Susan Brown rescued an Indian one winter who later intervened when she was captured. In addition to recounting the Brown family's capture and release in 1862, Allanson punctuates his narrative with information on and photographs of later family visits to historic sites, providing a sense of continuity with the past and a willingness to engage with it. For instance, the booklet includes a photograph of the remains of Joseph and Susan Brown's home and mentions visits to it; to the ruins of Fort Ridgely; and to Little Crow's house, which was still standing in 1920. There is a much greater sense in this publication that it concerns the entire family unit, rather than just Samuel or even Susan.

The background and biography of Joseph Godfrey (Otakle, sometimes also called Gussa) are much different from Samuel Brown's. For Godfrey was mixed-race by heritage, Dakota by culture, and nonelite by class. Although Heard's *History* comprises the best-known source for his story, other resources extend our knowledge of him. These include Godfrey's verbatim evidence before the Sioux War Trials Commission hearings, his testimony regarding other prisoners, and information that whites and Dakotas provided about him. Yet although he exists as subject and object, informational and interpretive gaps remain. He may have wanted it that way; he may have had no other choice.[27]

To begin with, it is unclear exactly when Godfrey was born. One major reason is that he was a slave in the territory that became Minnesota, and records of slave births were often indeterminate.[28] Most studies use his opening statement in Heard, that he was twenty-seven when war broke out, and thus infer that he was born in 1834 or 1835. When Godfrey was called upon to give his age in a series of Santee census reports, it was always consistent with these dates.[29] Thus the birth date of 1827 on his gravestone at the Santee Indian Reservation is almost certainly wrong, which is not surprising, as it was erected many years after he died. It does, however, list the correct date of death, 1909.

Godfrey's place of birth and parentage, however, are certain: he was born in Mendota to a French Canadian voyageur also named Joseph Godfrey and an enslaved black woman owned by Alexis Bailly, a fur trader. Brought up as a slave in Bailly's household, Godfrey moved with him to several Minnesota locations but then, as a teenager, "ran away from an abusive master, seeking sanctuary among the Dakotas as a fugitive slave."[30] He was in his twenties, living at the Lower Sioux Agency, when he married Wakpaduta's daughter Takanheca, of Wabasha's Mdewakanton Dakota band.[31]

As a Dakota, Godfrey farmed and wore European dress. Like some other part-black, part-Native people, his status as an Indian was better than his status as an African slave.[32] While Samuel Brown was physically captured by prowar Dakotas, Joseph Godfrey claims that he was psychologically pressured to join the Dakota war effort and then jailed by the military for his actions. He was charged with murdering at least seven whites and with fighting in key battles. As Walt Bachman, Godfrey's biographer, says, in court he "told his story eloquently in a soft-spoken and respectful voice, in lilting French-accented English" that magnetized the tribunal and helped sway it to change the original death sentence.[33]

Right from the opening statement that an armed Indian approached and threatened him, Godfrey's testimony weaves a consistent thread of Dakota coercion: "He asked which way would I go, he said it twice. I said I couldn't tell. I had my wife and children and didn't want to be killed."[34] Challenged by the warring Dakotas to take sides, Godfrey conveys his dilemma to the court. He then provides more rhetorical clues to what he swears was involuntary behavior, although he dressed and acted as a combatant during the war. For example, often he indicates that he was "told" to do things—to follow the Dakotas; to kill or be killed; and to join the war parties at New Ulm, Birch Coulee, and Wood Lake. At other times, such as when he approached New Ulm, he says he resisted involvement in the fighting. Although he admits being present and armed at several skirmishes, he asserts that he either did not shoot or shot at random—in other words, that he took evasive action.

Following Godfrey's testimony, Mary Schwandt, Mattie Williams, and several others provided additional but ambivalent data. Mary Schwandt's testimony both exonerated ("I didn't see him have any arms," "I didn't see him lay his hands on any of the persons," "Never saw the prisoner treat anyone harshly") and incriminated him ("He acted to me as if he was there willingly, he acted just the same as the Indians did").[35] Mattie Williams agreed that he "appeared to be a willing member of the party." And one of the other witnesses, Franco Dakota captive David Faribault Sr., damned Godfrey for the following reasons: fighting in several battles, admitting that he had tomahawked seven men, killing children, and being part of the Dakota war party.

The first-person account in Heard is fleshed out with more details and is regularized in terms of grammar and word choice. This strongly suggests editorial intervention; in fact, Heard's parenthetical or asterisked comments occasionally correct Godfrey's information. But Heard also apparently obtained additional post-trial data from Godfrey, because there are references to Dakotas who were convicted later. This lapse may also have given Godfrey even more incentive and opportunity to present himself as an unwilling participant. For instance, he further rationalizes his motivation for joining the prowar Dakotas by saying that he bowed to pressure from his wife's relatives and by reinforcing that he was terrified to refuse. He admits using violence but depicts himself as an accessory to crime rather than a killer, and sometimes he even claims to be a rescuer, as when he helped Mary Schwandt and the other two girls taken with her. When he recalls speaking with the dying Mary Anderson, he makes this significant statement: "I said I was a prisoner too. She asked what would be done with them. I said I didn't know; perhaps we would all be killed."[36] Thus he puts himself on a par with the captive girls, despite appearing to be allied with their captors.

While Godfrey's primary concern is self-fashioning within the pages of Heard's history (regardless of whether that persona is true or false), through extended description he also displays his verbal power to arrest, convict, or reprieve other Dakotas. These include Mazabomdu shooting an old lady and kicking several children; Wakantanka mutilating a dying man; and Wakpaduta, his father-in-law, shooting a bedridden woman. All three of them were hung at Mankato. But a good word from Godfrey was worth its weight in gold. When he and an old Indian named Wazakuta saw two dead girls whose "clothes were turned up" (i.e., who had been raped), Godfrey says that Wazakuta expressed concern and "put them [the clothes] down"; Godfrey then adds: "He is now in prison. . . . He is a good old man."[37] Wazakuta was not only removed from the execution list, he was acquitted.

Godfrey's testimony against others and their responses to him in the court transcripts reveal tensions and inconsistencies that may never be fully explained. He supplied evidence—much of it amazingly detailed—in fifty-five of the cases, and he testified in the trials of eleven of the thirty-eight Dakotas who hung.[38] Some of the convicts agreed with Godfrey's version of events or changed their stories after he challenged or prompted them. But other prisoners contradicted Godfrey, such as Mazabomdu and Wakpaduta. Godfrey's father-in-law categorically stated that Godfrey fought and killed willingly: "The colored man went of his own free will. with us [sic]. Ta-o-pe brought word that the Indians were all going below to New Ulm—that they were going to kill all the Whites. The Negro then went because willing."[39]

The court initially agreed with Wakpaduta's version and sentenced Godfrey to death despite credible gaps in his testimony and despite his service to the state. This was followed by a plea for clemency, but a handwritten note from General Sibley states, "Recommendations for commutation of punishment not adopted."[40] However, a renewed recommendation, dated 5 November 1862, reads: "His testimony has been invaluable to the State, for without it a very large number of men of the very worst character would have gone unpunished. His evidence has always proved truthful. His services warrant the exercising of judicial clemency."[41]

In 1886 a series of articles appeared in the St. Paul Dispatch questioning whether or not Godfrey had been executed. Memories were short among the Minnesota white populace about individual Dakotas' postwar fate. Even when a reporter questioned Sibley himself on the matter, he could only say that "to the best of his recollection" Godfrey had been spared. The article continued, "Godfrey was much the most valuable witness in the case" because "he made such clear, decisive statements on the witness stand, and questioned the Indians so closely regarding their evidence, that they were forced to speak the truth. The negro, the general said, was a bright, smart scoundrel" whose own evidence should have hung him.[42]

A day later R. O. Sweeny responded to this article. In 1862 he had sketched some of the imprisoned Dakotas, including Godfrey, and he recalled, "The officers seemed to like the fellow, and I think it

Figure 13. Joseph Godfrey (Otakle), 26 December 1862. Ink wash, by Robert O. Sweeny. Original in the Minnesota Historical Society Art Collection. From the Collections of the Minnesota Historical Society. Used with permission.

was through their recommendation he escaped the fate of the others, who were largely convicted through his aid and assistance."[43] Several scenarios might explain the officers' interest. First, Godfrey could have convinced them that he really was compelled to fight but that he evaded participation where possible, in other words, that he was innocent. Quite a few other Dakotas made the same claim of compulsion, and many were telling the truth. As further support, we now know that two other black men feared the Dakotas' wrath as war broke out: one was killed on the first day, and the other left his Dakota wife and sought refuge among whites.[44] Second, Godfrey could have completely manipulated the court despite the fact that he was guilty of both participation and murder, as originally charged. Obviously

Godfrey's ability to elicit confessions from the accused, or failing that, to provide seemingly incontrovertible proof of their guilt through his own testimony, was the surest evidence to secure convictions. Indeed, his role evolved from "the key state's evidence witness into a bilingual inquisitor."[45]

But perhaps the most interesting theory for Godfrey's attraction appears in the pages of Heard's history (repeated in Bryant and Murch), where he is compared to a providential instrument: "He seemed a 'providence' specially designed as an instrument of justice."[46] His accusers even gave him the benefit of the doubt when they questioned him about his Indian name, Otakle, which means "Many kills." It would indeed seem to refer to his having killed many people. But Godfrey convinced the court that he was given this name when he entered a house where many whites had been killed—by others. Again there is a potentially plausible explanation, namely that his presence near so many dead was an example of "counting coup" in Dakota culture, in which the first one to approach or make contact with an enemy was considered to have killed him.[47]

Godfrey was a more shrewd and powerful incarnation of someone else from a slave background who turned state's evidence under duress. During the Salem Witch Trials of 1692 Tituba, an Indian slave from South America transported to New England via the West Indies, named names and bought herself enough time to avoid the death penalty for witchcraft. Like Godfrey, Tituba came up with extremely detailed information that was used to convict others. In fact, it was so descriptive that she probably fabricated it. If the legal proceedings during the Salem Witch Trials had not been so irregular (another similarity that both sets of trials share), Tituba's evidence might not have been so influential. Still imprisoned when the hysteria died down, she was sold to pay for her keep while jailed, as was common in the seventeenth century for all prisoners, and disappeared from the white historical record.[48]

Godfrey served a prison term at Davenport, Iowa, from 1863 to

1866, until he was pardoned. He removed to the Santee Reservation in Nebraska, where he lived until his death in 1909. Similar to Tituba after her moment of fame, Godfrey became invisible to white society following his imprisonment, but unlike her, he became visible once again in old age. In 1907 Clarence Paine lodged some notes on Godfrey at the Nebraska State Historical Society and observed: "He has lived for upwards of forty years as a peaceable, industrious and temperate man. Indeed, his conduct has been so exemplary that his guilt of the murders with which he was charged, has been a matter of debate."[49]

The *Morton (Minnesota) Enterprise*, however, printed an inflammatory article on 23 July 1909 titled, "Gusa Godfrey Is Dead," and characterized him in its subtitle as "The Man Who Was the Leading Actor in That Blood Thirsty Drama." It concluded, "He was despised by the whites and Indians alike and for 47 years lived a horrible existance [*sic*], —a prisoner from his own conscience."[50] Both whites and Dakotas had reason to loathe him, whites for his violence and Dakotas for his betrayal. The comments by Paine and by the *Enterprise* reporter reach diametrically opposite conclusions: was Godfrey a reformed prisoner or a captive of his conscience?

Prompted by Godfrey's death and by the *Morton Enterprise* articles, Minnesota banker and Dakota War veteran Theodore Carter sent a letter to the Santee Indian Agency Superintendent, Major F. E. McIntire. Carter was also an amateur historian, and he wanted information on Godfrey for an article he was preparing about the Conflict. McIntire spoke to Dr. George Quinn, son of Dakota War participant George Quinn (Wakandayamani), and sent a letter back.[51] However, considerable doubt exists about Quinn's reliability, and at the very least the information McIntire passed on was second- or thirdhand.

Dr. Quinn had known Godfrey since they were young and said that Godfrey spoke French, German, English, and Dakota quite well (it is not likely, however, that Godfrey could read and write, as Quinn also claimed). He stated that Godfrey did not have enough status among

Figure 14. Gravestone of Joseph Godfrey at the Santee Sioux Indian Reservation, Nebraska. Photo taken by Elroy E. Ubl, New Ulm, Minnesota. Used with permission.

the Dakotas to be part of war plans and that in fact "he was treated like a dog while among the Indians. He was talked to by the Indians and told that everyone who married into the tribe as he did was expected to exhibit his bravery."[52] Godfrey supposedly did this by killing an entire family near New Ulm and bragging about it, something that Quinn not only knew about but that another Santee had verified. Quinn gave other details about Godfrey's precise involvement that corroborated some of Godfrey's claims, for example, his role in helping the three captured girls Mary Schwandt, Mattie Williams, and Mary Anderson.

On Godfrey's postwar life Quinn had this to say: "He was treated like a fugitive from justice by both Indians and whites, and many attempts were made to kill him, and his life was undoubtedly prolonged by the intervention of Major Stone, Acting Indian Agent, who told the Indians that any one who killed Godfrey would be hung. On this account no attempts were made on his life while on the reservation but as soon as he was off they were after him and he had many narrow escapes."[53] Godfrey married three times; all his wives were Dakota women. At his death he left several sons, including his namesake eldest son, Joseph, a farmer on the Santee Reservation.

A coda to Godfrey's story further shrouds his posthumous reputation. His gravestone, in one of the Episcopal graveyards on the Santee Indian Reservation, reads:

Joseph Godfrey

1827–1909

God's finger touched him and he slept.

His descendents erected the stone long after his death and presumably chose the epitaph. The quotation comes from section LXXX of Alfred, Lord Tennyson's elegy *In Memoriam*, published in 1850. Tennyson was well-known in the United States, where it was popular to use his elegiac poetry in epitaphs and memorials. However, it is also possible that the epitaph adapts chapter 19 of the First Book of Kings, where Elijah, who killed the false prophets on God's command, fled into the wilderness to protect himself from Jezebel's fury. He sat under a tree and prayed to die because he despaired of his ability to continue God's work. As he slept an angel touched him twice and told him to wake up, eat, and take the forty-day journey to Mount Sinai. There Elijah vented his anger against God, saying that although he had done God's will, the Israelites did not heed him, so that he was left alone: "I, *even* I only, am left; and they seek my life, to take it away."[54] But God revealed his power to Elijah, encouraged him, and gave him more holy tasks. The biblical allusion could refer to Godfrey's belief that he was doing God's work by sending Dakotas to the gallows, even though he later felt isolated and vulnerable.

A final note on Godfrey needs to extend the issue of race. All the nineteenth-century white commentaries define him as partly or wholly black. In other words, they always refer to him as "black" or "negro" and emphasize his difference. A good example can be found in General Sibley's order dated 28 September 1862, appointing the military commission to "try summarily the Mulatto, and Indians, or mixed bloods . . . and pass judgment upon them."[55] Even some of the Dakota testimony uses these terms. So, for instance, despite the fact that Godfrey had lived at the Redwood Agency for six or seven years before war broke out, was culturally Dakota by marriage, and belonged to Wakpaduta's immediate family, his own father-in-law's evidence includes the terms "colored man" and "Negro," though they may signify interpolations or Anglo translations of other Dakota words.

The negative portrayals of Godfrey created a particularly frightening figure for most readers at the time by emphasizing what they saw as the double liability of his African race and Indian culture. This is evident in the pejorative article "Gusa Godfrey Is Dead," examined earlier, which incorrectly defines him as "a full blooded negro" who "joined the Indians."[56] The positive depictions often state that he had light skin, as seen in extracts from R. O. Sweeny's 1886 newspaper letter: "He was light colored and seemed bright, intelligent and rather prepossessing—not appearing in the least like the bloody wretch he was said to have been in the massacres."[57] Both destructive and constructive characterizations merely replicate the traditional rhetorical device of coloring morality into light/good and dark/bad. They also reinforce both overly negative and overly positive stereotypes of Native Americans and African Americans by the dominant culture.

8. Paul Mazakutemani
Captivity and Spiritual Autobiography

The accounts by and about Samuel Brown and Joseph Godfrey fall into Western generic or literary forms (Godfrey's admittedly owing to the restrictions of testimony or the realities of mediation). But the narrative of the next figure, Paul Mazakutemani, partakes of both European and Dakota conventions of self-narration or oratory in distinctive ways. Paul Mazakutemani, also known as Little Paul, was a Dakota leader and orator who played an important role before, during, and after the Conflict. Born about 1806 at Lac Qui Parle, he was an early member of Thomas Williamson's mission school there. He learned to read and write in Dakota, converted to Christianity, took up farming, and helped to organize the Hazelwood Republic of assimilationist Dakotas.[1] In 1869 he wrote an autobiographical narrative in Dakota that he sent to Stephen Riggs, who translated and published it in the *Collections of the Minnesota Historical Society*. Riggs accompanied his translation with the following note: "I received this personal narrative of PAUL, written by himself in the Dakota Language. Among other things, *it gives an inside view of the late Sioux outbreak, by a loyal Dakota man.* I think, therefore, it will be valuable."[2]

To better understand Mazakutemani's text, it is helpful to consider Penelope Kelsey's theories on Native American autoethnography. Her dissertation analyzes the autobiographies of five Indian writers, including Dakota Charles Eastman, and following Arnold Krupat, she characterizes the works as "bicultural composite compositions."[3] Her selected texts exemplify not just autobiography but autoethnography, in other words, "instances in which the colonized subjects undertake

Figure 15. Paul Mazakutemani (Ma-za-Ku-te-Ma-ni), ca. 1858–59. Photo by Julian Vannerson. Denver Public Library, Western History Collection, x–32440. Used with permission.

to represent themselves in ways that engage with the colonizer's own terms."[4] So the authors Kelsey examines use European American and Native American literary traditions that initially may seem incompatible. The non-Indigenous textual elements suggest assimilation and modification, while the Indigenous ones suggest tradition and continuity.

Applying this principle to Paul Mazakutemani, we can see that although his narrative adopts the Western forms of the spiritual autobiography and the captivity narrative and seems to privilege white culture and identity, it also preserves Dakota forms of oratory and oral tradition and thus encodes and endorses Native culture too. In this way, while seeming to be hemmed in by European genres, Mazakutemani escapes complete discursive captivity and illustrates a still underaccepted truth: that "assimilation and 'being Indian' are not mutually contradictory."[5]

Captivity narratives often merged with spiritual autobiographies in the traditional stories of whites taken by Indians, especially during the seventeenth and eighteenth centuries. Rowlandson's account is the prime example, but many other texts used the occasion of physical capture to explore spiritual enslavement. And some Christian denominations like Puritanism interpreted captivity as a punishment for sin and an opportunity for religious growth. Sinfulness and redemption applied to the individual captive, of course, but also sometimes to the community at large. Beyond the connections between these genres in the European American literary tradition, some scholars specifically link the captivity narrative and the spiritual autobiography with Native American autobiography.[6]

Mazakutemani's account entwines these two genres, the captivity narrative and the spiritual autobiography. Mazakutemani shows that rescuing captives during the Spirit Lake (Iowa) attacks of 1857 and the Dakota War of 1862 allowed him to apply and deepen his Christian faith, for although he had already converted, he realized that the war against sin was ongoing. Whites were the physical captives at the same time that he continued to be the spiritual captive, so liberating them also entailed liberating and renewing his spirit. In this way he becomes a living example of Christian charity to the audience he designates at the beginning of his text: "I desire that the American people, who are my friends, should listen to this my personal narrative."[7]

The story focuses mostly on Mazakutemani's conversion to Christianity at age twenty-nine and his understanding that to follow this path he must "be like a white man" by cutting his hair, giving up his traditional dress, and relinquishing other Native practices.[8] But it took the catalyst of the Spirit Lake attack in 1857, in which Inkpaduta (Scarlet Point) killed and captured several dozen settlers, for Mazakutemani to find the answer to his question: "What shall I do to be saved?"[9] So he and two others rescued Abbie Gardner, the last surviving Spirit Lake captive, for which he received official thanks and an invitation to be part of an Indian delegation to Washington. These formalities helped to strengthen his ties to the Anglo world.

The outbreak of war in 1862 reinforced Mazakutemani's resolve to save vulnerable captives as part of his Christian mission. Thus the first part of his narrative is filled with the rhetoric of rescue. First, realizing that the Riggs family and other missionaries at Hazelwood were in danger, he rushed there and urged them to escape before they were caught up in the mayhem. He interprets this impulse providentially: "O God, my Father," he prays, "thou hast shown to me thy favor, in that thou hast enabled me to save alive my friends."[10] While this kind of language could signify Riggs's editorial mediation, Mazakutemani was an elder in the church by the time he was writing, so he was well-versed in the Dakota Bible, which Riggs and others had translated.

Next, saddened and sickened (his words) by the large number of women and children held in the Dakota camp, he determined to help "these captives."[11] His narrative reenacts through dialogue and speeches his various attempts to secure the hostages' release. In one speech that he gave at the end of August in a council debate before a thousand or so pro- and antiwar Indians, he asked why the soldiers had begun the fight; questioned procedure; and challenged the rebel faction to fight the U.S. military, not intimidate women and children. To escalate the negotiations he feasted the warriors at the Sisseton Wahpeton village so they would feel obligated to honor his request to relinquish the prisoners. In his speeches and other acts Mazakutemani was acting as a civil leader. Patricia C. Albers comments: "The civil leaders negotiated disputes with neighboring groups, and they arbitrated internal conflicts. In both bands and villages, these leaders had no real author-ity. They led by persuasion and their power was only as great as their ability to represent their followers' interests and to achieve consensus among them."[12]

In the second part of his narrative he shows Dakotas caught in their own spiritual and social captivity. Once again he re-creates speeches he delivered hoping to save his people from their distrust of government authority in matters political and religious and thus ensure their survival. In fact, Heard re-creates several of Mazakutemani's speeches in his history within a chapter called "The Captives," but Mazakutemani's own recall of his words is obviously more reliable. For Mazakutemani understood that resistance in the wake of the Conflict would likely result in the Dakotas' further destruction. He drives home this point in the final incident he recounts, when, like Samuel Brown, he served as a scout. At a scouting camp at the head of the Coteau des Prairies, in late 1863, the commanding officer told Dakotas that they must stop fighting, and he rewarded those who surrendered with provisions and blankets. Mazakutemani felt sorry for the ones who tried to hold out and attempted to persuade them to concede because winter was approaching and they would probably die otherwise.

While this sounds like selling out in the short term, Mazakutemani may have seen white/Dakota relations in the long term. Speaking to the resistant Dakotas, he says that if they lived on the reservations, accepted the gospel, and gave up certain traditional customs, "the *sacred brotherhood* may grow."[13] But what is "the *sacred brotherhood*"? Is it merely Christianized Dakotas? Perhaps he is just telling his Euro-pean American readership what they want to hear, namely that he is a leader among assimilationist Dakotas. Or perhaps he is preaching the radical message that fundamental—true—Christianity requires everyone to accept God's will and establish a confraternity regardless of culture.

Mazakutemani was also likely drawing on the relationship between

Dakota kinship and Christianity. As Sioux author Ella Deloria points out when discussing a hymn written by a Christian Dakota in the 1870s, "It identifies Christian brotherhood with the old Dakota kinship system and its laws of interpersonal responsibility and loving kindness."[14] We should remember too that the European American readers of *Minnesota History* formed Mazakutemani's original audience. Certainly, at the same time he was writing, radicals like Sojourner Truth in the African American community were also urging equality. As were Martha Riggs and Sarah Wakefield, the Anglo captives discussed in the previous section, who likewise found in the Conflict's aftermath reason to spread an inclusive Christian message. It is clear then that Mazakutemani's narrative can be viewed through the lens of two Western print genres. It contains elements of the captivity narrative and of the spiritual autobiography, and it conforms to many of their structural and thematic expectations.

However, the account also incorporates several Native oral forms to provide a literary representation of its author's own status in two cultures. According to Penelope Kelsey, Charles Eastman's two autobiographies can be said to exhibit four major strands of Indigenous self-narration, including "educational, naming, spiritual, and bravery narratives."[15] Eastman's autobiographies are much longer than Mazakutemani's or those of any of the other Dakotas in this section, and they were published for national, not regional, readerships. Furthermore, together Eastman's works trace a life from boyhood within traditional Dakota culture to adulthood within the white world. Mazakutemani's much briefer narrative, covering the years 1835 to 1869, does not, strictly speaking, contain educational or naming accounts, which are more appropriate when referring to a subject's youthful experiences. (However, it is possible to see his spiritual guidance by "the sacred men," as he calls the missionaries, as a kind of education narrative.) But his text does contain both spiritual and bravery narratives; indeed, they inform its basic structure.

Acquiring names and also spiritual power through ceremonies like the vision quest are defining aspects of Dakota male experience.[16] And retelling both the visions that came to men in dreams as well as tales of raids and war parties documented "the coups which made the raconteur a leader of his people."[17] Mazakutemani's account of his Christian conversion early in his narrative falls within the spiritual-powers genre for a man long accustomed to playing a leading role in Dakota life and to revealing his powerful position by a vision quest. We have already examined his words, "So the question came up, 'What shall I do to be saved?' and morning and night I sought by prayer how I could be saved," in the light of spiritual autobiography.[18] But this also forms an instance of the vision quest, as Mazakutemani gradually comes to realize that rescuing captives will deepen his spirituality, previously tied to Native religion but now to Christianity. These traditional vision-quest narratives, whose telling proved that "warriors and leaders" possessed the necessary qualities of "courage, endurance, and self-sacrifice," are newly reconstituted within a Christian framework.[19] But there is continuity between the Indian and the European revelations of faith and works.

Mazakutemani also uses the bravery narrative when he focuses on three separate incidents in his account: rescuing Abbie Gardner, overseeing the handover of several hundred captives at Camp Release, and confronting the rebel Dakotas at Coteau des Prairies. All these events show his courage in dangerous situations and his ability to prevail through oratory and action. Missionary Samuel Pond published a classic and still well-regarded ethnography of the Dakotas, which first appeared in *Collections of the Minnesota Historical Society* in 1908. He says that the best speeches were precipitated by crisis, and he comments on their significance in Dakota culture: "Speeches well made and well timed had a great influence over the minds of the Dakotas, and a few words fitly spoken often changed the purposes of the inhabitants of a whole village."[20]

Reproducing briefer versions of his actual speeches allows Mazakutemani to show his authority over various Dakota groups as an
adult. And he also includes verbal exchanges with opposing Indians
over whom he prevails in persuasive and therefore political power.
Yet readers should be aware that Native orators "were not privileging
themselves nor their own positions, rather they were emphasizing
the larger story that their words related, attempting to connect in
meaningful ways with their listeners through deeply conversive oratory that is more akin to conversation than to monologue."[21]

That Mazakutemani had oratory and performance in mind when he
wrote is obvious from his opening, which asks readers to "listen" to
his narrative, and also from his conclusion: "I am *fifty-eight* years old
when I write this which you hear. My friends of the Great Nation, one
and all, I shake hands with you."[22] He imagines people hearing his
words, although he knows they read them, and he parts by metaphorically shaking their hands in friendship, although he understands they
cannot reciprocate this performative action. Further, it is also true
that in Dakota culture "'I shake hands with you' is a very common
greeting expressing the goodwill of the speaker," and it is "often used
when addressing groups."[23] Among Dakotas, then, "to shake hands
with someone is an act of respect, courtesy, or friendship"; it is not
just a perfunctory ritual.

As we have seen, Paul Mazakutemani's narrative, written seven
years after the war, merges captivity and spirituality. An even clearer
rhetorical link exists in a letter Mazakutemani wrote to Governor
Ramsey during the war. Quoted in John and Mary Renville's *A Thrilling
Narrative of Indian Captivity*, the letter discusses his attempts to liberate
the other captives and observes, "But, my Father, we are all captives;
a small band of Christians surrounded by our persecuting neighbors,
and whither, oh whither, shall we flee?"[24] Able to span both white and
Dakota worlds, he was designated "chief of the farmer Wahpeton band"
of Dakota Indians in 1866 and "chief councilor" for the Sissetons and

Wahpetons on the Lake Traverse Reservation in 1872.[25] Well-known as an orator and active in the Dakota Presbyterian Church after the Conflict and up to his death, his speaking skills must have extended to preaching as well as political polemic. He died at the Sisseton Agency, Dakota Territory, in 1885.

9. Cecelia Campbell Stay and Nancy McClure Faribault Huggan

Captivity and Bicultural Women's Identity

How might narrating captivity incorporate questions about bicultural women's identity? The next two subjects, Cecelia Campbell Stay and Nancy McClure Faribault Huggan, both raise issues about Native women's autobiographies as seen through the lens of captivity that also apply to the other first-person female accounts by Maggie Brass (Snana), Good Star Woman (Wicahpewastewin), and Esther Wakeman (Mahpiyatowin), examined later. A useful distinction between male and female Indian autobiographies is observed by Gretchen Bataille and Kathleen Mullen Sands: "The autobiographies of male narrators usually center on historic events and crisis moments in individual lives and tribal history. Many of the day-to-day activities are given only cursory attention, and family and personal relationships are sometimes omitted. The autobiographies of American Indian women are generally concerned with the more private and intimate aspects of their lives and cultures and with the partnership women share in the structuring and preserving of traditions within their societies."[1]

However, non-Native readers should obviously avoid interpreting this comment as analogous to the "separate spheres" ideology of nineteenth-century European American society and should also reject any residual stereotypes of Indian women as drudges, princesses, or rescuers. Such mythologizing has overshadowed the complex role women played during the course of contact between whites and Indians.[2] One remedy to such oversimplification is to access the historical experiences of Native women through tribal culture, for example by

Figure 16. Cecelia Campbell Stay, ca. 1865. Chippewa County Historical Society, Montevideo, Minnesota. Used with permission.

focusing on autonomous concepts of the self (different from European notions of individuality); deemphasis of male/female social hierarchy (unlike gender relations in Western culture); gender balance in tribal belief systems (as opposed to rigid gender roles in most Christian denominations); and greater opportunity for women to adopt powerful political positions (unlike the restrictions for many European American females).[3] Accessing the roles of Cecelia Stay and Nancy Huggan in these ways proves illuminating.

Cecelia (often called Celia) Campbell Stay was born into a Franco-

Irish-Dakota family in 1848. The Campbells moved from St. Paul to Traverse des Sioux and then in 1855 to the Redwood Agency, where her father, Antoine J. Campbell, was a government interpreter.[4] During the war the family was captured along with others from a mixed cultural background, especially those with ties to the state or federal government. Like the Browns, the Campbells were defended by pacifist Dakotas and protected by Little Crow, among others. As the warring Dakotas retreated Antoine Campbell served as an intermediary between the prowhite faction and General Sibley, an act in which Celia took enormous pride. She was an observant thirteen-year-old in 1862 and recalled events later on from that vantage point. Similar to many captives, she mulled over the traumatic times she had lived through and provided several written and oral accounts as an adult. In a 1925 letter to the curator of manuscripts at the Minnesota Historical Society she states, "I have written much but it seems some is afraid of the truth so not published," and she signs off, "Always Yours for Minn. History."[5]

Between 1882 and 1925 she provided at least three English versions of her family's role in the war. Putting them together reveals her sharp memory, ability to sequence events, and interest in showing daily life under duress. Thus her stories conform to the defining features of Native women's autobiographical texts detailed above. The earliest account of 1882 is titled "The Massacre at the Lower Sioux Agency"; the next is based on an interview conducted in 1924; and the third is a more polished, written version titled "Camp Relief [sic] in 1862," which is undated.[6] Although there is some repetition of events, the three texts focus on different aspects of Stay's observations during and immediately after the war.

In 1882 Stay comments on what prompted her to write down her story, not for the first time apparently: "I was not quite fourteen years of age when this happened and remembered every word and act and day in different camps for years[.] Data gradually [has] left my memory[;] by and by everything may be forgotten so I rewrite my narrative before it is too late."[7] Although she was concerned with memory lapses, in fact she provides many details about who lived where at the Lower Sioux Agency and what they were doing when war broke out. One standard opening for Indian captivity narratives depicts a stable environment—often characterized as a "home"—followed by a sudden attack that disrupts daily affairs. This is rhetorically effective because it conveys the terror of capture and contrasts the ensuing chaos with a previously settled life. It also mirrors a historically accurate military strategy of Indians catching opponents off-guard, frequently in a morning ambush. Stay covers the experiences of many family members on 18 August, the first day of the war, and credits eight Dakotas who saved her father and her uncle Baptiste from harm. She establishes that they did this partly from kindness and partly from kinship, since they were all related to Celia's grandfather, Scott Campbell, and through him to the rest of the family.[8]

As Stay's statement about her rationale for writing indicates, she is most concerned with setting down events in as much detail as possible. Only occasionally do her spiritual or political beliefs intrude. For example, reiterating Christian doctrine about sin and punishment, she says that many of those killed in the attacks did not deserve a brutal death even if they were sinners and that those innocents who died did so for the sins of the world. Also, she challenges readers as to why prowhite Indians like her father's rescuers were not listed on the Camp Release Monument, one of many memorials erected to commemorate the war.[9] In other words, she asks why the historical record tends to privilege a European American version of history. Though she sees herself and her family as white, she realizes that others in the European American community do not necessarily see them that way.

In August 1924 several New Ulm residents traveled to Dakota War sites to gather historical information. After visiting and photographing what was left of Camp Release, they stopped to talk to Cecelia

Campbell Stay near Montevideo and recorded verbatim the story of her
capture and her experiences at Camp Release. The transcript shows
that seventy-five-year-old Stay was initially prompted to answer a series of questions, but that once the ball got rolling, she gave an almost
uninterrupted verbal account. Alex Seifert, the reporter, notes that he
made virtually no changes because he wanted "to secure the Indian
conversational style of delivery and retain the original words."[10] And
the effect is certainly colloquial, associative, and spontaneous. It is
an excellent example of the ethnographic type of oral autobiography
discussed earlier. This account, which picks up where the 1882 one
leaves off, includes several versions of captivity.

First, Stay shows how she and her family were virtually trapped for
days in and around their house at the Redwood Agency and depended
on Dakota friends and relatives for help. She effectively conveys the
conflicting loyalties of a man like Little Crow, who wanted to aid the
Campbells but knew that his influence was limited. "You could see
Little Crow was a banished man, so far as a man goes," she recalls.
"His eyes looked like they were faded and he shook his hands and then
he talked to mother. He was so pleased, I suppose, that they were alive,
that he talked around there for a while, and then he walked off."[11]

Also, Stay describes the cultural changes wrought by captivity that
required some of the Campbell womenfolk to adopt Native rather than
European dress while they were with their Dakota relatives. But the
Campbells still risked being killed, as shown by Celia's recollection
that at one point Little Crow's wife kept back Celia's sister Emily to
save her from what looked like inevitable death for the rest of the family. But then another of Little Crow's soldiers intervened and said he
would kill anyone who harmed the Campbells. These incidents reveal
the psychological uncertainty of captivity, so well described in some
of the white narratives examined in previous chapters. The account
also shows how Antoine Campbell and other Indians rescued several
white women from captivity at great personal risk and how Celia and

her mother helped Mary Anderson before she died and tried to comfort Mattie Williams, even though they could not intervene with her captor. Stay goes on to describe the conditions at Camp Release and probably would have continued talking except that one of the visitors stopped her by saying they had to leave because it was getting late.

The third and last version is an undated manuscript by Stay titled "Camp Relief [*sic*] in 1862," which accompanies two letters she wrote to the Minnesota Historical Society in 1925. Thus it may have been written the same year, and interestingly it expands on the family's experiences at Camp Release, which the other two accounts only gloss over. Stay intended to publish the story, as shown by several comments such as the following, indicating how her father endangered his life when he approached Sibley to arrange the handover of captives: "Perhaps they [readers] will think more of him when they read this little volume, and feel, 'What if they had been in his place, standing between two fires as it were, Indians watching [*sic*] to kill him, the 3rd Regiment wanting to kill him.'"[12]

In fact, much of this version exhorts readers to recognize the actions of Antoine Campbell, as well as other likeminded Dakotas, and essentially write them into history. His heroism denied, or at least withheld, by whites as well as by traditionalist Dakotas, Antoine Campbell is liberated into deserved recognition within the pages of his daughter's text. She undertakes to recover his reputation with such comments as: "How carefully that noble man's name has been kept from history. When he did so much to alleviate the wrongs of the Red Man. How he soothed wounded feelings, by kind words, and wise counsels and material aid. He could not see one come to him for naught, and risking his own life and welfare for these prisoners."[13]

She explains her father's overtures to Little Crow, first asking him to surrender and await Sibley's arrival, which he refused to do, and then asking him to release the hundred or so captives, which he agreed to do. Celia's eye for detail is extremely effective as she describes the

ex-captives who "trotted" after Antoine Campbell, hauling posses-
sions in heavy white sheets and tablecloths, carrying little ones, and
bombarding him with questions about other family members. Knowing that many of the captives' kin were dead, he thoughtfully fended
off their inquiries rather than tell them "the sad facts."[14] Next, she
mentions her father's daring rescue of a fourteen-year-old Swedish
girl in another war party heading west, whose captor did not want to
relinquish her and who almost shot Antoine.

Celia's narrative ends with the picture of Antoine Campbell and
Henry Sibley going through Camp Release side by side, and with these
words: "The proudest incident of my life to have seen a duty well performed and well ended so far, and to see those two men neither could
have done without the other in that last dark day of trouble of death
and devastation."[15] Elements of this account are more consciously
literary and retrospective than the two other versions, as shown, for
example, by the ending's alliteration ("dark day," "death and devastation") and apocalyptic texture.

Nancy Winona McClure Faribault Huggan: all the next subject's
names suggest her complex bicultural status but also her primary
print identity within European American culture. For like many of the
figures examined in this section, Huggan understood at some level
that written accounts intended for a white audience empowered her.
She could try to fashion a persona for herself and establish her own
interpretation of the Conflict, which would hopefully withstand any
editorial intervention. Nancy Winona McClure was born in 1836 at
Mendota, a thriving community of fur traders and Natives near the
confluence of the Minnesota and Mississippi rivers. Her parents were
an Indian woman also named Winona (meaning "firstborn," if a female
child) and Lieutenant James McClure, a white officer stationed at Fort
Snelling who had graduated from West Point. In fall 1837 McClure
was transferred to Florida and died the next spring. However, a note
to Huggan's captivity narrative in *Collections of the Minnesota Historical*

Society states that McClure showed "great affection and solicitude for his daughter, for whose care and education he provided."[16] This is evident from his letters, preserved in the Sibley Papers at the society, and from information Huggan herself gives, that her father made financial provisions for her, even though the white men to whom he entrusted the money pocketed some—perhaps much—of it themselves.[17]

Though Huggan lost sight of her father's side of the family until editors William Marshall and Return Holcombe made contacts on her behalf while compiling her story, she knew a great deal about her mother's background and status. Huggan's great-great-grandfather was a principal Dakota chief named Tate Mani (Walking Wind), and her great-grandfather was also a Dakota dignitary, called Magaiyake (Alighting Goose). Two years after James McClure died Nancy's mother married trader Antoine Renville, and Nancy lived with them at Lac Qui Parle until she was about fourteen, when her mother passed away after a long illness. She learned traditional Dakota women's ways from her mother, as well as white women's domestic skills from the various mission schools she attended.[18] After her mother's death Huggan stayed with her grandmother at Traverse des Sioux, where one of her schoolmates was Martha Riggs. Indeed, Stephen Riggs's compilation of the families associated with the ABCFM Dakota Mission in its early days, which Martha copied down for publication, indicates that at this time Huggan "made progress in learning to read English, and could understand nearly all that was said to her, but did not speak it much," presumably because Dakota and French were her first languages.[19]

Although only about fourteen, Huggan was well-developed and very pretty: "I was often flattered," she admits, "and I am afraid I became a little vain. I know that I used to try to dress myself well and to appear well."[20] Her looks attracted the attention of a prominent Franco Dakota widower more than twice her age, David Faribault Sr. They were married on 11 July 1851, during the festivities following the signing of the Treaty of Traverse des Sioux. In a letter to Holcombe,

Figure 17. Nancy McClure, 1851. Sketch by Frank B. Mayer, in Sketchbook No. 41, p. 102. Reproduced courtesy of Edward E. Ayer Collection, The Newberry Library, Chicago.

one of eight on which her Minnesota Historical Society account was based, she says, "I never would of [sic] married David Faribault I was to young my Indian relatives were against it but Gen Sibley talked me into it telling me David always made money and so on and he came of a good family."[21] Historian Walt Bachman concurs: "Henry Sibley was the matchmaker, urging a reluctant Nancy to wed his longtime friend and trading associate."[22]

Romanticized versions of the marriage found their way into con-

temporary newspapers and into the pages of artist Frank Blackwell
Mayer's sketchbooks and diary.[23] Mayer made pleasing sketches of
Nancy herself and also of the ceremony, and in his diary he left a detailed though patronizing testament to Nancy's extraordinary beauty:
"On a mattress covered by a neat quilt sat Winona, the most beautiful
of the Indian women I have yet seen. . . . She possesses Indian features
softened into the more delicate contour of the Caucasian & her figure
is tall, slender & gracefully girlish. Her eyes are dark & deep, a sweet
smile of innocence plays on her ruby lips, & silky hair of glossy black-
ness falls to her dropping [sic] shoulders. . . . She has been visited by
most of our camp, the rarity of her beauty being the attraction, & the
purchase of mocassins [sic] the ostensible object."[24]

David Faribault's trading business with the Indians caused him and
his new wife to move frequently, and she describes her many travels
in her Minnesota Historical Society narrative, including a business
trip to St. Louis, during which she was feted. When the Conflict began
the Faribaults were living between the Lower Sioux Agency and Fort
Ridgely, both sites the militant Dakotas targeted. They and their only
child, Mary Ann, were thus vulnerable and became 3 of the approximately 160 bicultural captives freed at Camp Release.[25] Initially held
prisoner by Little Crow, they were then rescued and protected by their
Dakota relatives and friends, like so many other bicultural captives.
In this way they exchanged "by force" captivity for "sanctuary-type
'captivity' among their Dakota kin."[26]

During spring 1894 Return Holcombe visited Dakota Conflict sites to
interview Natives still living there on behalf of the *St. Paul Pioneer Press*
and the Minnesota Historical Society. He then continued to Flandreau,
South Dakota, to visit Nancy Huggan (as she was then, having remarried) and ask her to recount her war experiences. As indicated in the
previous section, on European American texts, the Historical Society
became particularly interested at this time in preserving survivors' and
participants' stories, including Dakota perspectives. As with those of

Jannette DeCamp Sweet and Mary Schwandt Schmidt, among others, Huggan's account first appeared in the *St. Paul Pioneer Press* as a series of pioneer historical sketches. This trio of women's captivities then came out in the 1894 edition of *Collections of the Minnesota Historical Society*. The newspaper appearances were merely advance releases of the *Collections* narratives.

Huggan sent eight letters to Holcombe between 13 April and 14 June 1894, with piecemeal remembrances. Her letter of 27 May recognizes her haphazard approach, because she says she keeps remembering more things only after she has mailed her letters. Sometime in May she wrote a sixteen-page response to William Marshall's request for further details about the Conflict itself than had appeared in her letters to Holcombe up to then. From these two sources Holcombe compiled a continuous narrative and even visited the Huggans in late June for additional information—though more particularly to interview Big Eagle with Huggan and her son-in-law, John Eastman, as interpreters. Huggan's letter to Holcombe on 14 June says: "If you will just ask the questions I will try and answer them the best I can, or if you will come out we will try and do the best we can for you. Both my husband and I feel as if you were a very old friend instead of a new one."[27] While Huggan's letters and personal statement fall into Bataille and Sands's definition of the Indian-written life story, the edited version that appeared in *Collections of the Minnesota Historical Society* is more consciously literary.

The letters to Holcombe, the account to Marshall, and the resulting published narrative reveal Huggan's particular take on the Conflict, namely that the Dakota war faction treated Anglo and Franco Dakotas harshly because they tended to be prowhite. As Huggan states in one of her letters, "I have one thing the Indians are against the half bloods to day for the part they took in the out break of 1862 and I would like to have this part appear in my sketch."[28] After seeing the *Pioneer Press* story a week later, she wrote Holcombe, "I have always wanted to give the Indians a going over and I feel satisfied now."[29]

For example, when the Faribaults were captured and taken to Little Crow's camp, Huggan recalls that the men "said we were worse than the whites, and that they were going to kill all of us."[30] On word that same evening that Little Crow's soldiers were beginning to murder mixed-blood captives (which turned out to be a false alarm), Huggan and her daughter ran seven miles to find refuge at Shakopee's camp. When she returned to Little Crow's encampment the next day for her husband, she discovered him in the hands of a drunken Native holding a butcher's knife. Faribault said the man had terrorized him all night. Several more times in her narrative, and in the Holcombe/Marshall correspondence from which it is constructed, Huggan talks about the death threats to prisoners. Once she even overheard a young Indian boasting that she would become his wife when men like Faribault were killed.[31]

Huggan's interpretation of the Conflict is tied to her self-representation as a bicultural woman with a white primary identity, a depiction that Return Holcombe further heightened in the published version. Yet even in her own letters to Holcombe, which of course were written when she was almost sixty and had been married to a white man for many years, she "whitens" herself as a young girl. For instance, her letter of 24 May 1894 recalls what she terms her "first Indian scare" as a schoolgirl, when an Indian killed tame calves for food in missionary Thomas Williamson's yard (even though these same animals when mature would likely have been eaten by the Williamson family) and mentions that when Huggan's mother was on her deathbed she told her "not to stay among the Indians."[32] Thus to Huggan the term "Indian" represents a culture different from the one in which she was, in fact, brought up.

The published captivity narrative further plays on Huggan's white identity, to the point of including this statement about her feelings after her mother died: "How much I longed to be with some of my father's people then, I cannot tell you. I was always more white than

Indian in my tastes and sympathies, though I never had cause to blush for my Indian blood on account of the character of my family."[33] She presents herself during captivity as a brave, assertive, resourceful woman, demanding, for example, that an Indian in the hostile camp return her stolen horse, protecting white captives and helping several to escape, and lambasting a Dakota woman who insulted her. Recounting the last incident she (or perhaps Holcombe ghosting her voice) comments: "I flew at that woman and routed her so completely that she bore the marks for some time. . . . Perhaps it was not a very lady-like thing to do, but I was dreadfully provoked."[34] Whoever composed these lines wished to gentrify Huggan by indicating that this one lapse from "ladylike" behavior was uncharacteristic. On this kind of class distinction among Indians Devon Mihesuah observes that "after Indians adopted new value systems, members of a single tribe often viewed each other from different economic and social classes. Indians with a high 'level of acculturation' might have viewed themselves as more enlightened than others whom they deemed less enlightened, uncivilized, or heathens."[35]

By this point in the war Huggan was protected by her uncle Rdayamani (Rattling Walker), yet she still characterizes her overall captivity experiences as "sad and hard times [that] fell upon us and nearly crushed us."[36] Following the Conflict the Faribaults experienced real hardship, and their only material possession of any worth was the rescued horse, Jerry. The narrative states that their actual losses amounted to three thousand dollars.[37] Six years later, after they had begun to recover financially, the mail station and travelers' rest they were operating fell prey to another Indian attack, and they found themselves destitute once again.[38]

The published story, detailing physical, cultural, and economic captivity, breaks off after this information with the words, "My life since then is hardly worth writing about."[39] But as in many other accounts the final paragraph that follows details personal and generational continuity beyond captivity: a second marriage; a settled life; grandchildren from her only child, Mary Ann (who, Huggan reminds readers, was a captive with her); and commitment to Christianity.[40] After Huggan saw the narrative in the *St. Paul Pioneer Press* she wrote to Holcombe: "I think the sketch all very nice and thank you very much for taking so much pains to have It so. Their are one or two little mistakes but It is all right [sic]."[41]

However, this was not the last time she told her story. In the fall of 1926 Frank Hopkins interviewed Huggan; titled his notes "Statement of Nancy Huggins, Wa-Pa-Let [Hat]"; and published them in the *Fairfax (Minnesota) Journal* in 1927 under the title "Turkey's Egg Starts Ft. Ridgely Massacre."[42] Hopkins was a lawyer, and in 1926 he had gone to Flandreau, South Dakota, to question some of Little Crow's descendents whom he was representing in a lawsuit. He had also taken over the Fort Ridgely State Park and Historical Association and was thus a history buff. In a letter he wrote many years later, in 1951, he went over the interview process and explained why Huggan had signed his statement: not only did it suggest narrative authenticity, but it also gave him power of attorney to recoup money for her from one of Little Crow's treaties.[43]

They spoke in English, and Hopkins was surprised that she was so conversant in the language. He prompted her, "'You can tell me about your people, how they lived, what they believed and all about them.' 'I'll be glad to do so,' said she, 'You ask me questions.'"[44] The newspaper version includes ethnographic material and draws attention to the causes of the outbreak, primarily the fact that the Dakotas were desperate for food. "The Indians were starving and some of them had eaten their dogs and ponies. They did not believe they had been used right by the whites," Huggan comments.[45] She also believed that the trials and executions, with Natives informing on Natives, caused further cultural rifts in the Dakota community.

Hopkins was much affected by Nancy Huggan's story. In his 1951 letter

Figure 18. Nancy McClure Faribault Huggan at the Traverse des Sioux Treaty Rock in 1927. From the Collections of the Minnesota Historical Society. Used with permission.

he commented, "My contact with this Indian woman and the insight she gave me into the character of the true redman, how he decided every issue on honor . . . later became the foundation of a philosophy presented through experiences of real Indians, which changed my profession from law to teaching through public address."[46] He became a motivational speaker, one of a continuing line of Indian "wannabes." Indeed, the letterhead to his 1951 correspondence says, "FRANK HOP-KINS, Chief Minnesota Tribe America," with ersatz Native logos along the left margin including a tepee, a hatchet, and a canoe.

There is at least one more version of Huggan's captivity narrative, though it does not offer as much new information as the other two accounts. In July 1927 Huggan took her first train ride, to Traverse des Sioux, belatedly recognizing the seventy-fifth anniversary in 1926 of the treaty's signing and of her first marriage. An article published on 12 July 1927 in the *Minneapolis Journal* includes a photograph of her, then over ninety, standing by the commemorative monument. As it turned out, she died a month later at her daughter's home. But while she was at Traverse des Sioux, Thomas Hughes conducted an interview with her, which he supplemented generously with information from the 1894 published version and included in his 1929 book *Old Traverse des Sioux*. He titled it, "Notes by Nancy McClure Huggins" and added in the subtitle that it "recalls Indian lore."[47]

A letter he wrote describes Huggan's lack of interest in precise chronology when telling her story: "I simply took down the story in the order in which she told it to me and, of course, she did not intend it to be in any correct chronological order."[48] Thus for Hughes Huggan's role in the Treaty of Traverse des Sioux and the Dakota Conflict was just one more instance, essentially, of a bygone time and culture. Indeed, many of the "notes" were actually drawn from her narrative and thus situated her fairly and squarely at a time and place more than thirty years earlier.

Because Cecelia Campbell Stay and Nancy McClure Faribault Huggan came from a mixed heritage, the war tested their allegiances when they and their families were captured. In the stories they told later in life of their own and other people's captivities, they consolidated their European American identities as they became even more firmly entrenched in that world and its values.

10. Big Eagle, Lorenzo Lawrence, and Maggie Brass
Captivity and Cultural Stereotypes

A truism of white-centered captivity narratives is that they often portray stereotypically negative or, less often, stereotypically positive views of Native Americans. For example, part 1, "European Americans Narrating Captivity," illustrates the negative views in the texts of Jacob Nix and Harriet Bishop McConkey and the positive ones in those of Martha Riggs Morris and Sarah Wakefield. Indeed, reinforcing pejorative, essentially propagandist stereotypes is arguably the most pervasive cultural work the European American accounts performed. While this is a generalization, of course, some Native scholars believe that the overall legacy of the captivity narrative tradition has been so damaging to Native Americans that even a revised definition of the genre should not include Native texts.

Small wonder, then, that Native narratives might strive to present a more complex and constructive view of Indians' roles, behavior, and motivation, despite the mediation of white editors. Underlying this aim may also have been an attempt to show readers the social and spiritual ideology of Dakota culture. As Ella Deloria explains: "The ultimate aim of Dakota life, stripped of accessories, was quite simple: One must obey kinship rules; one must be a good relative. . . . To be a good Dakota, then, was to be humanized, civilized. And to be civilized was to keep the rules imposed by kinship for achieving civility, good manners, and a sense of responsibility toward every individual dealt with."[1] Among Christianized Dakotas the traits of a good Dakota might very well go hand-in-hand with those of a good Christian, and all the Dakota tellers in this chapter make that very point.

Figure 19. Big Eagle (Wamditanka), ca. 1863. Photo by Simon & Shepherd, Davenport, Iowa. From the Collections of the Minnesota Historical Society. Used with permission.

We have already seen that Huggan and Holcombe collaborated on Huggan's captivity narrative, but they also worked together on another Dakota War narrative, probably the most famous of them all and definitely the best-known of the Native ones: Big Eagle's account. It first appeared in the *St. Paul Pioneer Press* on 1 July 1894 and was reprinted in the 1894 volume of *Collections of the Minnesota Historical Society*, where it was titled "A Sioux Story of the War." Dakota Chief Big Eagle (Wamditanka) did not speak English, so Huggan and her son-in-law, Reverend John Eastman, acted as translators. Unfortunately the original manuscript of the interview has been lost, and the introduction to this text is written in the third person. Thus the prefatory remarks may be by another *Collections* editor or by Holcombe, attempting to sound objective by referring to himself as "a representative" from the *Pioneer Press*.[2] Regardless, the introduction includes information that Holcombe either passed on to its writer or that he composed himself. It states, "Big Eagle's story is here given substantially as related to the reporter by the two intelligent interpreters, or at least as it was understood."[3]

The likely scenario is that Big Eagle spoke; Huggan and Eastman translated his words out loud; and Holcombe, who had worked extensively as a journalist, wrote down what they said more or less verbatim and reworked it later into continuous, readable form. The potential for bias and change is substantial in any text involving two languages and three layers of telling. Yet at first glance this story seems to be a fairly literal redaction of what Big Eagle said, "at least as it was understood." Though it is hard to know whether Huggan and Eastman had anything to gain by misrepresentation, as a reporter Holcombe had much to lose. Recognizing the importance of such accounts, as well as his own skill in obtaining this one, Holcombe boasted, "To have been the first newspaper man to get the old hostiles to talk for publication is the feather in my cap of which I am vainest."[4]

How did he persuade Big Eagle to speak publicly in this exclusive interview? And what narrative measures did Big Eagle take to avoid being presented as the stereotypical "bad" Indian so familiar from earlier Dakota Conflict captivity narratives? That others still considered him in pejorative terms is evident from a letter Samuel Brown wrote to Holcombe in 1896: "I see you are considerably taken up with one Big Eagle. The old rascal has an interesting history—so had Cut Nose,

Little Six and Medicine Bottle. When you 'pump' him again try and find out why he should not be called Big Liar instead of Big Eagle."[5]

According to the introduction Big Eagle was told that his information would help readers better understand Dakota military strategy and would not be used to rekindle animosity. Though a new generation of Minnesotans knew his prominent wartime role, they also recognized "that he was now and had been for many years a quiet, industrious Christian citizen, respected by all who knew him, and he was assured that he would be correctly reported."[6] This story interprets the Conflict from the viewpoint of a Dakota chief who fought in all the important battles and who was, albeit reluctantly, prowar at the beginning. While other hawkish Dakotas also recounted their experiences, the value of Big Eagle's text cannot be overstated, because "there simply is no other major Indian account to compare with it."[7]

Of course it was to Holcombe's advantage to stress Big Eagle's honesty, because it made for better journalism. "The old man was very frank and unreserved," the introduction says. "He did not seem to wish to avoid or evade an answer to a single question. He is of more than ordinary intelligence and spoke candidly, deliberately and impassively, and with the air and manner of one striving to tell 'the whole truth and nothing but the truth.'"[8] Even if honesty was not the issue, subjectivity was inevitable. First, Holcombe probably led Big Eagle with his questioning; indeed, Samuel Brown used the significant word "pump" in his letter. And second, the sixty-seven-year-old leader recalled information from thirty years before and interpreted it within a Christian framework, as did his translators, one of whom was actually a minister.

In 1868, within "Evidence Taken by the Indian Peace Commission," Big Eagle himself had commented on the vagaries of memory: "When there is a long matter to state, and a single man designated to state it, there will be probably many things left out, as the memory is uncertain."[9] His later account portrays many of his people "captured" by a pre-Christian belief system before the war and literally incarcerated after the war. Thus his text is both a cultural captivity and physical confinement narrative, with both elements framing the beginning and end of his story and informing it in important ways.

For example, after giving biographical information on himself in the narrative proper's opening paragraph, Big Eagle states: "Of the causes that led to the outbreak of August, 1862, much has been said. Of course it was wrong, as we all know now, but there were not many Christians among the Indians then, and they did not understand things as they should."[10] However, he goes on to provide a very detailed and persuasive list of Dakota grievances against whites, so that even if the war itself was a mistake, the reasons for it were not. His rhetoric is precise: "Of course it was wrong" refers back to the singular noun in the previous sentence, "outbreak," not to the plural noun, "causes."

The narrative's two final paragraphs discuss Big Eagle's view of his unfair postwar treatment. Big Eagle explains that he gave himself up on the promise that he and other warriors "would only be held as prisoners of war a short time, but as soon as I surrendered I was thrown into prison."[11] No white witnesses testified to his having committed war crimes, only that he fought "in fair, open fight." He adds, "If I had known that I would be sent to the penitentiary I would not have surrendered."[12] When about to be released from prison after serving three years, he challenged the government by saying they could keep him longer if they wished, because "I did not like the way I had been treated." Then he abruptly concludes: "But all feeling on my part about this has long since passed away. For years I have been a Christian and I hope to die one. My white neighbors and friends know my character as a citizen and a man. I am at peace with every one, whites and Indians."[13]

While the surface meaning of the narrative's open and close is conciliatory and Christian-infused, the intervening selection of information and analysis of the war do not compromise Dakota history, culture, or language by spiritual bias. Rather, Big Eagle's Christian references throughout may indicate a subversive redefinition of the religion, namely a sense that true Christians do not behave toward each other as European Americans did toward the Dakotas before and after the Conflict. Many African Americans also preached this radical religious message as a way to boost abolitionist arguments and confound whites with their own source of moral authority, the Bible.

A closer look at the body of this text reveals both its surface and its underlying meanings. Big Eagle begins by rehearsing his genealogy, his life as a young man, and his experiences with the treaties of Traverse des Sioux and Mendota and reservation removal. He also establishes his ability to move within both red and white worlds, and thus his narrative credibility for a European American readership, for example in his mention of visiting Washington before the war as part of a Dakota delegation. The next several pages show his rhetorical skill, listing a litany of grievances while at the same time giving plausible rationales for war by inviting his readers to imagine themselves in the Dakotas' position: forced by treaties "to give up the old life and go to work like white men," which they found "distasteful."[14] This English word is ambiguous and euphemistic, though it is not clear whether it is an accurate translation of the original Dakota term.

Big Eagle then proceeds to indicate the many reasons for Dakota dissatisfaction leading to war. He frames them with the comment that because many Indians were not Christians then, "they did not understand things as they should."[15] Yet this statement seems deliberately ironic, since what follows shows a very clear comprehension of white/Indian interactions. If the Dakotas "did not understand things as they should," this probably means that they did not see the world as non-Natives wanted them to, not that they misunderstood what was going on.

First, treaty restrictions prevented Dakotas from fighting their traditional enemies, and although Big Eagle adds, "This was right, but the Indians did not then know it," the value judgment falls flat, since he provides no further explanation.[16] Second, the government wanted Dakotas to exchange cultural values overnight, but Big Eagle realizes that this was too abrupt a change to work. He plays on his readers' psychology by pointedly stating, "If the Indians had tried to make the whites live like them, the whites would have resisted, and it was the same way with many Indians."[17]

Third, European Americans put too much trust in the honesty of traders and of the entire trading system. As Big Eagle observes, many traders cheated the Indians, misused the legal system to collect debts, refused to extend repayment deadlines, and regularly cooked their books. Yet he is careful not to overgeneralize, because he admits that some traders were honest. Fourth, European Americans often abused Dakotas and treated them arrogantly and unkindly. While Big Eagle says that "perhaps they had excuse," his next comment suggests otherwise: "Then some of the white men abused the Indian women in a certain way and disgraced them, and surely there was no excuse for that."[18] Finally, treaty requirements fostered further disunity among Dakotas by rewarding those who changed their traditional way of life—particularly as regards farming practices—but penalizing those who did not.

Having dealt with many crucial contributing causes of the war, Big Eagle then reveals the internal political disunity in the tribe, typified by the three candidates lobbying for election as chief speaker in 1862: himself, Little Crow, and Traveling Hail (Wasuheyadan), who was actually elected. He contextualizes this information by clarifying that the principal hereditary chief at this time was Wabasha, not Little Crow, as many Minnesotans assumed; and that the death of old Shakopee in the summer of 1862 had altered the political balance. The leader of a large band, the elder Shakopee was succeeded by his son Little Shakopee (Eatoka), who did not share the same conciliatory approach to European Americans.

Further, Big Eagle states many times over how the Dakotas knew that massive Civil War deployments had left the Minnesota borderlands unprotected. This situation seemed to confirm that the South was getting the upper hand and that the time was ripe for a massive retaliatory response from the Dakotas, the Winnebagoes, and the Ojibwes. The recruitment of the Renville Rangers in particular sent the following signal: "The Indians now thought the whites must be pretty hard up for men to fight the South, or they would not come so far out on the frontier and take half-breeds or anything to help them."[19]

Big Eagle reiterates that although he fought in the Conflict, he did not believe the Dakotas would win, because the U.S. government was too powerful and too bent on conquest: "We might succeed for a time, but we would be overpowered and defeated at last," he states.[20] The delay in annuity payments, he points out, exacerbated existing tensions between farming and nonfarming Dakotas. With further delays and Civil War rumors swirling, many Dakotas who had pursued traditional subsistence practices and who had traveled to the Yellow Medicine Agency for their annuity payments ran out of food and patience. Big Eagle continues to state that he opposed fighting but did not want to desert his band and nation and thus led them into war when the influential prowar powerbrokers got the upper hand following the Acton incident.

With the outbreak of war Big Eagle places himself in the company of those Indians who tried to save the lives of particular friends, in his case George Spencer and another family. Yet he admits some embarrassment at claiming these deeds, since "so many Indians have lied about their saving the lives of white people."[21] What follows in his account is an overview of Dakota military strategy in major encounters, a balanced assessment of the weaknesses and strengths on both sides, and an examination of the advantages and disadvantages of certain maneuvers. For example, recalling the Battle of Birch Coulee, Big Eagle concludes that both sides fought well but that "owing to the white men's way of fighting they lost many men. Owing to the Indians' way of fighting they lost but few."[22] In the last conclusive battle, at Wood Lake, he reveals, an unauthorized group of white soldiers went out to dig potatoes and came so close to the hidden Dakotas awaiting General Sibley's main troop advance that the Indians had to fire or be run over by the soldiers' wagons. Once their positions were revealed, the Dakotas lost the advantage and were forced to retreat in disarray, yet they still managed to carry off all their wounded. He adds pointedly, "The whites scalped all our dead men—so I have heard."[23]

The account's final paragraph includes Big Eagle's sense of betrayal and outrage at being imprisoned after surrendering, when he had been assured that he would be treated as a prisoner of war. He served time at Davenport and Rock Island, but despite his wartime status as a soldier and his postwar mistreatment, he claims to be at peace with the world. He concludes by stressing family continuity following captivity, as in so many of the European American hostage accounts: "I am getting to be an old man, but I am still able to work. I am poor, but I manage to get along. This is my second wife, and this little girl is our adopted daughter. I will come and see you when I come to St. Paul. Good-bye," he signs off to Holcombe.[24]

Yet on 15 June 1868, a quarter of a century before this mediated and reflective account appeared in *Collections of the Minnesota Historical Society*, Big Eagle gave evidence to the Indian Peace Commission. He concurred with the statements that Wabasha, then chief of the Santees, had just given to the commissioners but indicated that he wanted to add "further particulars," since "the memory is uncertain" and a single spokesman could not recall everything. He clarified that he could no longer speak for his people because he had been deposed as chief while in prison; he could only give an individual assessment. And it was understandably angry and accusatory. On the morning of the outbreak, he said, when he saw militants bringing in women and children as prisoners, he thought it was wrong and confronted

Little Crow. After the leader refused to release them, Wamditanka and others "who pitied them got them in our possession and took care of them. I cared for five men, one woman, and four children, and others did the same."[25]

Thus he measures his capacity for compassion in terms of caring for captives: "These were our deeds to the whites, and we came in to them with every confidence. I can not think why the whites should forget these things."[26] Conversely he shows that the government ignored these good deeds and incarcerated large numbers of Dakotas who should have been treated fairly as prisoners of war, not jailed for long terms or executed. Again Big Eagle indicates that after formal surrender he and others who wanted appeasement gathered together all the white prisoners. The rhetoric of captivity and confinement permeates his testimony: Dakota militants captured white and mixed-blood prisoners; however, other Dakotas helped the captives. Meanwhile European Americans captured even compassionate and innocent Dakotas but did not help them. His final statement suggests that the government blackmailed the Dakotas economically, which resulted in a kind of financial captivity that (understandably) led to reaction and rebellion: "We were kept a long time waiting for the payment of our annuities, and were almost starved while waiting."[27]

Return Holcombe and Big Eagle himself were not, of course, the only ones who strove to overturn pejorative stereotypes of Dakotas' behavior during the Conflict. The story of Lorenzo Lawrence (Towanetaton)—as seen first in an 1862 postwar statement, then in a much longer account he titled "Story of Lorenzo Lawrence" in 1895, and finally in a 2005 reevaluation by his great-grandson, Elden Lawrence—reveals a man who by any standard was heroic.[28] And the measure of his heroism came, first, from helping ten captives reach the safety of Fort Ridgely and, second, from enduring economic captivity and privation after the war despite his courageous actions. Introducing the 1862 statement of Lorenzo Lawrence and three other Dakotas, Bishop Henry Whipple describes "the heroism" of these men "who, at the risk of life, saved helpless women and children."[29] But even before the war Lawrence was already known in white circles as an extraordinary man who defined stereotypically positive Indian attributes. By "stereotypically positive" I am not suggesting that Lawrence really lacked such commendable qualities, but rather that describing them performed specific cultural work in the European American community. A brief overview of his biography up to the war illustrates his standing in two societies.

Lorenzo Lawrence was born near Big Stone Lake about 1822. His mother, the well-respected Catherine Totidutawin, was one of the earliest Native converts at the Lac Qui Parle Mission. Skilled in traditional handicrafts and allowed entry to the medicine lodge at the Lac Qui Parle Wahpeton village as a young woman, she was baptized in 1837, became prominent among Christian Dakotas, and learned European women's domestic skills. Stephen Riggs's profile of her in 1858 praises her piety and observes that she clung to Christianity, "although for years she was hated, defamed, and threatened with death" by those who practiced Dakota spiritual traditions.[30] She exerted considerable influence over her children and encouraged Lorenzo's decision to put his Christianity into practice by rescuing captives during the Conflict.

Lorenzo Lawrence attended Thomas Williamson's mission school at Lac Qui Parle and became proficient in reading and writing English and Dakota and doing mathematics. He accompanied Riggs to Oberlin, Ohio, for additional schooling from 1842 to 1843. Yet he also was active in Dakota politics and remained loyal to Little Crow in 1845 during the quarrels over leadership. Lawrence moved to Pajutazee, near the Yellow Medicine River, about a decade later and was one of the founding members of the Hazelwood Republic on 4 July 1856.[31]

Like certain African Americans who seized the historical significance of Independence Day to signify that they were still captured and enslaved by an exclusionary legal system, these Dakotas founded the Hazelwood Republic on the day marking America's freedom from

British tyranny. In 1861 Stephen Riggs sponsored a group of Hazelwood Republic members to apply for American citizenship. That same year Lorenzo Lawrence became the first Dakota Indian to receive full American citizenship, and by 1862 he was an elder of the Presbyterian Church at Hazelwood. To understand the full political implications of Lawrence's status we have only to consider that American Indians in general did not obtain U.S. citizenship until 1924.

Lawrence's "Statement," made at the time the captives were liberated at Camp Release, tells the story of his flight to Fort Ridgely with his family and ten rescued hostages. Bishop Whipple did not publish it until 1912, within his memoir, *Lights and Shadows of a Long Episcopate*, but Lawrence refers to Whipple's story in his 1895 manuscript "Story of Lorenzo Lawrence," so either it was already in circulation or it had appeared in another venue.[32] Lawrence's 1895 reference corroborates Whipple's claim that the earlier "Statement" was indeed made in 1862, despite its lack of provenance. Though it preserves the spontaneity and straightforwardness of oral expression, it was fashioned into a more coherent and finished narrative than the taking down of oral testimony would suggest. It fits aspects of as-told-to oral autobiography, explained earlier.

The "Statement" opens by establishing that Lawrence and other prowhite Indians were essentially captives themselves among the militant Dakotas and felt as much need to protect themselves as the other hostages did. As Lawrence puts it, "Some days after the beginning of the massacre . . . I determined that the only safety of the friendly and Christian Indians was to escape if possible from the hostile camp."[33] Having made this decision, he agreed to aid Jannette DeCamp and her children because he believed God would show them all the way to freedom. Lawrence thus becomes the physical, spiritual, and moral leader of an escape party consisting of his own family, the DeCamp contingent, and Mrs. Robideaux and her children. He plays the part of a biblical hero—a patriarch—by helping the vulnerable women and children and risking his life on their behalf. Like Moses he leads his people out of the wilderness and saves religious relics, including the mission church bell and Bible, as well as the Dakota grammar and dictionary Riggs was compiling.

Some of his details are especially powerful, as when he had to kill his own dog for fear it would give him away: "I had a very savage watch-dog (a bull dog). I thought a great deal of him, but was afraid to take him lest he should make a noise by barking. I choked him with his collar, and then cut his throat."[34] This episode illustrates a very different kind of dog sacrifice from the one that prejudicial early twentieth-century readers of Whipple's book might have expected from Indians in 1862. It was an action signifying Lawrence's recognition that everyone's safety depended on his agreeing to give up this prized possession: a working dog as well as a companion animal. Indeed, it illustrates Christian sacrifice as well as self-survival.

Lawrence also describes the group's ongoing attempts to stave off hunger. For instance, hearing a tinkling bell he followed what he believed was a cow, hoping to kill it for food. It turned out to be a ram that outran him at first but was finally caught and killed. The "Statement" continues with a blow-by-blow account of the party's progress through a dangerous and devastated landscape. They reached the safety of Fort Ridgely, but only after enduring privations and dangers, including the near-drowning of one of the DeCamp boys and Lawrence's rescue of him. Often, as leader, Lawrence went on ahead of the others and risked discovery and death, but he was determined not to jeopardize the safety of his charges, who lagged behind, exhausted.

Lawrence's text concludes with these statements: "I rescued ten persons. The next day I went out with Mr. Marsh and a detachment of soldiers to find his brother's body. They promised to pay me for so doing, but I never received anything. This is all I have to say."[35] Although seemingly unconnected the comments actually follow a logical train of thought, namely that while Lawrence willingly delivered ten people from captivity by the hostile Dakotas, the military did not follow through on its promise to reward him. Jannette DeCamp Sweet acknowledges this inconsistency within her narrative when she says that Lawrence was never adequately recognized: "For his faithful kindness to me and mine I shall never cease to remember him as a true friend, albeit an Indian, and one who did not fear to sacrifice all he had for the safety of his white friends."[36] In the interview she gave to the *San Francisco Call* a year earlier than the 1894 publication of her narrative, she was even clearer about Lawrence's contributions: "No white man could have been kinder or more worthy of his Christian profession."[37]

The intervening years between Lawrence's 1862 "Statement" and 1895 "Story" only reinforce the sense that Lawrence was betrayed by white society in general. In 1863 he was exiled with other innocent Dakotas from Fort Snelling to Crow Creek and wrote a series of letters to Stephen Riggs about the starvation conditions there.[38] He visited Jannette DeCamp Sweet many times during 1866 at Fort Ridgely and homesteaded on the site of the Lac Qui Parle mission in 1868, but by 1877 he was in dire financial straits—so dire that one Sydney Cook published a testimonial in the *St. Paul Pioneer Press* asking for aid on his behalf. Titled "A Good Indian," Cook's letter designates Lawrence as "the old hero (yes, I might say God's nobleman)" and reminds readers that Lawrence could not live on the Sisseton Reservation because "his own tribe despises him for the course he took in 1862."[39] He made a living by farming, but like many others in Swift County, Minnesota, at that time he was destitute because grasshoppers had destroyed his crops. Lawrence removed again to the Lake Traverse Reservation in 1877 and died near Peever, South Dakota, in 1897.[40] But two years before his death he wrote a lengthy account in English focusing on his wartime role.

"Story of Lorenzo Lawrence" is a forty-one-page holograph manuscript that performs several narrative functions. First and foremost, it attempts "to tell the exact truth" about how he rescued ten captives and took them to Fort Ridgely.[41] Lawrence also hoped this text would establish his worth as "a good citizen" so he could request and receive aid from the state of Minnesota when he became so old that he could not provide for his family.[42] Aged seventy-three, Lawrence may have believed this point was near. He explains that his narrative offsets the exaggerated or fraudulent claims of having rescued large numbers of captives that some Indians made themselves or that others made about them. In this regard, he focuses especially on Taopi (Wounded Man), who saved 255 people, according to Bishop Whipple.[43] But Taopi alone was no more instrumental in the release of those hostages at Camp Release than were a dozen or so other Dakotas, including Lawrence. Instead of Taopi, Lawrence presents a trio of Christian Indians—himself, John Other Day, and Simon Anawangmani—who "performed the valiant deed of snatching poor White women and children from their Indian captors."[44]

Like his shorter "Statement," Lawrence's "Story" is primarily a captivity narrative showing his courage and perseverance as a fellow hostage, escaping with the others he rescued. The "Story" exhibits traits of the Native spiritual and bravery narratives examined earlier, in Paul Mazakutemani's account. Yet Lawrence subsumes these elements to an even greater degree than Mazakutemani within the Western forms of the spiritual autobiography and the captivity narrative. Their rhetoric and structure pervade the "Story" even more than the "Statement." Not only does he designate everyone in his escape party as captives, but he uses the captor/captive rubric ironically and deliberately.

For example, he recalls a conversation between Jannette DeCamp and his mother in which Totidutawin says of the Dakota captors, "If it is God's will, in less than a month all these Indians will be captives," to which Mrs. DeCamp responds, "Yes, they can kill the body but they can't kill the soul."[45] This dialogue plainly illustrates the traditional generic link between captivity narratives and spiritual autobiographies as representing the body and soul threatened respectively by physical and spiritual dangers. Thus individuals and their societies are measured by "grace under pressure," using "grace" in a religious not just an affective sense. Leading the captives to safety becomes a test of Lawrence's faith that he willingly embraces.

The length and literary nature of the "Story" allow Lawrence to develop the earlier account's religious rhetoric and spiritual elements. Thus there are many more typological references to the escape party pausing for prayers and hymns, as when they sang "All Hail the Power of Jesus' Name" shortly after the Robideaux family joined them and then prayed, "O Lord our God, watch over us this day, and turn the eyes of the Indians so they won't see us."[46] The biblical rhetoric is evident in Lawrence's frequent use of the term "behold" and in his story of saving young Willie DeCamp, which employs the language of miracles: "I said, Willie can you breathe, and he said, Yes. Then I said to his mother, Your son is alive. And she felt great joy. We were all frightened to think how near one of us came to dying, and our memory was refreshed, and we knew well that God was watching over us, and we were filled with gratitude to him."[47] Another intertextual marker between the "Story" and the Bible is a possible allusion to the miracle of the loaves and fishes when Lawrence asks the womenfolk to bake bread for the children and give it out in small bites so it lasts.

Lawrence's narrative also provides a history of the mission effort among the Dakotas. Looking at the destroyed church and at Riggs's burned house at Yellow Medicine in 1862, Lawrence recalled the building of the first mission church around 1844 at Lac Qui Parle, the funding of a bell through the sale of forty-eight pairs of moccasins, and the evangelizing efforts of the early ABCFM ministers Stephen Riggs and Thomas Williamson. He spends six pages detailing this information and then describes how he had the foresight to bury the mission bell and Dakota Bibles and hymn books before the attack on Yellow Medicine.

The last quarter of the text, told partly in first person and partly in third person, tells how Sibley and Riggs questioned Lawrence about his role in the Conflict. Indeed, the occasion of this interview may be the source of Lawrence's 1862 "Statement." Lawrence volunteers information to them on the beginning of the war, the Indian camps, and the large number of captives. Then, appealing to readers, he discusses the scouting role that he, John Other Day, and Simon Anawangmani played. This leads to his conclusion that because the three of them were early scouts who did particularly dangerous work, they should receive priority status for government compensation. He mentions that congressional scouting appropriations were still being made as late as 1895, the date of the "Story's" composition. Lawrence's final words reinforce his postwar economic captivity and social isolation: "I have never yet made an application for it [a government appropriation]. And among the Indians what I did brought me no credit, and I have few friends among them."[48]

In 2005 Lorenzo Lawrence's great-grandson Elden Lawrence (Ehanna Wicohan Oyake) reevaluated the role of Christian Dakotas in his book *The Peace Seekers: Indian Christians and the Dakota Conflict*. It focuses on the role of Lorenzo Lawrence during the war and reclaims Elden's own links to his heritage. In one of the epigraphs to the earlier "Historical Perspectives on the Dakota War," Elden Lawrence states his belief that "after sorting through the many documents, testimonials and historical accounts, in the final analysis . . . history must tell its own story."[49] In other words, there are so many competing interpretations of the war that readers must sift through the material to glean the truth for themselves.

A final measure of Lorenzo Lawrence's heroism concerns his recognition on the monument known as "the Faithful Indians Monument," completed in 1899. In *Sketches Historical and Descriptive of the Monuments and Tablets Erected by the Minnesota Valley Historical Society*, Return Holcombe devotes an entire section to this marker celebrating the "small but grandly noble element, who . . . signalized their

Figure 20. Loyal Indians Monument and Birch Coulee Monument near Morton, Minnesota, ca. 1930. From the Collections of the Minnesota Historical Society. Used with permission.

devotion by risking their lives for the preservation and salvation of those of the unfortunate white people."[50] The criteria for selection were stringent and required that those chosen must be full bloods, must have been loyal throughout the entire course of the war, and must have directly saved the life of at least one white person. Only five names were originally engraved on the monument, all of them

Figure 21. Maggie Brass (Snana), ca. 1880. From the Collections of the Minnesota Historical Society. Used with permission.

posthumously: Lorenzo Lawrence, John Other Day, Paul Mazakutemani, Simon Anawangmani, and Mary Crooks. A sixth was added later, that of the next figure examined in this chapter, Maggie Brass.

Chapter 4 notes that when the story of Mary Schwandt first appeared in Bryant and Murch's *History of the Great Massacre*, the role of both Maggie Brass (Snana) and her first husband, Andrew Good Thunder (Wakinyanwaste), was presented negatively. Schwandt and her editors conceded that the Dakota couple had adopted and protected her, but Schwandt described this experience as a compelled filial relationship—just another type of captivity—and one of many unpleasant or abusive aspects of her life among the Dakotas. Not until the first-person retelling of her captivity within the pages of the *St. Paul Pioneer Press* and the *Collections of the Minnesota Historical Society* in 1894 did Schwandt Schmidt portray Maggie (though not Andrew) Good Thunder as a loving parent and herself as a grateful child. By making this change Schwandt Schmidt acknowledged that her formal adoption involved reciprocal emotional ties as well as kinship status. The relationship between adopted mother and adopted child became particularly close, because each replaced a much-missed dead relative, Schwandt's mother and Snana's daughter. Indeed, both women later used the mother-child trope as a structuring narrative device.

When Return Holcombe helped to reunite the two women after many years apart, he was not only doing a good deed. As a shrewd journalist he undoubtedly recognized further publishing opportunities in bringing them together. First, he obtained information for, and may have actually written, a *Pioneer Press* article about the women's reconciliation.[51] Then he began trying to obtain Maggie Brass's own story to complement Schwandt Schmidt's and to furnish a rare example of a Dakota woman's perspective on the war. From 1895 until Brass's account actually appeared within the pages of *Collections of the Minnesota Historical Society*, both Holcombe and Schwandt Schmidt encouraged her to provide data about her family background, wartime role, and postwar life.

Dated fall 1894, from internal evidence, Maggie Brass's story, signed with her Anglo name, survives in a seven-page manuscript her son wrote in ink that is now almost too faint to read.[52] Brass told Schwandt Schmidt that the words were hers and that her son just copied them: "I make and wrote that story myself with my hand but my son he coppy for it," she said.[53] Since this quotation and the surviving letters in Brass's handwriting show some idiomatic departures from standard, edited English, and since a comparison of the manuscript and the printed version reveals very few changes, her son, rather than Holcombe, may have silently corrected most of her slips. However, the text still retains a distinctive narrative voice, as well as some unedited "authenticating" expressions. The most significant modification in the published story concerns the title: someone, presumably Holcombe, changed the neutral-sounding "The Story of Maggie Brass and Her Experience in the Sioux Outbreak" to the more emotionally charged "Narration of a Friendly Sioux. By Snana, the Rescuer of Mary Schwandt." In this way Maggie Brass is identified by her Dakota name and defined by the white girl she rescued. Holcombe also drafted copious notes on Brass's life, which he obtained from her and Schwandt Schmidt and included as annotations to her narrative.

Maggie Brass opens her "Narration" with the information that she was a childhood convert to Christianity who attended school and lived with missionary Thomas Williamson's family for several years. When she rejoined her mother her reintroduction to Dakota culture was difficult, she states, because "I thought of myself as a white lady in my mind and in my thoughts."[54] Like Nancy Huggan, Maggie Brass presents herself as belonging to a different ethnic and social group owing to her acculturation to Western ways. But Brass's telling comment also sets up her narrative credibility in stereotypically positive terms for readers of *Collections of the Minnesota Historical Society*. They had already been primed to view her this way by Schwandt Schmidt's representation of her and by newspaper reports of the two women's regular visits after their initial meeting. A *Pioneer Press* article dated 15 September 1895, for example, describes Brass's "brave and noble conduct in rescuing and preserving her helpless young charge from death." Another related article in the *Pioneer Press* appeared in fall 1906.[55]

Although Maggie Brass was little-known to the Minnesota public before Schwandt Schmidt's story appeared and her own story was published, she and her first husband had been discussed before, in the limited milieu of the 1861 and 1862 *Missionary Paper* of the Bishop Seabury Mission. The 1862 volume described the couple as devoted to their young daughter (the child whom Schwandt replaced) and characterized her thus: "Few children ever grow so rapidly in grace and we all feared our child would be early called—at last she sickened."[56] Maggie and Andrew Good Thunder remained steadfast in their faith despite harassment from non-Christian Dakotas who said the child was ailing because she had been hexed by and educated with Ojibwes, the Dakotas' traditional enemies.

As the parents took away their dying child they were given commendatory papers asking people to show them kindness as they made their way home. Indeed, later on Andrew Good Thunder is reported to have said, "When I was a wild Indian they drove me away, but now they treated me as a brother and laid my child on a good bed and gave her things to eat and I felt that I was no longer an Indian, because I was Christ's."[57] Thus this story becomes a contemporary parable of Christian sacrifice, faith, and fellowship and conforms to nineteenth-century sentimentalized conventions about the purity and authority of the dying female child ("our child," the text says) who preaches toleration and forgiveness. While these claims may well have been true, they also helped to justify Episcopal evangelism among the Dakotas to the *Missionary Paper*'s readers and supporters. After the war Bishop Whipple used a similar tactic in claiming that converts like Maggie and Andrew Good Thunder showed Christian, "civilized" morality when they saved the lives of captives.

Early in her own account Brass too emphasizes her identity as an educated Christian whose beliefs "led me from the darkness of superstition to the light of Christianity in those dark days among my people."[58] Spiritual autobiography—one of the many subgenres within the captivity narrative tradition—undergirds her "Narration." But the dominant narrative structure is the Indian captivity narrative, in which Brass retells Schwandt's story focusing on the relationship between mother and child and the interventions necessary to keep Schwandt from harm. In emphasizing this intimate relationship Brass's narrative exhibits a characteristic of Native women's autobiographies, namely that they are generally concerned with "the partnership women share in the structuring and preserving of traditions within their societies."[59]

Because Brass's eldest daughter had died about a week before the hostilities erupted, Brass told her uncles that if they saw a needy girl they should "bring her to me that I might keep her for a length of time."[60] Tending to a captive girl would assuage Brass's grief and assure protection to an otherwise vulnerable person. The uncles did not return with a hostage but instead informed her that "there was a young man who brought a nice looking girl" (the terms "young man," "brought," and "nice looking girl" could be Brass's euphemisms for a girl at risk of sexual harassment).[61] So Brass exchanged her pony for Mary Schwandt, explaining: "The reason why I wished to keep this girl was to have her in place of the one I lost. So I loved her and pitied her, and she was dear to me just the same as my own daughter."[62]

But Brass not only helped Schwandt, she decided to adopt her. With the Sioux and many other Native peoples, "captives were adopted to take the place of deceased relatives," and in the case of adopted children the adult assumed a full parental role.[63] Captive children in particular "were commonly adopted into the family of the captor and underwent ceremonial adoption similar to that carried out in the child-replacing rite."[64] Thus once Schwandt became part of Good Thunder's family, she was not harmed. Brass reports that whenever she heard of captives being hurt, she not only hid Schwandt but also protected herself and her two biological children against reprisals. The family bonding extended to Brass's mother, who helped care for Schwandt, but not to Good Thunder himself, who "never helped me in any way to take care of this girl."[65] A significant textual marker showing how much Brass cherished Schwandt during captivity concerns the same words she uses to express her grief when her daughter died and when she relinquished Schwandt at Camp Release: she says that her "heart was still aching" for her biological daughter when the war began and that her "heart ached again" when she turned over Schwandt—"this dear child"—to the U.S. military.[66]

Yet Brass ends her narrative not with this sundering but with the women's reunion thirty-two years later: "Soon I went to visit her, and I was respected and treated well. It was just as if I went to visit my own child."[67] Indeed, the mother-child rhetoric is not just a structural device for her narrative; it signals the enduring reality of her relationship with Schwandt. Many letters from Brass to Schwandt Schmidt survive in the Mary Schwandt Schmidt Papers, housed at the Minnesota Historical Society. Some are undated, but the dated ones range from 1895 to 1907, the year before Brass died. Almost all of them open with the salutation "My Dear Adopted daughter" and close with such expressions as "your poor adopted mother," "your true adopted mother," and "your poore Indian mother."

Brass visited the Schmidt family a number of times over the years and was particularly fond of Schmidt's son Carl, whom she sometimes wrote to separately and addressed as "my Dear grandson." The letters contain news about gifts both sent and received, progress in writing her story, messages for Return Holcombe, financial worries, old age, and her increasing health problems. She often talks about how much she cares for and misses her adopted daughter. The last dated letter, written on 11 March 1907, opens: "My Dear daughter I want to answer your kind letter that you wrote to me. I want to tell you that I was very sick this winter while I was sick I always think of you but I cant write to you."[68] The strong emotional connection between the two women survived, even grew, over the years. It showed that both parties respected the Dakota ideal that "the dictates of kinship demanded of relatives that they . . . be aware of their reciprocal obligations."[69] Presumably they also acted in this way out of Christian fellowship.

As we have seen, Maggie Brass's account is a captivity narrative that focuses on someone else's captivity. It does not mention the fact that she and her family endured their own virtual captivity after the Conflict, at the compound near Fort Snelling. Stephen Riggs compared the situation in the Mankato prison, where the Dakotas sentenced to be hung were incarcerated, with that at the encampment: "The conditions in both places were a good deal alike. In the camp as well as in the prison, they were in trouble and perplexity."[70] Two of Brass's children died at the compound, and perhaps from the strain of so much suffering, in about 1865 she and Good Thunder separated. A few years later she moved from Faribault to the Santee Sioux Reservation in Nebraska, where she worked at the government school and married Charles Brass (Mazazezee), another Dakota. They had one son and adopted two Indian girls. But her second husband had died by the time she and Schwandt Schmidt met again in 1895.

Maggie Brass's own death, on 24 April 1908, was reported three weeks later in the *Pioneer Press*, under the headline "Saved White Girl in Massacre / Death of Mrs. Maggie Brass Recalls Touching Incident of the Sioux Uprising."[71] Here Brass is presented as an example of Indian assimilation into white cultural norms, beginning with her early mission education and baptism and continuing with her life as Good Thunder's young wife. The article rehearses the by now familiar story of how the two women met during the war and were reunited decades after it and points out that Brass's name will be added to the Faithful Indians' Monument. It ends with information on her later life as further evidence of her family's integration: "Mrs. Brass died in comfortable circumstances. She was intelligent and prudent, owned considerable real estate and other property, which she managed well. She left one son, now a sergeant in the artillery branch of the regular army, and two foster daughters."[72]

These claims of material comfort are not corroborated by Brass's letters, where frequently she says that she cannot afford to visit Schwandt Schmidt as often as she would like, occasionally she asks if Schwandt Schmidt can send her some wild rice, and once she signs an informal promissory note borrowing ten dollars from her adopted daughter. Although Brass does mention land sales, it sounds as if they were needed to generate income rather than to invest in real estate, as the obituary suggests. Two large photographs supplement the verbal text, one of Maggie Brass as a young woman in European dress, taken about 1860, and another of the two women together in 1899, titled "The Rescuer and the Rescued" (reproduced on page 112). The latter image especially forms a visual equivalent of Brass's captivity narrative: each text reinforces positive cultural stereotypes but also signifies the reality of cultural cooperation and exchange.

11. Good Star Woman
Captivity and Ethnography

The subjects of the next two chapters—Good Star Woman (Wicah-pewastewin, Dorine Blacksmith), Esther Wakeman (Mahpiyatowin, Blue Sky Woman), and Joseph Coursolle (Joe Gaboo, Joe Caboo, Joe Gabbro)—could conceivably be included in a single chapter on oral history and traditions. Esther Wakeman and Joseph Coursolle told their stories to family members who passed down the accounts to succeeding generations before they appeared in print form. But I am placing Good Star Woman in a separate chapter because she told her story to an early professional ethnographer and ethnomusicologist, Frances Densmore.[1] Good Star Woman is the only Dakota in my book whose narrative was recorded in this way. All the other non-Native intermediaries to whom Dakotas gave their accounts, like Stephen Riggs and Return Holcombe, might be called amateur, or perhaps accidental, ethnographers.

In using these terms I do not mean that the amateurs' methods were necessarily more shoddy or skewed than those of the professionals but that their prime motives for information gathering were different. The amateur ethnographers favored a hands-on, personal approach to promote a specific agenda, such as conversion. The data they collected were a means to an end. But the professionals tried to adopt a more impersonal approach, with information itself as the main goal. In fact, the data they gathered underlay the fledgling discipline of anthropology in general and ethnography in particular. Both sets of information gatherers were prone to their own subjectivities, which might either hold the Indians' stories captive to non-Native intermediaries or at the very least offset claims of authenticity.

Frances Densmore is a transitional figure spanning ethnography's evolution and professionalization as a discipline. She had no formal training when she began her fieldwork in the 1890s, although she had received an academic musical education at Oberlin and Harvard. The extensive Web archive for Minnesota Public Radio's 1997 program *Song Catcher: Frances Densmore* aptly labels her "the White-Gloved Ethnologist" during these early years.[2] She had first become interested in Indian music after visiting the 1893 Columbian Exposition in Chicago and hearing performances there. But she found ample fieldwork opportunities closer to home, at the Prairie Island Dakota Reservation and at the Cass Lake, White Earth, and Grand Portage Ojibwe Reservations. By 1906 and 1907, when she was attending ceremonies among the Dakotas and Ojibwes using a phonograph to record information and music, her status might more accurately be described as semiprofessional. Over the decades she worked with many other Native peoples, but she continued to expand her knowledge of the Lakotas and Dakotas, as well as the Ojibwes.

Densmore was still an important figure in the field when she interviewed Good Star Woman in 1938. By then her peers accepted her as a self-educated professional, though her influence was waning with the growth of the (mostly male) academic ethnological establishment. Exactly how the two women met is unclear, but they certainly lived in the same general area. Densmore grew up in Red Wing, Minnesota, and used it as a base until her death in 1957. Good Star Woman lived with the Dakota band at Prairie Island, on the Mississippi River, about fourteen miles north of Red Wing. The Prairie Island band's musical compositions and performances greatly interested Densmore. So it is likely that on one of her field trips to collect music she encountered the octogenarian Good Star Woman and decided to record the old lady's wartime remembrances.

Densmore's introduction to the story of Good Star Woman opens by commenting on its significance: "There are few Indian survivors of the outbreak in Minnesota who can recall the details of the tragedy. One woman, however, remembers it clearly, though she was only eight years old at the time."[3] And Densmore was right that by the 1930s a Dakota woman's firsthand account provided an unusual perspective on the war, since few Indian women had spoken publicly of their experiences up to then. Yet Densmore also recorded reminiscences of non-Natives in Red Wing, so she may have valued Good Star Woman's contributions to local history as well as ethnography—a local history both women shared.

Like many of the other Dakota accounts, this narrative is a multi-layered bicultural collaborative text. For instance, Densmore strives to write an objective introduction and conclusion, but her subjectivity intrudes. She also indicates before the narrative itself that the story "is presented exactly as translated" by Good Star Woman's daughter Mrs. John Bearskin, with input from another daughter, Mrs. Peter Logan.[4] A handwritten note on the manuscript (presumably Densmore's) states that Bearskin suggested some minor changes, and the text itself includes the comment that these two women, the interviewer and the translator, discussed the story together. Such statements raise the possibility that one or both daughters influenced the basic tale. They might even have changed their mother's words and told Densmore what they thought she would want to hear. Finally, Densmore writes the account in the third person and includes one small parenthetical interpolation of her own. Although third-person narration could aptly signal to readers that the text is mediated, Densmore's decision not to write the narrative in the first person counters her statement that she presents an exact translation. Whose precise words are these: Good Star Woman's or her daughters'?

Similarly conflicting or compromised methodologies in Densmore's ethnomusicology lay her open to criticism among later anthropologists and activists. For instance, Michael F. Brown's book *Who Owns Native Culture?* discusses Densmore in light of "the difficulty of assessing the current moral status of information collected in other eras."[5] Brown questions whether she should be admired as a pioneering female anthropologist who preserved data, artifacts, and traditions that otherwise might have been lost or denounced as "a butterfly collector" who removed things from their cultural context and placed them in a sterile museum setting. Her ethical relationship to her subjects is also problematical, since different constituencies polarize her as a friend and protector of the Indians—particularly of the Prairie Island band—or as an elitist who exploited vulnerable people.[6] Similar charges, of course, continue to be leveled against anthropologists and ethnographers.

First, I will examine Densmore's frame to the narrative of Good Star Woman, which holds the intervening text rhetorically captive by priming readers before and after. Historically many captivity narratives were similarly enclosed by the words of an editor or some other authority, like a minister. This strategy is also evident in other texts presented here, such as Big Eagle's "A Sioux Story of the War." Then I will consider information in the narrative proper, focusing on its many references to literal kinds of captivity.

Deconstructing Densmore's title and assignation of authorship—"A Sioux Woman's Account of the Uprising in Minnesota by Frances Densmore"—reveals her sense that she "owned" a text worth preserving for posterity. The introductory paragraph describes Good Star Woman at the time of the interview as someone who "sews industriously all day," although practically blind.[7] Densmore also comments on her interesting face, long braids, and unusual vigor for her age. Noting Good Star Woman's bag of tobacco, the interviewer adds, "When she had finished her narrative she lit her long pipe as deftly as the woman of today lights a cigarette."[8] Through this analogy Densmore presents a figure joining two worlds: the storyteller who recalls details of a distant war when she was only a child, and the subject who survives into peaceful and productive old age. However, we must be clear that this dualism represents Densmore's sentimental interpretation, rather than the reality of reservation life at this time.

Next come basic biographical data the family supplied on Joseph Blacksmith, Good Star Woman's father, and finally a note on methodology: "No attempt has been made to harmonize it with history. It stands as the narrative of one who remembers the Sioux 'massacre' and shared in its sufferings."[9] The assurance that Densmore will not try to "harmonize" the story with history befits an anthropologist but also has other ramifications that I will discuss later. The one-sentence conclusion after the narrative proper, also in Densmore's voice, states simply, "Such is the story of Good Star Woman, one of the Friendly Sioux who remembers the uprising of the hostile Indians."[10] It reiterates the presentation of Good Star Woman throughout the narrative as one of "the Friendly Sioux."

Many Native and non-Native captivity narratives open by summarizing the general causes of hostilities before reaching specific firsthand reminiscences. This strategy, also adopted by Good Star Woman, helps confer credibility on narrators by contextualizing their experiences. As an eight-year-old in 1862 she could not have understood the chain of events then. So her later evaluation of the war's contributing causes must have evolved from family and community stories—from oral history—that she melded with her own sense of causation. In this way her narrative may also exhibit the workings of memory, discussed in the earlier "Historical Perspectives on the Dakota War," regarding traumatic and nontraumatic incidents encoded into "semantic" memory (remembrances that Good Star Woman did not know how she learned) and "episodic" memory (remembrances that she could clearly assign to a particular time and place).[11]

For example, she folds what were actually discrete events into a single timeframe in observing, "There were three outbreaks at once, the first being at Granite Falls, the second at Birch Coulee, and the third at Big Stone Lake."[12] Using composite history to collapse time is a common strategy in Indigenous historical narratives, where the essence of what happened is more important than distracting details or fixed chronology. Good Star Woman deflects attention from the Mdewakantons by claiming that the Sissetons started the war and by saying that those Mdewakantons who were involved received a disproportionate amount of blame. This information sets up her assertion that the Hemnica Mdewakanton band, to which her father belonged, did not initially want to fight.

She then interprets from a Dakota perspective several key events contributing to the outbreak of war. For example, she tells of an incident eighteen months before the Battle of Birch Coulee, in which white people brutally killed a hungry Indian. Despite this outrage, she says, Dakotas did not seek revenge. Next, she assesses the role of corrupt traders in fostering distrust between European Americans and Native Americans but again declares that many Natives overlooked this exploitation. Finally she retells the Acton incident that triggered the war. Surely many Dakota families passed down their own versions of this same story. Yet again, however, Good Star Woman is at pains to say that the chiefs disapproved of what the young men had done "and said the trouble must not go any further."[13] A page later she describes how Dakotas meted out punishment to these youths by killing them. She therefore implies that over time certain whites created the conditions under which one lone incident could cause all-out war. This in turn leads Good Star Woman to conclude that the militant Dakotas tried to hold the pacifist faction morally hostage to the decision to wage war.

The story becomes more vivid once Good Star Woman moves to concrete recollections of her family's whereabouts when war erupted. They were not at home, she says, but staying with her aunt and initially mistook the shots they heard that morning for an Ojibwe attack. After a messenger told them that the Dakotas were killing settlers, the children awoke and began to cry. She then details how two Indians who killed a white farmer were shot by other Dakotas specifically because they had caused the women and children so much suffering.[14] The womenfolk and children she refers to may have been Dakotas or other captives. Regardless, she continues by showing war's impact on innocent parties, and from this point on in her narrative she defines war's capacity to inflict pain by focusing on women and children; on sundered families; and on confinement, imprisonment, and captivity.

Good Star Woman is typical of the wartime generation of Dakota youth who underwent repeated family fractures and dislocations, and perhaps this helps to explain such a narrative focus. For example, she describes her memory of mothers and children being confined and sheltered inside wigwams while men crouched in a nearby trench they had dug below the line of fire. The earth that had been excavated formed an embankment outside the wigwams. This was the way Dakotas traditionally defended themselves against Ojibwe attacks, but in this case Good Star Woman's family and others used it to protect themselves from other Dakotas. Her recollection therefore involves a kind of self-imposed captivity for the women and children, ironically from dangers within their own community.

The narrative also includes Good Star Woman's remembrance of Camp Release, of the forced march to Fort Snelling, of white Minnesotans' violence along the way, and of her father's attempts to protect his family from the settlers' hostility. The story states that when the Dakotas "passed through towns the people brought poles, pitchforks and axes and hit some of the women and children in the wagons. Her father was struck once and almost knocked down."[15] While the rhetoric of forced confinement pervades this section of the narrative, the rhetoric of protection—meaning enclosure that could be beneficial—does so too. Both Joseph Blacksmith and the soldiers are described as shielding the Native women and children from attempts at vigilante justice by Dakotas as well as displaced settlers. But why would Good Star Woman link her father with these white authority figures?

The narrative's final sections deal specifically with captivity: first, the incarceration at Fort Snelling of "the pitiful column of friendly Sioux," including noncombatants like Good Star Woman and her family; and second, the series of internments and relocations as these same Dakotas left Fort Snelling for Crow Creek.[16] The section on Fort Snelling describes an enclosed space staffed by seemingly kind representatives, such as soldiers who "gave crackers to the children and bread to the older people" and a Catholic priest who fed the children and arranged formal burials for the Indian dead.[17] Yet Good Star Woman likely had a more subversive agenda than praising these male authorities. For, as she says, the "high fence" the soldiers erected did not protect Dakotas from greedy settlers stealing their horses and oxen, nor did it keep out the measles, which killed as many as fifty in a single day.[18]

Furthermore the Catholic priest may have been essentially bribing the children to convert. Good Star Woman states, "He was good to the children and told them to come to church and he gave them candy and apples."[19] Certainly Densmore seems to have taken this statement at face value, since it prompts a surprisingly emotional interpolation within the narrative: "(Who was this priest? Doubtless his name is recorded in history but the Sioux remember only his good deeds)."[20] Good Star Woman may have meant these details to be ironic, for anyone culturally sensitive enough to pick up on them, or at least may have questioned the efficacy and appropriateness of such palliative measures.

The final paragraph of the narrative proper recalls that in late 1862 some Dakotas left Fort Snelling in chains, while the rest stayed at the fort during the brutal winter months. In the spring of 1863 the latter group left in two contingents on 4 and 5 May. From details in her account Good Star Woman and her relatives must have left on 5 May, on a leaky steamboat named the *Northerner*. It was headed down the Mississippi River for Hannibal, Missouri, appropriately enough a slave-trading town. Then, as Good Star Woman remembers, the people were driven into railroad boxcars and taken to St. Joseph, on the Missouri River, where they joined the 4 May group on the dangerously overcrowded steamboat the *Florence*. For those who survived the journey, the destination was Fort Thompson, on the Crow Creek Reservation.[21] Missionary John P. Williamson, who accompanied the group on the *Florence*, said the inhuman conditions were "nearly as bad as the Middle Passage for slaves."[22]

At Fort Thompson, Good Star Woman recalls, her relations and others "were kept in a stockade for three years. Many starved to death there. The Indians were almost naked. They wound burlap around their legs to keep warm."[23] This section of the narrative most clearly conforms to the definition of a traditional captivity or slave narrative, with empowered captors holding disempowered captives in bondage physically, culturally, and emotionally. But as in some other participant captivity narratives, this captive lives to tell her tale and speaks many years later from her stable home base.

Knowing the history of the Prairie Island band is important for understanding Good Star Woman's narrative and her father's role in the story. The booklet "Transformation of an Island: A Historical Perspective on the Prairie Island Indian Community," available on the Prairie Island Mdewakanton Dakota Indian Community's Web site, points out that Mdewakanton Dakotas had lived on the island for many generations, until the diaspora in 1862. Several decades later "the Prairie Island Reservation was created when the Secretary of the Interior purchased land and placed it into trust. About 120 acres was purchased at Prairie Island for the landless Mdewakanton residing in Minnesota on May 20, 1886. Subsequent purchases by the Secretary under congressional appropriations and later the Indian Reorganization Act expanded the reservation's borders. Under the Indian Reorganization Act of 1934, an additional 414 acres was purchased for other Indian residents whose names appeared on the Minnesota Sioux rolls."[24]

Yet other historical records suggest that most of the postwar founders of Prairie Island had been tried and imprisoned for participation in the Conflict. This assertion must immediately be tempered by the

fact that "trial records indicate their crimes were anything but hei-
nous" and indeed that some had been wrongfully convicted.[25] After
their release from Davenport they gradually migrated back to Prairie
Island to practice traditional life ways, since it had not then been
designated as a reservation and was not subject to the same government strictures. Despite the treaty annulments of 1863, some Dakotas
had returned to Minnesota sooner than the 1880s because they were
under the protection of a particular church, and a few hundred brave
souls had never left the state.[26] But the Prairie Island Dakotas did not
have such sponsorship. Their land grant in the 1880s was probably the
result of legislation passed on behalf of the prowhite Dakotas during
the Conflict whose churches had sponsored them soon after. In effect
the same legislation also grandfathered in the Prairie Island Dakotas
and allowed them a formal land base.[27]

This information has ramifications for the narrative's reiterated
claims that Good Star Woman's family members, including her father, were among the pacifist faction and that they traveled together
to Fort Snelling and then to Crow Creek. The Dakota name of Good
Star Woman's father was Hepi Wakandisapa, but he adopted the Anglo name Joseph Blacksmith when he learned the blacksmith's trade.
Samuel Pond remembers Hepi and his brother Cantan (Chantan) as
early converts at his school in Lake Calhoun. He also mentions that
"both these men were condemned to death for participation in the
outbreak of 1862, but in the revival in the prison they were among the
most active in persuading their fellow captives to become Christians.
. . . Hepi was released after a time and located at Flandreau with many
of his kindred."[28]

If Joseph Blacksmith had marched to prison in Mankato with the
other convicted Dakotas, then he could not have accompanied his
family to Fort Snelling, since the two groups of Dakotas (condemned
prisoners and noncombatants) took separate routes to different des-
tinations.[29] Hepi's sentence, of course, does not necessarily mean that

he was guilty of anything, since the trial process was so flawed. Instead, in her narrative Good Star Woman may have articulated her father's true antiwar stance, as well as her own desire to have been protected by him on the way to Fort Snelling. Then she apparently ghosted him alongside the other close relatives who went there.

Eventually the family was reunited, but in 1886 John P. Williamson reported Blacksmith's mission work and death in the *Annual Report of the Commissioner of Indian Affairs*: "The [Dakota] laborers this past year have been Rev. W. O. Rogers and wife, at Wood Lake, and Elder Joseph Blacksmith, at Crow Hill. The society laments the loss of Mr. Blacksmith, who died in March last."[30] As Densmore says in her introduction, she does not try to resolve, or "harmonize," historical inconsistencies like the role of Joseph Blacksmith. Instead she is much more interested in his daughter's story as oral history.

At the time of this interview with Good Star Woman forty-five years had passed since Densmore's first exposure to ethnography at the Columbian Exposition. Her interest must have been prompted back then by a memorable exhibit organized by Franz Boas, who essentially founded the scientific study of American Indians.[31] Boas had done fieldwork among the Haida, Kwakiutl, and Bella Costa Indians of the Northwest. So, as is well-known, for the exposition he assembled a spectacular selection of masks and tools in a pavilion labeled "Anthropology" and installed a Kwakiutl group in two houses outside.[32] He intended these exhibits to help establish a more systematic basis for anthropology.

But instead of European Americans sympathetically absorbing data about other cultures, they responded at a far more primitive level to the Boas display and to nearly a hundred other "living exhibits" from such far-flung places as Egypt and Labrador. In fact, "the Chicago fair was a colossal freak show—a racist phantasmagoria, with commercial interests under the guise of 'anthropology' catering to every cheap and lurid prejudice."[33] Thus the young anthropologist's objective methodologies and idealistic politics made little impression on the national frame of reference. The impact of the exposition on ordinary European Americans was not unlike the impact of many written captivity narratives on the same constituency: they reinforced existing, usually negative, stereotypes of ethnic others.

Boas eventually obtained a position at Columbia, where he trained several generations of ethnographers, including Dakota/Lakota Ella Deloria, whom he recruited to do fieldwork among the Dakotas and to translate manuscripts at Columbia. Although Boas spoke Dakota and Lakota, "he trusted more to the authority of the native speaker than to the linguist."[34] Through Frances Densmore's influence Deloria did fieldwork at Prairie Island in 1936.[35] She may even have met Good Star Woman. At the very least trained Indigenous anthropologists like Deloria would help to further professionalize the discipline and liberate data from non-Native interviewers like Frances Densmore. Good Star Woman's oral history, with its many references to captivity, would have been a different text if Deloria had interviewed the old lady herself and recorded her words.

12. Esther Wakeman and Joseph Coursolle
Captivity and Oral History

The accounts of Esther Wakeman (Mahpiyatowin) and Joseph Coursolle (Joe Gaboo, Joe Caboo, Joe Gabbro) were passed down within their respective families until they were finally preserved in written form during the 1960s. This chapter concerns the transmission of these accounts, the information they convey, and the narrative adaptations they demonstrate. I focus on oral history in this chapter because a standard defining element of tribal memory involves oral history.[1] Waziyatawin Angela Wilson's definition of oral history as it pertains to Dakotas is particularly helpful:

> For my purposes here, from a Dakota perspective, I would suggest that the definition of oral history is contained within that of the oral tradition. For the Dakota and, I suspect, for many other Indigenous nations, "oral tradition" refers to the way in which information has been passed on rather than to the length of time something has been told. Hence, personal experiences, pieces of information, events, incidents, and so forth can become a part of the oral tradition at the moment they happen, or the moment they are spoken of, as long as the person adopting the memory is part of an oral tradition. Oral history can also exist outside the oral tradition since many individuals may provide authoritative oral-historical accounts based on their own experiences without necessarily belonging to an oral tradition themselves.[2]

In Wilson's terms Esther Wakeman and Joseph Coursolle provided "oral-historical accounts" that also became part of the oral tradition.

But the mediation involved in the stories' appearance in print moved them beyond the oral cultural context.

Elizabeth Wakeman repeated her story to her daughter Elizabeth (Wakeman) Lawrence (Morning Star), who retold it within the book *Minnesota Heritage*, published in 1960.[3] Elizabeth Lawrence then expanded and confirmed this information in an interview five years later. Joseph Coursolle's story was passed down to his grandson Clem Felix, who recounted it to a non-Native history buff, F. J. Patten. Patten seems to have embroidered the story and embellished the style when he wrote "The Ordeal of Hinhankaga" about 1962.[4] It remained unpublished until 1988. Supplementary information on Coursolle's life exists in testimony Coursolle gave in 1885 and in the Coursolle family's oral history, which is available via an interview with Joseph's grandson Naz Coursolle.[5]

As this background on the two original storytellers suggests, Wakeman's story remained in the family until they were ready to go public with it. On the other hand, Coursolle's life story spans several versions: his own oral testimony (1885); Patten's captivity narrative, with its editorial mediation (1962); and the family's oral transmission through several generations (1971). Only the Patten version constitutes a full-fledged captivity narrative; later analysis will explore the reasons why Coursolle's escape from the Lower Sioux Agency was recast in this way, blending Native oral history traditions with non-Native written ones.

Esther Wakeman was born in 1845 at a Dakota village near modern-day Bloomington, Minnesota.[6] She removed with her parents to the Lower Sioux Reservation in 1853 and married White Spider (John C. Wakeman, Big Thunder), Little Crow's half brother, about 1861. Esther Wakeman's story is thus particularly valuable because she viewed events as a close relative of Little Crow. Indeed, she and her family fled with Little Crow after his defeat at the Battle of Wood Lake in late September 1862 and then moved north to Canada. But starvation forced them to surrender at Fort Pembina, Dakota Territory, in January 1864, after which they were confined at Fort Snelling. The women in the family were sent to Crow Creek, while White Spider remained in prison at Davenport until 1866. The Wakemans reunited at the Santee Reservation; removed to the new Dakota settlement in Flandreau, South Dakota; and finally returned to Minnesota in the 1880s.[7] Esther's date of death cannot be confirmed, but John lived until 1902.[8]

Esther Wakeman's story, as told by Elizabeth (along with data from Elizabeth's husband, Harry Lawrence), appeared as part of the chapter "The Indian Nations of Minnesota," within the trade/coffee-table book *Minnesota Heritage: A Panoramic Narrative of the Historical Development of the North Star State*. Their section of the chapter is titled "The Sioux Uprising" and is designated, "By Mr. and Mrs. Harry Lawrence, Edited by Eugene T. Newhall." It is based on a 1958 tape transcription, about which Newhall says, "Much of the direct detail [is] as told to Mrs. Lawrence by her mother."[9] Newhall provides background information at the beginning of "The Sioux Uprising" and later quotes a comment about Little Crow from *Minnesota History*, but his intervention elsewhere seems limited.[10] Certainly Elizabeth Lawrence did not object to anything in the chapter. Interviewed elsewhere five years after "The Sioux Uprising" was published, she privileges information in it, refers people to it, and even quotes from it. She clarifies during the interview that one of her "great ambitions" within the pages of *Minnesota Heritage* was to provide "the true picture" of Little Crow's role in the Dakota War.[11]

The opening to Esther Wakeman's account establishes that in 1862 Little Crow dressed European-style, attended church, and lived in a frame house. For these activities, she says, he became the target of his own people's anger and was ousted as chief three months before the hostilities began. Historically accurate information like this undercuts the many accounts that blamed Little Crow for the Conflict, predisposes readers to view him more sympathetically, and reveals "the complex pressures" weighing on him as war began.[12] Throughout her story Esther Wakeman focuses on her brother-in-law rather than herself, trying to reclaim his role as a peacemaker, particularly through his attempts to save captives.

So, for example, she describes how he "divided some white women and children who found it difficult to escape among his friends to protect them from the renegades," and adds, "Little Crow wanted to make peace, but the majority of the people wanted him to lead them in a war."[13] The chapter ends with this statement: "After the massacre began and before he was drafted into the war by the angered people . . . Little Crow did not permit a single woman or child to be killed or injured at the lower agency, but permitted 32 of them, mostly adults, to escape to Fort Ridgely."[14] Not only does the text refer repeatedly to captives that Little Crow protected, but it also infers that the prowar faction essentially held him hostage and forced him to take part in the hostilities.

Still other information is reminiscent of many non-Native Indian captivity narratives, for instance the emphasis on daily routines before the war, the frantic search for family separated by fighting, the concern for injured relatives, and the utter chaos caused by the hostilities: "Like a destructive storm, the war struck suddenly and spread rapidly. Everything was confusion."[15] She also narrates White Spider's protective escort of several white women and children to a ravine through which they could travel by night and reach safety. One of them, Mrs. John Nairn, offered him her wedding ring, which he refused. Instead he replied, "Just look at my face and if anything happens, remember it."[16] What Nairn was being asked to recall was the face of an Indian who rescued captives rather than took them.

Esther Wakeman does devote one brief paragraph to her family's own captivity and confinement. Returning from Canada, she states that she and her husband "were imprisoned for three years. Our treatment was terrible. All the food was mixed in one big pot and it wasn't fit to eat. Three of my brothers died of smallpox while in prison."[17] She thus combines in historical memory the confinements of herself, her husband, and other close family at Fort Pembina, Fort Snelling, Crow Creek, and Davenport. Everyone was a captive of one kind or another, and everywhere, she indicates, the treatment was inhumane, the food inedible, and the dangers of sickness and starvation extreme. Captivity forms a common bond of suffering, as it does in many white-authored captivity narratives.

The oral transmission of Esther Wakeman's story follows a direct line to her daughter. But this account is also complemented by one that her husband told and published many years earlier. "Big Thunder's Story" appeared in 1886 in the *St. Paul and Minneapolis Pioneer Press*.[18] The byline reads, "He Makes a Statement Concerning the Massacre at Redwood Agency, Aug. 18, 1862, and Declares That Neither He Nor Little Crow Were to Blame."[19] The text opens with the salutation "To the Editor," so his words are characterized as a letter to the editor, not as an interview by reporters, and the newspaper seems to have produced John Wakeman's words verbatim, including some repetition and some nonstandard sentence constructions. But the precise role of translators and interpreters in this version is not known.

Eleven years later the same story was published unchanged as something novel, under the title "The Story of the Sioux Outbreak." It came out in the *Minneapolis Sunday Times* with a note that John Wakeman had narrated it to Return Holcombe and Edward Bromley with help from bilingual teacher Mary Whipple, Bishop Whipple's sister-in-law.[20] Did these white mediators, or others, help with the original 1886 account? Did John Wakeman tell the same story in the same words in 1897? Answers to these questions are not forthcoming. Neither the 1886 nor the 1897 account constitutes oral transmission in the same way that Esther Wakeman's does. Further, the role of intermediaries (Bromley, Holcombe, Whipple, if not other people) in both versions by John Wakeman is unclear. Therefore I am interested in his text mainly because it emphasizes the same things found in his wife's account, namely that John Wakeman himself saved white captives and that Little Crow, his brother, was extremely concerned with the captives' fate. It should be no surprise that the versions of husband and wife bolster each other.

"Big Thunder's Story" presents Wakeman and Little Crow taking the initiative in protecting white women and children after war began. This claim is most evident in the following extract, where Little Crow's words to White Spider reiterate the term "captive," though the biblical allusion, as well as the historical reality, is complicated by the fact that the Dakota word "Wayaka" can be translated as "captive" or "slave": "'The captives at my house this morning are crying and I feel very sorry. I have heard that God will have pity on poor captives, and, my brother, I have heard that God will be hard on those who are hard on captives. My brother, the captives in my house have nothing to eat, and so they are crying. I think you could find some flour where the Indians first commenced fighting.' . . . I agreed with what Little Crow said and rose up quickly and brought some flour for the captives."[21]

The Old Testament books of Ezra, Jeremiah, Ezekiel, and Amos contain the most instances of the keywords "captive," "captives," and "captivity" and mention the captivity of women and children. But Little Crow and John Wakeman may echo the captivity typology in Jeremiah 15:2, reflected in Revelation 13:10:

> Thus saith the LORD; Such as are for death, to death; and such as are for the sword, to the sword; and such as are for the famine, to the famine; and such as are for the captivity, to the captivity. (Jeremiah 15:2, King James Version)

> He that leadeth into captivity shall go into captivity: he that killeth with the sword must be killed with the sword. Here is the patience and the faith of the saints. (Revelation 13:10, King James Version)

Because Wakeman and Little Crow helped the captives, and because biblical precedent reveals that mercy should be shown to those who show mercy, John Wakeman concludes that the president himself should "look with pity on those who had mercy on the captives and sought to save them."[22] Specifically Wakeman believes his actions justify an appropriation now that he is old and poor. Together then the stories of Esther Wakeman and John Wakeman reinterpret the roles of Little Crow and of themselves through various means, including the treatment of captives and captivity rhetoric.

Although the Wakemans and the Coursolles both lived around the Lower Sioux Agency in 1862, their allegiances and experiences were radically different during wartime. John and Elizabeth Wakeman were loyal to Little Crow because they were kin: they fought and fled with him. But Joseph Coursolle was progovernment, and although he narrowly avoided capture by the Dakotas, his two young daughters (and possibly one of his sons) did not. Joseph Coursolle was born about 1832, the son of a French Canadian man and a Dakota woman. After Joseph's parents died in the 1840s Henry Sibley brought him up, educated him, and employed him for a while in Mendota.

When war erupted Joseph was working as a clerk and interpreter at the Lower Sioux Agency and was the father of five living children by three different women: Henri, his son by Marguerite Garceau, a French Canadian woman; Joseph, his son by Hapan, a Dakota woman; and three children by his wife, Jane Killcool, whose background was Scottish—Elizabeth Nancy, born in 1856; Philomene (Minnie), born in 1858; and another Joseph, who was born on 9 August and died on 18 August 1862.[23] His two older sons, Henri and Joseph, lived with their mothers, though there is some evidence that Joseph may have been with his father and stepmother, Joseph and Jane Coursolle, at the Lower Sioux Agency in August 1862, because he was entitled to an annuity payment and had to be physically present to receive it.

I rehearse the Coursolle genealogy in such detail, first, because family relationships are the essence of the oral history told by Joseph's grandson Naz Coursolle and, second, because the genealogical data authenticate parts of the captivity narrative that Clem Felix related to Patten.[24] Despite romantic touches and inconsistencies in "The Ordeal of Hinhankaga," the text is factually credible, as seen, for example, in the fact that the three Coursolle children mentioned there—Elizabeth Nancy, Minnie, and baby Joe—do indeed have the names of Joseph and Jane's children at that time. But "The Ordeal of Hinhankaga" shares with some other non-Native captivity narratives a tendency for fictionalized textual elements to overpower factual ones. When this happens readers may incorrectly doubt the validity of the entire captivity experience.[25]

Coursolle's own testimony in 1885 before the Special Commission of the Indian Division of the Secretary of the Interior tells briefly how he, his wife, and several children fled the Redwood Agency on 18 August and reached the safety of Fort Ridgely that night. But "The Ordeal of Hinhankaga" is a much longer narrative cast as an adventure story complete with suspense, revenge, heartbreak, humor, and resolution. While there is no reason to doubt that Clem Felix told Coursolle's story to F. J. Patten, there is good reason to doubt that he told it in this way.

"The Ordeal of Hinhankaga" sounds as if it was embellished by someone conversant with Western storytelling traditions. Indeed, examining other texts about the Dakota War that Patten penned reveals that he had a penchant for transforming stories into romanticized frontier tales.[26] The cultural reference points of both interviewer and interviewee are crucial "when assessing the factual credibility of oral history accounts today, for as the communicative chain from then to now will have invariably come under severe strain, if it was broken it is important to ascertain how it was rebound."[27] In the case of Patten and Felix I contend that the "communicative chain . . . was rebound" as something resembling a tale of the American frontier. And one of the prime genres that advanced such stories was the Indian captivity narrative.

Consider the opening to "The Ordeal of Hinhankaga," whose title recalls the often sentimentalized and sensationalized titles given to non-Native stories of captivity: "During the whole of the night—I shall never forget the date, August 18, 1862,—a strange foreboding kept sleep away. Marie, my fair-skinned French-Sioux wife, lay still beside me but I knew that she, too, was awake. Cistina Joe (Little Joe) my son, nine days old, kicked in his crib. My slender, black-eyed girls, Elizabeth, six, and Minnie, four, breathed quietly. Duta, my red setter, rumbled low growls outside the open door. Something was out of place, but what could it be?"[28]

As in many a good story, the opening introduces all the important characters in the rest of the narrative. Yet the information is rhetorically and historically uneven, suggesting that Clem Felix, or more likely F. J. Patten, made adaptations to strengthen narrative impact: some details are factually correct (the children's names and ages), but some are patently incorrect (Joseph's wife at this time was Jane, and he swore on oath elsewhere that she was white; furthermore, even if the name of Joseph's first love, Marguerite, morphed into "Marie," Naz Coursolle's oral history and other records indicate that she was not "French-Sioux" either). The authenticity of other data is unknown. Did Joseph really have a dog named Duta? Were the two girls really "black-eyed"? What is the effect of referring to the girls in this way here and elsewhere in the narrative? But disregarding these questions, the opening of "The Ordeal of Hinhankaga" is similar to that of many other captivity narratives, including many already examined in this book, that depict peaceful family life about to be ruptured.

As the story continues it reveals even more familiar captivity narrative elements, such as the sudden escape of some family members from their home (Joseph, Marie, and the baby), the captivity of others (the two girls Elizabeth and Minnie), the uncertainty of what was going to happen to the captives, the death of some of the family (the baby), the search for and discovery of the living captives, and the reconnected family sobered by their experience but ready to begin life anew at the end of the account. Alongside these elements, which provide suspense and then resolution, Joseph is presented as a hero who joins state and government forces at Camp Release to fight against the Dakota offensive. While he identifies himself as Franco Dakota and draws on Native knowledge to save himself from harm—for example by digging a shallow hole to protect himself against Dakota attacks and using kinnikinick to wad his gun—he also characterizes the Dakota warriors in stereotypically negative ways. One instance occurs when he speculates on what might have happened to his daughters: "I was gripped in an agony of fear as I pictured my black-eyed little girls in the hands of these blood-crazed warriors."[29]

Other narrative traces concern the deliberate sentimentalization of people and events, another defining aspect of much traditional captivity literature. The narrative tells how Joseph kills Duta, his dog, so the dog will not give away his presence by barking. Lorenzo Lawrence also describes killing his prized dog but does not narrate the incident in the same heightened way. Here is the account in "The Ordeal of Hinhankaga": "I was forced to do the cruelest task of my life. I slipped off my belt and pulled it tight around Duta's neck. Tears ran from my eyes as I felt him struggle for breath. Finally he was dead. I knelt down, took his head in my lap and whispered, 'Forgive me Duta, forgive me.'"[30] Reunited with his girls at Camp Release, Coursolle informs them that their baby brother has died but adds: "I couldn't bear to tell them how Duta died. I told them only that he had gone to a happy land where he was playing every day with Cistina Joe."[31] Presumably Coursolle really did have a dog that he killed, but the way that the narrative uses this detail to humanize the hero and sentimentalize the story carries more emotional weight than the information itself.

Another fact mentioned at the end of the narrative reinforces the sense of family continuity despite the war. As a member of Captain Anderson's Mounted Men and then the Sixth Minnesota Regiment, Coursolle served alongside a man called Denais (Dennis) Felix. When Denais Felix sees Coursolle with his daughters at Camp Release, he says of Elizabeth: "You have lips red like strawberries and sparkling black eyes! You will be a lovely lady bime-by [by and by] pretty soon!"[32] Let's remember that in 1862 Elizabeth was six, and it strains credulity to think that a fellow soldier would describe his comrade's child like this; it is far more likely evidence of Patten's editorialization. However, the narrative concludes by noting that thirteen years later Denais married Elizabeth. This is historically accurate; in fact, their ninth child was Clem Felix, who was born in 1892. So this romantic reference actually predicts the future relationship of Denais and Elizabeth and also makes for a neat conclusion to the entire story.

Despite these emotive narrative strategies "The Ordeal of Hinhankaga" presents other information more factually. For instance, like some of the white captives, including Sarah Wakefield, Joseph Coursolle felt that Sibley moved his soldiers too slowly, so Coursolle "was tormented with worry" about his daughters for longer than necessary.[33] Once Sibley arrived at Fort Ridgely, he spent too long drilling troops instead of ending the hostilities and rescuing the captives. And Coursolle exclaims that when he did set off with reinforcements, including Coursolle's regiment, "We moved like snails. I could have crawled on my stomach and made faster time. Again we cursed Sibley. He was so slow!"[34] The presentation of historically accurate information amid personal details or fictionalized elements is also found in the non-Native captivity literature.

The real Joseph Coursolle underwent other ordeals, especially in middle and old age. In February 1875 he wrote an urgent letter to Sibley asking for help, since grasshoppers had destroyed his crops the previous year and he and his family were starving and destitute. "You will doubtless be surprised to hear from me," the letter opens, "but I *am compelled to* write you and ask for aid of some kind." It concludes: "I understand that you have money to distribute to the 'Grasshopper sufferers'—if so I surely am one of them. Please write me and let me know if you cannot do something for me."[35] We do not know if Sibley ever responded to this heartrending and persuasive request. Soon after, Coursolle moved with his family to the Santee Reservation, where he was living when he gave testimony in 1885 concerning Nathan Myrick's claim for trade goods lost in the Conflict. Joseph Coursolle must have died before 1893, as the Mdewakanton Annuity Roll for that year lists his wife, Jane Coursolle, but not him.[36]

13. Virginia Driving Hawk Sneve
Captivity and Counter Captivity

Virginia Driving Hawk Sneve is a widely published contemporary author and National Humanities Medalist who began her writing career focusing on juvenile literature.[1] Originally she wanted to write on Native American subjects for adults but couldn't find a market for her work. By the early 1970s, however, "there was a demand for truthful ethnic stories for children written by minority writers," and so in 1972 she published her award-winning first novel, *Jimmy Yellow Hawk*, about a modern Sioux boy living on a reservation in South Dakota.[2] She followed up this success with dozens of fictional and nonfictional works for young adults, including the historical novel *Betrayed* (1974), which is based on the 1862 Lake Shetek incident.

Sneve describes her complex identity in *Completing the Circle*, her family story blending history, myth, and autobiography: "My Sioux heritage is from all three groups [Dakota, Lakota, and Nakota], blended with Ponca, French, Scots, and English."[3] The desire to represent both the Native American and the European American sides of her ancestry is evident not only in children's books such as *Betrayed* and *Grandpa Was a Cowboy and an Indian and Other Stories*, but also in works for adults such as her preface to volume 3 of *Daughters of Dakota: Stories of Friendship between Settlers and the Dakota Indians* and *Completing the Circle*. As she explains, recalling her great-grandmother's words:

> "They were starving in Minnesota," is how Hannah Howe Frazier began her story of the 1862 Uprising, and I remembered this when I wrote *Betrayed*. The story began in Minnesota and ended in Dakota Territory, just as the Frazier chronicle did, and I told

my story from the Santees' and Tetons' view of their relationships with the whites. Yet my mixed-blood heritage led me to include as well the non-Indian point of view, a dilemma I've faced not only in my writing but in all my life. Walking the path between two cultures has given me perspective on both ways, which can be confusing.[4]

However, Sneve also understands that traditionally the non-Native perspective has dominated popular culture and children's literature, particularly the stereotypical presentations of Native Americans in genres like the captivity narrative and the dime novel. In *The Dakota's Heritage*, for example, she observes, "I learned the history of my people from non-Indian sources."[5] Although this misinformation was balanced by "traditional oral Dakota education" from her relatives, she "still felt frustrated by the inaccuracies presented in Indian historical and creative literature, and by misperceptions perpetrated by non-Indian authors."[6] So although she is fair when writing about whites, she prefers to privilege a balanced representation of the Indian characters in her works. For this reason her publications have been well-received by educators and librarians, who are increasingly sensitive to the impact of Native American stereotypes in young adult books. The Association for the Study of American Indian Literatures discussion list, for instance, regularly announces information about culturally sensitive and insensitive juvenile literature.[7]

The children's literature arising from the Dakota War—which includes the dime novel *Indian Jim*, discussed in chapter 3—has until recently been written for a white readership and has often demonized the Dakotas. Captivity narratives have certainly played their part in this kind of cultural propaganda. An article titled "American Indians in Children's Historical Fiction" includes information on Dakota War children's books and identifies seven that appeared between 1912 and 1969.[8] None of the authors of these young adult books was Native, and none was interested in moving beyond stereotypical Indian and white characters: the former were either sympathetic or hostile to whites, and the latter were invariably heroic.[9] These reactionary assumptions underscore the radical achievement of *Betrayed*, especially when first published, which presents "honest images that honor and authenticate the Native experience."[10] Sneve continues, "In my books, I always try to write about something from the past that still affects us today and will in the future." Thus in *Betrayed* she retells an incident from the Dakota War in order to suggest and modify its continued ramifications.

As described earlier, *Betrayed* covers events at Lake Shetek, in which the Fool Soldiers, or Crazy Band, rescued the captives that White Lodge (Wakeyeska) took there, namely Julia Wright and two of her children; Martha Duley and three of her children, one of whom died during captivity; and three young girls, Rosa and Ellen Ireland and Lillian Everett.[11] The Fool Soldiers were led by Waanatan, the Charger, and also included Kills Game and Comes Home, Four Bear, Swift Bird, Mad Bear, Pretty Bear, One Rib, Strikes Fire, Sitting Bear, Red Dog, and Charging Dog.[12] The official Fool Soldiers Web site defines their past and present functions:

We are a warrior society of the Lakota Nation from the Sans Arc Band. We are sworn to protect peace, to serve our country, and to help those in need. . . . The drums of the Akicita Heyoka have been beating for peace, nonviolence, and justice since 1862, the year that 10 young Lakota men risked their lives in the name of peace. These 10 young men—ranging from 16 to 21 years old—were led by WaAnnatan, the Charger. During the Minnesota Uprising of 1862, a time of war among the Native American nations and White settlers, WaAnnatan and his Fool Soldiers negotiated the release of several women and children from the warring Dakota White Lodge, and returned the captives to St. Pierre, South Dakota.[13]

Figure 22. Martin Charger (Waanatan). Photo Courtesy of the South Dakota State
Historical Society—State Archives.

The current leader is Chief Harry Charger, a descendent of the original
Waanatan, whose English name was Martin Charger.

A few accounts by the Lake Shetek survivors exist, though most are
from those who lived through the initial attack but were not captured.
In fact, Lillian Everett's brief version, examined in chapter 5, and a story
recounted in old age by one of the Ireland girls are the only known
first-person responses from White Lodge's prisoners.[14] Sneve wanted
to present a dual perspective in *Betrayed*, but to recover the Dakota
one she had to go beyond the non-Native narratives and histories. The

resulting research, letters to and from the editors of her young adult
books at Holiday House, and reviews of the book are now available
at the extensive Virginia Driving Hawk Sneve Papers at South Dakota
State University. Understandably Sneve was particularly interested in
uncovering information about Waanatan.

And she managed to obtain a great deal of relevant material, including Martin Charger's own account, given to Doane Robinson in 1900
and inserted in Robinson's *Encyclopedia of South Dakota*.[15] Although this
version is written in the third person and is likely editorialized, it and
material from another publication by Robinson, *History of the Dakota or
Sioux Indians*, formed the structural and informational basis of Sneve's
novel. Sneve also contacted two of Charger's grandchildren, Rufus M.
Charger and Louise Gray Bear High Bear Green, and other descendents
of his to verify data, including the fact that he really was the grandson
of explorer Meriwether Lewis and a Lakota woman. For background
she read a good deal of primary and secondary material on the Dakota
Conflict, as evidenced by her careful handwritten notes.

In January 1974 Sneve submitted the manuscript to Holiday House
using the working title "In Addition to Brutality." A few weeks later
she responded to her editors' comments and admitted that she had
almost abandoned the project "as being too difficult an undertaking
for a novice to attempt."[16] She added that the characters were all
real and that she had followed the known chronology of the episode
as accurately as possible "after slicing through the bigotry of white
historians."[17] But she agreed with her editors that the book's abrupt
ending was problematic, although she was uncertain how to resolve
this. Sneve later retitled the book *Betrayed* and referred throughout it
to the successive betrayals that the Dakotas experienced at the U.S.
government's hands.

The entire novel is essentially a captivity narrative about the Lake
Shetek settlers that dramatizes their abduction by White Lodge and
their rescue by the Fool Soldiers. But it is a captivity narrative with a

twist, as its Native author provides her own perspective on the captivity of white hostages. After a brief historical introduction needed for background, especially since her young adult readership would not be familiar with the Dakota War, let alone this particular incident, the novel's four core chapters proceed by careful alternation of plot, setting, character, and viewpoint among the white and Indian groups. Specifically Sneve counterpoints two characters, nineteen-year-old Waanatan and twelve-year-old Sarah Duley. She uses Sioux words and phrases to authenticate Native culture and educate readers and also lists them in a glossary, though context or in-text translation usually conveys the meaning well enough for her designated audience.

Chapter 1, "Waanatan, the Charger," introduces Waanatan and presents his decision to rescue the white captives as a vision quest undertaken with other youths to prove their bravery and leadership potential. He is therefore privileged in being the first major character introduced in the novel. The chapter opens as an emissary from Little Crow arrives in the village of the Two Kettles Lakota band, where Waanatan lives, and tries to obtain support for the Dakota War. However, the Lakotas remain neutral, and most show concern and compassion for the captive white women and children whom the Dakotas are holding. Waanatan and Kills and Comes go into trances during which they decide to rescue White Lodge's hostages, and they then undergo a purification ceremony in preparation for their task. Charger's own account in Robinson's *Encyclopedia* does not present this decision as a vision quest but does indicate that he and his companions were prompted by "sentiments of humanity."[18]

Chapter 2, "Slaughter Slough," begins with a sensitive description of the Duley family going about their morning routines. As discussed several times before, a standard opening trope of many Indian captivity narratives shows a settled life about to be sundered. But Sneve adapts this pattern by making it part of the second—not the first—chapter in *Betrayed*. Thus initially she provides a description of the sympathetic

Lakotas before she details the attack by the hostile Dakotas. The story then follows White Lodge's capture of the two women and children, the help given the hostages by a mission-schooled Dakota named Anna, their dispersal among various Dakota families, and the march to find a safe winter encampment. In writing a captivity narrative focusing on women and children Sneve also plays into another component of the traditional captivity literature, in which female hostages figure prominently. Yet the women on whom she focuses, Sarah Duley and Julia Wright, are not presented stereotypically as victimized women. They both adapt to their situation and take appropriate actions in order to survive.

In this chapter and elsewhere Sneve handles controversial subject matter skillfully. She does not dwell on violence, but she not flinch from it either. For example, in the following description Sneve infers that Sarah Duley is raped: "She struggled to rise and screamed in terror as a dark, painted face loomed above her. Sarah scratched, kicked and bit at the Indian, whose teeth gleamed in a grotesque smile. A sharp blow in her belly knocked the wind out of her. She gasped for air as she felt a smothering weight upon her, and then she knew nothing."[19] When Sarah comes to she discovers that "only a remnant of cloth covered her nakedness."[20] But Sneve says nothing more about the episode and leaves readers to reach their own conclusions. Contrasting her method with some of the euphemisms for or exaggerations of women's treatment in other Dakota War captivity narratives (within Heard and Bishop, for example) shows her verbal restraint. Decisions like this prompted Cathleen Elmer, in the *New York Times Book Review*, to praise Sneve for her ability to "deal even-handedly" with story and style.[21]

Chapter 3, "White Lodge," is most concerned with individualizing and humanizing the Dakota chief. Once again Sneve modifies traditional Indian captivity narratives, in which the captor is more likely to be demonized than presented as a credible and even sympathetic character. Sneve complicates White Lodge partly by relating the story through his restricted third-person viewpoint and partly by showing his interactions with other Indians and with the captives. For example, Sneve conveys the tremendous responsibility he bears in making decisions for his people's welfare, and she also reveals his uncertainty about how to deal with the captives in the long run. Such descriptions as the following indicate a man torn by cares: "Ruefully, he recalled how briefly fired with energy he had been as he fought as well as a young man in the battle at Lake Shetek. He had even a youth's desire to take a new wife. But now he felt old, tired, and full of sorrow."[22] He is lulled into thinking that Julia Wright, whom he has taken as his third wife, is content in her new role, until the chapter ends dramatically with her call for help to Major Galpin's passing canoe, an act that White Lodge punishes severely.

Chapter 4, "Fool Soldiers," involves the complex negotiations between the Fool Soldiers and White Lodge in exchanging the prisoners for food and horses. It shows White Lodge's dilemma in needing to accept provisions, because his own supplies were so limited, but wanting to retain control of the captives, particularly of Julia Wright. Sneve includes the true historical information that White Lodge gave up Julia Wright reluctantly and later tried to recapture her.[23] The chapter then follows the difficult journey back to Charlie Primeau's trading post with the ragged and hungry captives. It ends with a meaningful conversation and connection between the two different cultural representatives, Waanatan and Sarah Duley, after Sarah says that she forgives White Lodge: "Charger's heart was stirred by the girl's compassion for her captors. He knew that her feelings for Indians were unacceptable to most white people. He thought she would be considered as foolish by her people as he was by the Two Kettles. Charger felt a bond between himself and the white girl."[24]

And that leaves the five-page conclusion, "Mankato." Sneve's editors had been concerned about her decision to end *Betrayed* with the mass execution at Mankato, in which Sarah's father, William Duley—introduced only briefly in the opening chapter—springs the trip rope that hangs all thirty-eight condemned men simultaneously. Although Sneve considered omitting this incident and following Sarah's and/or Waanatan's lives, ultimately she kept it. Ending her novel this way allows her to portray the vengeful settlers as savage and thus destabilize, once again, the prevailing stereotype of violent Indians in so many white-authored captivity narratives. Specifically she conveys Duley's desire for vengeance in not only agreeing to cut the rope but refusing to be paid for it: "'No money needed,' Duley said grimly. 'I'll do it for nothing. One hundred times that amount wouldn't be enough for the pleasure it will give me to send those red devils to hell.'"[25] Some reviewers, however, criticized this final chapter as overly didactic when they felt rest of the book had maintained cultural balance.[26]

What Sneve did not do is end her story with the fate of the Fool Soldiers, which admittedly would have complicated her novel considerably but would have continued the captivity trope. In ironies that are almost too extreme to contemplate, after returning the captive women and children, most of the Fool Soldiers were reportedly imprisoned at Fort Randall and shot. This information is available in a remarkable series of interviews conducted in 1972.[27] Many of the thirteen people interviewed claim that President Lincoln himself ordered up to seven of the Fool Soldiers to be executed, while others were released to join the removed Dakotas at Crow Creek. Treated as outcasts there, the remaining Fool Soldiers left when they could. Martin Charger's cabin, before he moved on, was reputedly painted white by angry Indians.[28] He settled on the Cheyenne River Reservation, became an Episcopalian in the 1880s, and died in 1900 aged sixty-six.[29]

In *Betrayed* Virginia Driving Hawk Sneve realigns the Indian captivity narrative and reverses many of its traditionally negative associations. The white hostages are initially captured by White Lodge, but they are recaptured by the Fool Soldiers. So Sneve's text enacts both hostile and benevolent forms of captivity. Going beyond fiction to the historical record shows that after returning the women and children to safety, the Fool Soldiers themselves experienced other forms of captivity, including imprisonment and cultural captivity. For going against so many literary conventions *Betrayed* could more accurately be termed a "counter captivity narrative" than a captivity narrative. It redefines the originally European American genre of the Indian captivity narrative by incorporating a Native perspective on the Indian captors (White Lodge and his band, as well as the Fool Soldiers) and the white captive women and children. This young adult historical novel represents one way that the Dakota War was remembered a little more than a century after it was fought. The conclusion to my book explores other ways in which this war haunts identity and memory.

Conclusion
Captive to the Past? The Legacy of the Dakota War

A quarter-century after the Vietnam War, I spent five years interviewing
350 people on all sides of the conflict. I was continually struck by how
visceral the memories of the war remain and how important it is to remind
ourselves that war produces a countless variety of wounds that do not
heal, even years and decades after the shooting stops—wounds to the
body and the soul, to witnesses and survivors, to public trust and every
human relationship, to the land itself, and even to the generations that
follow. | Christian G. Appy, "The Ghosts of War"

These questions, which have engaged so many, have troubled all of my
work. How to be both free and situated; how to convert a racist house
into a race-specific yet nonracist home. How to enunciate race while
depriving it of its lethal cling? They are questions of concept, of language,
of trajectory, of habitation, of occupation, and, although my engagement
with them has been fierce, fitful, and constantly (I think) evolving, they
remain in my thoughts as aesthetically and politically unresolved. | Toni
Morrison, "Home"

We owe it to our ancestors to commemorate their suffering and their
sacrifice by having the courage to stand up and speak the truth, to examine honestly the events of 1862, unencumbered by the shackles that have
bound our historical consciousness. This telling of the truth is the first
step to our own true healing. After seven generations, it is about time. |
Waziyatawin Angela Wilson, *In the Footsteps of Our Ancestors*

The epigraphs above signify several key areas raised by this study of
Dakota War captivity narratives. The first area concerns the visceral
memories and residual wounds that remain after all wars but particularly after such unresolved hostilities as the Vietnam War and the
Dakota Conflict: physical, spiritual, psychological, political, ecologi-
cal, and generational scars that just don't heal or don't heal properly.
These injuries are not only a constant reminder of the past; they also

affect present and future relationships. The second area confronts the role of race in American literature and life. Nobel Prize winner Toni Morrison admits that her work cannot resolve how to both claim racial identity and counteract the historically racist implications of doing so. Yet she is convinced that "domesticat[ing] the racial project," while fraught with paradox, is "a manageable, doable, modern human activity."[1] A particular challenge in this book has been to frame a discussion of race and ethnicity but at the same time deconstruct binaries by problematizing individual identity. And the third area connects the past with the present and indicates the importance of oral history—telling the past—especially within Native communities. In this conclusion I explore how hurt, healing, memory, race, ethnicity, identity, and storytelling hold history captive but also offer hope for liberation and renewal.

The Legacy of the Dakota War

Recognizing the war's continuing after-effects, Minnesota Public Radio broadcast a series of stories on 26 September 2002 collectively (and cleverly) titled *Minnesota's Uncivil War*.[2] On that date 140 years earlier, General Sibley had reached Camp Release and coordinated the formal handover of many of the captives. The series also performed a public service by providing balanced and accessible reporting for new generations unaware of how the Dakota War has shaped modern life in Minnesota and the Dakota diaspora.[3] Disseminating this kind of information is particularly important since Minnesota has seen an influx of newcomers in the twentieth and twenty-first centuries and since school curricula often slight local history in favor of national and international history.

Comments included in *Minnesota's Uncivil War* from descendents of Dakotas involved in the Conflict suggest the war's lasting legacy within the Indigenous community. For example, Ed Red Owl believes that Dakotas have "never really come out of that grief and mourning.

We are yet afflicted with that."[4] Waziyatawin Angela Wilson stresses that "[the events] of 1862 are very real to us as Dakota people today. . . . The problems that we have in our contemporary communities are a direct consequence of losing our homeland, having attempts at cultural eradication perpetrated against us—and it needs to be addressed."[5] And Chris Mato Nunpa sums up the feelings of many of his people: "For us, these aren't old wounds. . . . These are still new and festering wounds. We had all this land. Now someone else has it. Somebody else enjoys the bounty of this land, and we are treated like strangers in our own land."[6]

Along with *Minnesota's Uncivil War*, the 2006 imprint *In the Footsteps of Our Ancestors: The Dakota Commemorative Marches of the 21st Century* contains reflections on the Conflict from a Dakota point of view. This collection of essays, creative responses, historical and contemporary photographs, and maps stresses the need for healing and commemorates the Dakotas' forced march in 1862. But in a particularly ironic and divisive development, Dakotas' treatment by the government during the Conflict is the basis for a continuing lawsuit filed in 2003. The case, titled *Wolfchild, et al. v. United States* (Minnesota Mdewakanton Dakota Oyate Litigation), pits Dakotas against Dakotas over land-ownership claims and casino revenues regarding the Lower Sioux Community, the Prairie Island Indian Community, and the Shakopee Mdewakanton Community in Minnesota.[7] The war's legacy for European Americans seems more muted. Generally they are less knowledgeable and less concerned than Native Americans because the long-term effects have not been as damaging to them.

Home

Yet all those who originally took part in the Dakota War clashed over a place they called, or wanted to call, home. As indicated earlier in this book, the Dakota War captivity narratives enact the struggle over birthright and homeland by using captivity as a metonymy for white/

Indian wars. This struggle was not only geographic and political: "home" also referred to the human relationships, which were as significant as the ties to place. In fighting their own verbal wars after the fact these narratives attest to survival and continuity through storytelling, and they articulate the search for home.

Toni Morrison's essay "Home" analyzes the liberating and imprisoning effects of language and experience. For Morrison the freedom of writing is continually mitigated by the realization that she is "an already- and always-raced writer."[8] Therefore, she says, none of us has ever lived "in a world in which race did not matter."[9] When authors have imagined a race-free world, it has usually been a dreamlike or utopian place that of its very nature is unreal and otherworldly. Morrison rejects these constructs and attempts to convert the historically "racist house into a race-specific yet nonracist home" by using language "that insists on race-specificity without race prerogative."[10]

So many of the discussions on race, she believes, are really "about home: an intellectual home; a spiritual home; family and community as home; forced and displaced labor in the destruction of home; dislocation of and alienation within the ancestral home; creative responses to exile, the devastations, pleasures, and imperatives of homelessness as it is manifested in discussions on feminism, globalism, the diaspora, migrations, hybridity, contingency, interventions, assimilations, exclusions. The estranged body, the legislated body, the violated, rejected, deprived body—the body as consummate home. In virtually all of these formations, whatever the terrain, race magnifies the matter that matters."[11] She recognizes that critics who misunderstand her will simplify her thinking and accuse her of trying to transcend or trivialize race. But her goal is far more radical than they can conceive: she is determined to "take what is articulated as an elusive race-free paradise and domesticate it."[12]

In much of her fiction Morrison uses the form of the slave narrative—one of the types of captivity narrative discussed in earlier chapters of my book—to interrogate free and unfree subjects and states of being. The authors of the Dakota War captivity narratives I have examined also explore their own or others' captivities in a war that destroyed a stable sense of home and resulted in multiple forms of displacement. In the immediate aftermath of the Dakota Conflict thousands of white settlers abandoned their homesteads and left the state. Many returned within a few years and began to rebuild their lives. But those Dakotas who had not already fled north and west became transient and at times culturally conflicted. Some Dakotas became scouts for the U.S. military precisely because they could not bear to leave their homelands (working for the government made it easier for them to stay), and a tiny number were able to remain because they lay low or because missionaries interceded for them. Helen Horsbeck Tanner refers to those few who stayed in Minnesota as "landless outcasts."[13]

A Thrilling Narrative of Indian Captivity, by John and Mary Renville

Home was a deep concern for John B. Renville and Mary B. Renville, who in 1863 published a little-known captivity narrative titled *A Thrilling Narrative of Indian Captivity*.[14] The narrative is noteworthy for several reasons. First, it was one of the earliest book-length narratives on the Conflict to be published. Second, it captures many of the dualities raised collectively by later texts. And third, it provides an unusual perspective because it was written by an Anglo woman and her Dakota husband who were protected by the progovernment faction and lived in what they and others called "The Friendly Camp" throughout the war. Sometimes they had to conceal themselves, and often they worried because their situation was uncertain, but compared to many other captives they were fairly safe. Their position allowed them to interact with other captives and rescuers in the camp: Jannette DeCamp, Mary Schwandt, the Brown family, Urania White, Lorenzo Lawrence, and Paul Mazakutemani, for example. Indeed, John Renville played a role in helping hostages himself, while Mary Renville fed and comforted some of those who were passing through.

John was born at Lac Qui Parle in 1831, the son of Mary and Joseph Renville Sr. He attended the mission school founded there by Stephen Riggs and Thomas Williamson under the auspices of his father, Joseph, and then furthered his education in Galesburg, Illinois. He was one of the original members of the Hazelwood Republic and taught at the Upper Sioux Agency. Mary's early history is not known, but she attended the high school associated with Knox College in Galesburg and taught elsewhere in the town.[15] The preface to their narrative says that they both left Galesburg in 1859 and came to Minnesota "as Teachers among the Indians."[16] When they sought sanctuary with the Dakotas, their young daughter, Ella, was with them.

The narrative first appeared in the *Berlin (Wisconsin) Courant* from 25 December 1862 to 9 April 1863.[17] The Renvilles had moved to Berlin after the war and were probably staying temporarily with family or friends. The almost weekly installments were titled "The Indian Captives Leaves from a Journal," and the final installment carried the names "J. B. and M. A. Renville." But only "Mrs. Mary B. Renville" appears as author on the title page of the book version, published in Minneapolis in 1863 (though the dual signature still appears at the end). While the book has a more hyped-up title—*A Thrilling Narrative of Indian Captivity*—and while the name of a single female author might have fanned contemporaneous readers' expectations of sensationalism, the book and newspaper versions are virtually identical and relatively restrained, with the book's chapters corresponding to the *Courant*'s weekly selections. The narrative's first chapter says that the text is based on "the Journal of one who was a captive during the late trouble," suggesting that there is one major author, presumably Mary.[18] External evidence might seem to corroborate this, as Mary wrote a letter to Stephen Riggs in February 1863 talking about the series of stories she was putting together for the local newspaper, and in August 1863

Mary Riggs commented in her diary, "Mrs. Renville is publishing her book in Minneapolis."[19]

But other data, in addition to the dual signature, suggest that the account really was a joint production. In one of seven extant letters Mary wrote to Stephen Riggs between 1862 and 1864, she mentions that John was helping her reconstruct events in the narrative.[20] Indeed, from information in the account as well as testimony John Renville gave in 1901 during litigation the Sisseton and Wahpeton bands brought against the U.S. government, we know that the family stayed together during the war and underwent the same experiences. For example, John Renville's 1901 evidence stated, "My wife was a white woman, and I stayed right with her."[21]

Also, the *Narrative* contains far more information than the journal on which it is based, including speeches and letters that augment the original journal but must have been added later. Further, both John and Mary were involved in writing strategic letters, reprinted in the narrative, from progovernment Dakotas like Lorenzo Lawrence, Paul Mazakutemani, and Simon Anawangmani (fellow members of the Hazelwood Republic) to Governor Ramsey and General Sibley. The narrative describes the Renvilles' composition process while they were captives, which definitely applies to the letters and probably to the journal too:

We have already given one letter dictated by Paul. We now copy one from some other chiefs. Before doing so, we will state that we endangered our lives by writing, and had to be very cautious so as not to be discovered. If in the day time, we usually secreted ourselves in the tent some way; but generally the Indians wished us to write in the night. Sometimes we have waited until we thought every one ought to be asleep, and then putting out the fire, Mr. R. [John Renville] would hold a blanket over us and the candle, so as to keep the light from shining through the tent; besides this caution, a guard was placed outside the tent to report any intruder who might be approaching.

If Mary was usually the scribe, John contributed through discussion and translation.[22]

More compelling evidence of joint authorship concerns the ambiguous use of "we" throughout the entire narrative. Sometimes "we" seems like a "royal we" applied to Mary alone, as in these examples: "We had an attack of the pleurisy, and suffered extremely for several days," and "When about half through [washing clothes] Ella cried so much we carried her up the long hill, hoping to find her father there."[23] But elsewhere the use of "we" in terms of composition and experience appears to apply to both parties. Take this description of the journal on which the longer narrative is based: "This little book, in the providence of God, may fall into other hands, for we are in jeopardy every moment, and are so closely watched that we scarcely dare use the pen for fear of being suspected of trying to get letters to friends at home. With a full sense of the danger we are in, we forthwith subscribe the names of our family and those of our friends in Illinois, Wisconsin and Iowa."[24]

What seems to be operating here is an unassigned or free-floating "we" that not only applies sometimes to Mary and sometimes to Mary and John but also concerns "multiple subjectivity" and "multiple subject positions" spilling over to the work's readers as well.[25] These multiple selves are made overt in *A Thrilling Captivity*, because the Renvilles were trying to establish for themselves and for their audience where their identity and sympathy lay: "we" were the Renville family; "we" were teachers; "we" were Christians; "we" were captives; "we" were "white persons"; "we" were Dakotas by blood or marriage; "we" were propagandists running down militant Dakotas and New Ulm's German population; "we" were writers and readers.[26] "We" were also pining for home.

A Thrilling Narrative speaks to the loss of home at many points. Sheltering from a huge storm a few days after they had fled Hazelwood, the

Renvilles describe taking refuge in an unfinished house: "Here we were seated on the few goods we had saved from *home*, wishing, nay praying, that some way would open for our escape from such a miserable life."[27] A few days later, when they occupied the empty mission buildings at the Upper Agency, they lamented, "It is impossible to describe the desolation, confusion and destruction that had been made at these houses, and the feelings that took possession of us when we thought of the many families that had thus been driven from their homes."[28] Washing some clothes at what had been missionary Jonas Pettijohn's house, they were glad they could use the soap "we saved from our own dear home."[29] And toward the end of their captivity they sighed, "We try to clear up the tent, but cannot make it look like home."[30]

But where was home? Before the war it had been at Hazelwood, but after the war it was unclear for a while where they would settle. Mary's letters to Stephen Riggs between 1862 and 1864 reveal that she was more traumatized by her experiences in 1862 than the narrative might suggest.[31] She was torn by her desire to support John, who wanted to teach the Dakotas at Fort Snelling, and her need to wait a while longer before returning to the site of such turmoil. But they did return to Minnesota, and by 1865 John had become the first Sioux minister to be ordained, ironically enough at Mankato, site of the hangings three years earlier.[32] He continued to minister to the Indians, traveling far and wide from his new home base at Ascension Church in Big Coulee, South Dakota, where he was pastor for over thirty years from about 1870 to about 1901. An obituary of his death on 20 December 1903 announced that his remains would be "laid to rest in Big Coulee cemetery beside those of his first wife [Mary], who died several years ago."[33]

The Future

Recent decades have seen renewed efforts at appeasement and forgiveness in the Dakota and non-Dakota communities. In 2002 an article titled "Mending the Wounds" in the *Mankato Free Press* celebrated the continuation of a thirty-one-year tradition begun in 1972. In that year, through the efforts of white businessman Bud Lawrence and Dakota tribal leader Amos Owen, the first Mahkato [sic] Wacipi, or Pow-wow, was held at Mankato, long a site of sadness to the Dakotas, since the 1862 executions there.[34] The Minnesota-based Diversity Foundation is also determined to overturn the Conflict's legacy by fostering human rights, racial harmony, and conciliation programs. Recent initiatives include the group's involvement in the 2004 Wapasha Prairie/Dakota Homecoming and Gathering, which brought together Dakotas from all over the Midwest and Canada in association with the City of Winona's National 2004 Grand Excursion. Local news stories in the *Winona Daily News*, the *Dakota Journal*, and elsewhere carried such titles as "Atoning for Henry Sibley's Sins," "City Leaders Seek Dakota Forgiveness," "A Truthful Journey Home for the Dakotah People," and "Dakota Homecoming and Reconciliation Prompt Reflection."[35]

As part of its continuing features on the Dakota War, Minnesota Public Radio ran a story on 26 April 2006 titled *Historic Sites Reopen*.[36] It focused on the Lower Sioux Agency site, which was closed to visitors in 2004 owing to budget cuts but which was set to reopen on Memorial Day weekend 2006 after the state legislature restored funding. "Many historians," the article reported, "consider it the most important soil in the state," because the Dakota War began there.[37] The manager of the Lower Sioux Agency at that time was Tom Sanders, who comes from a bicultural background. "There's still healing that needs to be done, in both sides and within communities," Sanders said in the news story. "And this place can facilitate that." He continued: "The healing's going to come from true understanding. It's that gaining a respect for the different communities and different ways of thinking about things, the different cultures. If we can do that, then we've accomplished a great deal. And we're going to do that, I fully believe that."[38]

Notes

Preface

1. In later sections of the book I discuss the complexities of naming this war. Current designations include the Dakota War, the U.S.-Dakota War of 1862, the Dakota Conflict, and the Conflict. I use these terms interchangeably.

2. Funding also allowed me to publish two articles using earlier versions of material on Sarah Wakefield and Edward Ellis. See Derounian-Stodola, "'Many persons say,'" and Ramsey and Derounian-Stodola, "Dime Novels."

3. I delivered a longer version of this information as the presidential address at the Society of Early Americanists Conference in March 2004. It was published as "The Accidental Colonialist: Notes on Academic Choice and Identity."

4. Bandura, "Exploration of Fortuitous Determinants," 95.

5. Bandura, "Exploration of Fortuitous Determinants," 95.

6. Giddens, *Modernity and Self-Identity*, 53 (original emphasis).

7. Giddens, *Modernity and Self-Identity*, 243–44.

8. Young, *Three Bags Full*, ix.

List of Narratives and Their Chronological Contexts

1. Let me clarify how I try to be consistent when naming people in this book. First, the married names of women who were captured or whom I write about when they were young or when they were married to earlier spouses cause problems in citation. Where possible I have tried to use the last name *they* used at specific times in their life (e.g., "Mary Schwandt" for when this German immigrant to Minnesota was still unmarried and when she told the first version of her captivity narrative; "Mary Schwandt Schmidt" for after she married and usually used both last names). With all Indians on first citation I give the major names by which they were known but then use their own preferred names, meaning the ones they used, whenever possible. Sometimes this means that I refer to them by their Anglo, rather than Native, names. For instance, after she converted to Christianity, Snana, the Dakota woman who rescued Mary Schwandt, used Margaret (Maggie) as her first name and the last names of her first husband, Andrew Good Thunder, and later her second husband, Charles Brass. At the time of the war she called herself Maggie Good Thunder; when she published her narrative decades later she was Maggie Brass.

2. Some of the Dakota narratives that I refer to in my book are reprinted in Anderson and Woolworth, *Through Dakota Eyes*. Because the editors break up the texts according to different stages of the war addressed in specific passages, change punctuation, and do not always include complete texts, I do not cite references to this collection in the bibliographical information in the "List of Narratives." Nevertheless this anthology is widely available, so readers wishing to read selected narratives that I discuss might find it useful as a resource.

3. For more information about the Columbian Exposition see Pierpont, "Measure of America." I will return to the subject of the Columbian Exposition later in the book. Carrie R. Zeman and I e-mailed back and forth about possible reasons why such a spate of captivity narratives appeared in 1894, but she was the one who made the initial connection between that date and the Columbian Exposition (personal e-mail to the author, 30 Mar. 2006). She also provided information that helped me construct the list of legal proceedings after the Dakota War that may have affected the appearance of published narratives (personal e-mail to the author, 19 Aug. 2006).

4. For an extensive discussion of the Military Commission Trials and other legal proceedings concerning the Dakota War, see Chomsky, "United States–Dakota War Trials."

Methodology

1. Naming this war is still contested, as evident from a story on Minnesota Public Radio, dated 26 Sept. 2002, under the general title *Minnesota's Uncivil War*. A sidebar on the Minnesota Public Radio Web site includes a link to "What Should We Call It?" See http://news.minnesota.publicradio.org/features/200209/23_steilm_1862-m/name.shtml.

2. For example, the winter 2004 special issue of *American Indian Quarterly* (vol. 28) is entirely devoted to oral and written accounts of, and information on, the Dakota Conflict, mostly by contemporary Dakotas involved in a 2002 commemorative march. Entitled "Walking for Justice: The Dakota Commemorative March of 2002," the special issue was edited by Angela Cavender Wilson (who now uses the name Waziyatawin Angela Wilson). A book based on the 2002 and the 2004 commemorative marches titled *In the Footsteps of Our Ancestors: The Dakota Commemorative Marches of the 21st Century*, edited by Waziyatawin Angela Wilson, is available as a 2006 imprint from Living Justice Press. See also Westerman, "Floyd Red Crow Westerman."

3. Felman and Laub, *Testimony*, xiv–xv.

4. Todorov, *Conquest of America*, 250.

5. In his compilation "Narratives of the Flight of the Missionary Party from Yellow Medicine, 1862," Woolworth lists ten narratives about the missionary party's flight from the Upper Sioux Agency. In "Known Personal Narratives from the Lower Sioux or Redwood Indian Agency, on August 18, 1862," Woolworth lists nineteen accounts—the largest number of narratives by non-Natives from the same location. These numbers are only the tip of the iceberg, however, as there are also accounts from New Ulm, Lake Shetek, and other sites, as well as a mass of secondhand versions by nonparticipants, and even these are only some of the narratives by white peoples and a few of those by mixed-race and Dakota peoples. Marken and Hoover, *Bibliography of the Sioux*, also contains useful listings. Additionally Namias, *White Captives*, includes a partial list of American captivity narratives, including some Dakota War ones (see her appendix "Guide to Captives"). In 1933 the Minnesota Tourism Bureau conducted a contest on the Dakota War of 1862 that generated at least twenty-one manuscript responses by individuals, some of which can be classified as captivity narratives. I accessed these references through a computer search of the Minnesota Historical Society Library

catalog, using the keywords "Minnesota Tourism Bureau 1933." Other Dakota accounts of captivity and confinement exist, for example, in the Dakota Prison Letters Project, undertaken by tribal members in Flandreau, South Dakota, and at Sisseton Wahpeton Community College, which seeks to translate from the Dakota language approximately two hundred letters written from 1863 to 1866 by prisoners at Mankato and Fort Snelling, Minnesota, and later at Camp McClellan in Davenport, Iowa. Those involved with the translation project include Bill Bean, Clifford Canku, Elden Lawrence, Mona Miyasato, and Marla Worth.

6. Regarding the extensively discussed linguistic designations "Indian," "Native American," "American Indian," "native," "Native," "Indigenous peoples," and "First Nations" (as nouns), I use a tribal affiliation where appropriate but sometimes use these other terms. Postings about which name to use for non-Natives on the Association for the Study of American Indian Literatures discussion list, Jan. 2006, did not privilege any single word or phrase. Various synonyms, including "white" and "European American," are still in circulation and still widely accepted, so I employ both. I acknowledge the difficulty of finding the most culturally sensitive term to describe people from mixed racial or mixed tribal backgrounds. Sometimes I use the term "bicultural," but technically, in terms of the prefix "bi," this word is not appropriate for people from more than two racial backgrounds. See Forbes, *Black Africans*, for an extensive discussion of the language Europeans have used historically to designate shades of skin color and other supposedly racial markers. Terry P. Wilson, "Blood Quantum," also contains a helpful discussion of the politics of definition. More recent studies include Sturm, *Blood Politics*; and Saunt, *Black, White, and Indian*.

7. Logan, "'Cross-Cultural Conversations,'" 471.

8. Vizenor, *Fugitive Poses*, 46.

9. Strong, *Captive Selves*, 13.

10. Waziyatawin Angela Wilson, *Remember This!* 197.

11. Waziyatawin Angela Wilson, *Remember This!* 5.

12. Atkins, "Facing Minnesota," 35.

13. Atkins, "Facing Minnesota," 34.

14. See Feezor, "Mdewakanton Dakota Women."

15. Roediger, "Whiteness and Its Complications," B7.

16. Memmi, *Racism*, 10.

17. Ian Duncan, quoted in Howard, "Fragmentation of Literary Theory," A16.

18. Forbes, *Black Africans*, 191.

19. See Bieder, "Scientific Attitudes."

20. Bieder, "Scientific Attitudes," 17.

21. Quoted in Bieder, "Scientific Attitudes," 20.

22. Horsman, *Race and Manifest Destiny*, 192.

23. Smits, "'Squaw Men,'" 55–56.

24. Terry P. Wilson, "Blood Quantum," 118.

25. Diane Wilson, *Spirit Car*, 167–68.

26. See Marable, "We Need New and Critical Study." See also Marable's edited essay

collection, *Dispatches from the Ebony Tower*, from which I take some of the material in this chapter. There are far too many scholars working on race and ethnicity to list them, but Marable's essay mentions some of the leading voices, and his collection contains contributions by them.

27. Marable, "We Need New and Critical Study," B6.

28. Gardner, "Not for Publication."

29. I am grateful to one of my manuscript reviewers for clarifying this point about asserted identities.

30. Kolchin, "Whiteness Studies."

31. Jacobson, *Whiteness of a Different Color*, 14.

32. Brooks, "Working Definitions," 314.

33. Zeman, "Historical Notes," 14.

34. Clemmons, "Satisfied to Walk," 242.

35. Kolchin, "Whiteness Studies."

36. Barnett, "Reading 'Whiteness' in English Studies," 14.

37. Morrison, "Introduction," xii.

Historical Perspectives on the Dakota War

1. Gauper, "River with a Past."

2. One of my manuscript reviewers suggested, for example, that I extend the chronology to include two other events: the death of Little Crow, on 3 July 1863; and the illegal and unethical mid-December 1863 attack on an Indian camp by a detachment from Major Edwin Hatch's cavalry battalion, resulting in the death of several Indians and the capture of the rest.

3. See the following publications, arranged alphabetically by author, for more detailed overviews of the war: Gary Clayton Anderson, *Kinsmen of Another Kind* and *Little Crow*; Anderson and Woolworth, *Through Dakota Eyes*; Carley, *Sioux Uprising of 1862*; Richard N. Ellis, *General Pope and U.S. Indian Policy*; Lass, "Removal from Minnesota"; Elden Lawrence, *Peace Seekers*; Oehler, *Great Sioux Uprising*; Satterlee, *Detailed Account of the Massacre*; and Angela Wilson, *In the Footsteps of Our Ancestors*. A very good recent overview of Dakota customs, traditions, and tales can also be found in Oneroad and Skinner, *Being Dakota*. Also note that some of my information about Dakota culture, politics, and history comes from internal documents at the Minnesota Historical Society (MHS), written and compiled by MHS Research Fellow Emeritus Alan R. Woolworth. Further, in 1992 the *St. Paul Pioneer Press* published a series of stories by Nick Coleman and John Camp collectively called "The Great Dakota Conflict" that it later collected into a single pamphlet, also titled *The Great Dakota Conflict*. This forty-eight-page pamphlet, part of the newspaper's "Pioneer in Education Supplements" series, provides a great deal of valuable information. Also see the essay collection *Trails of Tears*, edited by Bakeman and Richardson (not yet available at the time *The War in Words* went to press). This collection examines two marches, one of condemned Dakotas and the other of their families and dependents, that took place at the end of the Dakota War. Forthcoming publications by independent scholars Carrie

R. Zeman and Walt Bachman will also add considerably to a reevaluation of the Dakota War's historical, political, legal, and military aspects.

4. Mato Nunpa, "Letter to the Editor." Much information from a Dakota point of view is also now available on tribal Web sites.

5. Mato Nunpa, "Letter to the Editor."

6. Cook-Lynn, *Anti-Indianism in Modern America*, 165.

7. Cook-Lynn, *Anti-Indianism in Modern America*, 145.

8. Cook-Lynn, *Anti-Indianism in Modern America*, 148.

9. Blight, "Civil War in History and Memory," B7.

10. Blight, "Civil War in History and Memory," B7.

11. Bates, *Wars We Took to Vietnam*, 2.

12. Engel, *Context Is Everything*.

13. Engel, *Context Is Everything*, 129, 7.

14. Engel, *Context Is Everything*, 12.

15. Nichols, "Other Civil War."

16. Russo, "Time to Speak Is Over," 99.

17. Clemmons, "Satisfied to Walk," 322.

18. Assessing the total number of dead is impossible, though scholars have tried to do so. Marion Satterlee's detailed statistics state that 490 whites died (413 civilians and 77 soldiers) and that 71 Indians either died in combat or were executed (see the appendix in Satterlee, *Detailed Account*). Following Satterlee the much more recent work by Anderson and Woolworth says that "nearly five hundred" whites died, as well as "an unknown but substantial number" of Indians (*Through Dakota Eyes*, 1). Of course subjective white accounts published closer to the events were more likely to exaggerate the number of European Americans who died than later publications.

19. See Elden Lawrence, *Peace Seekers*, 150; Gilman, "History and Peopling of Minnesota," 3.

20. Dee Brown, *Bury My Heart at Wounded Knee*, 65.

21. Red Owl, "Brief Historical Overview." For more specialized information on the Eastern Dakotas see DeMallie, *Plains*.

22. Zeman, "Historical Notes," 7–8. Other information in this paragraph also comes from Zeman's historical notes.

23. Zeman, "Historical Notes," 8–9.

24. Big Eagle, "Sioux Story of the War," 384.

25. Woolworth, "Setting at the Redwood," 5.

26. Woolworth, "Setting at the Yellow Medicine," 5–6.

27. Kolodny, "Letting Go Our Grand Obsessions," 11–12, 13.

28. Blaeser, "Y2K Indians."

29. Limerick, "Haunted America."

30. Angela Cavender Wilson, "Grandmother to Granddaughter," 35.

31. Felman and Laub, *Testimony*, xv.

32. Diane Wilson, *Spirit Car*, 10.

33. Florestine Kiyukanpi Renville, "Dakota Identity Renewed," 100.

34. Florestine Kiyukanpi Renville, "Editor's Note," 4.

35. See Angela Wilson, *In the Footsteps of Our Ancestors*.

36. Red Owl, "Brief Historical Overview."

37. Interestingly Elizabeth Cook-Lynn argues in her essay "Reconciliation, Dishonest in Its Inception, Now a Failed Idea" that the term "Dakota Conflict" is euphemistic; that the hostilities unequivocally amounted to war; and that a more candid term is probably the one used in the nineteenth century: "Little Crow's War." See Cook-Lynn, *Anti-Indianism in Modern America*, 100.

38. In the 1990s, in another gesture of appeasement, KTCA, Twin Cities Public Television, aired two documentaries that are now available as videocassettes: *The Dakota Conflict*, narrated by Garrison Keillor and Floyd Red Crow Westerman, and *Dakota Exile*. The back-cover copy of *Dakota Exile* says that the video is the first television documentary that "has gathered and presented stories of Dakota people and their disparate paths after the war." The narrators and commentators are mostly Dakota elders and tribal historians.

39. Limerick, "Haunted America," 129–33. Note that these pages cover the first and second of Limerick's twelve points.

40. "Learning from the Dakota."

41. Limerick, "Haunted America," 131.

42. For more information on the connections between the Dakota Conflict and the Civil War see Henig, "Neglected Cause of the Sioux Uprising."

43. Quoted in Hubbard and Holcombe, *Minnesota in Three Centuries*, 396.

44. Limerick, "Haunted America," 133–37. Note that these pages cover the third, fourth, and fifth of Limerick's twelve points.

45. Limerick, "Haunted America," 134.

46. "Lightning Blanket's Account," 154.

47. Anderson and Woolworth, *Through Dakota Eyes*, 20; Zeman, "Historical Notes," 11.

48. Big Eagle, "Sioux Story of the War," 388–89.

49. Diane Wilson, *Spirit Car*, 14, furnishes the names of these four Dakotas.

50. Limerick, "Haunted America," 134.

51. Ernest Wabasha, quoted in Coleman and Camp, "Great Dakota Conflict," 6G.

52. Limerick, "Haunted America," 135–36.

53. Nix, *Sioux Uprising in Minnesota*, 77.

54. Nix, *Sioux Uprising in Minnesota*, 81, 114.

55. Limerick, "Haunted America," 136.

56. Zeman, "Historical Notes," 12.

57. Henig, "Neglected Cause of the Sioux Uprising," 108.

58. Bryant and Murch, *History of the Great Massacre*, 54–55.

59. Stephen R. Riggs, *Tah-Koo Wah-Kan*, 63.

60. Big Eagle, quoted in Hubbard and Holcombe, *Minnesota in Three Centuries*, 338.

61. Limerick, "Haunted America," 137–46. Note that these pages cover the sixth, seventh, eighth, and ninth of Limerick's twelve points.

62. Limerick, "Haunted America," 138.

63. Anderson and Woolworth, *Through Dakota Eyes*, 7.

64. Gideon Pond, "True History of the Indian Outbreak."

65. Anderson and Woolworth, *Through Dakota Eyes*, 168–69.

66. Anderson and Woolworth, *Through Dakota Eyes*, 4.

67. Limerick, "Haunted America," 140–42.

68. The fact that the American Board of Commissioners for Foreign Missions considered work with the Dakotas equivalent to mission work in a foreign land is certainly significant for its recognition of the cultural and physical challenges that missionaries faced.

69. Martha T. Riggs, "Flight of the Missionaries."

70. Limerick, "Haunted America," 142–43.

71. See F. E. McIntire to Theodore G. Carter, 14 Feb. 1910.

72. Limerick, "Haunted America," 146–51. Note that these pages cover the tenth, eleventh, and twelfth of Limerick's twelve points.

73. Limerick, "Haunted America," 147.

74. Heard, *History of the Sioux War*, 147.

75. Heard, *History of the Sioux War*, 148.

76. Heard, *History of the Sioux War*, 148.

77. Limerick, "Haunted America," 148–49.

78. Heard, *History of the Sioux War*, 188.

79. Quoted in Anderson and Woolworth, *Through Dakota Eyes*, 233.

80. Angela Cavender Wilson, "Grandmother to Granddaughter," 31.

81. An exhaustive legal analysis of the postwar trials can be found in Chomsky, "United States–Dakota War Trials." The platform that allowed all thirty-eight condemned men to hang simultaneously was considered a technological innovation. See Zalusky, "Why—What," for two models of the scaffolding. Although the weather was too cold in December 1862 to allow cameras of that era to take photographs, several famous on-site drawings were published, notably those by W. H. Childs, for *Frank Leslie's Illustrated Newspaper* (24 Jan. 1863, 285) (see fig. 2) and those by a Mr. Herman for *Harper's Weekly* (17 Jan. 1863). The *St. Paul Pioneer* (18 Feb. 1863) advertised copies of Child's drawing for five or fifteen cents, depending on the quality of the paper. The *Mankato (Minnesota) Record*, in 1865, 1867, and 1902, also advertised the availability of lithographs or photographs of the execution. See Woolworth, "Accounts, Drawings, and Photographs."

82. Nichols, "Other Civil War," provides more details on Lincoln's response to the U.S.-Dakota Conflict.

83. Chomsky, "United States–Dakota War Trials," 27.

84. Chomsky, "United States–Dakota War Trials," 15.

85. *Dakota Exile*.

86. Audoin-Rouzeau and Becker, *14–18*, 100.

Part 1. Introduction

1. See Slotkin, *Regeneration through Violence*; VanDerBeets, *Held Captive by Indians*; and Pearce, "Significances of the Captivity Narrative"—an old but very influential article.

2. For full bibliographical information for these thirty captivity narrative books see the works cited list. While I have made every effort to cover the most important recently published books concerning captivity narratives, I apologize for inadvertent omissions. For example, I only learned of Scott Zesch's *The Captured: A True Story of Abduction by Indians on the Texas Frontier* (2004) when my book was in press.

3. Historically many Indian captivity narratives were bestsellers, including those by Mary Rowlandson and John Williams. See Derounian-Stodola, *Women's Indian Captivity Narratives*, xvii–xviii; Mott, *Golden Multitudes*; Amory and Hall, *Colonial Book in the Atlantic World*.

4. Ebersole, *Captured by Texts*, 2.

5. For example, Dakotas were sometimes held captive when fort commanders or even Indian superintendents used them as pawns to try to force other Dakotas accused of insurgency to surrender (Zeman, "Historical Notes," 16).

6. Faery, *Cartographies of Desire*, back-cover copy.

7. *Publishers Weekly*, review of *Captives*.

8. The Native response to captivity narratives will receive closer examination in the introduction to part 2, "Native Americans Narrating Captivity."

1. Martha Riggs Morris and Sarah Wakefield

1. Mary Schwandt Schmidt to Marion P. Satterlee, 19 Dec. 1915.

2. Audoin-Rouzeau and Becker, *14–18*, 37.

3. Bauer, "Creole Identities in Colonial Space," 667.

4. Bauer, "Creole Identities in Colonial Space," 672.

5. Watts, *American Colony*, presents a related argument regarding the Midwest's identity as a regional colony within the United States. See also Dean, "Nameless Outrages," which reaches conclusions similar to mine about the authority of the participant narrator, particularly Sarah Wakefield, in the Dakota Conflict. I had already drafted part 1 of my book when I read Dean's article.

6. Warner, *Our Martha*, "Foreword," n.p.

7. Warner, *Our Martha*, 6–8.

8. Martha's mother, Mary Ann (Longley) Riggs, wrote many letters about her life as a missionary, some of which appear in an edition her great-granddaughter compiled. See Maida L. Riggs, *Small Bit of Bread and Butter*.

9. Woolworth, *Santee Dakota Indian Legends*.

10. *First Fifty Years*, "Appendix," xv.

11. Warner, *Our Martha*.

12. Warner, *Our Martha*, 16.

13. The "Donner Party" refers to a group of California-bound emigrants who left Springfield, Illinois, in April 1846. Along the way their number grew to eighty-seven, but bad luck and poor judgment dogged them from the very beginning. While it is true that Paiute raiders drove off many of the wagon train's cattle in October, no one was actually captured by Indians. Instead they found themselves trapped in the Sierra

Nevadas as winter approached, captive to the harshness of nature and human nature. A splinter group wintered in a remote camp, where starvation drove some to become cannibals, but other expeditionary parties left to find help. One of these groups killed two Indians for food in an ironic reversal of the captivity paradigm in which Indians kill whites. Although forty-six people survived, the Donner Party's macabre story remains one of the most memorable frontier tragedies. See Johnson, "New Light on the Donner Party."

14. Maida L. Riggs, *Small Bit of Bread and Butter*, 246.

15. Margaret Fuller Ossoli (1810–1850), the best-known female Transcendentalist, is also considered the first American woman to serve as a foreign correspondent and, later, as a foreign war correspondent. Her articles from war-torn Italy, in the late 1840s, appeared in the *New York Tribune*.

16. Martha Riggs, in Stephen R. Riggs, *Mary and I*, 173 (original emphasis).

17. Martha Riggs, in Stephen R. Riggs, *Mary and I*, 174.

18. Martha Riggs, in Stephen R. Riggs, *Mary and I*, 174. See Woolworth, "Adrian J. Ebell," which provides biographical and other information. Ebell also published eight newspaper reports in the *St. Paul Daily Press* and an article in *Harper's New Monthly Magazine*, which Woolworth calls "the first substantial account of the early aspects of the war by a participant" (92). The *Harper's* piece is one of the more inflammatory and inaccurate accounts of the Conflict. See Ebell, "Indian Massacres and War of 1862."

19. Martha Riggs, in Stephen R. Riggs, *Mary and I*, 175.

20. Martha Riggs, in Stephen R. Riggs, *Mary and I*, 178 (original emphasis).

21. Martha's recording of "Sweet Grass' Story" is included in Woolworth, *Santee Dakota Indian Legends*, 89–93.

22. Much of my information on the early history of the Dakota missions comes from Clemmons, "Satisfied to Walk," 29–40.

23. Clemmons, "Satisfied to Walk," viii.

24. Clemmons, "Satisfied to Walk," ix.

25. Clemmons, "Satisfied to Walk," 249.

26. Tinker, *Missionary Conquest*, 4, 20.

27. Florestine Kiyukanpi Renville, "Dakota Identity Renewed," 115.

28. Cook-Lynn, *Anti-Indianism in Modern America*, 47–48.

29. Tinker, *Missionary Conquest*, 97, 110.

30. Zanger, "'Straight Tongue's Heathen Wards,'" 212.

31. These essays and others are reprinted in Vine Deloria Jr., *For This Land*.

32. Vine Deloria Jr., *For This Land*, 22.

33. Bluestone, "From My Grandmother I Learned," 75.

34. Berkhofer, *Salvation and the Savage*, 69.

35. See Lewis, *Creating Christian Indians*.

36. All quotations from Wakefield's captivity narrative come from the second edition as published in Derounian-Stodola, *Women's Indian Captivity Narratives*, 241–313. See also Derounian-Stodola, "'Many persons say,'" for the full texts of the previously unpublished letters to Riggs. The originals are in the Stephen R. Riggs and Family Papers,

MHS. Some of the information on Wakefield in *The War in Words* originally appeared in this article. However, my theory (in "'Many persons say'") that Stephen Riggs should bear the brunt of the blame for Chaska's death now seems overstated. For the full text of Wakefield's extremely interesting letter to Abraham Lincoln, see Sarah F. Wakefield to Abraham Lincoln, 23 Mar. 1863.

37. Wakefield to Lincoln, 23 Mar. 1863.

38. *The Oxford English Dictionary* lists the earliest use of "monomania" in 1823, when its medical meaning was "a form of insanity in which the patient is irrational on one subject only." But by 1834 a more widespread meaning of the term denoted "an exaggerated enthusiasm for or devotion to one subject; a craze." Either definition could apply to Wakefield's usage. While she could have learned the medical term from her husband, she seems to use the word in its more popular form.

39. Sarah F. Wakefield to Stephen R. Riggs, 9 Apr. 1863, in Derounian-Stodola, "'Many persons say,'" 19.

40. Sarah F. Wakefield to Stephen R. Riggs, 25 Apr. 1863, in Derounian-Stodola, "'Many persons say,'" 21.

41. Wakefield to Riggs, 25 Apr. 1863, in Derounian-Stodola, "'Many persons say,'" 22.

42. Wakefield to Lincoln, 23 Mar. 1863.

43. Wakefield, *Six Weeks in the Sioux Tepees*, 255.

44. For more biographical information on Wakefield see Derounian-Stodola, "'Many persons say'"; June Namias's introduction to Wakefield, *Six Weeks in the Sioux Tepees*.

45. Namias, introduction, 26–27.

46. Wakefield, *Six Weeks in the Sioux Tepees*, 244.

47. Wakefield, *Six Weeks in the Sioux Tepees*, 248.

48. Dakota naming practices are complex. The following information comes from the "Learning from the Dakota" social studies unit compiled by the Shakopee Mdewakanton Dakota Community's Education and Outreach Department (http://www.ccsmdc.org/crp/edu.html). In a box on the department's Web site, labeled "Dakota Birth Order Names," the ordinal name is described as indicating a child's order of birth among all his or her siblings, not just those of the same gender:

	Girl	Boy
First born	Winuna	Caske
Second born	Hapan	Hepan
Third born	Hapstin	Hepi
Fourth born	Wanske	Catan
Fifth born	Wihake	Hake

Many men named Chaska were imprisoned after the Conflict. Wakefield's protector was actually a Dakota Indian named We-Chank-Wash-ta-don-pee, but the precise identity of Hepan has not been determined.

49. Wakefield's testimony can be found in U.S. Army, Military Commission, Sioux War Trials.

50. Zeman's unpublished essay "'I Am Sure of It in My Own Mind,'" which she sent me, makes a compelling case that Wakefield exhibited classic symptoms of Stockholm Syndrome during and after captivity. Zeman also extends other evidence that John Wakefield abused Sarah during their marriage and that her resulting emotional vulnerability made her more likely to suffer from identification with the oppressor. Such a psychological profile could certainly explain some of Wakefield's more bizarre and rash acts. Perhaps more important, it would cast doubt on the strong narrative voice and moral stance she adopts in her letters and her captivity narrative. While I am persuaded that Sarah Wakefield was an abused wife, I cannot discount her overt narrative voice. Instead I see her as a strong, self-conscious moral force whose writing empowered her, rather than a person in the thrall of a psychological condition. Also, when a dominant culture ascribes Stockholm Syndrome to a survivor, it sometimes overlooks for social-disciplinary purposes the very real possibility that even as a hostage an individual might become truly sensitized to a different culture and that this change might be long-lasting.

51. Wakefield, *Six Weeks in the Sioux Tepees*, 271.

52. Schwandt-Schmidt, "Story of Mary Schwandt," 472–73.

53. Wakefield, *Six Weeks in the Sioux Tepees*, 273.

54. Wakefield, *Six Weeks in the Sioux Tepees*, 285, 299.

55. Here are pertinent quotations from a letter Sibley wrote to his wife on 27 Sept. 1862: "One rather handsome woman among them [the captives] had become so infatuated with the redskin who had taken her for a wife that, although her white husband was still living at some point below and had been in search of her, she declared that were it not for her children, she would not leave her dusky paramour." The next day Sibley continued: "The woman I wrote you of yesterday threatens that if *her* Indian, who is among those who have been seized, should be hung, she will shoot those of us who have been instrumental in bringing him to the scaffold, and then go back to the Indians." See Carley, "Sioux Campaign of 1862," 109.

Although Sibley does not identify this woman by name, perhaps for confidentiality, two details all but confirm that she was Wakefield. First, she does indeed state in the letter to Riggs dated 25 Apr. 1863, "If I had no Children I would go with the Indians and become as one of them, for I do believe they would take some interest in my welfare" (Derounian-Stodola, "'Many persons say,'" 21). Second, Sibley retells the story that Wakefield narrates in her own captivity account of threatening to shoot anyone involved in sending Chaska to the gallows. Since we know that no other woman publicly defended an accused Dakota Indian, this fact alone proves that Sibley must be referring to Sarah Wakefield. Her hasty remark, as she herself admits in her narrative, eventually circulated throughout the state and reinforced her reputation as a traitor.

56. Wakefield, *Six Weeks in the Sioux Tepees*, 298.

57. Wakefield, *Six Weeks in the Sioux Tepees*, 301.

58. Wakefield, *Six Weeks in the Sioux Tepees*, 308.

59. The letter from Lincoln's private secretary, John Nicolay, to Henry Sibley can be found in the National Archives. I am grateful to Walt Bachman for bringing it to my attention.

60. Walt Bachman, personal e-mail to the author, 6 July 2005.

61. A second person executed by mistake was apparently a mentally impaired Indian youth, Wasicun, who also answered for someone of the same name. It was fairly well-known at the time that some of the Dakotas who were executed or imprisoned were innocent. For example, Bishop Whipple says this, apparently referring to Chaska's death: "The marshall of the prison told the Rev. Dr. Knickerbacker and myself that a man was hanged by mistake. 'The day after the execution,' said the marshall, 'I went to the prison to release a man who had been acquitted for saving a woman's life, but when I asked for him, the answer was, "You hung him yesterday." I could not bring back the redskin.'" See Whipple, *Lights and Shadows*, 131–32.

62. Three other pieces of external evidence confirm that Riggs met We-Chank-Wash-ta-don-pee on several occasions and certainly should have recognized him. First, in a letter to his daughter Martha on 27 Sept. 1862, written from Camp Release, Riggs spoke of questioning captive Julia Laframbois: "I had her in before the military commission today to testify in the case of the Indian who had Mrs. Wakefield. That is a curious case but I cant tell you about it now." Unfortunately Riggs did not elaborate on what was so "curious." Next, at the end of her third letter to Riggs, dated 25 Apr. 1863, Wakefield made this request: "I wish when you see Chaska's Mother that you would explain to her how her Son was executed," suggesting by her use of "when," not "if," that he knew the family (see Wakefield to Riggs, 25 Apr. 1863, in Derounian-Stodola, "'Many persons say,'" 22). Third, lawyer Isaac Heard, the recorder of the military commission trials, included in his popular *History of the Sioux War* (1863) extensive discussions of Riggs's role in the court proceedings and executions and even went so far as to say, "He was, in effect, the Grand Jury of the court" (Heard, *History of the Sioux War*, 251).

In a Dec. 1863 newspaper review of Heard's book, Stephen Riggs objects to this designation of his "Grand Jury" role and states, "In no way was I the *accuser* of the Indians" (Stephen R. Riggs, "History of the Sioux War" [original emphasis]). Although he claims not to have known three-quarters of the accused Indians, he agrees that "there were a few cases, and but a few, in which I felt a personal interest either for condemnation or acquittal" ("History of the Sioux War"). He explains that many Indians implicated themselves by admitting their presence at battles or their ownership of firearms, which the commission deemed sufficient evidence for a death sentence. And then he confesses to being part of "a common erring humanity" that, in the heat of recrimination, convicted Indians against "Military Regulations and the spirit of Christianity. . . . Many were more guilty than they appeared to be, while many were condemned to death on insufficient evidence" ("History of the Sioux War"). Riggs can also be faulted for secretly obtaining evidence to accuse other Dakotas while taking the confessions of men on death row; in so doing "he was blurring the line between parson and prosecutor" (Bachman, personal e-mail to the author, 6 July 2005). The unwitting combination of the powerful politician Brown and the conflicted missionary Riggs contributed to the hanging of a man who had been removed from the execution list.

63. Wakefield, *Six Weeks in the Sioux Tepees*, 308–9. There may be another reason to add to the others showing that Riggs knew We-Chank-Wash-ta-don-pee. One of Mary

Ann Riggs's letters to Stephen, dated 5 Nov. 1862, responds to information he had given her in an earlier letter: "May God help you to bear the burden of sorrow you must feel for *Chaske* & others. I hope your other duties, will not prevent your taking time to visit the poor condemned criminals. . . . Surely *Chaske* was not bound to criminate himself by confession. Were there no palliating circumstances? How came he to go to Birch Coolie? I am very sorry on his account & for Sarah also." Stephen's earlier letter to Mary describes how Robert Chaskay (or Chaskaydan) had incriminated himself at trial. Mary Riggs's letter almost certainly refers to either Robert Chaskay or Robert Hopkins, but it is possible that she may have misinterpreted her husband's letter and assumed he was talking about Sarah Wakefield and We-Chank-wash-ta-don-pee. See Maida L. Riggs, *Small Bit of Bread and Butter*, 249.

64. Stephen R. Riggs, *Mary and I*, 184.

65. Wakefield, *Six Weeks in the Sioux Tepees*, 308.

66. Wakefield to Lincoln, 23 Mar. 1863.

67. The unanswered question is why Dr. John Wakefield would accuse Joseph Brown of such a deliberate act. It is true that Wakefield's appointment was a political one, along with that of Thomas Galbraith, and that Galbraith, as the new Sioux agent, had replaced Joseph Brown, the old one. Were there tensions between Brown and Galbraith that spilled over to their employees, in this case John Wakefield? We do know that Joseph Brown superintended the prison at Mankato and employed some of his Dakota relatives there. This left Brown open to the charge of nepotism but allowed him considerable oversight if not actual control of conditions in the prison (Walt Bachman, personal e-mail to the author, 10 July 2005). But it is not clear why the Wakefields persisted in making these allegations beyond the effort to clear themselves of the scandal surrounding Sarah's relationship with Chaska and its embarrassing backlash for her entire family. It is possible, though conjectural at this point, that the man called Chaskadon (number 121), who had killed a pregnant woman and was on the execution list, was related to Joseph Brown through his Dakota kin and that Brown found a way to save him. Indeed, Wakefield stated clearly in the letter she wrote to Lincoln that "this man is now at Mankato living" (23 Mar. 1863).

68. The *Mankato (Minnesota) Weekly Record*, 3 Jan. 1863, contains the following information under the subheading "'The Resurrection'": "On the day of execution, a number of physicians from different parts of the State were here to procure bodies for scientific purposes. Before midnight on Friday, at least eight or ten bodies were taken up and carried off. Others were taken on Saturday, Sunday and Monday nights, for the same purpose; and very few, if any, remain in the grave at the present time."

69. John F. Meagher to J. Fletcher Williams, 26 Dec. 1887.

70. Another famous Dakota War atrocity concerns the scalping, dismemberment, and appropriation of the bones of Little Crow, which were finally returned to his grandson in 1971 and buried privately. In 1971 the Minnesota Historical Society noted that it had "returned skeletal remains formerly in its collections to appropriate tribal people." See *Minnesota History News* 28 (Nov.–Dec. 1987): 2, as quoted in Namias, *White Captives*, 364n145. See also Haga, "Another Burial for Dakota Leader."

Two other executed Dakotas, including Cut Nose, were preserved, apparently by taxidermy (see "Resurrection").

71. Harran and Harran, "Remembering a Loved One."

72. Wakefield to Riggs, 25 Apr. 1863, in Derounian-Stodola, "'Many persons say,'" 20.

73. Carrie R. Zeman, personal e-mail to the author, 15 July 2005.

74. Liberal theology was the product of German thinker Friedrich Schleiermacher (1768–1834), who was influenced by Romanticism to focus on individual experience, intuition, and feeling, rather than knowledge or ethics, as the basis of religion. Schleiermacher believed that piety does not need to be expressed through doctrinal sophistication because religion is experienced, not learned, and that church teachings "are really explanations or explications of Christian experience" exemplified in "the liberal spirit." See Dillenberger and Welch, *Protestant Christianity Interpreted*, 185, 188, 211. It seems unlikely that Wakefield consciously applied these theological beliefs as a result of her own reading, though she may have heard them expressed from the pulpit. Rather, her personal spiritual development led her in the same direction and encouraged her to see that the evidence of individual religious experience lay in the social expression of faith. In an ideal world, she suggests, she should not be criticized according to dry spiritual doctrine (she had not been baptized) or prejudicial social stigma (she had shown kindness to Indians).

But Vine Deloria Jr.'s 1997 essay "On Liberation" sees liberation theology as "simply the latest gimmick to keep minority groups circling the wagons with the vain hope that they can eliminate the oppression that surrounds them." He believes that true liberation can only come about with "the destruction of the whole complex of Western theories of knowledge and the construction of a new and more comprehensive synthesis of human knowledge and experience," which he admits is no easy task. See Vine Deloria Jr., *For This Land*, 100, 106.

75. For details on marital problems between John and Sarah Wakefield before she was captured, see Derounian-Stodola, "'Many persons say,'" 7–9; Zeman, "'I Am Sure of It in My Own Mind.'"

76. Namias, *White Captives*, 248.

77. Namias, *White Captives*, 248–51.

78. *St. Paul Pioneer Press*, 29 May 1899, 8. Carrie R. Zeman is currently engaged in further research on Sarah Wakefield's pre- and postcaptivity life, including the possibility that she remarried after John's death.

79. Namias, introduction, 31, 137n65.

80. Wakefield, *Six Weeks in the Sioux Tepees*, 241.

81. Wakefield, *Six Weeks in the Sioux Tepees*, 268.

82. Wakefield, *Six Weeks in the Sioux Tepees*, 259.

83. Castiglia, *Bound and Determined*, 57.

2. Harriet Bishop McConkey and Isaac Heard

1. The texts are Heard, *History of the Sioux War*; McConkey, *Dakota War Whoop*; and Bryant and Murch, *History of the Great Massacre*.

2. Sommerdorf, "No Grass beneath Her Feet," 21.

3. Zeman, "Historical Notes," 27.

4. Sommerdorf, "No Grass beneath Her Feet," 20.

5. See the following notices, all on the front page of various editions of the *St. Paul Pioneer Press*: one untitled paragraph, 20 Sept. 1863; "Heard's *History of the Sioux War*," 22 Oct. 1863; "The Sioux War and Massacres of 1862–3," 14 Nov. 1863.

6. Quoted in Bolin, "Harriet E. Bishop," 8.

7. Bishop, *Floral Home*, 52–54.

8. Bolin, "Harriet E. Bishop," 8.

9. Bolin, "Harriet E. Bishop," 12.

10. Sommerdorf, "No Grass beneath Her Feet," 18.

11. Sommerdorf, "No Grass beneath Her Feet," 16–19.

12. Philecclesian Society Papers, 1857–58, MHS.

13. Bishop, *Floral Home*, 71.

14. Harriet E. Bishop McConkey to Henry H. Sibley, 19 and 20 Oct. 1864.

15. McConkey to Sibley, 20 Oct. 1864.

16. Return I. Holcombe, at bottom of letter from McConkey to Sibley, 19 Oct. 1864.

17. McConkey, *Dakota War Whoop*, 30; Sommerdorf, "No Grass beneath Her Feet," 20.

18. McConkey, *Dakota War Whoop*, 82.

19. Audoin-Rouzeau and Becker, *14–18*, 39.

20. McConkey, *Dakota War Whoop*, 257–96.

21. McConkey, *Dakota War Whoop*, 106. Burnham, *Captivity and Sentiment*, also explores connections between captivity narratives and expressions of sentiment.

22. Elsewhere I have identified the general historical development of Indian captivity narratives as moving from factive (tending toward fact) to fictive (tending toward fiction). However, the impulse to fictionalize was present even in the earliest accounts, like Mary Rowlandson's, and to factionalize even in the later narratives, though the latter existed alongside novels and short stories that used captivity plots. See Derounian-Stodola, *Women's Indian Captivity Narratives*, xii–xiii.

23. McConkey, *Dakota War Whoop*, 17.

24. McConkey, *Dakota War Whoop*, 17–18.

25. Rowlandson, "True History of the Captivity and Restoration," 13 (original emphasis).

26. McConkey, *Dakota War Whoop*, 46–48.

27. For more information on these anthologies see Derounian-Stodola and Levernier, *Indian Captivity Narrative*, 35; Castiglia, *Bound and Determined*, 106–8.

28. See McConkey, *Dakota War Whoop*, 24, 27–29, 38, 73, 132, 156, for some of her many references to Indian atrocities. See Chomsky, "United States–Dakota War Trials," 20n39, for a recent assessment of how claims of Dakota atrocities were wildly exaggerated.

29. Audoin-Rouzeau and Becker, *14–18*, 110.

30. Audoin-Rouzeau and Becker, *14–18*, 101.

31. Coward, *Newspaper Indian*, 5–6.

32. Culley, *American Women's Autobiography*, 7 (original emphasis).

33. Bishop, *Minnesota*.

34. Bishop, *Minnesota*, 65.

35. Sommerdorf, "No Grass beneath Her Feet," 20–21.

36. Moss, "Miss Harriet E. Bishop," 159.

37. Newson, *Pen Pictures of St. Paul*, 346–47.

38. Heard, *History of the Sioux War*, [v].

39. Heard, *History of the Sioux War*, [v].

40. "Literary Notices," 851.

41. "Review of *History of the Sioux War*," 266.

42. "Review of *History of the Sioux War*," 267.

43. "Review of *History of the Sioux War*," 270.

44. Stephen R. Riggs, "History of the Sioux War," 2.

45. Stephen R. Riggs, "History of the Sioux War," 2.

46. Heard, *History of the Sioux War*, 13.

47. Heard, *History of the Sioux War*, 13.

48. I will discuss Godfrey and his story in more detail in part 2, "Native Americans Narrating Captivity."

49. Heard, *History of the Sioux War*, 13. For Godfrey's appearances throughout the text see 189–90, 199, 251–71, 278–82.

50. Heard, *History of the Sioux War*, 189.

51. Heard, *History of the Sioux War*, 254.

52. Heard, *History of the Sioux War*, 266.

53. Heard, *History of the Sioux War*, 267.

54. Heard, *History of the Sioux War*, 116.

55. I discuss the Lake Shetek incident in more detail later and analyze two specific works concerning it: a letter by Lillian Everett Keeney later in part 1, and a novel by contemporary Sioux author Virginia Driving Hawk Sneve in part 2.

56. Heard, *History of the Sioux War*, 102, 111.

57. Heard, *History of the Sioux War*, 110–11.

58. Heard, *History of the Sioux War*, 101, 111.

59. Heard, *History of the Sioux War*, 130, 177–78.

60. Stephen R. Riggs to Mary Riggs, 23 Sept. 1862.

61. Heard, *History of the Sioux War*, 69, 75–76.

62. Heard, *History of the Sioux War*, 31.

63. Heard, *History of the Sioux War*, 342.

64. "Isaac Heard Dies at New York Home."

65. "Isaac Heard Dies at New York Home."

3. Edward S. Ellis

1. Edward S. Ellis, *Indian Jim*.

2. Cox, *Dime Novel Companion*, xiii.

3. Cox, *Dime Novel Companion*, xiv.

4. Johanssen, *House of Beadle and Adams*, 2:93–96.

5. Bill Brown, *Reading the West*, 165.

6. Bill Brown, *Reading the West*, 166.

7. Brummond, "Litchfield Man," 14.

8. Bill Brown, *Reading the West*, 6.

9. Edward S. Ellis, *Indian Jim*, 11, 15.

10. Edward S. Ellis, *Indian Jim*, 10.

11. Edward S. Ellis, *Indian Jim*, 19.

12. See Norwood, "Fragments, Ruins and Artifacts," for an extensive discussion of constructing meaning from reading landscape signs and reading books in *The Deerslayer*.

13. Edward S. Ellis, *Indian Jim*, 53.

14. Edward S. Ellis, *Indian Jim*, 57.

15. Edward S. Ellis, *Indian Jim*, 72, 78 (original emphasis).

16. Edward S. Ellis, *Indian Jim*, 9–10.

17. Edward S. Ellis, *Indian Jim*, 26.

18. Edward S. Ellis, *Indian Jim*, 76.

19. Edward S. Ellis, *Indian Jim*, 77, 80, 83.

20. Edward S. Ellis, *Indian Jim*, 20 (original emphasis).

21. Edward S. Ellis, *Indian Jim*, 77, 93.

22. Edward S. Ellis, *Indian Jim*, 98.

23. Edward S. Ellis, *Indian Jim*, 100.

24. Edward S. Ellis, *Indian Jim*, 10, 14, 30.

25. Stowe, *Uncle Tom's Cabin*, 2:113.

26. Edward S. Ellis, *Indian Jim*, 25.

27. Edward S. Ellis, *Indian Jim*, 66, 75.

28. Edward S. Ellis, *Indian Jim*, 90–91.

29. Johanssen, *House of Beadle and Adams*, 2:94–97.

30. Edward S. Ellis, *Indian Wars of the United States*.

31. Edward S. Ellis, *Indian Wars of the United States*, 2, 484.

32. Edward S. Ellis, *Red Plume*. I am grateful to Carrie R. Zeman and Walt Bachman for providing some contextual information on this novel (Bachman, personal e-mails to the author, 14 and 15 June 2007; Zeman, personal e-mails to the author, 14 and 15 June 2007).

33. Edward S. Ellis, *Red Plume*, 385. A clear example of the specific cultural work that Indian captivity performed, and continues to perform, in popular fiction concerns the 1964 romance by Frederick Manfred set during the Dakota War, *Scarlet Plume*. Manfred, who writes about a region he calls Siouxland, may have read Ellis's books on the Dakota War and appropriated the name of one of Ellis's Dakota characters (Red Plume becomes Manfred's Scarlet Plume), or he may have taken the name of a real Dakota warrior and chief called Scarlet Plume (Wamdiupidata), who led one of the Upper bands in 1862 (see various references to Scarlet Plume in Samuel J. Brown, *In Captivity*). Manfred also did some research and based his main female character, Judith Raveling, on Sarah Wakefield (Zeman, personal e-mail to the author, 30 May 2007). Yet this book reflects

the 1960s, when it appeared, with its emphasis on counterculture: Scarlet Plume is the Noble Indian, symbolic of "back-to-the-earth" sentiment; Raveling is the initially repressed but then sexually liberated flower child; and the entire book presents every romantic stereotype imaginable. Although the 1960s also saw the rise of the women's movement and the American Indian Movement, Manfred's book shows that there was still an audience for sensationalized racial and gender typecasting.

34. Edward S. Ellis, *Red Feather*.

35. Zeman, personal e-mails to the author, 14 and 15 June 2007.

36. For more information on dime novels in general and the place of *Malaeska* and *Indian Jim* within this tradition see Ramsey and Derounian-Stodola, "Dime Novels."

4. Mary Schwandt Schmidt and Jacob Nix

1. See Bryant and Murch, *History of the Great Massacre*. Although the title page of the 1864 edition says "2nd edition," I have not been able to find a copy of the first edition of 1863. An extract from the "advance sheets," as well as notice of the first edition's publication, appeared in the *Mankato (Minnesota) Weekly Union*, 25 Sept. 1863, and a notice from Red Wing, Minnesota in Dec. 1863 indicates that the book has 504 pages. Bryant and Murch do not refer to a first edition in their preface to the 1864 edition, which is dated Nov. 1863. I am assuming that the 1864 edition is actually a reprint, since it too has 504 pages, and that the earlier edition had a limited circulation. When it came out relative to Bishop's and Heard's histories is not completely clear either.

2. See these figures and further census information at http://www.census.gov/prod/www/abs/decennial/1860.htm and http://www.census.gov/prod/www/abs/decennial/1890.htm, accessed online, 6 July 2007, and forwarded to me by Carrie R. Zeman ("Historical Notes," 30–31).

3. Tolzmann, *Sioux Uprising in Minnesota*, xii.

4. Calloway, Germunden, and Zantop, *Germans and Indians*.

5. Tolzmann, *Sioux Uprising in Minnesota*, xi.

6. In discussing the site for a monument to Schwandt's family, a 25 June 1915 article in the *Morton (Minnesota) Enterprise* mentioned that Schwandt Schmidt was "at present engaged in printing a book telling of her experience." Also, in a letter dated 4 Sept. 1927 that Schwandt Schmidt wrote to Frank Hopkins, president of the Fort Ridgely Association and the Fort Ridgely Historical Society, she said that she would write up her story for him and that it was "a fine Idea to have a little booklet printed of my Captivity. I think it would sell fine." If anything was printed, it must have been a pamphlet rather than a book and must have had very limited local circulation. In 2002 Schwandt Schmidt's 1894 account, along with that of Minnie Buce Carrigan, was republished in a small press edition by historian Don Heinrich Tolzmann titled *German Pioneer Accounts of the Great Sioux Uprising of 1862*. Note that Mary Schwandt Schmidt's name is variously spelled as two surnames and as a single hyphenated one (the latter is the way her 1894 story appeared). The Minnesota Historical Society has cataloged her with the two separate surnames, so I have adopted this version, except where I quote from her 1894 story.

7. Lepore, *Name of War*, x.

8. Maggie Brass's account and the role of Return I. Holcombe will receive more attention in part 2, "Native Americans Narrating Captivity." It is clear that after she converted to Christianity, Snana preferred the name "Maggie." Return Holcombe seems to be the person who wanted to assign the Native name "Snana" to her when he published Schwandt Schmidt's account and then Maggie Brass's a few years later. Using Snana's Dakota name dramatized the cultural differences between her and Mary Schwandt. Interestingly Pocahontas has gone down in history under a name that was actually a nickname; her formal Native name was Matoaka and, after she was baptized and married, Rebecca Rolfe. European Americans have always appropriated the names they want to use for ethnic others.

9. See the Mary Schwandt Schmidt Papers, MHS. See also the Fort Ridgely State Park and Historical Association Papers, MHS.

10. Bonney, "Was There a Single German-American Experience?" 20.

11. Bonney, "Was There a Single German-American Experience?" 21.

12. Bonney, "Was There a Single German-American Experience?" 25.

13. Schwandt-Schmidt, "Story of Mary Schwandt," 462.

14. Zeman, "Historical Notes," 31.

15. Calloway, "Historical Encounters across Five Centuries," 60.

16. Zeman, "Historical Notes," 32.

17. Schmidt, "Recollections of My Captivity."

18. Arnold, *Poets and Poetry of Minnesota*, 305–6.

19. Bryant and Murch, *History of the Great Massacre*, iv; Henig, "Neglected Cause of the Sioux Uprising," 109.

20. Bryant and Murch, *History of the Great Massacre*, iv.

21. Bryant and Murch, *History of the Great Massacre*, iv–v.

22. Arnold, *Poets and Poetry of Minnesota*, 301.

23. Arnold, *Poets and Poetry of Minnesota*, 302.

24. Bryant and Murch, *History of the Great Massacre*, iii.

25. Bryant and Murch, *History of the Great Massacre*, [i], title page.

26. Bryant and Murch, *History of the Great Massacre*, 504.

27. Bryant and Murch, *History of the Great Massacre*, 339–40.

28. Bryant and Murch, *History of the Great Massacre*, 340.

29. Sweet, "Mrs. J. E. De Camp Sweet's Narrative," 362.

30. Only two women in the entire trials process in 1862 gave evidence against their rapists. Apart from Mattie Williams (in trial 4), Margaret Cardinal accused Tehedhonecha of raping her (in trial 2). Schwandt did not accuse anyone of rape. It is also significant of European American cultural priorities that the Indians accused of rape were among the earliest men tried. In addition to other legal irregularities during the trials process, Abraham Lincoln used the fact that only two men were convicted of rape, versus the widespread but unsubstantiated claims of gang rape, to winnow the original number of Dakota men to be executed to thirty-nine.

31. For further discussion of rape among women captured by Indians see Castiglia,

Bound and Determined, 122–23; Derounian-Stodola and Levernier, *Indian Captivity Narrative*, 127–30; Ebersole, *Captured by Texts*; Namias, *White Captives*.

32. Audoin-Rouzeau and Becker, *14–18*, 46.

33. Bryant and Murch, *History of the Great Massacre*, 341–42.

34. Schmidt, "Recollections of the Indian Massacre," 24.

35. Schmidt, "Recollections of the Indian Massacre," 11.

36. Schmidt, "Recollections of My Captivity," 47–48. This particular manuscript is the topic of an article appearing in the *St. Paul Pioneer Press*, 9 Aug. 1931, titled "Girl's Capture by Sioux Told in Copybook." Schwandt Schmidt was eighty-three at the time.

37. Schmidt, "Recollections of My Captivity," 48–49.

38. Schmidt, "Recollections of My Captivity," 51.

39. Schwandt-Schmidt, "Story of Mary Schwandt," 470.

40. Schwandt-Schmidt, "Story of Mary Schwandt," 470–71.

41. Mihesuah, *American Indians*, 9.

42. Green, "Pocahontas Perplex."

43. Schmidt, "List of Talks Given by Mary Schwandt Schmidt."

44. Upham, "For the Dedication of the Schwandt Monument."

45. For more information on this monument see Holcombe, "Faithful Indians' Monument."

46. Nix, *Sioux Uprising in Minnesota*. I reference Nix's text under Nix, and Tolzmann's introduction under Tolzmann, but use the same book title for each.

47. Tolzmann, *Sioux Uprising in Minnesota*, x.

48. Iverson, *Germania, U.S.A.*, 33.

49. Quoted in Tolzmann, *Sioux Uprising in Minnesota*, x.

50. Tolzmann, *Sioux Uprising in Minnesota*, x; Iverson, *Germania, U.S.A.*, 53.

51. Iverson, *Germania, U.S.A.*, 6.

52. Nix, *Sioux Uprising in Minnesota*, 152.

53. Nix, *Sioux Uprising in Minnesota*, vii.

54. Nix, *Sioux Uprising in Minnesota*, vii.

55. Nix, *Sioux Uprising in Minnesota*, vii.

56. Tolzmann, *Sioux Uprising in Minnesota*, xi; Neill, *History of the Minnesota Valley*, 722.

57. McConkey, *Dakota War Whoop*, 51.

58. McConkey, *Dakota War Whoop*, 51; Nix, *Sioux Uprising in Minnesota*, 129.

59. McConkey, *Dakota War Whoop*, 53.

60. Tolzmann, *Sioux Uprising in Minnesota*, xiv.

61. Heard, *History of the Sioux War*, 80.

62. Bryant and Murch, *History of the Great Massacre*, 170.

63. Hubbard and Holcombe, *Minnesota in Three Centuries*, 389.

64. See Flandreau, *Minnesota in the Civil and Indian Wars* (1891); Berghold, *Indians' Revenge* (1891) (Carrie R. Zeman, personal e-mail to the author, 4 July 2006).

65. Tolzmann, *Sioux Uprising in Minnesota*, xix–xx, note 16.

66. Nix, *Sioux Uprising in Minnesota*, 96, 97, 102.

67. Nix, *Sioux Uprising in Minnesota*, 102.

68. Nix, *Sioux Uprising in Minnesota*, 77, 105.

69. Nix, *Sioux Uprising in Minnesota*, 114, 115, 130.

70. Nix, *Sioux Uprising in Minnesota*, 91.

71. Nix, *Sioux Uprising in Minnesota*, 82.

72. Nix, *Sioux Uprising in Minnesota*, 130–31.

73. "Captain Jacob Nix," quoted in Tolzmann, *Sioux Uprising in Minnesota*, xi.

5. Jannette DeCamp Sweet, Helen Carrothers Tarble, Lillian Everett Keeney, and Urania White

1. The stories by Sweet, Huggan, and Schwandt Schmidt were sponsored by the Minnesota Historical Society but published initially in the *St. Paul Pioneer Press* with the society's permission, presumably to reach a larger audience than would read the *Collections of the Minnesota Historical Society*. An earlier typescript version of Jannette DeCamp Sweet's narrative exists in the Brown County (Minnesota) Historical Society. Titled "In the Hands of the Sioux: A California Woman's Captivity among Savages," it is dated Apr. 1892 and from internal evidence seems to have appeared in the *San Francisco Call*. At the time Sweet was living in Centerville, California. Other information and provenance concerning the document are not available. The 1892 version definitely has the feel of journalism rather than antiquarianism and is also based on an interview, not a written document by Sweet herself. The unnamed reporter-interviewer makes some wild generalizations, perhaps for the benefit of the California readership, saying, for example, that in 1862 "the Indians in Minnesota rose against the whites and went upon that awfulest war-trail [*sic*] that has ever been known to the history of this country." The expanded information within the 1894 accounts published in Minnesota is considerably more detailed and authoritative and exists within a more finished piece of writing based on an eighty-one-page holograph document by Sweet at the Minnesota Historical Society.

2. Quoted in Fridley, "Critical Choices," 131.

3. Fridley, "Critical Choices," 131–32.

4. Fridley, "Critical Choices," 133.

5. Fridley, "Critical Choices," 136.

6. Upham, "Return I. Holcombe."

7. Hubbard and Holcombe, *Minnesota in Three Centuries*.

8. Upham, "Return I. Holcombe," 11.

9. Jannette DeCamp Sweet to William R. Marshall, 28 July 1894.

10. Jannette DeCamp Sweet to William R. Marshall, 10 July 1894.

11. Sweet, "Mrs. J. E. De Camp Sweet's Narrative," 355.

12. Sweet to Marshall, 10 July 1894; Sweet, "Mrs. J. E. De Camp Sweet's Narrative," 354.

13. Even Schwandt's first account, in Bryant and Murch, *History of the Great Massacre*, came from testimony rather than a voluntary desire to recount her experiences.

14. Sweet, "Mrs. J. E. De Camp Sweet's Narrative," 356.

15. Sweet, "Mrs. J. E. De Camp Sweet's Narrative," 356.

16. Sweet, "Mrs. J. E. De Camp Sweet's Narrative," 358–59.

17. Sweet, "Mrs. J. E. De Camp Sweet's Narrative," 364, 367.

18. Sweet, "Mrs. J. E. De Camp Sweet's Narrative," 376.

19. Sweet, "Mrs. J. E. De Camp Sweet's Narrative," 367.

20. Sweet, "Mrs. J. E. De Camp Sweet's Narrative," 378.

21. Sweet, "Mrs. J. E. De Camp Sweet's Narrative," 380.

22. Sweet, "Mrs. J. E. De Camp Sweet's Narrative," 380. For more information on the significance of shaking hands in Dakota culture see chapter 8, "Paul Mazakutemani: Captivity and Spiritual Autobiography," note 23.

23. Schwandt-Schmidt, "Story of Mary Schwandt," 468.

24. Bryant and Murch, History of the Great Massacre, 283–97; "Escaped from the Sioux"; Tarble, Story of My Capture and Escape.

25. Bryant and Murch, History of the Great Massacre, 297.

26. Bryant and Murch, History of the Great Massacre, 296.

27. Bryant and Murch, History of the Great Massacre, 283.

28. Tarble, Story of My Capture and Escape, 3.

29. Bryant and Murch, History of the Great Massacre, 28; Tarble, Story of My Capture and Escape, 7.

30. Tarble, Story of My Capture and Escape, 7, 12, 8, 13.

31. Schlissel, Women's Diaries, 45, 51.

32. Schlissel, Women's Diaries, 51.

33. Tarble, Story of My Capture and Escape, 16.

34. Tarble, Story of My Capture and Escape, 16.

35. Tarble, Story of My Capture and Escape, 17.

36. Tarble, Story of My Capture and Escape, 19.

37. Gary Clayton Anderson, Kinsmen of Another Kind, 264.

38. Tarble, Story of My Capture and Escape, 21.

39. Tarble, Story of My Capture and Escape, 22; Zeman, "Historical Notes," 36–37.

40. Tarble, Story of My Capture and Escape, 33.

41. Tarble, Story of My Capture and Escape, 28.

42. Tarble, Story of My Capture and Escape, 23.

43. Tarble, Story of My Capture and Escape, 44.

44. Tarble, Story of My Capture and Escape, 44.

45. Countless studies of Indian captivity narratives address these two dominant (though by now stereotypical) models of captive women. See especially Castiglia, Bound and Determined; Derounian-Stodola and Levernier, Indian Captivity Narrative; Namias, White Captives.

46. Tarble, Story of My Capture and Escape, 34.

47. Tarble, Story of My Capture and Escape, 16.

48. Tarble, Story of My Capture and Escape, 49.

49. Tarble, Story of My Capture and Escape, 51.

50. See Kolodny, *Lay of the Land* and *Land before Her*.

51. Tarble, *Story of My Capture and Escape*, 64.

52. Workman, "Early History." The manuscript by Workman contains 197 leaves and includes his history of the Lake Shetek area in Murray County, Minnesota, along with a list of settlers living there at the time of the Conflict; biographical sketches of and letters from them; information about their experiences during the war; and a map showing important war sites. Work by Neil Currie complements and repeats some of Workman's data. Keeney's original typescript letter appears to be in the Currie documents; it looks as if it was retyped for inclusion in Workman's manuscript. See Currie, "Information on Victims."

53. Lillian Everett Keeney to Harper M. Workman, 2 Aug. 1894, in Currie, "Information on Victims."

54. Keeney to Workman, 2 Aug. 1894.

55. Keeney to Workman, 2 Aug. 1894.

56. Keeney to Workman, 2 Aug. 1894.

57. Keeney to Workman, 2 Aug. 1894.

58. Keeney to Workman, 2 Aug. 1894.

59. Zeman, "Historical Notes," 36. Some other information in this paragraph comes from Woolworth, "Lake Shetek Massacre."

60. Mariah Kock Hohnmuth, who was captured at Lake Shetek but who escaped, says in an undated letter, "The Ireland girls were abused while in captivity; I will not talk about my treatment by the Indians, while most that is written is untrue, the treatment of Mrs. Duley and myself could not be told." See Currie, "Information on Victims."

61. "Arrival of Mrs. Duly and Children."

62. Workman, "Early History of Lake Shetek Country," 57.

63. White, "Captivity among the Sioux," 395.

64. Some of the other accounts in the captivity literature that deal overtly with psychological trauma are Mary Rowlandson's "A True History of the Captivity and Restoration" (1682), Emeline Fuller's *Left by the Indians* (1892), and Minnie Buce Carrigan's Dakota War narrative (not one of my core texts) *Captured by the Indians* (1907).

65. White, "Captivity among the Sioux," 399.

66. White, "Captivity among the Sioux," 404–5. The Indian woman who helped Urania White and her baby was Mary Crooks. Like that of Maggie Brass, her name was placed on the monument to the loyal Indians in Morton, Minnesota.

67. White, "Captivity among the Sioux," 405–6.

68. White, "Captivity among the Sioux," 407–8.

69. White, "Captivity among the Sioux," 403.

70. White, "Captivity among the Sioux," 406.

71. White, "Captivity among the Sioux," 417.

72. White, "Captivity among the Sioux," 418.

73. White, "Captivity among the Sioux," 414.

74. See Ben-zvi, "Discovering a 'Native' American Genre."

75. Ben-zvi, "Discovering a 'Native' American Genre."

76. White, "Captivity among the Sioux," 417.

6. Benedict Juni

1. Twain's unfinished work was published by the University of California Press in 1989, having first appeared in *Life Magazine* in 1968. In 2003 contemporary author Lee Nelson obtained permission from the Mark Twain Foundation and the University of California Press, which held the copyright to the manuscript, to finish the novel. See Twain, *Huck Finn and Tom Sawyer*; Twain and Nelson, *Huck Finn and Tom Sawyer*.

2. Twain, *Adventures of Huckleberry Finn*, 388.

3. It is quite possible of course that Juni had read Twain's masterpiece, though I do not have any definitive proof of this.

4. Juni, *Held in Captivity*.

5. Benedict Juni to William M. Folwell, 13 Jan. 1908.

6. "Ben. Juni Passes Thursday Evening."

7. Juni, *Held in Captivity*, 1.

8. Juni, *Held in Captivity*, 7.

9. Juni, *Held in Captivity*, 5.

10. Juni, *Held in Captivity*, 15.

11. Juni, *Held in Captivity*, 13.

12. Juni, *Held in Captivity*, 9.

13. Juni, *Held in Captivity*, 14.

14. Juni, *Held in Captivity*, 11.

15. Juni, *Held in Captivity*, 18.

16. Juni, *Held in Captivity*, 15.

17. Zeman, "Historical Notes," 37–38.

18. Juni, *Held in Captivity*, 19.

19. Juni, *Held in Captivity*, 21.

20. Juni, *Held in Captivity*, 7.

21. Juni, *Held in Captivity*, 16.

22. Juni, *Held in Captivity*, 22.

23. "Ben. Juni Passes Thursday Evening."

24. Audoin-Rouzeau and Becker, *14–18*.

25. Quoted in Martin, *American Indian and the Problem of History*, 158.

Part 2. Introduction

1. Davis and Gates, *Slave's Narrative*.

2. Bataille and Sands explore other connections among the slave narrative, the Indian captivity narrative, and Indian autobiography in *American Indian Women*, 7–8.

3. Cook-Lynn, *Anti-Indianism in Modern America*, 198–99.

4. See Stoll and Arias, *Rigoberta Menchu Controversy*.

5. Cook-Lynn, *Anti-Indianism in Modern America*, 203.

6. Kelsey, "Native American Autoethnography," 4.

7. Pulitano, *Toward a Native American Critical Theory*, 79. For a particularly interesting recent publication suggesting a Native engagement with captivity narratives and the oral tradition, see Chebahtah and Minor's 2007 book, *Chevato: The Story of the Apache Warrior Who Captured Herman Lehmann*. In addition to providing biographical information on Chevato, this oral history "provides a Native American point of view on both the Apache and Comanche capture of children and specifics regarding the captivity of Lehmann known only to the Apache participants" (jacket copy).

8. The session was titled "Indians Re-Visioning the Captivity Narrative." It was chaired by Stephanie Fitzgerald and organized by the Association for the Study of American Indian Literatures at the 2004 American Literature Association Conference, San Francisco. The panel featured three papers: my own "Virginia Driving Hawk Sneve's *Betrayed*: Historical and Cultural Contexts"; Betty Donohue's "Live Indians Talking: Native Voices Embedded in Mary Rowlandson's Captivity Narrative"; and Theresa Gregor's "Louise Erdrich's and Sherman Alexie's Captivity: Revising Rowlandson, Reaffirming the Indian in the Captivity Narrative Tradition."

9. Gregor, "Louise Erdrich's and Sherman Alexie's Captivity."

10. The session at the 2004 Native American Literature Symposium, Mystic Lake, Minnesota, was titled "Capturing Captivity: Retaking American Indian Captivity." It was chaired by Stephen Brandon and featured two papers: Adam Ruh's "Captivity and the Captivity Narrative: Opening the Gap" and Stephen Brandon's "The American Indian Captivity Narrative: (Re)Telling Captivity from the Native Point of View."

11. Gregor, "Louise Erdrich's and Sherman Alexie's Captivity."

12. Owing to space limitations I restrict my examination of the trope and rhetoric of captivity to selected contemporary Native authors and theorists. But other instances certainly go further back. One particularly interesting example comes from the famous Sioux author Gertrude Bonnin (Zitkala-Ša). In the *National Council of American Indians, Inc. Newsletter*, 25 Jan. 1933, Bonnin discusses the Depression and says that all Americans, including Native Americans, would prefer to work than to accept handouts. She explicitly connects the reservation system with captivity and silence because it fosters dependency: "Indians do not expect food and clothing doled out to them indefinitely. What they want is an opportunity to work and make a living, as do the 14 million men unemployed. When Columbus visited our continent, Indians were working out their own salvation but immediately after their treaty agreements with the government, the red race fell into voiceless captivity under the Indian reservation system" (Brigham Young Library, L. Tom Perry Special Collections, Bonnin Collection). I am extremely grateful to P. Jane Hafen, University of Nevada at Las Vegas, for making available to me her transcription of this newsletter before its publication in her forthcoming edition of Bonnin's later writings.

13. Vizenor, *Fugitive Poses*, 47.

14. "Ishi: The Last Yahi," at http://www.library.ucsf.edu/collres/archives/hist/ishi/, contains much information and many links on Ishi. In 1996 Steven Shackley, a research anthropologist at the Hearst Museum of Anthropology, challenged the claim that Ishi was the last Yahi Indian. Shackley provides compelling evidence that while Ishi was

culturally Yahi, he was not the last full-blood Yahi Indian but was of mixed Indian descent, probably part Yahi and part Wintu or Nomlaki. This information is significant because it complicates simplistic notions that Ishi was "the last of the Yahi" and makes his biography into a longer story of cultural adaptation. See Shackley, "Stone Tool Technology."

15. Lyons, "Captivity Narrative," 88.
16. Angela Cavender Wilson, "Grandmother to Granddaughter," 30.
17. Bluestone, "From My Grandmother I Learned."
18. Westerman, "Floyd Red Crow Westerman," 126.
19. Pulitano, *Toward a Native American Critical Theory*, 102.
20. Kelsey, "Native American Autoethnography," 17.
21. Brumble, *Annotated Bibliography*, 1.
22. Chapman, "Use of Oral History."
23. Bataille and Sands, *American Indian Women*, 10–11.
24. Bataille and Sands, *American Indian Women*, 11.
25. Bataille and Sands, *American Indian Women*, 12–13.
26. Florestine Kiyukanpi Renville, "Dakota Identity Renewed," 101.
27. Big Eagle, "Sioux Story of the War," 385–86.
28. Clemmons, "Satisfied to Walk," 330–33.
29. Szasz, *Between Indian and White Worlds*, 3.
30. Terry P. Wilson, "Blood Quantum," 119.
31. Anderson and Woolworth, *Through Dakota Eyes*, 5.

7. Samuel J. Brown and Joseph Godfrey

1. Walzer, *Obligations*, 147.
2. Rowlandson, "True History of the Captivity and Restoration," 46.
3. Gary Clayton Anderson, *Little Crow*, 190.
4. Gary Clayton Anderson, *Little Crow*, 107.
5. Heard, *History of the Sioux War*, 202.
6. Heard, *History of the Sioux War*, 202.
7. Heard, *History of the Sioux War*, 208.
8. Heard, *History of the Sioux War*, 205–6.
9. Woolworth, "Samuel Jerome Brown."
10. Red Owl, "Brief Historical Overview."
11. Clifton, *Being and Becoming Indian*, 23.
12. Florestine Kiyukanpi Renville, "Dakota Identity Renewed," 101.
13. Samuel J. Brown, *In Captivity*, 2.
14. Samuel J. Brown, *In Captivity*, 2.
15. Samuel J. Brown, *In Captivity*, 5.
16. Samuel J. Brown, *In Captivity*, 5.
17. Gary Clayton Anderson, *Little Crow*, 156–57.
18. Samuel J. Brown, *In Captivity*, 11.
19. Samuel J. Brown, *In Captivity*, 8.

20. Samuel J. Brown, *In Captivity*, 25.

21. In 1901, when the Sisseton and Wahpeton Dakotas from the Upper Reservation claimed back-annuity payments from the U.S. government, Samuel Brown gave evidence on their behalf. He stated that about two thousand innocent Sissetons and Wahpetons had fled because "they were afraid the soldiers would make no discrimination between the guilty and those that were not guilty." See "Evidence for the Claimants."

22. Dale, "Sam Brown's Ride," 6–8.

23. "Scout Sam J. Brown."

24. Anderson and Woolworth, *Through Dakota Eyes*, 5.

25. Angela Cavender Wilson, "Decolonizing the 1862 Death Marches."

26. Allanson, *Stirring Adventures*, [2].

27. I am grateful to Walt Bachman for sharing some of the considerable information he has gathered on Joseph Godfrey, which will appear in his forthcoming biography.

28. Bachman, "Joseph Godfrey," 377.

29. Walt Bachman, personal e-mail to the author, 24 July 2006.

30. Bachman, "Joseph Godfrey," 377.

31. Bachman, "Joseph Godfrey," 377.

32. Terry P. Wilson, "Blood Quantum," 114.

33. Bachman, "Joseph Godfrey," 379.

34. Godfrey, Testimony.

35. Schmidt, Testimony; Mattie Williams, Testimony.

36. Heard, *History of the Sioux War*, 198.

37. Heard, *History of the Sioux War*, 196–97.

38. Chomsky, "United States–Dakota War Trials," 50.

39. Quoted in *Notes from the Trials*, 16.

40. *Notes from the Trials*, 7.

41. *Notes from the Trials*, 7. See also Bachman, "Joseph Godfrey," 381.

42. "Godfrey Not Hanged."

43. "Mankato Hanging."

44. Bachman, "Joseph Godfrey," 377.

45. Bachman, "Joseph Godfrey," 380.

46. Heard, *History of the Sioux War*, 267; Bryant and Murch, *History of the Great Massacre*, 449.

47. Bachman, "Joseph Godfrey," 379.

48. For further information on Tituba see Breslaw, *Tituba*.

49. Paine, "Biographical Data on Joseph Godfrey."

50. "Gusa Godfrey Is Dead."

51. McIntire to Carter, 14 Feb. 1910.

52. McIntire to Carter, 14 Feb. 1910.

53. McIntire to Carter, 14 Feb. 1910.

54. Guzik, Bible commentary.

55. Quoted in Chomsky, "United States–Dakota War Trials," 23.

56. "Gusa Godfrey Is Dead."

57. "Mankato Hanging."

8. Paul Mazakutemani

1. Anderson and Woolworth, *Through Dakota Eyes*, 194.

2. Paul Mazakutemani's thirty-two-page handwritten manuscript, in Dakota, as well as Stephen Riggs's twenty-page handwritten manuscript translation, are available at the Minnesota Historical Society, in the Dakota Conflict of 1862 Manuscripts Collections. They are printed in Mazakutemani, "Narrative," 82–90.

3. Kelsey, "Native American Autoethnography," 3. Kelsey's book, *Tribal Theory in Native American Literature: Dakota and Haudenosaunee Writing and Indigenous Worldviews*, was published by the University of Nebraska Press in 2008.

4. Pratt, *Imperial Eyes*, 7.

5. See Terry P. Wilson, "Blood Quantum," 124; Baird, "Are There 'Real' Indians in Oklahoma?"

6. Bataille and Sands, *American Indian Women*, 5.

7. Mazakutemani, "Narrative," 82.

8. Mazakutemani, "Narrative," 83.

9. Mazakutemani, "Narrative," 83.

10. Mazakutemani, "Narrative," 84.

11. Mazakutemani, "Narrative," 84.

12. See Mazakutemani, "Narrative," 84–86; Gary Clayton Anderson, *Kinsmen of Another Kind*, 271; Albers, "Santee," 767.

13. Mazakutemani, "Narrative," 89.

14. Ella Deloria, *Speaking of Indians*, 106.

15. Kelsey, "Native American Autoethnography," 56.

16. Kelsey, "Native American Autoethnography," 57.

17. O'Brien, *Plains Indian Autobiographies*, 7.

18. Mazakutemani, "Narrative," 82.

19. Brumble, *American Indian Autobiography*, 44.

20. Samuel W. Pond, *Dakota or Sioux in Minnesota*, 78.

21. De Ramirez, review, 81.

22. Mazakutemani, "Narrative," 90 (original emphasis).

23. I am grateful to Beth Brown, program assistant, American Indian Studies, University of Minnesota, for her detailed explanation of the significance of shaking hands in Dakota culture (personal e-mail to the author, 28 Aug. 2007). I quote from her e-mail in this and in the next sentence.

24. Paul Mazakutemani to Alexander Ramsey, 2 Sept. 1862, as quoted in Renville and Renville, *Thrilling Narrative of Indian Captivity*, 16.

25. Quoted in Woolworth, "Notes on Paul Mazakutemani."

9. Cecelia Campbell Stay and Nancy McClure Faribault Huggan

1. Bataille and Sands, *American Indian Women*, 9.

2. Kidwell, "Indian Women as Cultural Mediators," 98.

3. Maltz and Archambault, "Gender and Power in Native North America," 246.

4. Anderson and Woolworth, *Through Dakota Eyes*, 44. For recent work on the Campbell family see Atkins, *Creating Minnesota*, chapters 3 and 5.

5. Cecelia Campbell Stay to Grace L. Nute, 6 July 1925.

6. Cecelia Campbell Stay's story also appeared in the *Madison Independent Press*, 15 June 1923. I have not been able to examine this version.

7. Stay, "Massacre at the Lower Sioux Agency," 47.

8. Stay, "Massacre at the Lower Sioux Agency," 51.

9. There is a discrepancy in the dating of the first manuscript. Although the record at the Provincial Archives of Manitoba dates it 1888, Stay's reference to names on the Camp Release Monument, which was not dedicated until 1894, strongly suggests that it must have been written (or perhaps only revised) after 1894. Also, Stay was only forty in 1888, and so her concern about fading memory does not necessarily ring true. But six-plus years later, in 1894, her recall of decades-old incidents might have dimmed. Since I cannot definitively disprove the original dating, however, I continue to use 1888 as the date of her earliest text. Even if it was written in or shortly after 1894, it is still her earliest extant account.

10. Cecelia (Celia) Campbell Stay, interview with Alexander Seifert et al., 5 Aug. 1924.

11. Stay, interview with Seifert et al., 5 Aug. 1924.

12. Stay, "Camp Relief."

13. Stay, "Camp Relief," [2].

14. Stay, "Camp Relief," [4].

15. Stay, "Camp Relief," [5].

16. Huggan, "Story of Nancy McClure," 439.

17. Huggan, "Story of Nancy McClure," 441–42.

18. Woolworth, "Nancy's Life and Travels."

19. Stephen R. Riggs, "Tableau of the Families."

20. Huggan, "Story of Nancy McClure," 445.

21. Nancy Huggan to Return I. Holcombe, 13 Apr. 1894.

22. Walt Bachman, personal e-mail to the author, 3 July 2005.

23. Published as *With Pen and Pencil on the Frontier in 1851: The Diary and Sketches of Frank Blackwell Mayer*, edited by Bertha L. Heilbron.

24. Heilbron, *With Pen and Pencil*, 167–78.

25. Number quoted in Samuel J. Brown, *In Captivity*, 23.

26. Walt Bachman, personal e-mail to the author, 1 July 2005.

27. Nancy Huggan to Return I. Holcombe, 14 June 1894.

28. Nancy Huggan to Return I. Holcombe, 27 May 1894.

29. Nancy Huggan to Return I. Holcombe, 11 June 1894.

30. Huggan, "Story of Nancy McClure," 452.

31. Huggan, "Story of Nancy McClure," 453.

32. Nancy Huggan to Return I. Holcombe, 24 May 1894.

33. Huggan, "Story of Nancy McClure," 445.

34. Huggan, "Story of Nancy McClure," 455.

35. Mihesuah, "Commonality of Difference," 39.
36. Huggan, "Story of Nancy McClure," 448.
37. Huggan, "Story of Nancy McClure," 459.
38. Huggan, "Story of Nancy McClure," 459.
39. Huggan, "Story of Nancy McClure," 459.
40. Huggan, "Story of Nancy McClure," 460.
41. Huggan to Holcombe, 11 June 1894.
42. Hopkins, "Turkey's Egg Starts Ft. Ridgely Massacre."
43. Frank Hopkins to Mrs. Sidney A. Peterson, 18 Nov. 1951.
44. Hopkins to Peterson, 18 Nov. 1951.
45. Huggan, "Statement of Nancy Huggins."
46. Hopkins to Peterson, 18 Nov. 1951.
47. Hughes, *Old Traverse des Sioux*.
48. Thomas Hughes to W. C. Brown, n.d.

10. Big Eagle, Lorenzo Lawrence, and Maggie Brass

1. Ella Deloria, *Speaking of Indians*, 25.
2. Return I. Holcombe, introduction to Big Eagle, "Sioux Story of the War," 383.
3. Holcombe, introduction to Big Eagle, "Sioux Story of the War," 383.
4. Return I. Holcombe, *St. Paul Pioneer Press*, 21 Jan. 1906, quoted in Carley, "As Red Men Viewed It," 128.
5. Samuel J. Brown to Return I. Holcombe, 6 Feb. 1896.
6. Holcombe, introduction to Big Eagle, "Sioux Story of the War," 383.
7. Carley, "As Red Men Viewed It," 128.
8. Holcombe, introduction to Big Eagle, "Sioux Story of the War," 383.
9. *Papers Relating to Talks and Councils*, 93.
10. Big Eagle, "Sioux Story of the War," 384.
11. Big Eagle, "Sioux Story of the War," 399.
12. Big Eagle, "Sioux Story of the War," 399-400.
13. Big Eagle, "Sioux Story of the War," 399-400.
14. Big Eagle, "Sioux Story of the War," 384.
15. Big Eagle, "Sioux Story of the War," 384.
16. Big Eagle, "Sioux Story of the War," 384.
17. Big Eagle, "Sioux Story of the War," 384.
18. Big Eagle, "Sioux Story of the War," 385.
19. Big Eagle, "Sioux Story of the War," 387.
20. Big Eagle, "Sioux Story of the War," 387.
21. Big Eagle, "Sioux Story of the War," 390.
22. Big Eagle, "Sioux Story of the War," 394.
23. Big Eagle, "Sioux Story of the War," 399.
24. Big Eagle, "Sioux Story of the War," 400.
25. *Papers Relating to Talks and Councils*, 94.

26. *Papers Relating to Talks and Councils*, 94.
27. *Papers Relating to Talks and Councils*, 94.
28. The three texts are: Lorenzo Lawrence, "Statement of Lorenzo Lawrence"; Lorenzo Lawrence, "Story of Lorenzo Lawrence"; and Elden Lawrence, *Peace Seekers*.
29. Whipple, *Lights and Shadows*, 110.
30. Stephen R. Riggs, "Toteedootawin."
31. Woolworth, "Notes on Lorenzo Lawrence." Some of this information also comes from notes on Lorenzo Lawrence's life dated about 1894, which may be in his own handwriting. These notes are partly reproduced in Richards, "Biographic Notes of 'Wasicu.'"
32. It is not known how or why Lawrence's statement was made at Camp Release. Whipple was certainly not at Camp Release to take it. Carrie R. Zeman surmises that however Whipple obtained the statement, he may have originally used it, along with the other three included in *Lights and Shadows of a Long Episcopate* and other testimonies from Camp Release, to obtain awards for thirty-five Indians who had aided whites in 1862. From 1866 to 1867 Congress appropriated money to reward these "loyal" Indians. Lorenzo Lawrence received five hundred dollars. Yet Lawrence makes it clear in both his texts that he did not *ask* for a reward (Zeman, personal e-mail to the author, 13 Feb. 2006).
33. Lorenzo Lawrence, "Statement," 114.
34. Lorenzo Lawrence, "Statement," 116.
35. Lorenzo Lawrence, "Statement," 118.
36. Sweet, "Mrs. J. E. De Camp Sweet's Narrative," 380.
37. "In the Hands of the Sioux."
38. A note by Laura Anderson about these letters and a translation of one of them, dated 1864, are included in Alan Woolworth's research folder on Lorenzo Lawrence at the Minnesota Historical Society. In this one translated letter Lawrence entreats Riggs to intercede on his behalf by reminding the authorities at Crow Creek of what he did during the war. He says that he and his family, as well as many other Dakotas, were starving to death.
39. Cook, "Good Indian."
40. Woolworth, "Notes on Lorenzo Lawrence."
41. Lorenzo Lawrence, "Story," [1] (page numbers refer to manuscript pages).
42. Lorenzo Lawrence, "Story," [2].
43. One problem in making such assertions involves the role of Bishop Whipple rather than Taopi himself and the competition for converts between the Episcopalians and the Presbyterians. Whipple may have been overly zealous in claiming public credit for his Episcopalian Dakota converts saving lives during the war and may have appropriated Taopi in particular to further the Episcopalian missionary cause. Through Whipple's intervention Taopi and his family were not removed to Crow Creek. However, the Presbyterian missionaries were arguably not as successful in intervening for their converts. Thus Lawrence and his family, who were Presbyterians, were indeed removed to Crow Creek. This does not mean, of course, that the Episcopalian converts did not save lives,

just that others did too and acted as heroically as those singled out for special praise and preferential treatment (Zeman, personal e-mail to the author, 13 Feb. 2006).

44. Lorenzo Lawrence, "Story," [39].

45. Lorenzo Lawrence, "Story," [4].

46. Lorenzo Lawrence, "Story," [17].

47. Lorenzo Lawrence, "Story," [27–28].

48. Lorenzo Lawrence, "Story," [41].

49. Elden Lawrence, *Peace Seekers*, 162.

50. Holcombe, "Faithful Indians' Monument," 47. The monument was renamed the Sioux Indians State Monument in 2008.

51. This newspaper story is headlined, "After Many Years. Noble Indian Squaw Meets Again a Girl Rescued in 1862."

52. The manuscript, titled "The Story of Maggie Brass and her Experience in the Sioux Outbreak," is in the Minnesota Historical Society Institutional Archives Libraries and Archives Division, Publications and Research Monograph Files, Box 151.

53. Maggie Brass to Mary Schwandt Schmidt, n.d.

54. Brass, "Narration of a Friendly Sioux," 428.

55. "After Many Years." The 1906 article appeared on 23 Oct. in the *St. Paul Pioneer Press* and is titled "Indian Woman Visits Mrs. Mary Smith Whom She Rescued from Death Half a Century Ago."

56. *Missionary Paper*, n.p.

57. *Missionary Paper*, n.p.

58. Brass, "Narration of a Friendly Sioux," 429.

59. Bataille and Sands, *American Indian Women*, 9.

60. Brass, "Narration of a Friendly Sioux," 429.

61. Brass, "Narration of a Friendly Sioux," 429.

62. Brass, "Narration of a Friendly Sioux," 429.

63. DeMallie, "Sioux until 1850," 727.

64. Hassrick, *Sioux*, 101.

65. Brass, "Narration of a Friendly Sioux," 430.

66. Brass, "Narration of a Friendly Sioux," 429, 430.

67. Brass, "Narration of a Friendly Sioux," 430.

68. Maggie Brass to Mary Schmidt, 11 Mar. 1907.

69. Ella Deloria, *Speaking of Indians*, 29.

70. Stephen R. Riggs, *Mary and I*, 190.

71. "Saved White Girl in Massacre."

72. "Saved White Girl in Massacre."

11. Good Star Woman

1. Technically "ethnography" refers to a branch of anthropology that describes ethnic groups, has a theoretical dimension, and is based in fieldwork. Cultural anthropology evolved from ethnography. "Ethnology" analyzes and compares different cultures and also deals with origins and characteristics of human racial groups.

2. See the extensive Web support that Minnesota Public Radio provides to supplement its program *Song Catcher: Frances Densmore*, which first aired on 1 Feb. 1997. These links include a huge Densmore bibliography, a biographical profile, and a list of field trips Densmore took from 1905 to 1954: http://news.minnesota.publicradio.org/features/199702/01_smiths_densmore/.
Another excellent source of information is "The Densmore Project: Music of the Native Peoples of North America": http://www.music-cog.ohio-state.edu/Densmore/Densmore.html. Also, "History Topics," at the Minnesota Historical Society Web site, includes a profile of Densmore and other links: http://www.mnhs.org/library/tips/history_topics/124frances_densmore.html.3.
3. Densmore, "Sioux Woman's Account."
4. Densmore, "Sioux Woman's Account," 2.
5. Michael F. Brown, *Who Owns Native Culture?* 25. Brown has constructed an impressive Web site to supplement his book and provide updated links on the topic of Native knowledge. Called "Who Owns Native Culture? Resources for Understanding Current Debates about the Legal Status of Indigenous Art, Music, Folklore, Biological Knowledge, and Sacred Places," it can be found at http://www.williams.edu/go/native/.
6. Michael F. Brown, *Who Owns Native Culture?* 25.
7. Densmore, "Sioux Woman's Account," [1].
8. Densmore, "Sioux Woman's Account," [1].
9. Densmore, "Sioux Woman's Account," 2.
10. Densmore, "Sioux Woman's Account," 9.
11. Engel, *Context Is Everything*, 129, 7.
12. Densmore, "Sioux Woman's Account," 2.
13. Densmore, "Sioux Woman's Account," 4.
14. Densmore, "Sioux Woman's Account," 6.
15. Densmore, "Sioux Woman's Account," 7.
16. Densmore, "Sioux Woman's Account," 8.
17. Densmore, "Sioux Woman's Account," 8.
18. Densmore, "Sioux Woman's Account," 8.
19. Densmore, "Sioux Woman's Account," 8. I am reminded of images from the current Iraq War showing soldiers distributing candy to children whose homes have been bombed and whose lives have been traumatized.
20. Densmore, "Sioux Woman's Account," 8.
21. Carley, *Sioux Uprising of 1862*, 78–79.
22. Quoted in Meyer, *History of the Santee Sioux*, 146.
23. Densmore, "Sioux Woman's Account," 8–9.
24. "Transformation of an Island."
25. Carolyn Ruth Anderson, "Dakota Identity in Minnesota," 237.
26. Carolyn Ruth Anderson, "Dakota Identity in Minnesota," 222.
27. Carolyn Ruth Anderson, "Dakota Identity in Minnesota," 237.
28. Samuel W. Pond, *Two Volunteer Missionaries*, 237–38.
29. Carrie R. Zeman, personal e-mail to the author, 16 Oct. 2005.

30. John P. Williamson, quoted in *Annual Report of the Commissioner of Indian Affairs* (1886), 59.

31. For a very interesting assessment of Franz Boas and the Columbian Exposition see Pierpont, "Measure of America."

32. Pierpont, "Measure of America."

33. Pierpont, "Measure of America."

34. See the Web site "Our Languages," sponsored by the Saskatchewan Indian Cultural Centre, and follow the appropriate link to "Ihanktonwan Dakota": http://www.sicc.sk.ca/heritage/sils/ourlanguages/ihanktonwan/history/early_study.html. This site contains a noteworthy discussion of the contributions of Frances Densmore, Franz Boas, and Ella Deloria to the study of the Dakota/Nakota/Lakota language.

35. Carolyn Ruth Anderson, "Dakota Identity in Minnesota," 354.

12. Esther Wakeman and Joseph Coursolle

1. An extensive discussion of the complex theoretical dimensions of Native oral history and storytelling is beyond this book's scope. See Allen, *Sacred Hoop*; Chapman, "Use of Oral History"; Ruoff, *American Indian Literatures*; Wiget, *Critical Essays on Native American Literature*. See also a large Web site, part of the Transcriptions Project, called "Weaving Webs: Native American Literature, Oral Tradition, Internet," which provides many other links: http://transcriptions.english.ucsb.edu/archive/topics/weaving-webs/home.html.

2. Waziyatawin Angela Wilson, *Remember This!* 27.

3. Mr. and Mrs. Harry Lawrence, "Indian Nations of Minnesota," 80–82; Elizabeth (Wakeman) Lawrence, "Interview."

4. Felix, "Ordeal of Hinhankaga."

5. Naz Coursolle, family interview.

6. Anderson and Woolworth, *Through Dakota Eyes*, 53–54.

7. Woolworth, "Notes on Esther and John Wakeman," 53–54.

8. Esther Wakeman and John Wakeman appear on the Records of the Bureau of Indian Affairs Mdewakanton Enrollment and Annuity Roll, 1885, Record Group 75, so Esther obviously died after 1885.

9. About halfway through this article Esther Wakeman's voice seems to conclude her story, but the article continues with other information in quotation marks, specifying "the Indian account relates," "the Indian account continues," and "the Indian account concludes." I assume that in the second half of the article both Elizabeth and Harry Lawrence furnished data, with the greatest "direct detail"—as editor Newhall had already indicated—coming through the stories Esther Wakeman told her family. See Mr. and Mrs. Harry Lawrence, "Indian Nations of Minnesota," 80.

10. Mr. and Mrs. Harry Lawrence, "Indian Nations of Minnesota," 81.

11. Elizabeth (Wakeman) Lawrence, "Interview."

12. Mr. and Mrs. Harry Lawrence, "Indian Nations of Minnesota," 80.

13. Mr. and Mrs. Harry Lawrence, "Indian Nations of Minnesota," 81.

14. Mr. and Mrs. Harry Lawrence, "Indian Nations of Minnesota," 82.

15. Mr. and Mrs. Harry Lawrence, "Indian Nations of Minnesota," 81.

16. Mr. and Mrs. Harry Lawrence, "Indian Nations of Minnesota," 81.

17. Mr. and Mrs. Harry Lawrence, "Indian Nations of Minnesota," 81.

18. Wakeman, "Big Thunder's Story"; Bromley, "Story of the Sioux Outbreak."

19. Wakeman, "Big Thunder's Story."

20. Anderson and Woolworth, *Through Dakota Eyes*, 60.

21. Wakeman, "Big Thunder's Story." See Williamson, *English-Dakota Dictionary*, 28, 210.

22. Wakeman, "Big Thunder's Story."

23. Naz Coursolle, family interview; Anderson and Woolworth, *Through Dakota Eyes*, 57.

24. Considerable confusion exists about which Joseph Coursolle was really called Hinhankaga (The Owl). Clem Felix and F. J. Patten assign this name to Joseph Coursolle (Joe Gaboo, Joe Caboo, Joe Gabbro); hence his story is titled "The Ordeal of Hinhankaga." But Ernest W. Coursolle, Joseph Coursolle's great-great-grandson, with whom I have corresponded, is convinced that Hinhankaga is actually the Dakota name of Joseph Coursolle's son by Hapan, also named Joseph. Regardless, the story told in "The Ordeal of Hinhankaga" is that of Joseph Coursolle, the father. According to Ernest W. Coursolle, it seems likely that Joseph Coursolle's Dakota name was Kabupi (The Drummer) and that this was phonetically transposed into Gaboo, Caboo, or Gabbro.

25. For example, until recently historians and critics strongly suspected that *A True Narrative of the Sufferings of Mary Kinnan*, published in 1795, was fictional because of its extreme sentimentalism and melodrama. But as in "The Ordeal of Hinhankaga," these elements are more likely the result of editorial tampering. The basic content of *A True Narrative* is indeed true. See Derounian-Stodola, *Women's Indian Captivity Narratives*, 107–16.

26. Patten, *1862*, 1–12.

27. Chapman, "Use of Oral History," 1.

28. Felix, "Ordeal of Hinhankaga," 1.

29. Felix, "Ordeal of Hinhankaga," 8.

30. Felix, "Ordeal of Hinhankaga," 3.

31. Felix, "Ordeal of Hinhankaga," 14.

32. Felix, "Ordeal of Hinhankaga," 15.

33. Felix, "Ordeal of Hinhankaga," 8.

34. Felix, "Ordeal of Hinhankaga," 12.

35. Joseph Coursolle to Henry H. Sibley, 5 Feb. 1875.

36. Woolworth, "Joseph Coursolle."

13. Virginia Driving Hawk Sneve

1. For more information on Sneve see the Web site "Native American Authors Project," at http://www.ipl.org/div/natam, which is arranged by author, title, and tribe. There is also an excellent entry with links on the Web site "Voices from the Gaps: Women Writers of Color," at http://voices.cla.umn.edu.

2. Sneve, *Completing the Circle*, 7.

3. Sneve, *Completing the Circle*, xii–xiii.

4. Sneve, *Completing the Circle*, 59.

5. Sneve, *Dakota's Heritage*, ix.

6. Sneve, *Dakota's Heritage*, ix.

7. See "American Indians in Children's Literature," hosted by Deborah Reese, who teaches American Indian Studies at the University of Illinois at Urbana–Champaign. It can be found at http://americanindiansinchildrensliterature.blogspot.com, and it contains links to recommended books and print resources, online articles, Web sites with reviews of books, and other topics. See also "Native American Children's and Young Adult Literature," at http://www.library.uiuc.edu/edx/nativeamericanchildrens .htm, and http://www.oyate.org.

8. Murphy, "Starting Children," 295n7, 295n8.

9. Murphy, "Starting Children," 290.

10. "Native Writers."

11. Robinson, *Encyclopedia of South Dakota*, 649.

12. There is some discrepancy concerning the number (ten or eleven) and names of the Fool Soldiers. Sebastian LeBeau lists their names as Martin Charger, Four Bear, Swift Bird, Kills Game and Comes Home, Mad Bear, Pretty Bear, Sitting Bear, One Rib Strikes Fire, Red Dog, and Charging Dog. See LeBeau, "'Tribal History.'" In Charger's account in Robinson's *Encyclopedia of South Dakota* they are identified as Charger, Kills and Comes, Four Bear, Swift Bear, Mad Bear, Pretty Bear, One Rib, Strikes Fire, Sitting Bear, Red Dog, and Charging Dog (650–51).

13. "Who Are the Fool Soldiers?"

14. "Pioneer Recalls the Massacre at Shetek." See also Currie, "Information on Victims."

15. Martin Charger's account contains a good deal of factual information, assessment of the Fool Soldiers' motivation, and also re-creations of speeches by White Lodge and Waanatan. Told in the third person, the account presents the entire episode sympathetically and also includes didactic commentary on the Fool Soldiers' courage and humanity. See Robinson, *Encyclopedia of South Dakota*, 650–53.

16. Virginia Driving Hawk Sneve to Eunice Holsaert, 4 Feb. 1974.

17. Sneve to Holsaert, 4 Feb. 1974.

18. Robinson, *Encyclopedia of South Dakota*, 651.

19. Sneve, *Betrayed*, 47.

20. Sneve, *Betrayed*, 48.

21. Elmer, review.

22. Sneve, *Betrayed*, 67.

23. At several points in his account Martin Charger discusses White Lodge's wish to keep Julia Wright. For example: "White Lodge, who had given but grudging consent to the proceeding thus far, now absolutely refused to surrender Mrs. Wright upon any terms, and the boys [i.e., the Fool Soldiers] were equally as determined to procure possession of her." The day after the Fool Soldiers obtained control of the captives,

Charger says, "White Lodge appeared, accompanied by five warriors, and demanded the return of Mrs. Wright, but after a long parley the boys bluffed him out, and he gave up the pursuit" (Robinson, *Encyclopedia of South Dakota*, 652–53).

24. Sneve, *Betrayed*, 112.

25. Sneve, *Betrayed*, 120.

26. *Betrayed* was extensively reviewed and widely praised. Regarding the conclusion, Cathleen Elmer drew attention to the "less-than-satisfactory ending, which is not so much a resolution as an abrupt dislocation of an otherwise forthright and logical story line" (review). Molly Wright stated, "The last chapter feels 'added on' to show white cruelty to Indians" (review).

27. See "Fool Soldiers," in "Oyate Iyechinka Woglakapi: An Oral History Collection," which is part of the American Indian Research Project at the South Dakota Oral History Center, the University of South Dakota. Volume 4 of the collection contains thirteen entries under the category "Fool Soldiers."

The editor's note prefacing the summaries of these interviews states, "Because of the sensitive nature of these interviews, a majority of the informants asked that they remain anonymous" ("Fool Soldiers," 40). Respecting the continued sensitivity of this information, I have chosen not to reveal any further details in my book. However, the oral histories powerfully reinforce the Dakotas' belief that, first, heroic deeds to save whites during the war ultimately meant little or nothing to the authorities and, second, the blame for injustice to the Dakotas should go all the way to the top, to the president himself.

28. "Fool Soldiers."

29. "Burial Record" of Martin Charger.

Conclusion

1. Morrison, "Home," 3–4.

2. See Steil and Post, *Minnesota's Uncivil War*. The main story is subdivided into individual segments following the course of the war and its aftermath.

3. The Dakota diaspora now includes eight tribal centers in three states: the Lower Sioux, Upper Sioux, Prairie Island Sioux, and Shakopee Mdewakanton Sioux Communities in Minnesota; the Santee Sioux Community in Nebraska; and the Crow Creek Sioux, Sisseton Wahpeton Sioux, and Flandreau Santee Sioux Communities in South Dakota. Other communities exist in Canada.

4. Quoted in Steil and Post, *Minnesota's Uncivil War: The Remnants of War*.

5. Quoted in Steil and Post, *Minnesota's Uncivil War: Execution*.

6. Quoted in Steil and Post, *Minnesota's Uncivil War: Dakota Walk*.

7. For an excellent overview of this legal situation see Stinson, "Land, Lineage and Lawsuits." For more detailed information see the *Minnesota Mdewakanton Dakota Oyate Litigation Wolfchild, et al. v. United States*. See also Barbara Feezor Buttes to Kevin Gover, 6 Mar. 2000, letter entitled "The Shakopee Mdewakanton Sioux Community Enrollment Problems and the Minnesota Mdewakanton Sioux Identity."

8. Morrison, "Home," 4.

9. Morrison, "Home," 3.

10. Morrison, "Home," 5.

11. Morrison, "Home," 5.

12. Morrison, "Home," 8.

13. Tanner, *Atlas of Great Lakes Indian History*, 181.

14. Carrie R. Zeman is preparing an edition of John B. Renville and Mary B. Renville's *A Thrilling Narrative of Indian Captivity*. I am grateful to her for sharing some of the information on the Renvilles that she has found in doing research for this edition.

15. Carrie R. Zeman, personal e-mails to the author, 17 and 23 Dec. 2005; Zeman, "Historical Notes," 55.

16. Renville and Renville, *Thrilling Narrative of Indian Captivity*, n.p.

17. Carrie R. Zeman, personal e-mail to the author, 15 Jan. 2006.

18. Renville and Renville, *Thrilling Narrative of Indian Captivity*, [5].

19. Mary Riggs, quoted in Maida L. Riggs, *Small Bit of Bread and Butter*, 256.

20. The Minnesota Historical Society possesses letters from John Renville and Mary Renville to Stephen Riggs, written between 1862 and 1868. According to Carrie R. Zeman, Mary probably corresponded with Riggs as early as 1858 or 1859 and continued to do so after 1868, even though such letters are not currently identified. In the period immediately following the war and covering publication of the narrative, Mary wrote Riggs seven letters in English, and John wrote him four letters in Dakota (Riggs was fluent in both languages) (Zeman, personal e-mails to the author, 23 and 24 Dec. 2005; Zeman, "Historical Notes," 57–58). John's decision to write in Dakota should not necessarily be taken to mean that his English was poor; after all he had attended an English-language school. Perhaps, too, like some other prominent Hazelwood Republic members who also knew English but who wrote to Riggs the same time as John in Dakota, John Renville chose to use the Dakota language so he could reveal sensitive information. The Renvilles' letters to Riggs are in the Stephen R. Riggs Papers, MHS.

21. "Evidence for the Claimants," 129.

22. Renville and Renville, *Thrilling Narrative of Indian Captivity*, 29–30.

23. Renville and Renville, *Thrilling Narrative of Indian Captivity*, 19, 29.

24. Renville and Renville, *Thrilling Narrative of Indian Captivity*, [5].

25. Spahr, *Connective Reading and Collective Identity*, 76.

26. Renville and Renville, *Thrilling Narrative of Indian Captivity*, 22, 6–9, 19, 43, 14, 29. These pages indicate places where the Renvilles specifically speak to these different identities.

27. Renville and Renville, *Thrilling Narrative of Indian Captivity*, 8 (original emphasis).

28. Renville and Renville, *Thrilling Narrative of Indian Captivity*, 12.

29. Renville and Renville, *Thrilling Narrative of Indian Captivity*, 29.

30. Renville and Renville, *Thrilling Narrative of Indian Captivity*, 35.

31. Zeman, personal e-mail to the author, 23 Dec. 2005.

32. ["Rev. John B. Renville"].

33. ["Rev. John B. Renville"].
34. Tougas, "Mending the Wounds."
35. "Redefining Humanity through Diversity."
36. Steil, *Historic Sites Reopen.*
37. Steil, *Historic Sites Reopen.*
38. Tom Sanders, quoted in Steil, *Historic Sites Reopen.*

Works Cited

"After Many Years. Noble Indian Squaw Meets Again a Girl Rescued in 1862." *St. Paul Pioneer Press*, 15 September 1895.

Albers, Patricia C. "Santee." In *Plains*, edited by Raymond J. DeMallie, vol. 13, part 2, *Handbook of North American Indians*, 761–76. Washington DC: Smithsonian, 2001.

Alexie, Sherman. *First Indian on the Moon*. Brooklyn: Hanging Loose Press, 1993.

Allanson, George G. *Stirring Adventures of the Joseph R. Brown Family*. 1933. Rpt., Wheaton MN: Wheaton Gazette, 1947.

Allen, Paula Gunn. *The Sacred Hoop: Recovering the Feminine in American Indian Traditions*. Boston: Beacon, 1986.

Amory, Hugh, and David D. Hall, eds. *The Colonial Book in the Atlantic World*. Vol. 1, *A History of the Book in America*. New York: Cambridge University Press, 1999.

Anderson, Carolyn Ruth. "Dakota Identity in Minnesota, 1820–1995." PhD diss., Indiana University, 1997.

Anderson, Gary Clayton. *Kinsmen of Another Kind: Dakota-White Relations in the Upper Mississippi Valley, 1650–1862*. 1984. Rpt., St. Paul: Minnesota Historical Society Press, 1997.

———. *Little Crow: Spokesman for the Sioux*. St. Paul: Minnesota Historical Society Press, 1986.

Anderson, Gary Clayton, and Alan R. Woolworth, eds. *Through Dakota Eyes: Narrative Accounts of the Minnesota Indian War of 1862*. St. Paul: Minnesota Historical Society Press, 1988.

Annual Report of the Commissioner of Indian Affairs. Washington DC: Government Printing Office, 1886.

Anzaldua, Gloria. *Borderlands/La Frontera: The New Mestiza*. San Francisco: Aunt Lute Books, 1987.

Appy, Christian G. "The Ghosts of War." *Chronicle of Higher Education*, 9 July 2004, B12–B13.

Armstrong, Nancy, and Leonard Tennenhouse. *The Imaginary Puritan: Literature, Intellectual Labor, and the Origins of Personal Life*. Berkeley: University of California Press, 1992.

Arnold, Mrs. W. J., ed. *The Poets and Poetry of Minnesota*. Chicago: Rounds, 1864.

"Arrival of Mrs. Duly and Children." *Mankato (Minnesota) Weekly Record*, 31 January 1863.

Atkins, Annette. *Creating Minnesota: From the Inside Out*. St. Paul: Minnesota Historical Society Press, 2007.

———. "Facing Minnesota." *Daedalus* 129, no. 3 (2000): 31–53.

Audoin-Rouzeau, Stephane, and Annette Becker. *14–18: Understanding the Great War*. New York: Hill and Wang, 2002.

Bachman, Walt. "Joseph Godfrey: Black Dakota." In *Race, Roots and Relations: Native and African Americans*, edited by Terry Straus, 375–83. [Chicago]: Albatross Press, 2005.

Baepler, Paul, ed. *White Slaves, African Masters: An Anthology of American Barbary Captivity Narratives*. Chicago: University of Chicago Press, 1999.

Baird, W. David. "Are There 'Real' Indians in Oklahoma? Historical Perspectives of the Five Civilized Tribes." *Chronicles of Oklahoma* 68 (1990): 4–23.

Bakeman, Mary H., and Antona M. Richardson, eds. *Trails of Tears: Minnesota's Dakota Indian Exile Begins*. Roseville MN: Prairie Echoes, 2008.

Bandura, Albert. "Exploration of Fortuitous Determinants of Life Paths." *Psychological Inquiry* 9 (1998): 95–99.

Barnett, Timothy. "Reading 'Whiteness' in English Studies." *College English* 63 (2000): 9–37.

Bataille, Gretchen, and Kathleen Mullen Sands. *American Indian Women: Telling Their Lives*. Lincoln: University of Nebraska Press, 1984.

Bates, Milton J. *The Wars We Took to Vietnam: Cultural Conflict and Storytelling*. Berkeley: University of California Press, 1996.

Bauer, Ralph. "Creole Identities in Colonial Space: The Narratives of Mary White Rowlandson and Francisco Nunez Pineda y Bascunan." *American Literature* 69 (1997): 665–95.

"Ben. Juni Passes Thursday Evening." *New Ulm (Minnesota) Journal*, 25 February 1922.

Ben-zvi, Yael. "Discovering a 'Native' American Genre: Literary and Ethnographic Authenticities of Indian Captivity Narratives." Paper delivered at the American Literature Association Conference, Summer 2004, San Francisco.

Berghold, Alexander. *The Indians' Revenge; or, Days of Horror: Some Appalling Events in the History of the Sioux*. San Francisco: P. J. Thomas, 1891.

Berkhofer, Robert F. *Salvation and the Savage: An Analysis of Protestant Missions and American Indian Response, 1787–1862*. New York: Atheneum, 1972.

Bieder, Robert E. "Scientific Attitudes toward Indian Mixed-Bloods in Early Nineteenth-Century America." *Journal of Ethnic Studies* 8, no. 2 (1980–81): 17–30.

Big Eagle, Jerome (Wamditanka). "A Sioux Story of the War." *Collections of the Minnesota Historical Society* 6 (1894): 382–400.

Bishop, Harriet E. *Floral Home; or, First Years of Minnesota*. New York: Sheldon, 1857.

———. *Minnesota; Then and Now*. St. Paul: D. D. Merrill, 1869.

———. *See also* Harriet E. Bishop McConkey.

Blaeser, Kimberly. "Y2K Indians: Native Literatures Spanning the Centuries." Keynote address, Sequoyah Research Center Symposium, 2001, Little Rock.

Blight, David W. "The Civil War in History and Memory." *Chronicle of Higher Education*, 12 July 2002, B7–B10.

Bluestone, Rose. "From My Grandmother I Learned about Sadness." In *Messengers of the Wind: Native American Women Tell Their Life Stories*, edited by Jane Katz, 69–77. New York: Ballantine, 1995.

Bolin, Winifred D. Wandersee. "Harriet E. Bishop: Moralist and Reformer." In *Women of Minnesota: Selected Biographical Essays*, edited by Barbara Stuhler and Gretchen Kreuter, 7–19. Rev. ed. St. Paul: Minnesota Historical Society Press, 1998.

Bonney, Rachel A. "Was There a Single German-American Experience?" In *A Heritage Deferred: The German-Americans in Minnesota*, edited by Clarence Glasrud, 20–31. Moorhead MN: Concordia College, 1981.

Brandon, Stephen. "The American Indian Captivity Narrative: (Re)Telling Captivity from the Native Point of View." Paper presented at the Native American Literature Symposium, 2004, Mystic Lake MN.

Brass, Maggie. Letter to Mary Schmidt. 11 March 1907. Mary Schwandt Schmidt Papers. Minnesota Historical Society.

———. Letter to Mary Schwandt Schmidt. N.d. Mary Schwandt Schmidt Papers. Minnesota Historical Society.

———. "Narration of a Friendly Sioux: By Snana, the Rescuer of Mary Schwandt." *Collections of the Minnesota Historical Society* 9 (1898–1900): 427–30.

———. "The Story of Maggie Brass and Her Experience in the Sioux Outbreak." Miscellaneous Manuscripts. Minnesota Historical Society Manuscripts.

Breslaw, Elaine. *Tituba: Reluctant Witch of Salem.* New York: New York University Press, 1996.

Bromley, Edward A. "The Story of the Sioux Outbreak." *Minneapolis Sunday Times,* 15 August 1897.

Brooks, Joanna. "Working Definitions: Race, Ethnic Studies, and Early American Literature." *Early American Literature* 41 (2006): 313–20.

Brown, Bill, ed. *Reading the West: An Anthology of Dime Westerns.* Boston: Bedford, 1997.

Brown, Dee. *Bury My Heart at Wounded Knee: An Indian History of the American West.* New York: Henry Holt, 1970.

Brown, Michael F. *Who Owns Native Culture?* Cambridge: Harvard University Press, 2004.

Brown, Samuel J. *In Captivity: The Experience, Privations, and Dangers of Samuel J. Brown. . . .* 56th Congress, 2nd session, 1900, Senate Document 23. Washington DC: Government Printing Office, 1900.

———. Letter to Return I. Holcombe, 6 February 1896. Minnesota Historical Society.

Brumble, H. David. *American Indian Autobiography.* Berkeley: University of California Press, 1998.

———, comp. *An Annotated Bibliography of American Indian and Eskimo Autobiographies.* Lincoln: University of Nebraska Press, 1981.

Brummond, Kathryn Smith. "Litchfield Man One of Last Indian Scouts: Al DeLong Looks Back on Colorful Career as Frontiersman and Indian Fighter." *Southern Minnesotan* 1, no. 3 (1931): 13–14, 21.

Bryant, Charles S., and Abel B. Murch. *A History of the Great Massacre by the Sioux Indians, in Minnesota.* 2nd ed. Chicago: Rickey and Carroll, 1864. Rpt., Millwood NY: Kraus, 1973.

"Burial Record" of Martin Charger. Copy of original record. Vol. 4, *The Register,* Cheyenne River Mission of the Episcopal Church, Eagle Butte SD, p. 214, no. 308.

Burnham, Michelle. *Captivity and Sentiment: Cultural Exchange in American Literature, 1682–1861.* Hanover: University Press of New England, 1997.

Busch, Fritz. "Dakota Share Their Story of the 1862 Conflict at Conference." *New Ulm (Minnesota) Journal,* 12 June 2001.

Buttes, Barbara Feezor. "The Shakopee Mdewakanton Sioux Community Enrollment

Problems and the Minnesota Mdewakanton Sioux Identity." Letter to Kevin Gover, Assistant Secretary–Indian Affairs, 6 March 2000. Reprinted in *Native American Press/Ojibwe News*, 27 September 2002. Accessed online at http://www.maquah .net/press/Buttes_letter.html, 6 September 2006.

———. *See also* Barbara Feezor.

Calloway, Colin G. "Historical Encounters across Five Centuries." In *Germans and Indians: Fantasies, Encounters, Projections*, edited by Colin Calloway, Gerd Germunden, and Suzanne Zantop, 47–81. Lincoln: University of Nebraska Press, 2002.

———, ed. *North Country Captives: Selected Narratives of Indian Captivity from Vermont and New Hampshire*. Hanover: University Press of New England, 1992.

Calloway, Colin, Gerd Germunden, and Suzanne Zantop, eds. *Germans and Indians: Fantasies, Encounters, Projections*. Lincoln: University of Nebraska Press, 2002.

"Captain Jacob Nix: Early New Ulm Pioneer." *New Ulm (Minnesota) Review*, 4 October 1947.

Carley, Kenneth, ed. "As Red Men Viewed It: Three Indian Accounts of the Uprising." *Minnesota History* 38 (1962): 126–49.

———. "The Sioux Campaign of 1862: Sibley's Letters to His Wife." *Minnesota History* 38 (1962): 99–114.

———. *The Sioux Uprising of 1862*. 1961. Rpt., St. Paul: Minnesota Historical Society Press, 1976.

Carroll, Lorrayne. "'My Outward Man': The Curious Case of Hannah Swarton." *Early American Literature* 31 (1996): 45–73.

———. *Rhetorical Drag: Gender Impersonation, Captivity, and the Writing of History*. Kent OH: Kent State University Press, 2007.

Castiglia, Christopher. *Bound and Determined: Captivity, Culture-Crossing, and White Womanhood from Mary Rowlandson to Patty Hearst*. Chicago: University of Chicago Press, 1996.

Chapman, Serle L. *Of Earth and Elders: Visions and Voices from Native America*. 1998. 2nd ed., Missoula MT: Mountain Press, 2002.

———. "The Use of Oral History in Contemporary Literature." Paper delivered at the Sequoyah Research Center Symposium, 2005, Little Rock.

Chebahtah, William, and Nancy McGown Minor. *Chevato: The Story of the Apache Warrior Who Captured Herman Lehmann*. Lincoln: University of Nebraska Press, 2007.

Chomsky, Carol. "The United States–Dakota War Trials: A Study in Military Injustice." *Stanford Law Review* 43, no. 1 (1990): 13–95.

Clemmons, Linda Marie. "Satisfied to Walk in the Ways of Their Fathers: Dakotas and Protestant Missionaries, 1835–1862." PhD diss., University of Illinois at Urbana-Champaign, 1998.

Clifton, James A. *Being and Becoming Indian*. 1989. Rpt., Prospect Heights IL: Waveland Press, 1993.

———. "Cultural Fictions." *Society* 27 (May–June 1990): 19–28.

Coleman, Nick, and John Camp. *The Great Dakota Conflict*. Pioneer in Education Supplement series. St. Paul: St. Paul Pioneer Press, 1992.

————. "The Great Dakota Conflict." Part 1. *St. Paul Pioneer Press Dispatch*, 19 July 1987.

Colley, Linda. *Captives: Britain, Empire, and the World, 1600–1850.* New York: Anchor/ Doubleday, 2004.

Cook, Sydney. "A Good Indian." Letter published in *St. Paul Pioneer Press*, 10 February 1877.

Cook-Lynn, Elizabeth. *Anti-Indianism in Modern America: A Voice from Tatekeya's Earth.* Urbana: University of Illinois Press, 2001.

Coursolle, Joseph. Letter to Henry H. Sibley, 5 February 1875. Return I. Holcombe Papers. Minnesota Historical Society.

————. Testimony before the Special Commission of the Indian Division of the Secretary of the Interior. As recorded in RG 75, Office of Indian Affairs Special Files No. 274, Folio 9, pp. 10–12.

Coursolle, Naz. Family interview conducted in 1971. Transcribed by Ernest W. Coursolle. Accessed online at http://www.mninter.net/~dakota1/naz.htm, 25 August 2006.

Coward, John M. *The Newspaper Indian: Native American Identity in the Press, 1820–90.* Urbana: University of Illinois Press, 1999.

Cox, J. Randolph. *The Dime Novel Companion: A Source Book.* Westport CT: Greenwood, 2000.

Culley, Margo, ed. *American Women's Autobiography: Fea(s)ts of Memory.* Madison: University of Wisconsin Press, 1992.

Currie, Neil, comp. "Information on Victims of the Lake Shetek Massacre Obtained by Correspondence and Personal Testimony." 25 pages. 1894, 1946. Dakota Conflict of 1862 Manuscripts Collections. Minnesota Historical Society.

Curtiss, Lillian E. Letter to Marion P. Satterlee. [9 May 1914]. Marion P. Satterlee Papers. Minnesota Historical Society.

The Dakota Conflict. Narrated by Garrison Keillor and Floyd Red Crow Westerman. Videocassette. KTCA, 1992.

Dakota Exile. Produced by Kristian Berg. Videocassette. KTCA, 1995.

Dale, Ludvig S. "Sam Brown's Ride to Save St. Paul." *Boy's Life*, March 1913, 6–8.

Davis, Charles T., and Henry Louis Gates. *The Slave's Narrative.* New York: Oxford University Press, 1985.

Dean, Janet. "Nameless Outrages: Narrative Authority, Rape Rhetoric, and the Dakota Conflict of 1862." *American Literature* 77 (2005): 93–122.

Deloria, Ella. *Speaking of Indians.* New York: Friendship Press, 1944.

Deloria, Vine, Jr. *For This Land: Writings on Religion in America.* Edited by James Treat. New York: Routledge, 1999.

————. "The Subject Nobody Knows." *American Indian Quarterly* 19 (1995): 143–47.

DeMallie, Raymond J., ed. *Plains.* Vol. 13, part 2, *Handbook of North American Indians.* Washington DC: Smithsonian, 2001.

————. "Sioux until 1850." In *Plains*, edited by Raymond J. DeMallie, vol. 13, part 2, *Handbook of North American Indians*, 718–60. Washington DC: Smithsonian, 2001.

Demos, John. *The Unredeemed Captive: A Family Story from Early America.* 1994. New York: Knopf, 1995.

Densmore, Frances. "A Sioux Woman's Account of the Uprising in Minnesota." 1934 [1938]. Typescript. Frances Densmore Papers. Minnesota Historical Society Library.

"Deposition of Mrs. Maggie Brass." Evidence for Defendant, Court of Claims No. 22524. *Sisseton and Wahpeton Bands of Sioux Indians v. the United States*, 1901–7, part 2, 379–85.

De Ramirez, Susan Berry Brill. Review of *Oratory in Native North America*, by William M. Clements. *Studies in American Indian Literatures* 16, no. 2 (2004): 88–92.

Derounian, Kathryn Zabelle. "Puritan Orthodoxy and the 'Survivor Syndrome' in Mary Rowlandson's Indian Captivity Narrative." *Early American Literature* 22 (1987): 82–93.

————. *See also* Kathryn Zabelle Derounian-Stodola.

Derounian-Stodola, Kathryn Zabelle. "The Accidental Colonialist: Notes on Academic Choice and Identity." *SEA Newsletter* 17, no. 2 (2005): 3–7.

————. "'Many persons say I am a "Mono Maniac"': Three Letters from Dakota Conflict Captive Sarah F. Wakefield to Missionary Stephen R. Riggs." *Prospects: An Annual of American Cultural Studies* 29 (2004): 1–24.

————. "Virginia Driving Hawk Sneve's *Betrayed*: Historical and Cultural Contexts." Paper presented at the American Literature Association Conference, Summer 2004, San Francisco.

————, ed. *Women's Indian Captivity Narratives*. New York: Penguin, 1998.

————. *See also* Kathryn Zabelle Derounian.

Derounian-Stodola, Kathryn Zabelle, and James A. Levernier. *The Indian Captivity Narrative, 1550–1900*. New York: Twayne, 1993.

Dillenberger, John, and Claude Welch. *Protestant Christianity Interpreted through Its Development*. New York: Scribner's, 1954.

Donohue, Betty. "Live Indians Talking: Native Voices Embedded in Mary Rowlandson's Captivity Narrative." Paper delivered at the American Literature Association Conference, Summer 2004, San Francisco.

Doyle, Robert C. *Voices from Captivity: Interpreting the American POW Narrative*. Lawrence: University Press of Kansas, 1994.

Durand, Paul. *Where the Waters Gather and the Rivers Meet: An Atlas of the Eastern Sioux*. Prior Lake MN: For the Author, 1994.

Ebell, Adrian J. "The Indian Massacres and War of 1862." *Harper's New Monthly Magazine*, June 1863, 1–24.

Ebersole, Gary L. *Captured by Texts: Puritan to Postmodern Images of Indian Captivity*. Charlottesville: University of Virginia Press, 1995.

Ellis, Edward S. *Indian Jim: A Tale of the Minnesota Massacre*. London: Beadle and Co., 1864.

————. *The Indian Wars of the United States from the First Settlement at Jamestown, in 1607, to the Close of the Great Uprising of 1890–91*. New York: Cassell, 1892.

————. *Red Feather: A Tale of the American Frontier*. New York: McLoughlin, 1908.

————. *Red Plume*. New York: Grosset and Dunlap, 1900.

Ellis, Richard N. *General Pope and U.S. Indian Policy*. Albuquerque: University of New Mexico Press, 1970.

Elmer, Cathleen Burns. Review of *Betrayed*, by Virginia Driving Hawk Sneve. *New York Times Book Review*, 19 January 1975.

Engel, Susan. *Context Is Everything: The Nature of Memory*. New York: Freeman, 1999.

"Escaped from the Sioux: A Girl Wife's Adventures in the Outbreak of '62." *St. Paul Pioneer Press*, 18 November 1894.

"Evidence for the Claimants." *Sisseton and Wahpeton Bands of Dakota or Sioux Indians v. the United States, 1901–07*. U.S. Army Court of Claims No. 22524.

"Evidence for the Defendants." *Sisseton and Wahpeton Bands of Dakota or Sioux Indians v. the United States, 1901–07*. U.S. Army Court of Claims No. 22524.

"Evidence Taken by the Indian Peace Commission . . . June 15, 1868." Big Eagle's Testimony. In *Papers Relating to Talks and Councils Held with the Indians in Dakota and Montana Territories in the Years 1866–1869*, 93–94. Washington DC: Government Printing Office, 1910.

Faery, Rebecca Blevins. *Cartographies of Desire: Captivity, Race, and Sex in the Shaping of an American Nation*. Norman: University of Oklahoma Press, 1999.

Feezor, Barbara Y. "Mdewakanton Dakota Women: Active Participants in Mdewakanton Cultural Transformations, 1860–1900." PhD diss., University of California, Los Angeles, 1994.

———. *See also* Barbara Feezor Buttes.

Felix, Clem. "The Ordeal of Hinhankaga." As told to F. J. Patten. Ca. 1962. Minnesota Historical Society Library.

Felman, Shoshana, and Dori Laub. *Testimony: Crises of Witnessing in Literature, Psychoanalysis, and History*. New York: Routledge, 1992.

The First Fifty Years: Dakota Presbytery to 1890. 1886, 1892. Rpt., Freeman SD: Pine Hill Press, 1984.

Flandrau, Charles E. *Minnesota in the Civil and Indian Wars*. N.p.: 1891.

Folwell, William Watts. "The First Battle of New Ulm." In *A History of Minnesota*, 2:362–74. St. Paul: Minnesota Historical Society, 1924.

"Fool Soldiers." In "Oyate Iyechinka Woglakipi: An Oral History Collection." Vol. 4, *American Indian Research Project*, 40–51. Vermillion: University of South Dakota, 1973.

Forbes, Jack D. *Black Africans and Native Americans: Color, Race and Caste in the Evolution of Red-Black Peoples*. Oxford: Blackwell, 1988.

Foster, William Henry. *The Captors' Narrative: Catholic Women and Their Puritan Men on the Early American Frontier*. Ithaca: Cornell University Press, 2003.

Fridley, Russell W. "Critical Choices for the Minnesota Historical Society." *Minnesota History* 46 (1978): 130–46.

Fritsche, Louis A., ed. "Seven Weeks' Captivity of Benedict Juni." In *History of Brown County Minnesota: Its People, Industries and Institutions*, 1:111–22. Indianapolis: B. F. Bowen, 1916.

Gardner, Susan. "Not For Publication, or: On Not (Yet, Anyway) Producing Bicultural Lumbee Auto-Ethnography." *Studies in American Indian Literatures* 8, no. 2 (1996): 29–46. Accessed online at http://oncampus.richmond.edu/faculty/ASAIL/SAIL2/82.html, 2 April 2006.

Gates, Charles M. "The Lac Qui Parle Indian Mission." *Minnesota History* 16 (1935): 133–51.

Gauper, Beth. "River with a Past." *St. Paul Pioneer Press*, 6 August 2006. Accessed online at http://www.twincities.com/mld/twincities/living/travel/15191864.htm, 14 August 2006.

George, Suzanne. "Nineteenth Century Native American Autobiography as Captivity Narrative." *Heritage of the Great Plains* 30 (Spring–Summer 1997): 33–48.

Giddens, Anthony. *Modernity and Self-Identity: Self and Society in the Late Modern Age.* Stanford: Stanford University Press, 1991.

Gilman, Rhoda R. "The History and Peopling of Minnesota: Its Culture." *Daedalus* 129, no. 3 (2000): 1–29.

Godfrey, Joseph. Testimony. U. S. Army, Military Commission, Sioux War Trials: 1862. Original Transcripts of the Records of Trials of Certain Sioux Indians Charged with Barbarities in the State of Minnesota. Senate Records 37A–F2. Original documents at National Archives, Washington DC.

"Godfrey Not Hanged." *St. Paul (Minnesota) Dispatch*, 26 March 1886.

Green, Rayna. "The Pocahontas Perplex: The Image of Indian Women in American Culture." *Massachusetts Review* 16 (1976): 698–714.

Greenberg, Kenneth S., ed. *The Confessions of Nat Turner and Related Documents.* Boston: Bedford, 1996.

Gregor, Theresa. "Louise Erdrich's and Sherman Alexie's Captivity: Revising Rowlandson, Reaffirming the Indian in the Captivity Narrative Tradition." Paper delivered at the American Literature Association Conference, Summer 2004, San Francisco.

"Gusa Godfrey Is Dead." *Morton (Minnesota) Enterprise*, 23 July 1909.

Guzik, David. Bible commentary. Accessed online at http://www.enduringword.com/commentaries, 22 June 2005.

Haefeli, Evan, and Kevin Sweeney, eds. *Captive Histories: English, French, and Native Narratives of the 1704 Deerfield Raid.* Amherst: University of Massachusetts Press, 2006.

———. *Captors and Captives: The 1704 French and Indian Raid on Deerfield.* Amherst: University of Massachusetts Press, 2003.

Haga, Chuck. "Another Burial for Dakota Leader." *Minneapolis Star Tribune*, 16 July 2000.

Harran, Susan, and Jim Harran. "Remembering a Loved One with Mourning Jewelry." *Antique Week*, December 1997. Accessed online at http://www.hairworksociety.org, 18 June 2004.

Hartman, James D. *Providence Tales and the Birth of American Literature.* Baltimore: Johns Hopkins University Press, 1999.

Hassrick, Royal B. *The Sioux: Life and Customs of a Warrior Society.* Norman: University of Oklahoma Press, 1964.

Heard, Isaac V. D. *History of the Sioux War and Massacres of 1862 and 1863.* 1863. 2nd ed., New York: Harper, 1864. Rpt., Millwood NY: Kraus, 1975.

Heilbron, Bertha L., ed. *With Pen and Pencil on the Frontier in 1851: The Diary and Sketches of Frank Blackwell Mayer.* St. Paul: Minnesota Historical Society Press, 1986.

Henig, Gerald S. "A Neglected Cause of the Sioux Uprising." *Minnesota History* 45 (1976): 107–10.

Hillar, Marian. "Liberation Theology: Religious Response to Social Problems. A Survey." In *Humanism and Social Issues: An Anthology of Essays*, edited by Marian Hillar and H. R. Leuchtag. Houston: American Humanist Association, 1993. Accessed online at http://www.socinian.org/liberty.html, 12 August 2005.

Holcombe, Return I. "The Faithful Indians' Monument." In *Sketches Historical and Descriptive of the Monuments and Tablets Erected by the Minnesota Valley Historical Society*, 46–63. Morton MN: Minnesota Valley Historical Society, 1902.

———. ["Notes on Snana."] Minnesota Historical Society Library. Minnesota Historical Society.

Hopkins, Frank. Letter to Mrs. Sidney A. Peterson, 18 November 1951. Fort Ridgely State Park and Historical Association Papers. Minnesota Historical Society.

———. "Turkey's Egg Starts Ft. Ridgely Massacre." *Fairfax (Minnesota) Journal*, 9 September 1927. In Fort Ridgeley State Park and Association Papers. Minnesota Historical Society.

Horsman, Reginald. *Race and Manifest Destiny: The Origins of American Racial Anglo-Saxonism.* Cambridge: Harvard University Press, 1981.

Howard, Jennifer. "The Fragmentation of Literary Theory." *Chronicle of Higher Education*, 16 December 2005, A12–A16.

Hubbard, Lucius F., and Return I. Holcombe. *Minnesota in Three Centuries.* Vol. 3, *Minnesota in Three Centuries, 1655–1908.* Mankato: Publishing Society of Minnesota, 1908.

Huggan, Nancy McClure Faribault. Eight letters to Return I. Holcombe, 13 April–14 June 1894. Return I. Holcombe Papers. Minnesota Historical Society.

———. Letter to William R. Marshall. May 1894. Dakota Conflict of 1862 Manuscripts Collections. Minnesota Historical Society.

———. "Statement of Nancy Huggins, Wa-Pa-Let (Hat)." Interview with Frank Hopkins. 29 October 1926. Manuscript Notebooks. Fort Ridgely State Park and Historical Association Papers. Minnesota Historical Society. Published in the *Fairfax (Minnesota) Journal*, 9 September 1927, under the title "Turkey's Egg Starts Ft. Ridgely Massacre."

———. "The Story of Nancy McClure: Captivity among the Sioux." *Collections of the Minnesota Historical Society* 6 (1894): 438–60.

Hughes, Thomas. Letter to Brigadier General W. C. Brown. N.d. Thomas Hughes, 1854–1934, and Family Papers, 1855–1946. SMHC Manuscript Collection 101, Southern Minnesota Historical Center, Memorial Library. Minnesota State University, Mankato.

———. Letter to Mr. H. M. Hitchcock. 8 August 1928. Thomas Hughes, 1854–1934, and Family Papers, 1855–1946. SMHC Manuscript Collection 101, Southern Minnesota Historical Center, Memorial Library. Minnesota State University, Mankato.

———. *Old Traverse des Sioux.* St. Peter MN: Herald, 1929.

"In the Hands of the Sioux: A California Woman's Captivity among Savages." Typescript of article possibly appearing in *San Francisco Call*, April 1892. Brown County (Minnesota) Historical Society. New Ulm MN.

"Isaac Heard Dies at New York Home." *St. Paul (Minnesota) Dispatch*, 20 June 1913.

Iverson, Noel. *Germania, U.S.A.: Social Change in New Ulm, Minnesota*. Minneapolis: University of Minnesota Press, 1966.

Jacobson, Matthew Frye. *Whiteness of a Different Color: European Immigrants and the Alchemy of Race*. Cambridge: Harvard University Press, 1998.

Johanssen, Albert. *The House of Beadle and Adams and Its Dime and Nickel Novels: The Story of a Vanished Literature*. 3 vols. Norman: University of Oklahoma Press, 1950.

Johnson, Kristen. "New Light on the Donner Party." Accessed online at http://www.utahcrossroads.org/DonnerParty/Chronology.htm, 7 June 2004.

Juni, Benedict. *Held in Captivity*. New Ulm MN: Liesch-Walter Printing Company, 1926. Rpt., New Ulm MN: Kemske, 1961.

———. Letter to William M. Folwell. 13 January 1908. Folwell Papers. Minnesota Historical Society.

Keeney, Lillian Everett. Letter to Dr. Harper M. Workman. 2 August 1894. In "Information on Victims of the Lake Shetek Massacre Obtained by Correspondence and Personal Testimony," comp. Neil Currie. Dakota Conflict of 1862 Manuscripts Collections. Minnesota Historical Society.

———. *See also* Lillian E. Curtiss.

Kelsey, Penelope. "Native American Autoethnography, Sovereignty, and Self: Tribal Knowledges in New Genres." PhD diss., University of Minnesota, 2002.

———. "A 'Real Indian' to the Boy Scouts: Charles Eastman as a Resistance Writer." *Western American Literature* 38 (2003): 30–48.

Kidwell, Clara Sue. "Indian Women as Cultural Mediators." *Ethnohistory* 39, no. 2 (1992): 97–107.

Kolchin, Peter. "Whiteness Studies: The New History of Race in America." *Journal of American History* 89, no. 1 (2002). Accessed online at http://www.historycooperative.org/journals/jah/89.1/kolchin.html, 10 July 2003.

Kolodny, Annette. *The Land before Her: Fantasy and Experience of the American Frontiers, 1630–1860*. Chapel Hill: University of North Carolina Press, 1984.

———. *The Lay of the Land: Metaphor as Experience and History in American Life and Letters*. Chapel Hill: University of North Carolina Press, 1975.

———. "Letting Go Our Grand Obsessions: Notes toward a New Literary History of the American Frontiers." *American Literature* 64 (1992): 1–18.

Lass, William E. "The Removal from Minnesota of the Sioux and Winnebago Indians." *Minnesota History* 38 (1963): 353–64.

Lawrence, Elden. *The Peace Seekers: Indian Christians and the Dakota Conflict*. Sioux Falls SD: Pine Hill Press, 2005.

Lawrence, Elizabeth (Wakeman). "Interview." By Mary P. Lindeke of the Minnesota Historical Society. Minnesota Historical Society.

Lawrence, Mr. and Mrs. Harry. "The Indian Nations of Minnesota: The Sioux Uprising." In *Minnesota Heritage: A Panoramic Narrative of the Historical Development of the North Star State*, 80–82. Minneapolis: Denison, 1960.

Lawrence, Lorenzo. "The Statement of Lorenzo Lawrence." In *Lights and Shadows of a Long Episcopate*, by Henry B. Whipple, 114–18. New York: Macmillan, 1912.

————. "Story of Lorenzo Lawrence." 1895. Lorenzo Lawrence Papers. Minnesota Historical Society Library.

"Learning from the Dakota." Shakopee Mdewakanton Dakota Community Education and Outreach Department. A unit guide for social studies classes. Based on *Painting the Dakota: Seth Eastman at Fort Snelling*, edited by Marybeth Lorbiecki. Afton MN: Afton Historical Society Press, 2000. Accessed online at http://www.ccsmdc.org/crp/edu.html, 8 July 2006.

LeBeau, Sebastian (Bronco). "'Tribal History' of the Good River Reservation." Accessed online at http://www.sioux.org/more_history.html, 22 July 2006.

Lepore, Jill. *The Name of War: King Philip's War and the Origins of American Identity*. New York: Knopf, 1998.

Lewis, Bonnie Sue. *Creating Christian Indians: Native Clergy in the Presbyterian Church*. Norman: University of Oklahoma Press, 2003.

"Lightning Blanket's Account." 1908. Rpt. in Anderson and Woolworth, *Through Dakota Eyes*, 153–57.

Limerick, Patricia Nelson. "Haunted America." In *Sweet Medicine: Sites of Indian Massacres, Battlefields, and Treaties. Photographs by Drex Brooks*, 119–63. Albuquerque: University of New Mexico Press, 1995.

————. "Making the Most of Words: Verbal Activity and Western America." In *Under an Open Sky: Rethinking America's Western Past*, edited by William Cronon, George Miles, and Jay Gitlin, 167–84. New York: Norton, 1992.

"Literary Notices." Review of *The Sioux War*, by Isaac Heard. *Harper's New Monthly Magazine*, June–November 1863, 851.

Logan, Lisa M. "'Cross-Cultural Conversations': The Captivity Narrative." In *A Companion to the Literatures of Colonial America*, edited by Susan Castillo and Ivy Schweitzer, 4764–79. Oxford: Blackwell, 2005.

Lyons, Scott. "A Captivity Narrative: Indians, Mixedbloods, and 'White' Academe." In *Outbursts in Academe: Multiculturalism and Other Sources of Conflict*, edited by Kathleen Dixon and William Archibald, 87–108. Portsmouth NH: Boynton/Cook, 1998.

Maddox, Lucy. *Removals: Nineteenth-Century American Literature and the Politics of Indian Affairs*. New York: Oxford University Press, 1991.

Maltz, Daniel, and JoAllyn Archambault. "Gender and Power in Native North America: Concluding Remarks." In *Women and Power in Native North America*, edited by Laura F. Klein and Lillian A. Ackerman, 230–49. Norman: University of Oklahoma Press, 1995.

Manfred, Frederick. *Scarlet Plume*. New York: Trident, 1964.

"The Mankato Hanging." *St. Paul (Minnesota) Dispatch*, 27 March 1886.

Marable, Manning, ed. *Dispatches from the Ebony Tower: Intellectuals Confront the African-American Experience*. New York: Columbia University Press, 2000.

————. "We Need New and Critical Study of Race and Ethnicity." *Chronicle of Higher Education*, 25 February 2000, B4–B7.

Marken, Jack W., and Charles L. Woodard, eds. *Shaping Survival: Essays by Four American Indian Tribal Women*. Lanham MD: Scarecrow Press, 2001.

Marken, Jack W., and Herbert T. Hoover. *Bibliography of the Sioux*. Metuchen NJ: Scarecrow Press, 1980.

Martin, Calvin, ed. *The American Indian and the Problem of History*. New York: Oxford University Press, 1987.

Mazakutemani, Paul. "Narrative of Paul Mazakootemane." Trans. Stephen R. Riggs. *Collections of the Minnesota Historical Society* 3 (1870–80): 82–90.

McConkey, Harriet E. Bishop. *Dakota War Whoop; or, Indian Massacres and War in Minnesota*. St. Paul: D. D. Merrill, 1863. Rev. ed., St. Paul: For the Author, 1864. Rpt., Chicago: Lakeside, 1965.

———. Two letters to Gen. Henry H. Sibley. 19 and 20 October 1864. H. H. Sibley Papers. Minnesota Historical Society.

———. *See also* Harriet E. Bishop.

McIntire, F. E. Letter to Theodore G. Carter. 14 February 1910. Theodore G. Carter Papers. Minnesota Historical Society.

Meagher, John F. Letter to J. Fletcher Williams. 26 December 1887. George Gleason Folder. Minnesota Historical Society.

Memmi, Albert. *Racism*. Minneapolis: University of Minnesota Press, 2000.

Meyer, Roy W. *History of the Santee Sioux: United States Indian Policy on Trial*. Lincoln: University of Nebraska Press, 1967.

Mihesuah, Devon A. *American Indians: Stereotypes and Realities*. Atlanta: Clarity Press, 1996.

———. "Commonality of Difference: American Indian Women and History." In *Natives and Academics: Researching and Writing about American Indians*, edited by Devon A. Mihesuah, 37–54. Lincoln: University of Nebraska Press, 1998.

Minnesota Mdewakanton Dakota Oyate Litigation Wolfchild, et al. v. United States. Accessed online at http://www.mklaw.com/mdewakanton.htm, 6 September 2006.

Missionary Paper. Number 23. Bishop Seabury Mission. Faribault MN: Alex Johnston, 1862.

Morris, Martha Riggs. "Sisseton Mission." In *The Dakota Mission: Past and Present*, 9–15. Minneapolis: Tribune Job Printing Company, 1886.

———. "Sweet Grass' Story." *Iape Oaye* 6, no. 11 (1876): 44 ff.

———. *See also* Martha T. Riggs.

Morrison, Toni. "Home." In *The House That Race Built: Black Americans, U. S. Terrain*, edited by Wahneema Lubiano, 3–12. New York: Pantheon, 1997.

———. "Introduction: Friday on the Potomac." In *Race-ing Justice, En-gendering Power: Essays on Anita Hill, Clarence Thomas, and the Construction of Social Reality*, edited by Toni Morrison, vii–xxx. New York: Pantheon, 1992.

Mortimer, Barbara. *Hollywood's Frontier Captives: Cultural Anxiety and the Captivity Plot in American Film*. New York: Garland: 1999.

Moss, Henry L. "Miss Harriet E. Bishop." Part of "Biographic Notes of Old Settlers." *Collections of the Minnesota Historical Society* 9 (1898–1900): 157–59.

Mott, Frank Luther. *Golden Multitudes: The Story of Best Sellers in the United States*. New York: Macmillan, 1947.

Murphy, Nora. "Starting Children on the Path to the Past: American Indians in Children's Historical Fiction." *Minnesota History* 57 (2001): 284–95.

Namias, June, ed. *A Narrative of the Life of Mrs. Mary Jemison*. By James E. Seaver. Norman: University of Oklahoma Press, 1992.

———, ed. *Six Weeks in the Sioux Tepees: A Narrative of Indian Captivity*. By Sarah Wakefield. Norman: University of Oklahoma Press, 1997.

———. *White Captives: Gender and Ethnicity on the American Frontier*. Chapel Hill: University of North Carolina Press, 1993.

"Native Writers: Interview Focus on Michael Dorris and Virginia Driving Hawk Sneve: BookPage [sic], 1992." Accessed online at http://www.wildewritingworks.com/int/native.html, 24 March 2003.

Neill, Edward D. *History of the Minnesota Valley, Including the Explorers and Pioneers of Minnesota*. Minneapolis: North Star, 1882.

Newson, T. M. *Pen Pictures of St. Paul, Minnesota, and Biographical Sketches of Old Settlers*. St. Paul: By the Author, 1886.

Nichols, David. "The Other Civil War: Lincoln and the Indians." *Minnesota History* 44 (1974–75): 3–15.

Nicolay, John. Letter to Henry H. Sibley. 9 December 1862. RG 94, Entry 173, Indian Prisoners. National Archives. Washington DC.

Nix, Jacob. *Der Ausbruch der Sioux-Indianer in Minnesota, im August 1862*. Milwaukee: Zahn, 1887.

———. *The Sioux Uprising in Minnesota, 1862: Jacob Nix's Eyewitness History*. Translated and edited by Don Heinrich Tolzmann. Indianapolis: Max Kade German-American Center, 1994.

Norwood, Lisa West. "Fragments, Ruins and Artifacts of the Past: The Reconstruction of Reading in *The Deerslayer*." Paper delivered at the American Literature Association Conference, Summer 2004, San Francisco. *James Fenimore Cooper Society Miscellaneous Papers* 18 (August 2003): 3–7.

Notes from the Trials of Dakota Indians Following the Outbreak of 1862. Minneapolis: Satterlee Printing Company, 1927.

Nunpa, Chris Mato. "Letter to the Editor." *New Ulm (Minnesota) Journal*, 8 January 2003.

O'Brien, Lynne Woods. *Plains Indian Autobiographies*. Caldwell ID: Caxton, 1973.

Oehler, C. M. *The Great Sioux Uprising*. 1959. Rpt., New York: Da Capo Press, 1997.

Oneroad, Amos, and Alanson B. Skinner. *Being Dakota: Tales and Traditions of the Sisseton and Wahpeton*. Edited by Laura L. Anderson. St. Paul: Minnesota Historical Society Press, 2003.

"Our Languages: Ihanktonwan Dakota." Sponsored by the Saskatchewan Indian Cultural Centre. Accessed online at http://www.sicc.sk.ca/heritage/sils/ourlanguages/ihanktonwan/history/early_study.html, 8 June 2006.

Paine, Clarence, comp. "Biographical Data on Joseph Godfrey." 4 October 1907. Dakota Conflict of 1862 Manuscripts Collections. Minnesota Historical Society.

Papers Relating to Talks and Councils Held with the Indians in Dakota and Montana Territories in the Years 1866–1869. Washington DC: Government Printing Office, 1910.

Patten, F. J. *1862: The Great Sioux Uprising*. Marshall MN: For the Author, 1962.

Peacock, Thomas D., and Donald R. Day. "Nations within a Nation: The Dakota and Ojibwe of Minnesota." *Daedalus* 129, no. 3 (2000): 137–59.

Pearce, Roy Harvey. "The Significances of the Captivity Narrative." *American Literature* 19 (1947): 1–20.

Philecclesian Society Papers, 1857–58. Minnesota Historical Society.

Pierpont, Claudia Roth. "The Measure of America: How a Rebel Anthropologist Waged War on Racism." *New Yorker*, 8 March 2004, 48–58, 60–63.

Pierson, A. T. C. Letter to C. G. Wycoff. 21 September 1861. Clark W. Thompson Papers. Minnesota Historical Society.

"Pioneer Recalls the Massacre at Shetek." Typescript of article from *Murray County (Minnesota) Herald* about Mrs. Albert Hotaling, daughter of Thomas Ireland, 15 October 1931. Virginia Driving Hawk Sneve Papers/Creative Writings. *Betrayed*: Research. South Dakota State University Archives and Special Collections.

The Poets and Poetry of Minnesota. Edited by Mrs. W. J. Arnold. Chicago: S. P. Rounds, 1864.

Pond, Gideon H. "True History of the Indian Outbreak in Minnesota." *Evangelist*, 5 March 1863, n.p.

Pond, Samuel W. *The Dakota or Sioux in Minnesota as They Were in 1834*. 1908. Rpt., St. Paul: Minnesota Historical Society Press, 1986.

———. *Two Volunteer Missionaries among the Dakotas: or, The Story of the Labors of Samuel W. and Gideon H. Pond*. N.p.: Congregational Sunday-School and Publishing Society, 1893.

Pratt, Mary Louise. *Imperial Eyes: Travel Writing and Transculturation*. London: Routledge, 1992.

Publishers Weekly. Review of *Captives: Britain, Empire, and the World, 1600–1850*, by Linda Colley. Accessed online at http://www.amazon.com, 29 June 2004, under Colley's book.

Pulitano, Elvira. *Toward a Native American Critical Theory*. Lincoln: University of Nebraska Press, 2003.

Ramsey, Colin T., and Kathryn Zabelle Derounian-Stodola. "Dime Novels." In *A Companion to American Fiction, 1780–1865*, edited by Shirley Samuels, 262–73. London: Blackwell, 2004.

"Redefining Humanity through Diversity." Diversity Foundation, Inc. Accessed online at http://www.diversityfoundation.org, 24 June 2005.

Red Owl, Ed. "Brief Historical Overview of the Sisseton-Wahpeton Oyate of the Lake Traverse Reservation South/North Dakota." Accessed online at http://www.earth skyweb.com/culture.htm, 23 June 2005.

Renville, Florestine Kiyukanpi. "Dakota Identity Renewed." In *Shaping Survival: Essays by Four American Indian Tribal Women*, edited by Jack W. Marken and Charles L. Woodard, 91–158. Lanham MD: Scarecrow Press, 2001.

———. "Editor's Note." *Ikce Wicasta Magazine* 5 (Fall 2002): 4.

Renville, Gabriel. "A Sioux Narrative of the Outbreak of 1862, and of Sibley's Expedition of 1863." *Collections of the Minnesota Historical Society* 10 (1905): 595–613. Rpt. in Anderson and Woolworth, *Through Dakota Eyes*, 100–105, 186–92, 230–34, 273–75.

Renville, Mary Butler, and John B. Renville. *A Thrilling Narrative of Indian Captivity*. Minneapolis: Atlas, 1863.

"The Resurrection." *Mankato Weekly Record*, 3 January 1863.

"Review of *History of the Sioux War and Massacres of 1862 and 1863* by Isaac V. D. Heard." *North American Review* 98 (1864): 266–70.

["Rev. John B. Renville."] Untitled obituary. *Redwood (Minnesota) Gazette*, 4 January 1904.

Richards, Bergmann, ed. "Biographic Notes of 'Wasicu': Lorenzo Lawrence, a Full Wahpeton." *Hennepin County (Minnesota) History* (Winter 1960): 7–9.

Riggs, Maida L., ed. *A Small Bit of Bread and Butter: Letters from the Dakota Territory 1832–1869*. South Deerfield MA: Ash Grove Press, 1996.

Riggs, Martha T. "The Flight of the Missionaries." *Cincinnati Christian Herald*, ca. 1 October 1862. Rpt. in Stephen R. Riggs, *Mary and I: Forty Years with the Sioux*, 171–78. Chicago: Holmes, 1880. Rpt., Williamstown MA: Corner House, 1971.

———. *See also* Martha Riggs Morris.

Riggs, Stephen R. "History of the Sioux War by Isaac V. D Heard" (review). *St. Paul Press*, 17 December 1863.

———. Letter to Mary Riggs, 23 September 1862. Stephen Return Riggs and Family Papers. Minnesota Historical Society.

———. Letter to Martha Riggs, 27 September 1862. Riggs Family Papers, 1834–1938. South Dakota State Archives.

———. *Mary and I: Forty Years with the Sioux*. Chicago: Holmes, 1880. Rpt., Williamstown MA: Corner House, 1971.

———. "A Tableau of the Families, and Single Persons, Connected with the A.B.C.F.M. in the Dakota Mission, During the Quarter of a Century from 1835 to 1860. With the Boarding Scholars." Prepared and copied by Martha S. Riggs. Hazelwood MN, September 1861.

———. *Tah-Koo Wah-Kan; or, The Gospel among the Dakotas*. Boston: Congregational Sabbath School and Publishing Society, 1869.

———. "Toteedootawin; or, Her Scarlet House." *Minnesota Free Press*, 16 June 1858. Rpt. in "Dakota Portraits." *Minnesota History Bulletin* 2 (November 1918): 542–47.

Robertson, Thomas A. "Reminiscences." Sioux Uprising Collection. Minnesota Historical Society.

Robinson, Doane. *Encyclopedia of South Dakota*. Sioux Falls SD: Beach, 1925.

Roediger, David R. "Whiteness and Its Complications." *Chronicle of Higher Education*, 14 July 2006, B6–B8.

Root, Maria P. P., ed. *Racially Mixed People in America*. London: Sage, 1992.

Rowlandson, Mary. "A True History of the Captivity and Restoration of Mrs. Mary Rowlandson." In Derounian-Stodola, *Women's Indian Captivity Narratives*, 3–51.

Ruh, Adam. "Captivity and the Captivity Narrative: Opening the Gap." Paper presented at the Native American Literature Symposium, 2004, Mystic Lake MN.

Ruoff, LaVonne Brown, ed. *American Indian Literatures: An Introduction, Bibliographic Review, and Selected Bibliography*. New York: MLA, 1990.

Russo, Priscilla Ann. "The Time to Speak Is Over: The Onset of the Sioux Uprising." *Minnesota History* 45 (1976): 97–106.

Sarris, Greg. *Keeping Slug Woman Alive: A Holistic Approach to American Indian Texts*. Berkeley: University of California Press, 1993.

Satterlee, Marion P. *A Detailed Account of the Massacre by the Dakota Indians of Minnesota in 1862*. Minneapolis: n.p., 1823.

———. *Outbreak and Massacre by the Dakota Indians in Minnesota in 1862*. Minneapolis: Marion P. Satterlee, 1923.

Saunt, Claudio. *Black, White, and Indian: Race and the Unmaking of an American Family*. New York: Oxford University Press, 2005.

"Saved White Girl in Massacre. Death of Mrs. Maggie Brass Recalls Touching Incident of the Sioux Uprising." *St. Paul Pioneer Press*, 17 May 1980.

Sayre, Gordon M., ed. *American Captivity Narratives*. Boston: Houghton Mifflin, 2000.

Schlissel, Lillian. *Women's Diaries of the Westward Journey*. New York: Schocken, 1982.

Schmidt, Mary Schwandt. Letter to Marion P. Satterlee. 19 December 1915. Marion P. Satterlee Papers, 1879–1937. Minnesota Historical Society.

———. "List of Talks Given by Mary Schwandt Schmidt 1910–1920." Holograph manuscript. Mary Schwandt Schmidt Papers. Minnesota Historical Society.

———. "Narrative of Mary Schwandt." In *A History of the Great Massacre by the Sioux Indians in Minnesota*, by Charles Bryant and Abel Murch, 335–42. Cincinnati: Rickey and Carroll, 1864.

———. "Recollections of My Captivity among the Sioux the Year of 1862." Ca. 1929 (n.d.). Mary Schwandt Schmidt Papers. Minnesota Historical Society.

———. "Recollections of the Indian Massacre of 1862 in Minnesota." Address before the Colonial Dames of America in Minnesota. St. Paul, 25 October 1915. Mary Schwandt Schmidt Papers. Minnesota Historical Society.

———. Testimony. U.S. Army, Military Commission, Sioux War Trials: 1862. Original documents at National Archives, Washington DC, Senate Records 37A–F2. Original Transcripts of the Records of Trials of Certain Sioux Indians Charged with Barbarities in the State of Minnesota.

———. *See also* Mary Schwandt-Schmidt.

Schultz, Nancy, ed. *A Veil of Fear: Nineteenth-Century Convent Tales*. West Lafayette IN: Purdue University Press, 1999.

Schwandt-Schmidt, Mary. "The Story of Mary Schwandt." *Collections of the Minnesota Historical Society* 6 (1894): 461–74. Reprinted in Don Heinrich Tolzmann, ed., *German Pioneer Accounts of the Great Sioux Uprising of 1862*, 8–25. Milford OH: Little Miami Publishing Company, 2002.

———. *See also* Mary Schwandt Schmidt.

"Scout Sam J. Brown Hero of Indian Wars Dies at Browns Valley." Unidentified, newspaper clipping. N.d. Thomas Hughes Papers. Minnesota State University, Mankato.

Seaver, James E. *A Narrative of the Life of Mrs. Mary Jemison*. Edited by June Namias. Norman: University of Oklahoma Press, 1992.

Shackley, Steven M. "The Stone Tool Technology of Ishi and the Yana of North Central California: Inferences for Hunter-Gatherer Cultural Identity in Historic California." *American Anthropologist* 102 (2001): 693–712.

Silko, Leslie Marmon. *Ceremony*. New York: Penguin, 1977.

Slotkin, Richard. *Regeneration through Violence: The Mythology of the American Frontier, 1600–1860*. Middletown CT: Wesleyan University Press, 1973.

Smits, David D. "'Squaw Men,' 'Half-Breeds,' and Amalgamators: Late Nineteenth-Century Anglo-American Attitudes toward Indian-White Race-Mixing." *American Indian Culture and Research Journal* 15, no. 3 (1999): 29–61.

Snader, Joe. *Caught between Worlds: British Captivity Narratives in Fact and Fiction*. Lexington: University Press of Kentucky, 2000.

Snana. *See* Maggie Brass.

Sneve, Virginia Driving Hawk. *Betrayed*. New York: Holiday House, 1974.

———. *Completing the Circle*. Lincoln: University of Nebraska Press, 1995.

———. *The Dakota's Heritage: A Compilation of Indian Place Names in South Dakota*. Sioux Falls SD: Brevet, 1973.

———. Letter to Eunice Holsaert, fiction editor at Holiday House. 4 February 1974. Virginia Driving Hawk Sneve Papers. South Dakota State University Archives and Special Collections. South Dakota State University.

———. "Preface." In *Daughters of Dakota: Stories of Friendship between Settlers and the Dakota Indians*, edited by Sally Roesch Wagner, 3: vii–viii. Yankton SD: Pine Hill Press, 1990.

Sommerdorf, Norma. "No Grass beneath Her Feet: Harriet Bishop and Her Life in Minnesota." *Ramsey County (Minnesota) History* 32 (1997): 16–21.

Song Catcher: Frances Densmore. Minnesota Public Radio. 22 November 1994. Accessed online at http://news.minnesota.publicradio.org/features/199702/01_smiths_densmore/, 20 August 2006.

Spahr, Juliana. *Connective Reading and Collective Identity*. Tuscaloosa: University of Alabama Press, 2001.

Stay, Cecelia (Celia) Campbell. "Camp Relief [Release] in 1862." Typescript. N.d. In Celia M. Campbell Stay, "Reminiscence and Biographical Data." Dakota Conflict of 1862 Manuscripts Collections. Minnesota Historical Society.

———. Interview with Alexander Seifert et al. 5 August 1924. In "Notes of Committee Selecting Historical Data from New Ulm, Minn," comp. Alexander Seifert. Typescript. Dakota Conflict of 1862 Manuscripts Collections. Minnesota Historical Society.

———. Letter to Grace L. Nute. 6 July 1925. In Celia M. Campbell Stay, "Reminiscence and Biographical Data." Dakota Conflict of 1862 Manuscripts Collections. Minnesota Historical Society.

———. "The Massacre at the Lower Sioux Agency, August 18, 1862." Typescript. 1882. Provincial Archives of Manitoba. Winnipeg MB. In Anderson and Woolworth, *Through Dakota Eyes*, 44–52.

Steil, Mark. *Dakota Walk into History*. Minnesota Public Radio, 7 November 2002. Accessed online at http://news.minnesota.publicradio.org/features/200211/08_steilm_march-m/, 28 July 2006.

———. *Historic Sites Reopen*. Minnesota Public Radio, 26 April 2006. Accessed online at http://minnesota.publicradio.org/display/web/2006/04/24/historicsites, 28 July 2006.

Steil, Mark, and Tim Post. *Minnesota's Uncivil War*. Minnesota Public Radio. 26 September 2002. Accessed online at http://news.minnesota.publicradio.org/features/200209/23_steilm_1862-m/, 15 August 2006.

Stinson, Duane. "Land, Lineage and Lawsuits." *Circle* 27, no. 2 (2006). Accessed online at http://www.thecirclenews.org/feb06cover.html, 10 June 2008.

Stoll, David, and Arturo Arias, eds. *Rigoberta Menchu Controversy*. Minneapolis: University of Minnesota Press, 2001.

Stowe, Harriet Beecher. *Uncle Tom's Cabin*. 2 vols. Boston: Jewett, 1852.

Strong, Pauline Turner. *Captive Selves, Captivating Others: The Politics and Poetics of Colonial American Captivity Narratives*. Boulder: Westview Press, 1999.

Sturm, Circe. *Blood Politics: Race, Culture, and Identity in the Cherokee Nation of Oklahoma*. Berkeley: University of California Press, 2002.

Sweet, Jannette DeCamp. Letter to William H. Grant. 10 July 1894. Return I. Holcombe Papers. Minnesota Historical Society.

———. Letter to William R. Marshall. 28 July 1894. Return I. Holcombe Papers. Minnesota Historical Society.

———. "Mrs. J. E. De Camp Sweet's Narrative of Her Captivity in the Sioux Outbreak of 1862." *Collections of the Minnesota Historical Society* 6 (1894): 354–80.

———. Untitled manuscript. 81 pages. Minnesota Historical Society Institutional Libraries and Archives Division. Publications and Research Monograph Files, Box 151.

Szasz, Margaret Connell, ed. *Between Indian and White Worlds: The Cultural Broker*. Norman: University of Oklahoma Press, 1994.

Tanner, Helen Horsbeck. *Atlas of Great Lakes Indian History*. Norman: University of Oklahoma Press, 1987.

Tarble, Helen M. *The Story of My Capture and Escape during the Minnesota Indian Massacre of 1862*. St. Paul: Abbott, 1904.

Tinker, George E. *Missionary Conquest: The Gospel and Native American Cultural Genocide*. Minneapolis: Fortress Press, 1993.

Tinnemeyer, Andrea. *Identity Politics of the Captivity Narrative after 1848*. Lincoln: University of Nebraska Press, 2006.

Todorov, Tzvetan. *The Conquest of America: The Question of the Other*. New York: Harper and Row, 1984.

Tolzmann, Don Heinrich, ed. *German Pioneer Accounts of the Great Sioux Uprising of 1862*. Milford OH: Little Miami, 2002.

———, ed. *The Sioux Uprising in Minnesota, 1862: Jacob Nix's Eyewitness History*. Indianapolis: Max Kade German-American Center, 1994.

Tougas, Joe. "Mending the Wounds." *Mankato (Minnesota) Free Press*, 27 July 2002. Reproduced on the Mahkato Mdewakantoan Association Web site, at http://www.mahkatowacipi.org/Press/July272002.htm, 24 June 2005.

Toulouse, Teresa A. *The Captive's Position: Female Narrative, Male Identity, and Royal Authority in Colonial New England*. Philadelphia: University of Pennsylvania Press, 2007.

"Transformation of an Island: A Historical Perspective on the Prairie Island Indian Community." Welch MN: Prairie Island Indian Community, n.d.

Twain, Mark. *The Adventures of Huckleberry Finn.* 1884. Vol. 13, *The Writings of Mark Twain.* New York: Harper, 1912.

———. *Huck Finn and Tom Sawyer among the Indians and Other Unfinished Stories.* Berkeley: University of California Press, 1989.

Twain, Mark, and Lee Nelson. *Huck Finn and Tom Sawyer among the Indians.* Springville UT: Council Press, 2003.

Upham, Warren. "For the Dedication of the Schwandt Monument, August 18, 1915." Mary Schwandt Schmidt Papers. Minnesota Historical Society.

———. "Return I. Holcombe." *Minnesota History Bulletin* 2 (February 1917): 7–11.

U.S. Army, Military Commission. Sioux War Trials: 1862, 1–150. Minnesota Historical Society.

VanDerBeets, Richard, ed. *Held Captive by Indians: Selected Narratives, 1642–1836.* 1973. Rev. ed., Knoxville: University of Tennessee Press, 1994.

Vizenor, Gerald. *Crossbloods: Bone Courts, Bingo, and Other Reports.* Minneapolis: University of Minnesota Press, 1990.

———. *Fugitive Poses: Native American Indian Scenes of Absence and Presence.* Lincoln: University of Nebraska Press, 1998.

Wakefield, Sarah F. Letter to Abraham Lincoln. 23 March 1863. Transcribed and annotated by the Lincoln Studies Center, Knox College, Galesburg IL. Abraham Lincoln Papers at the Library of Congress. Manuscript Division. Washington DC: American Memory Project, [2000–2002]. Accessed online at http://memory.loc .gov/ammem/alhtml/alhome.html, 10 January 2006.

———. *Six Weeks in the Sioux Tepees: A Narrative of Indian Captivity.* Minneapolis: Atlas, 1863. 2nd ed., Shakopee MN: Argus, 1864. In Derounian-Stodola, *Women's Indian Captivity Narratives,* 241–313.

———. Three Letters to Stephen R. Riggs. Stephen R. Riggs and Family Papers. Minnesota Historical Society. Rpt. in Kathryn Zabelle Derounian-Stodola, "'Many persons say I am a "Mono Maniac"': Three Letters from Dakota Conflict Captive Sarah F. Wakefield to Missionary Stephen R. Riggs." *Prospects: An Annual of American Cultural Studies* 29 (2004): 1–24.

Wakeman, John. "Big Thunder's Story." *St. Paul and Minneapolis Pioneer Press,* 28 January 1886.

Walzer, Michael. *Obligations: Essays on Disobedience, War, and Citizenship.* Cambridge: Harvard University Press, 1970.

"Wapasha Prairie/Dakota Homecoming and Gathering." Diversity Foundation, Inc. Accessed online at http://www.diversityfoundation.org, 24 June 2005.

Warner, Anna Riggs. *Our Martha.* Santee NE: Santee Normal Training School Press, [ca. 1910].

Watts, Edward. *An American Colony: Regionalism and the Roots of Midwestern Culture.* Athens: Ohio University Press, 2002.

Westerman, Floyd Red Crow. "Floyd Red Crow Westerman." In *Of Earth and Elders:*

Visions and Voices from Native America, by Serle L. Chapman, 2nd ed., 124–37. Missoula MT: Mountain Press, 2002.

Whipple, Henry B. *Lights and Shadows of a Long Episcopate*. New York: Macmillan, 1912.

White, Mrs. N. D. "Captivity among the Sioux, August 18 to September 26, 1862." *Collections of the Minnesota Historical Society* 9 (1901): 394–426.

"Who Are the Fool Soldiers?" Accessed online at http://www.angelfire.com/me4/charger10/FoolSoldiers.html, on 18 July 2006.

Wiget, Andrew, ed. *Critical Essays on Native American Literature*. Boston: G. K. Hall, 1985.

Williams, Daniel E., ed. *Liberty's Captives: Narratives of Confinement in the Print Culture of the Early Republic*. Athens: University of Georgia Press, 2006.

Williams, Mattie. Testimony. U.S. Army, Military Commission, Sioux War Trials: 1862. Original documents at National Archives, Washington, DC, Senate Records 37A–F2. Original Transcripts of the Records of Trials of Certain Sioux Indians Charged with Barbarities in the State of Minnesota.

Williamson, John P. *An English-Dakota Dictionary*. New York: American Tract Society, 1902. Rpt., St. Paul: Minnesota Historical Society Press, 1992.

Wilson, Angela Cavender. "Decolonizing the 1862 Death Marches." *American Indian Quarterly* 28 (2004): 185–215.

———. "Grandmother to Granddaughter: Generations of Oral History in a Dakota Family." In *Natives and Academics: Researching and Writing about American Indians*, edited by Devon A. Mihesuah, 27–36. Lincoln: University of Nebraska Press, 1998.

———. *See also* Waziyatawin Angela Wilson.

Wilson, Diane. *Spirit Car: Journey to a Dakota Past*. St. Paul: Borealis Books, 2006.

Wilson, Terry P. "Blood Quantum: Native American Mixed Bloods." In *Racially Mixed People in America*, edited by Maria P. P. Root, 108–25. London: Sage, 1992.

Wilson, Waziyatawin Angela, ed. *In the Footsteps of Our Ancestors: The Dakota Commemorative Marches of the 21st Century*. St. Paul: Living Justice Press, 2006.

———. *Remember This! Dakota Decolonization and the Eli Taylor Narratives*. Lincoln: University of Nebraska Press, 2005.

———. *See also* Angela Cavender Wilson.

Woolworth, Alan R. "Accounts, Drawings, and Photographs of the Execution of 38 Dakota Indians at Mankato, Minnesota, December 26, 1862." 19 May 1988. Alan R. Woolworth Research Collection. Minnesota Historical Society.

———. "Adrian J. Ebell, Photographer and Journalist of the Dakota War of 1862." *Minnesota History* 54 (1994): 87–92.

———. "Joseph Coursolle." N.d. Alan R. Woolworth Research Collection. Minnesota Historical Society.

———. "Known Personal Narratives from the Lower Sioux or Redwood Indian Agency, on August 18, 1862." N.d. Alan R. Woolworth Research Collection. Minnesota Historical Society.

———. "The Lake Shetek Massacre, August 20, 1862." Typescript. N.d. Alan R. Woolworth Research Collection. Minnesota Historical Society.

———. "A Listing of Family Units in the Riggs-Williamson Missionary Refugee Party from the Hazlewood [*sic*] and Yellow Medicine Missions, August, 1862." N.d. Alan R. Woolworth Research Collection. Minnesota Historical Society.

———. "Members of the Riggs-Williamson Refugee Party from Yellow Medicine, August, 1862." N.d. Alan R. Woolworth Research Collection. Minnesota Historical Society.

———. "Nancy's Life and Travels." N.d. Alan R. Woolworth Research Collection. Minnesota Historical Society.

———. "Narratives of the Flight of the Missionary Party from Yellow Medicine, 1862." N.d. Alan R. Woolworth Research Collection. Minnesota Historical Society.

———. "Notes on Esther and John Wakeman." N.d. Alan R. Woolworth Research Collection. Minnesota Historical Society.

———. "Notes on Lorenzo Lawrence." N.d. Alan R. Woolworth Research Collection. Minnesota Historical Society.

———. "Notes on Paul Mazakutemani." N.d. Alan R. Woolworth Research Collection. Minnesota Historical Society.

———. "Samuel Jerome Brown." N.d. Alan R. Woolworth Research Collection. Minnesota Historical Society.

———, ed. *Santee Dakota Indian Legends.* St. Paul: Prairie Smoke Press, 2003.

———. "The Setting at the Redwood or Lower Sioux Indian Agency and Individuals Present at the Start of the Dakota War, August 18, 1862." December 1986. Alan R. Woolworth Research Collection. Minnesota Historical Society.

———. "The Setting at the Yellow Medicine or Upper Sioux Indian Agency and the Individuals Present at the Start of the Dakota War August 18, 1862." December 1986. Alan R. Woolworth Research Collection. Minnesota Historical Society.

Workman, Harper M. "Early History of Lake Shetek Country." N.d. and 1924–30. Minnesota Historical Society.

Wright, Molly. Review of *Betrayed*, by Virginia Driving Hawk Sneve. Curriculum Advisory Service, Chicago. 10 April 1975. N.p.

Young, Philip. *Three Bags Full: Essays in American Fiction.* New York: Harcourt Brace, 1967.

Zalusky, Joseph W. "Why—What—When—How—Where—& Who." *Hennepin (Minnesota) County News* (Summer 1967): 11–14.

Zanger, Martin N. "'Straight Tongue's Heathen Wards': Bishop Whipple and the Episcopal Mission to the Chippewas." In *Churchmen and the Western Indians 1820–1920*, edited by Clyde A. Milner and Floyd A. O'Neil, 177–213. Norman: University of Oklahoma Press, 1985.

Zesch, Scott. *The Captured: A True Story of Abduction by Indians on the Texas Frontier.* New York: St. Martin's Press, 2004.

Zeman, Carrie R. "Descendents of Joseph Coursolle." 8 November 2005. To be deposited at the Minnesota Historical Society.

———. "Historical Notes on Drafts of *The War in Words*." 2005–7. To be deposited at the Minnesota Historical Society.

———. "'I Am Sure of It in My Own Mind': Sarah Wakefield's *Six Weeks in the Sioux Tepees* as a Manifestation of Stockholm Syndrome." 2005. N.p.

Index

fictive tendencies, 83, 149–50, 259, 299n22, 319n25. *See also* novels

Finn, Huck, 149–50, 153, 155

First Baptist Church of St. Paul, 79

First Mounted Rangers, 119

First World War, 44, 55, 115

Flandrau, Charles, 37, 82, 118–21

Flandreau SD, 207, 211, 249, 254, 287n5

"The Flight of the Missionaries" (M. Riggs), 58, 61, 63

Floral Home; or, First Years in Minnesota (Bishop), 80

Flora Township MN, 106, 107

food allocations, 29, 31–32, 68, 127, 175, 211, 221

Fool Soldiers, xxvi–xxvii, 91, 143, 266–73

Fort Abercrombie, 17

Fort Pembina, Dakota Territory, 254, 256

Fort Randall, 272

Fort Ridgely: Benedict Juni at, 151; Dakota attacks on, 16, 17, 34, 36, 143; Esther Wakeman on, 255; George Allanson on, 178; Helen Tarble at, xxviii, 130, 135–37; Jannette Sweet at, xxviii, 128, 227; Joseph Coursolle at, 259, 262; Lorenzo Lawrence at, 223, 225–28; Samuel Brown at, xix; staffing of, 33–34

Fort Ridgely Association, 302n6

Fort Ridgely Historical Society, 302n6

Fort Ridgely State Park and Historical Association, 211

Fort Sisseton, 173, 174

Fort Snelling, *18*; commemorative marches to, 27; Esther Wakeman at, xxix, 254, 256; Good Star Woman at, xxi, 246–47, 250; John Renville at, 283; Lorenzo Lawrence at, 227; Maggie Brass at, 237–38; Nancy Huggan at, xxii; prisoners at, 18, 19, 41, 163, 287n5

Fort Thompson, 163, 248

Fort Wadsworth, 173, 174

Franco Dakotas, 7, 167, 171, 199–200, 208, 261. *See also* mixed bloods

"Friendly Indians" monument. *See* Sioux Indians State Monument (Morton MN)

"From My Grandmother I Learned about Sadness" (Bluestone), 163

"frontier," 26

Fugitive Poses (Vizenor), 162

Galbraith, Thomas, 30, 34, 68, 126, 297n67

Galpin, Charles, 90–91, 271

gender, 11, 12, 76, 77, 86, 164, 171, 302n33. *See also* women

genocide, 19, 63, 86. *See also* Holocaust

The Generall History of Virginia (Smith), 114

German American Turner societies, 117, 119, 123

German Pioneer Accounts of the Great Sioux Uprising of 1862 (Tolzmann), 52, 302n6

Germans, xxxi, 11–12, 19, 52, 104–7, 116–17. *See also* European Americans; New Ulm; Nix, Jacob; Schwandt Schmidt, Mary E.

Germans and Indians: Fantasies, Encounters, Projections (Calloway et al.), 105

Gleason, George, 69, 72–73

Godfrey, Joseph (Otakle), 178–88, *183*; allegiances of, 38–39; background of, xx–xxi, 169, 178–79, 185–86; content of narrative, xxxiii; gravestone of, *186*, 187; Isaac Heard on, 88–90, 171; Jannette Sweet on, 128; name, 184; postwar life of, 182, 184–87; and race and ethnicity, 7, 187–88; reasons for telling story, 169–70; type of narrative by, xxx, xxxi, 189

Good Star Woman (Mahpiyatowin), 240–51; background of, xxi; Frances Densmore's presentation of, 243, 244; memories of, 241–42; publication of narrative, xxxii; type of narrative by, 165, 240

Lakota Indians, 20, 23, 38, 91, 241. *See also* Fool Soldiers
language, 11, 23, 134, 151, 156, 269, 278, 322n20
Lawrence, Elden, 1, 223, 230, 287n5
Lawrence, Elizabeth (Wakeman) (Morning Star), 253, 254, 256, 318n9
Lawrence, Lorenzo (Towanetaton), 223–32; aid from Minnesota, 228; American citizenship of, 225; attitude toward war, 36; background of, xxiii, 224; Christianity of, 65; content of narrative, xxxiii, 227–28; on dog sacrifice, 226; and Jannette Sweet, xxviii, 33, 127–29, 225, 227, 228; Martha Riggs on, 61; point of view of, 167; postwar life of, 223, 230; and publication of narrative, xxxii; and Renvilles, 279, 281; "Statement" of, 225–28, 230
Left by the Indians (Fuller), 307n64
liberation theology, 74, 298n74
Liberty's Captives (D. Williams), 53
Lights and Shadows of a Long Episcopate (Whipple), xxxiii, 223, 315n32
Limerick, Patricia Nelson, 26–30, 32, 35, 36, 39, 42. *See also* "Haunted America" (Limerick)
Lincoln, Abraham, 17, 30, 42, 66–69, 72, 82, 272, 297n67, 303n30
Little Big Horn, 23
Little Crow (Taoyateduta): and Acton incident, 31–32, 34; attitude toward war, 36; Big Eagle on, 223; and Browns, xix, 171–73, 175–77; and Cecelia Stay, xxvii, 202, 203; cultural identity of, 6; death of, 38; Edward Ellis's references to, 101, 102; election as chief speaker, 220; at Forest City and Hutchinson, 17; George Allanson on, 178; and Helen Tarble, 136; Isaac Heard on, 88; at Lower Sioux Agency, 16, 25, 31–32, 200; and Mary Schwandt Schmidt, 111, 113; and Nancy Huggan, 207, 209, 211;

portrayal in *Betrayed*, 269; portrayal in Bryant and Murch, 109; postwar conduct of, 39–40; remains of, 297n70; on Thomas Galbraith, 30; and Wakemans, xxix, 253–55, 257–58
"A Long Story" (Brant), 163
Lower Sioux Agency: and Acton incident, 31, 34; attacks on, 16, 58, 68, 118, 172; attitudes toward war at, 174–75; Cecelia Stay at, xxvii, 200–202; claims of Indians from, xxxiv; description of, 25; Esther Wakeman at, xxix, 253; Helen Tarble at, xxviii, 133–34; Jannette Sweet at, xxvii, 33, 126; Joseph Coursolle at, xix, 253, 258, 259; Joseph Godfrey at, 179, 188; march from, 19, 27; Mdewakantons at, 16, 36; postwar activities at, 284; settlement of reservation at, 24
Lower Sioux Community, 277
Loyal Indians Monument. *See* Sioux Indians State Monument (Morton MN)

Malaeska: The Indian Wife of the White Hunter (Stephens), 94–95, 102
Manheim narratives, 85
Manifest Destiny, 65, 80, 102
Mankato, 72, 151, 237–38, 249, 283, 284, 287n5, 297n67. *See also* execution of Dakotas
Marshall, William R., 125, 126, 174, 205, 208, 209
Mary and I: Forty Years with the Sioux (S. Riggs), xxx, 58
"The Massacre at the Lower Sioux Agency" (Stay), 200
Mato Nunpa, Chris, 18–19, 277
Mayer, Frank Blackwell, 206, 207
Mazakutemani, Paul (Little Paul), 190; 189–97; attitude toward war, 36; background of, xxiv, 189; Christianity of, 9–10, 65; and *Indian Jim*, 101; on Loyal Indians Monument, 232; point of view